At the Heart of Terror

At the Heart of Terror

Islam, Jihadists, and America's War on Terrorism

Monte Palmer and Princess Palmer

ROWMAN & LITTLEFIELD PUBLISHERS, INC.
Lanham • Boulder • New York • Toronto • Plymouth, UK

ROWMAN & LITTLEFIELD PUBLISHERS, INC.

Published in the United States of America
by Rowman & Littlefield Publishers, Inc.
A wholly owned subsidiary of The Rowman & Littlefield Publishing Group, Inc.
4501 Forbes Boulevard, Suite 200, Lanham, Maryland 20706
www.rowmanlittlefield.com

Estover Road, Plymouth PL6 7PY, United Kingdom

British Library Cataloguing in Publication Information Available

The hardback edition of this book was catalogued by the Library of Congress as follows:

Palmer, Monte.
  At the heart of terror : Islam, Jihadists, and America's war on terrorism / Monte
Palmer and Princess Palmer.
     p.   cm.
  Includes bibliographical references and index.
  1. Islam and politics—Middle East—History—20th century. 2. Islamic
fundamentalism. 3. War on Terrorism, 2001– I. Palmer, Princess, 1952– II.
Title.
  DS62.8.P347   2004
  909'.09767083—dc22

                                                                                    2004009249
ISBN-13: 978-0-7425-3602-9 (cloth : alk. paper)
ISBN-10: 0-7425-3602-5 (cloth : alk. paper)
ISBN-13: 978-0-7425-3603-6 (pbk. : alk. paper)
ISBN-10: 0-7425-3603-3 (pbk. : alk. paper)

Printed in the United States of America

♾™The paper used in this publication meets the minimum requirements of American National Standard for Information Sciences—Permanence of Paper for Printed Library Materials, ANSI/NISO Z39.48-1992.

CONTENTS

1 Who Is Attacking America?   1

2 Islam, Muslim Extremism, and Anti-Americanism   9
   Muslim Relations with Christians and Jews   10
   Unity and Turmoil within Islam   12
   The Evolution of Islamic Extremism   14
   The Sources of Muslim Discontent   20
   Gauging Popular Support for Muslim Extremists   23
   Levels of Islamic Religiosity   26
   Separating Islamic Extremism from Anti-Americanism   31

3 The Muslim Brotherhood and Hizbullah: Radical-Moderates   39
   The Muslim Brotherhood   41
   Hizbullah: A Tale of Three Countries   55
   Can the Muslim Brotherhood and Hizbullah Serve as a
      Counterweight to the Jihadists?   76

4 The Jihadist Movement and How It Evolved   85
   Egypt and the Origins of Modern Jihadism   85
   The Islamic Revolution   91
   Pakistan: The Jihadist Gateway to the Far East and Central
      Asia   92
   Afghanistan and the Making of a Muslim Hero   96
   The Sudan: An International Terrorist Network Takes Shape   100

The Battle for Algeria   106
The Palestinian Jihadists: Hamas and Holy Jihad   110
The Jihadist War Comes to America   116
From Turabi to bin Laden   118
The Continuing Evolution of the Jihadist Movement   123

5 The Jihadist War Plan   127
   Jihadist Strategy: The Psychology of Terror   129
   The Components of Terror   131
   Terror and the Propaganda War   140
   The Jihadist War Plan of the Future: Compelling Logic for
     Attacking America   143
   One War Plan or Several?   145

6 The Jihadist War Machine   149
   Organizing the Jihadists: The Pyramid of Terror   149
   Leadership in Jihadist Organizations   156
   The Jihadist Soldiers: Who Are They, What Motivates
     Them, and How Good Are They?   165
   The Physical Plant   172

7 The Allies of the Jihadists: Those Who Make Terror Possible   177
   Holy Allies: The Struggle for the Control of Islam   178
   Unholy Allies: Drug Lords, Mafioso, and Other Kindred
     Souls   189
   Governments as Allies of Terror   192

8 How Israel and Its Middle Eastern Neighbors Fight Terror   207
   The Israeli Experience in Fighting Terror   207
   The Basic Principles of Israeli Anti-Terrorist Strategy   212
   The Struggle against Jihadist Terror in the Islamic World   231
   Relevance of the Experience of Israel and the Islamic World
     to America's War on Terror   240

9 The Future: Winning the War on Terror   247
   U.S. Anti-Terrorist Strategy   247
   Assessment: How Well Is America Doing?   249

Why the Glitches?   255
Defeating the Jihadists   260

Selected Bibliography   273

Index   287

About the Authors   293

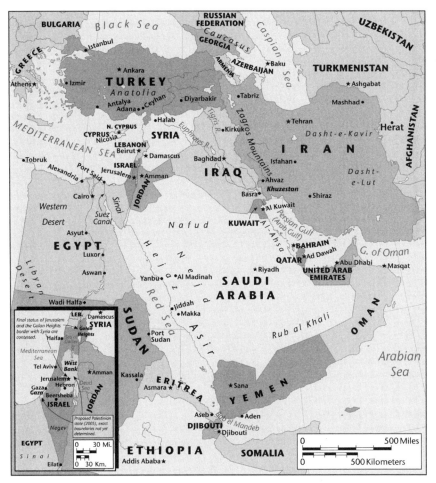

The Middle East

1

WHO IS ATTACKING AMERICA?

The greatest threat facing the United States today is terrorism by Muslim jihadists. The jihadists are a self-appointed collection of religious fanatics who have launched a holy war, a jihad, against the United States and everything American.[1] They have also declared war on Israel, Europe, and anyone else who opposes their vision of a world governed by Islamic law. Ironically, the foremost target of the jihadists has been the Muslim world itself. Most Muslims reject the jihadists' rigid interpretation of Islam, and few relish the austerity of jihadist rule. It is the Muslims who have borne the brunt of jihadist terror, with the past decade claiming more than 100,000 lives in Algeria alone. The jihadists may be Muslim, but few Muslims are jihadists.

The September 11, 2001, attacks on the United States made bin Laden's al Qaeda network the focal point of world attention. The jihadist movement, however, is much larger than bin Laden and his al Qaeda network. Jihadist groups flourish throughout the world, plotting violence and fueling civil unrest whenever the opportunity presents itself. Civil conflicts in Palestine, Chechnya, Kashmir, Kosovo, Bosnia, the Philippines, and elsewhere have all been infiltrated by jihadist groups of one form or another. Some jihadist groups have formed temporary alliances with al Qaeda. Others have not. Egypt alone once boasted some ninety diverse jihadist groups; rare is the country with a large Muslim population that does not possess several. Most of the groups are small and fluid, appearing and disappearing, splintering and reemerging in new alliances. Adding complexity to the picture has been the splintering of the al Qaeda network itself.

1

Rather than facing one bin Laden, the United States may now be facing several.

The jihadist war raged in the Middle East for more than three decades before targeting the United States. It was only in 1993, with the first jihadist bombing of the World Trade Center, that jihadist attacks on the United States began in earnest. Attacks on U.S. peacekeepers in Somalia followed in the same year. In 1995, the scene shifted to Saudi Arabia, as jihadists bombed facilities used by U.S. troops in Riyadh. The following year saw the demolition of the al-Khobar Towers, a U.S. marine facility in the Saudi Arabian city of Dhahran, the heart of Saudi Arabia's oil fields. Five U.S. soldiers were killed in the former incident, and nineteen in the latter. Scores were maimed by the intensity of these explosions. In 1998, the scene shifted to sub-Saharan Africa, as jihadists bombed U.S. embassies in Kenya and Tanzania. American losses were few, but the jihadists had made their point: "We can attack the United States at the time and the place of our choosing." September 11 removed all doubt. America was at war.

Despite the growing ferocity of jihadist violence in the Middle East, few people in the United States seemed concerned. Even after the 1993 bombing of the World Trade Center, no one seemed terribly alarmed. Events were noted, but countermeasures were few. Perhaps the American attitude reflected the arrogance of a global power unable to grasp the threat posed by roaming bands of bearded warriors. It may also have been the collective denial of a country relieved by the collapse of the Soviet threat and unwilling to acknowledge the emergence of a new and potentially more dangerous enemy. Far more likely than either of those is the historical reluctance of the United States to become embroiled in foreign conflicts until they reach crisis proportions. Muslims killing Muslims was unfortunate, but this was not a threat to the United States. That has now changed. Americans everywhere have become the preferred target of the jihadists.

Terrorism, of course, is a global problem. The British have long suffered the terror of the IRA, the Spanish the assassinations of the ETA, and the Israelis the relentless attacks of the Palestinian resistance. Lists of terrorist organizations abound and are revised daily, some having hundreds of entries. Of these, the major purveyors of terror are jihadist groups such as al Qaeda and independence movements such as the Tamil Tigers, the Real Irish Republican Army, and the Palestinian resistance. Other groups featured prominently on world terrorist lists include the Japanese Red Army and Peru's Shining Path as well as drug gangs who often masquerade as leftist bands. Of the latter, the most prominent is the Revolutionary Armed Forces of Colombia (FARC), a large quasi-military organization with an estimated ten to twenty thousand troops.

Of all the groups cited on the world's terrorist lists, only those associated with the jihadists and the drug gangs have systematically attacked American targets during the past decade. Even here, a sharp distinction exists between drug-related groups such as FARC and the jihadists. The drug terrorists are basically businessmen intent on maximizing profits. Americans are attacked when they pose a threat to drug operations. FARC could probably topple the Colombian government if it so chooses but it finds a weak and ineffective government more conducive to its operations than the burden of running a country known throughout the region as *la violencia*. FARC is not involved in terror within the United States, but it is violently opposed to U.S. efforts to strengthen the Colombian government. Its threat to American security is drugs, not terror.

The case of the jihadists is far different. The jihadists believe that the United States is the major obstacle to their control of the Islamic world. It is they who have declared war on the United States and its allies, and it is they who have become the focal point of America's war on terror.

The war being waged by the jihadists is unlike any war that the United States has ever encountered. There are no massed armies to bomb or front lines to fortify, only shadows that dissolve into throngs of the innocent. The enemy wears no uniforms except, perhaps, the ubiquitous beard, but even that can be abandoned for holy purposes. The jihadists fight for neither national pride nor wealth. Both are irrelevant. They fight for God. An eternity in paradise is the reward of those who die in defense of their faith.

The jihadist war against America is a war of maddening cycles. Brilliant attacks are followed by two or three year lulls as the jihadists regroup and lure their foe into a false sense of complacency. This strategy is part necessity and part psychology. It is a necessity because the jihadists are hounded by security forces and lack the physical capacity to occupy territory for sustained periods of time. It is psychological because the jihadists believe that terror will undermine the will of their opponents to resist. They don't have to field armies or occupy territory if they can terrorize their foe into submission.

Maddening, too, is the global nature of the jihadist war against America. No areas are secure from jihadist attack, least of all the United States itself. Nor is there a single jihadist country that can be obliterated with American weaponry. Much like a multinational corporation, the jihadists are mobile, shifting their base of operations from place to place as opportunities dictate.

All of this has been put into play by a jihadist enemy who represents a minute segment of the world's Muslims. How can so few do so much damage? The answer is simple. They have help. It is the supporters and allies of the jihadists who make it possible for them to carry out their deadly missions. By all appearances, the jihadists want for neither money nor protection. Weapons abound and supply lines transverse the world. It is the supporters and the allies of the jihadists that make them a threat to the United States and the Western world.

Who are the supporters and allies of the jihadists? The list is long and would surely include a narrow stratum of Islamic society that supports the jihadists with an all-consuming passion. It is this stratum of Islamic society that provides the jihadists with the majority of their recruits and much of their financial support. It is also this layer of hard-core supporters that shelters the jihadists and serves as a subversive fifth column within the institutions of the Muslim world.

To a lesser extent, sympathy for the jihadists can be found among moderate Muslims distraught by the moral decay of the Islamic world. They have little desire to live in a religious theocracy, but neither are they content with the rampant immorality and corruption of their societies. Many are also fearful that the United States has declared war on Islam. The jihadists symbolize resistance to both.

It would be a mistake to believe that support for the jihadists is motivated by religious emotions alone. People join extremist movements for a multitude of reasons, ranging from frustration and insecurity to humiliation and hopelessness. All are rife in the Islamic world. The governments of that world are corrupt, incompetent, and oppressive. Services are atrocious, jobs are few, and hope for a better future is minimal. Most people who do get ahead do so by connections and servility. Muslims blame the United States for keeping despotic governments in power as well as for a multitude of other sins ranging from support of Israel to economic exploitation. Inevitably, some of this frustration and anti-Americanism is translated into support for the jihadists.

In addition to a significant base of popular support, the jihadists also have powerful allies. Washington has accused a broad range of Muslim schools, charitable associations, banks, and businesses of supporting jihadist activities. Islamic groups that publicly reject anti-American violence have also been accused of supporting the jihadists. Of these, the most prominent are the Muslim Brotherhood and Hizbullah. Adding to the fray are drug gangs, gunrunners, secular terrorist groups, warlords, and various independence movements, each benefiting from the others.

In many ways, the most dangerous allies of the jihadists are the governments of the Islamic world, if not the world at large. Some governmental support has been intentional, but most has been unintentional or unforeseen. Iran proudly proclaims its support for Hizbullah and Hamas, as does Syria. Pakistan plays a major role in supporting jihadist groups in Kashmir and Central Asia. Saudi Arabia opposes jihadist terror but is the world's major sponsor of the Islamic schools and institutions that the United States accuses of fostering jihadist terror. Ironically, the United States, Pakistan, and Saudi Arabia all played a major role in promoting the jihadists as a counterweight to the Soviet occupation of Afghanistan. With the liberation of Afghanistan and collapse of the Soviet Union, it is now the United States that is their target.

It is the supporters and allies of the jihadists who make it possible for them to pose a sustained threat to the United States and the Western world. The jihadists themselves are an infinitesimally small group of individuals who lack the personnel and resources to do so. The world has always been plagued with terrorists in one form or another. The difference between those who have succeeded and those who have failed has been their level of support within the communities in which they operate. America's homegrown terrorists soon fade because they possess few allies and lack a base of popular support. The British struggle against the IRA has failed because the IRA had both.

Perhaps because of the strange and unfamiliar nature of the jihadist war, the United States has lashed out at its foe with indiscriminate ferocity, punishing the innocent as well as the guilty. In so doing, the United States has conveyed the impression that it has launched new crusades against the Islamic world. Indeed, soon after September 11, President Bush referred to America's war on terror as a "crusade," a turn of phrase that seemed to imply that the United States had renewed Christendom's conquest of the holy lands. He later apologized. Italian Prime Minister Silvio Berlusconi was particularly blunt, saying, "We must be aware of the superiority of civilization . . . in contrast with the Islamic countries," comments that seemed to suggest that Muslims were barbarians.[2] The European Union rushed to denounce Berlusconi's comments as unfortunate. Jerry Falwell weighed in on CBS's "60 Minutes" by calling the Prophet Mohammed a terrorist. Falwell's comments triggered protests throughout the Islamic world, with some observers blaming his statements for the victory of Islamic parties in Pakistan's subsequent elections.[3] Falwell later apologized.

Creating the impression that the United States had declared war on Islam was a mistake. Muslims constitute more than one-sixth of the global population, and Muslim communities are an integral part of almost every country in the world. Little is to be gained by pushing them into the hands of religious extremists. On the contrary, moderate Muslims, the majority, are the natural allies of the United States in its war on terror. It is they who bear the brunt of jihadist terror and is they who are threatened with the prospect of being locked in a time warp of the seventh century. The United States needs their help, not their animosity.

The objectives of this book are to provide a step-by-step guide through the intricacies of the jihadist movement, to highlight its vulnerabilities, and to suggest ways to confront it. These goals are addressed by a series of eight questions that constitute the organization of the book: Who are the jihadists? How do they fit within the broader context of Islamic religion? What is their war plan? How do they operate? Who are their allies? What are their weaknesses? What is the experience of Israel and other countries in fighting the jihadists? How can the jihadists be defeated?

Providing answers to these questions is not as complex as it would seem. We begin by examining Islam and Islamic fundamentalism. By and large, Muslim fundamentalists differ little from other fundamentalists throughout the world. All are referred to as fundamentalists because they base their values on the fundamentals of their religion, be it Islam, Judaism, Christianity, or Hinduism. Most fundamentalists demand a greater role for religion in their governance. A few extreme fanatics in all faiths attempt to impose their will by violence. In Islam, they are the jihadists.

We then turn to the radical Muslim groups who prefer reform to violence. Most possess the capacity for violence, but they find reform and non-violence to be a more effective means of achieving their goal of an Islamic state. The foremost members of this category are the Muslim Brotherhood, Hizbullah, and the multitude of Islamic political parties that have emerged as the major players in the Islamic world's sham democracies. All have disavowed anti-American terrorism, but all support the jihadist attacks on Israel. In the case of Hizbullah, that support is blatant. Are reformist Islamic groups the allies of the jihadists or their opponents? Probably both.

This will bring us to the jihadists: their evolution, their war plan, and their organization muscle. How good are the jihadists and where are they vulnerable? As in any war, the United States must be able to counter the strengths of its opponents and exploit their vulnerabilities. The jihadists have a multitude of both. Also to be examined are the allies of the jihadists, including countries that support jihadist terror.

Finally, we come to the task of fighting the jihadists. What works, what doesn't, and what should the United States do next? In addressing these questions, we draw on the experience of the Israelis, the Islamic world, and the world's major powers. Some may find the conclusions painful, but war is a painful business.

We have resisted the temptation to provide yet another definition of terrorism.[4] There is no generally accepted definition of the term, and the U.S. government uses several definitions simultaneously. Each of America's allies has its own definition of terrorism, most of which differ from those of the United States. Needless to say, this adds confusion to an already confusing war. Most definitions of terrorism in current use stress the execution of violent acts by small groups of individuals for political objectives. In the case of the jihadists, the goal of the terror is to drive the United States and its allies from the Islamic world. Such acts would certainly include highjacking, kidnapping, assassination, car bombing, and chemical attacks unleashed by small groups of operants. Biologic weapons and small nuclear devices may soon be added to the terrorist arsenal. Both are amenable to use by small groups of mobile terrorists.

We have also resisted the temptation to define the Middle East, a region that has nearly as many definitions as terrorism.[5] The definition used by Washington focuses on the Arab world as well as all neighboring countries that have large Muslim populations.[6] This list would certainly include Turkey, Israel, Iran, most of Central Asia, Pakistan, Afghanistan, and the predominantly Muslim regions of the Balkans. The Islamic world is global and includes predominantly Islamic countries such as Indonesia, Malaysia, and Bangladesh. Indeed, Indonesia is the world's most populist Islamic country. The Islamic world also includes countries in which Islam has become the second-largest religion, not the least of which are the United States, Canada, Russia, India, Israel, and most of Western Europe.

NOTES

1. It is important to note that the word "jihad" possesses a variety of meanings ranging from war in the name of God to the individual's internal struggle against evil. We have debated alternative expressions to characterize the narrow band of extremists who commit terror in the name of Islam, but find jihadists to be the least offensive. The term

jihadist also finds extensive use in the media of the Islamic world. We do not use the expression "Islamic extremists" or "Muslim extremists" to imply terrorists, for most extremists in the Islamic (Muslim) world are not terrorists.

2. "EU Deplores 'Dangerous' Islam Jibe," *BBCOnline*, 27 Sept. 2001, at http://news .bbc.co.uk/2/hi/europe/1565664.stm (accessed 7 Dec. 2002).

3. Todd Hertz, "Riots, Condemnation, Fatwa, and Apology Follow Falwell's CBS Comments," *Christianity Today Magazine*, 14 Oct. 2002, at http://www.christianity today.com/ct/2002/140/41.0.html (accessed 7 Dec. 2003).

4. For a general discussion of terrorism, we suggest Jonathan White, *Terrorism: An Introduction, 4th ed., 2002 Update* (Belmont, Calif.: Wadsworth, 2003).

5. General surveys of the Middle East are found in James Bill and Robert Springbord, *Politics in the Middle East* (New York: HarperCollins, 1997) and Monte Palmer, *Politics of the Middle East* (Belmont, Calif.: Wadsworth, 2002), formerly published by Peacock Publishing.

6. The United States Commission on National Security/Twenty-first Century, *New World Coming: American Security in the Twenty-first Century: Supporting Research and Analysis*. The Phase I Report on the Emerging Global Security Environment for the First Quarter of the 21st Century (15 Sept. 1999).

2

ISLAM, MUSLIM EXTREMISM, AND ANTI-AMERICANISM

Many Americans find the link between Islam and terrorism to be self-evident. The September 11, 2001, attacks on the United States originated in the Middle East and were perpetrated by Muslims. Adding to the impression that Muslims support terror were the seemingly endless television portrayals of Muslim groups cheering bin Laden and desecrating the American flag. Muslim countries have furthered this impression by dragging their feet on America's war on terror and opposing the U.S. occupation of Iraq.

Not shown on television was the overwhelming majority of the world's one billion Muslims who want nothing more than to live their lives in a normal and peaceful manner. While most would welcome a greater role for religion and morality in their societies, few support violence as a means for achieving that end. In their view, the jihadists are an aberration of Islam who offer little more than oppression, religious police, veiled women, and disavowal of modern science. This is not how the majority of Muslims want to live.

Given the hostility of moderate Muslims toward the jihadists, one might expect that they would embrace America's war on terror with open arms. This is not the case. Anti-Americanism is rampant in the Islamic world and the majority of the world's moderate Muslims remain passive in the face of the jihadist threat. This is tragic, for only the active support of the world's moderate Muslims can eliminate the global threat of jihadist terror. Passivity is not enough.

Why, then, haven't the world's Muslims joined America's war on terror? The objective of the present chapter is to answer this most perplexing of questions. We begin by examining Muslim relations with Christians and Jews as well as the tremendous diversity that exists within the Islamic faith. Following this discussion, we examine differing levels of religiosity among Muslims. Many Muslims are either secular or practice their faith in a perfunctory manner. Others exhort the faithful to prayer and incline toward extremism. Between these two poles is a large group of Muslims who are devout yet opposed to extremism of any variety. Levels of religiosity have much to say about who supports the jihadists and who should oppose them. Rough estimates are provided for each category. Finally, we look at the broader causes of anti-Americanism in the Islamic world. Anti-Americanism has a religious component, but it is much more. Focusing on Islam alone will not solve America's problems with the Islamic world.

MUSLIM RELATIONS WITH CHRISTIANS AND JEWS

Most Christians and Jews will be relieved to find that they already know more about the Islamic experience than they realize. Islam builds on Judaism and Christianity, and a clear line of progression exists between the three religions.[1] Much as Christians believe that God sent Christ to correct the deviations of the Jews, so Muslims believe that God sent Mohammed, his final prophet, to correct the deviations of the Christians. Islam acknowledges the major prophets of the Jews, including Adam, Noah, Moses, and Abraham. Christ is recognized as a major prophet but not as the Son of God. Islam does, however, accept the virgin birth of Christ and the Koran, the revealed word of God, devotes an entire chapter to Mary.[2]

Not only do Muslims worship the same God as Christians and Jews, but the Islamic experience parallels that of the Christians and Jews. Much like Christianity and Judaism, Islam is a religion of many parts. Islam is a creed based on the revealed word of God. It is also men of religion (*ulema*) who interpret that creed and a multitude of schisms resulting from those interpretations. Above all, Islam is a body of faithful attempting to achieve salvation by living in accordance with the word of God.

The institutions of Islam also parallel the institutions of Christianity and Judaism. Muslims are linked to their clergy by a network of mosques that differ little from churches and synagogues. Islamic schools, charities, and religious societies are similar to those of their sister faiths. Much like Christianity and Judaism, Islam is also an identity, a way of life, and a symbol of hope. Muslims, like Christians and Jews, struggle to find the proper means of expressing their faith. Most stress peace, but a very small minority of all three faiths have justified violence in the name of their religion. In Islam, these are the jihadists, the sworn enemies of America.

The holy book of Muslims is the Koran, a compilation of God's laws as revealed to the Prophet Mohammed by the Angel Gabriel. Mohammed is revered by Muslims as a prophet of God rather than as an extension of God. He was a mortal being chosen by God to receive his message of peace and enlightenment and, as such, possessed no supernatural powers. In addition to the Koran, Muslims seek guidance from the Sunna or "way of the prophet." When early Muslims encountered issues not fully addressed in the Koran, the logical procedure was to consult the traditions of the Prophet Mohammed and his associates. This process was quite effective during the years immediately following the Prophet Mohammed's death, but led to abuses as memories grew dim.

Much like the Torah and the Bible, the Koran provides Muslims with a guide to salvation. The Koran, however, far exceeds the Bible in instructing Muslims on the ordering of their political, economic, and social lives. The Prophet Mohammed was a political leader, and the Koran has much to say about how to organize a well-run society in a manner that will promote peace and justice. Unlike the Christian tradition, Islam does not draw a clear line between the sacred and the profane. Indeed, many Muslims find it absurd to separate religion from government. Why would human law be placed above the law of God?

The Koran refers to Christians and Jews as people of the book. Christians and Jews, from the Islamic perspective, had been converted to a belief in the one God by earlier prophets but refused to accept the teachings of the Prophet Mohammed, God's final prophet. As believers in the one God, both Jews and Christians are allowed to live in peace among Muslims.[3]

Islam calls on its adherents to protect their faith, as do all major religions. Barring this, there would be no faith. In Islam, protecting the faith is referred to as a jihad, an Arabic word used to sound the call for a holy war.[4] It is this, but so much more. Sheikh Atiyyah Saqr, an eminent Muslim scholar long associated with Cairo's venerable Al-Azhar Mosque, offers the following clarifications.

> The word "jihad" means exerting effort to achieve a desired thing or prevent an undesired one. . . . Among the types of Jihad are struggling against

one's desires, the accursed Satan, poverty, illiteracy, disease, and all evil forces in the world. . . . Jihad is also done to avert aggression on the home countries and on all that is held sacred, or in order to face those who try to hinder the march of the call of truth. In Islamic Shari'ah [law] Jihad in the Cause of Allah means fighting in order to make the Word of Allah most high and the means for doing so is taking up arms in addition to preparation, financing and planning strategies.[5]

Islam's relations with Christianity and Judaism, then, operate on a dual axis. One axis stresses tolerance toward Jews and Christians who live in their midst. Historically, the record of Muslim tolerance toward people of the book has been exemplary. It has certainly surpassed the Christian treatment of Jews in Europe.

The second axis centers on the Koranic scriptures enjoining Muslims to protect their faith and to bring nonbelievers into the fold. Conflict between Islam and the West has centered on this second axis and has occurred whenever Jews and Christians have challenged Muslim dominance in the predominantly Islamic countries of the world. This occurred during the Crusades and it has been a recurring theme in the violence that has devastated the Islamic world since the colonial era. Many Muslims believe that Christian and Jewish attacks on Islam are now reaching a level of fervor unknown since the Crusades. They also believe that those attacks are being spearheaded by Israel and the United States. Does this require a jihad? If so, what kind of jihad? These matters have yet to be resolved. Most Muslims see little need for a holy war. The jihadists believe that there is no other option.

UNITY AND TURMOIL WITHIN ISLAM

The evolution of Islam parallels the evolution of Christianity. In each case, a simple message of hope and faith was revealed to the masses by a prophet or Son of God. Organizational structures, such as they were, consisted of the prophet, a small band of disciples, and a gradually expanding body of the faithful. The evolution of Judaism was somewhat more complicated, but the basic principle was the same.[6]

With the passing of the founding prophet, simplicity gave way to complexity as a class of priests became the guardians of the faith, bickering over fine points of doctrine and preparing the way for eventual schisms. In the case of Islam, the most devastating schism occurred in 656 A.D. when Ali, the fourth caliph, or successor to the Prophet Mohammed, was challenged for the leadership of Islam by Muawiyah, the governor of Damascus. Ali was assassinated, giving way to a schism of enduring bitterness. As described by Yahya Armajani:

> Failing to establish their claim by politics or by war, the Shi'is separated permanently from the majority and founded a religion of their own complete with theology, philosophy, government, and ethics. Religiously, Shi'ism has Zoroastrian, Nestorian, and other overtones, and has supplied Islam with mysteries, saints, intercessors, belief in atonement, and a spirit of high cult, all of which are repugnant to the majority of Sunnis. The Sunnis consider the Koran infallible, while the Shi'is place infallibility in a man, the Imam who is sinless and has been considered as a man-God. The Shi'is believe in the doctrine of the Return. This has many things in common with the return of the deliverer of Zoroastrianism, the coming of the Messiah in Judaism, and the "second coming" of Jesus in Christianity. The majority of the Shi'is believe that there were twelve imams and that the twelfth, the Mahdi (messiah) has disappeared and shall return at the end of time when he will bring the whole world under the jurisdiction of Shi'i Islam.[7]

The Shi'a belief that the hidden Imam would reappear to lead the Muslim community to salvation resulted in the evolution of religious leaders empowered to rule the Shi'a community until the time of the Imam's return. Such individuals, often referred to as ayatollahs, were imbued with spiritual powers similar to if not greater than those of the Pope.[8] These powers have enabled the Shi'a clergy to control their followers by promising entrance into heaven for religious sacrifice.

In sharp contrast to the mysticism of the Shi'a, the Sunnis follow a more literal interpretation of the Sunna, or way of the Prophet. There are no hidden Imams, nor are Sunni spiritual leaders imbued with supernatural powers. Aside from the Caliphate, now vacant, the religious elites of Sunni Islam consist of learned scholars or *ulema*. The most senior of these are the mufti (senior religious judges), the directors of Waqfs or religious endowments, and the rectors of Islamic universities such as Al-Azhar University in Cairo. Aside from these positions, Sunni Islam lacks an overarching organizational structure and each congregation more or less selects its own preachers (*muazin*) and prayer leaders albeit with help from the government. In effect, the schism between the Shi'a and Sunni shares much in common with the schism between Catholics and Protestants.[9]

Each of the two main branches of Islam has generated diverse schools of thought, each with a multitude of interpretations. Some interpretations are liberal, allowing Muslims a large degree of freedom in ordering their daily lives. Others are severe, attempting to recreate life on earth much as it existed during the days of the Prophet. The Taliban in Afghanistan clearly fell into this latter category and created a society that forbade every symbol of modernity, with the exception of that linked to maintaining themselves in power. The Wahhabi interpretation of Islam applied in Saudi Arabia is also renowned for its severity, with religious police patrolling the country to apprehend laggards.[10]

The vast gulf that separates the Shi'a and Sunni makes cooperation within the Islamic world difficult. Many Sunni go so far as to suggest that Shi'a are not really Muslims. Be that as it may, Sunni and Shi'a share a common dedication to their faith and common fear that the United States has declared war on Islam. Distrust, however, runs deep between the two groups.

THE EVOLUTION OF ISLAMIC EXTREMISM

The evolution of all major religions has witnessed the emergence of extremist groups vowing to purify the faith. Islam is no exception. Indeed, extremism in Islam returns to the earliest days of the faith and was spawned by the debate over who should succeed to the leadership of Islam after the passing of the Prophet Mohammed. Many of the faithful believed that successors to the Prophet Mohammed should be drawn from his lineage and particularly that of Ali, the fourth caliph. This view was opposed by the Kharijites, who believed that the successor to the Prophet Mohammed should be selected by egalitarian and democratic procedures. They attacked those who opposed their views as heretics, and killed Ali in 661 A.D., as he bowed in prayer.

The roots of modern Islamic extremism are often traced to the works of Ibn Taymiyyah, a Muslim thinker who lived in Damascus during the thirteenth and fourteenth centuries. Ibn Taymiyyah lived in an era in which Islam was in danger of being dominated by the Mongols, and his writings are often credited with rallying the Arabs against the Mongol invaders. The Mongols had legitimized their rule by converting to Islam, but they had done so in an imperfect manner that mixed the creeds of several religions as the moment dictated, not the least of which was hailing their leader, Chengis Kahn, as a prophet of God. Ibn Taymiyyah declared the Mongols to be infidels (*kafirs*) and, as such, unfit to rule. Only the followers of the

Salafiya—the Koran and teachings of the Prophet Mohammed, his follow-ers, and their followers—were true Muslims and fit to rule, he maintained. All others had to be resisted. Among Ibn Taymiyyah's justifications was the saying of the Prophet, "The best of mankind is my generation, then those who follow them, and those who follow them."[11]

Far from being obscure, Ibn Taymiyyah's logic has often been used by Sunni extremists to justify their attacks on groups whose lax interpretations of Islam didn't conform to the Koran and the Sunna (Salaf). Muslim Broth-erhood propagandists, for example, openly quoted Ibn Taymiyyah during the Brotherhood's rebellion against Syria's Alawite leaders during the early 1980s.[12] The early eighteenth century saw the emergence of the Wahhabi doctrine in Saudi Arabia, as Abd al-Wahhab, a charismatic religious leader with a broad following in the region, joined forces with the founder of the first Saudi dynasty.[13] Much in line with Ibn Taymiyyah's earlier teachings, Abd al-Wahhab condemned the embellishment of Islamic practices with mystical beliefs, not the least of which were those of the Shi'a. The fortunes of both the Saudis and the Wahhabis ebbed and flowed over the ensuing centuries and surfaced again with the founding of the present Saudi King-dom at the turn of the twentieth century. Ibn Saud, the founder of modern Saudi Arabia, used Wahhabi teachings to fire his troops with holy zeal, but was himself threatened by the zeal of the Wahhabi extremists, know as Ikh-wan or brothers. As Robert Lacy describes these zealots:

> The Prophet condemned personal ostentation, so the Ikhwan shunned silk, gold, jewelry and ornaments, including the gold thread traditionally woven round the dark bhisht or mishlah, the outer robe and they also cut their robes short above the ankles. This was because the Prophet had declared clothes that brushed the ground to be an affectation, and the same went for luxuriant moustaches. So the Ikhwan clipped the hair on their upper lip to a mere shadow of stubbiness while adopting a different rule for hair on the chin. In this case, they argued, it would be affectation to trim and shape, so beards must be left to grow as long and to straggle as far as God might will them.[14]

The most recent crisis in Islam was provoked by Western colonization of the Islamic world, a process that was well under way by the end of nine-teenth century. While science and industrialization had transformed England, France and Germany into world powers, the Islamic empires of old were collapsing of their own weight. The Ottoman Empire, the remaining Islamic power at the time, survived largely because the European powers had already begun to fight over its corpse, each fearing an advantage for the others.

The power of Europe forced Muslim intellectuals to acknowledge that the Islamic world was in decay. The issue could not be dodged. Something had to be done, but what? Enlightened voices called for the accommodation of modern science within a religious framework. Science, as all things in life, they argued, was the will of God and should be accepted as such. Islam would enjoy the best of both worlds: scientific advancement provided by the West, and the moral strength provided by the Islamic faith. This was surely the formula for the revival of an Islamic empire long in decay.

Not all in the Islamic world shared this enlightened view. Conservative theologians feared that modern science would lead to secularism and eternal damnation. It was not the science of Europe that had lead to decay of Islam, they argued, but the perversion of basic Islamic teachings that had occurred over the course of Islamic history. Attempting to "modernize" Islam would weaken the Islamic faith, not strengthen it. The only solution to the decay that had beset Islam, in the view of the conservative theologians, was a return to the fundamental principles of the Koran and the way of the Prophet Mohammed. Everything not based on the fundamentals of Islam as preached by the Prophet would be jettisoned. That was the surest path to the revival of Islam.

Theologians debated while the Islamic world fell ever deeper under the control of the European colonialists. The crisis came to a head in the aftermath of World War I, when all of the Arab world, with the exception of Saudi Arabia and Yemen, fell under Western control. Turkey and Iran, the two non-Arab powers of the region, escaped Western domination but had become so dependent on Europe for arms and commerce that the result was much the same.[15] The time for debate had passed. It was time for action.

It was not the Islamic theologians who acted, but the generals. Stung by defeat and fired by national pride and the lust for power, it was they who plotted the future of the Islamic world. Muslims, in their view, had been defeated by the science, industrialization, and secularism of Europe. The countries of the Islamic world, they reasoned, could only defeat their adversaries by following suit. Islam, in their view, was passé, an obstacle to development. Nationalism, not religion, would be made the opiate of the masses.

The forced secularization of the Islamic world was spearheaded by Mustafa Kemal, a Turkish general who had seized power in the waning days of World War I in a desperate effort to stem the dismemberment of Turkey by the major powers of the day. Soon renamed Ataturk (Father of the

Turks), Kemal used the power of the army to forcibly transform Turkey into a clone of Europe.[16] The rush to industrialization was matched by a rush toward secularization. Islamic law was replaced by the Swiss legal code. Family names, a rarity during the Ottoman Empire, became mandatory. The fez and other forms of religious dress were forbidden. Latin script replaced Arabic script, the script of the Koran, as the medium for writing Turkish. Religious schools were also secularized and religion was relegated to the role of personal salvation. Did Ataturk succeed? This is an interesting question that may have much to say about America's war on terror. As of this writing, Turkey is governed by an Islamic political party that aspires to an Islamic state. It is also a party that blocked Turkish participation in the joint U.S. and British invasion of Iraq.

Particularly distressing to Muslim theologians was Ataturk's abolition of the caliphate in 1924. For some five hundred years, Turkish monarchs had ruled their massive empire as both sultan and caliph. Atatuk had shattered the unity of religion and state. Political leaders of the Muslim world continued to pay lip service to Islam, but the religious elites were on the defensive, their power fading much as the power of Christian leaders had faded in the Europe of an earlier era. Presidents and kings appointed religious leaders compatible with their views and changed them at will. The role of the Muslim *ulema* was now to justify a secular regime. In the final analysis, the modernizing generals would pose a greater threat to Islam than the colonial invaders.

It was in this environment that Hassan al-Bana, an Egyptian schoolteacher, launched the Muslim Brotherhood, an organization designed to enliven the Islamic spirit by encouraging Egypt's youth to follow the way of the Prophet Mohammed. Indeed, the initial name of al-Bana's organization was the Young Men's Muslim Association. The solution to Egypt's woes, according to al-Bana, was not secularism but a return to the basic principles of Islam and a system of government modeled on the Koran. As al-Bana's emphasis on basic principles seemed to have much in common with Protestant fundamentalism, it soon became common for Westerners to refer to groups such as the Muslim Brotherhood as fundamentalists.

Muslims have never been particularly comfortable with the term "fundamentalism" and believe that it is the obligations of all Muslims to follow the way of the Prophet. The Muslim experience was also far more complex than Protestant notions of redemption and rebirth. Muslims are born again every time they testify that there is no God but Allah and that Mohammed is His prophet, something that can happen several times a day. In contrast to Christian fundamentalists, the basic issue confronting Muslims is not the rededication of their faith but agreeing on the best way to serve God. Were prayer and good works adequate, or did their faith require political action?

Many chose political action. The Brotherhood flourished and become the largest and most dynamic fundamentalist organization in the region. Henceforth, the Islamic faith would be divided between two Islams: an "establishment Islam" consisting of religious leaders appointed by the government, and a "fundamentalist Islam" that sought to recapture the state.

The road, however, was not easy. The very success of the Muslim Brotherhood placed it in conflict with a new generation of secular generals intent on building a modern Arab empire. During the mid-1950s, the Brotherhood made an abortive attempt to assassinate Abdul Nasser, the president of Egypt and successor to Ataturk as the driving force of secularism and modernity in the Middle East. Nasser retaliated with vengeance. The Brotherhood's leaders were either killed or jailed, and the organization was driven into remission. Westernization and modernity had become the order of the day.

The Middle East, however, is a region of startling change. The Arab-Israeli War of 1967 saw the armies of Nasser humbled by Israeli forces in less than a week. The war is often referred to as the Six Day War, but the abject humiliation of the Arabs took only four. The promises of secular modernity had proven hollow and left the Arabs bitter and devoid of hope. Their despair was shared by the Muslim world as a whole, for the defeat of the Arabs was also a humiliation for Islam. Once again, the Jews and Christians had reigned supreme. In whom could Muslims place their faith and trust?

The Muslim Brotherhood provided the answer. "God is the Solution," proclaimed their slogan. It appeared everywhere: in mosques, on pamphlets passed from hand to hand, and on the walls unprotected by the watchful eyes of the police. The Muslim Brotherhood may have been in remission, but it was not dead.

The Brotherhood, however, had also changed. The Muslim Brotherhood that emerged in the ashes of the 1967 War was a chastised Brotherhood that stressed reform rather than assassinations and violence. Nasser and the generals had proven too powerful to be overthrown by a religious organization. Henceforth, the Brotherhood accommodated the secular leaders of Egypt and other countries on the condition that they be allowed to spearhead an Islamic revival not terribly different from the Christian revival sweeping the United States. Reform based on teaching, preaching, and good works was to be the key to success. Once the spirit of Islam had been revived among the masses, so the argument went, the political leadership would follow suit. They would have no choice.

Again, however, there were problems. The new moderation of the Muslim Brotherhood attracted a following with views so diverse that they defied incorporation into a single organization. The question of strategy was particularly divisive. Was it better to work within the system, as advocated by the new strategists of the Muslim Brotherhood, or to destroy it, as advocated by Sayeed Qutb, a leading Brotherhood thinker during the 1950s and 1960s? According to Qutb, Muslim society had been corrupted beyond the point of salvation and differed little from the era of ignorance that had prevailed in Arabia prior to the arrival of the Prophet Mohammed.[17] Just as the Prophet Mohammed had imposed the teachings of Islam on the citizens of Mecca by force, Qutb argued, so the obligation of today's Muslims was to reclaim Islam by force. There was no other choice. Working within the system served the devil and corrupted the faithful. A holy war, a jihad, had to be declared against secular regimes and those who supported them. Secular Muslim leaders had become infidels and were no longer fit to rule.

The jihadists excelled in zeal and violence, but found unity elusive. Some observers in Egypt charted the existence of some ninety Islamic jihadist groups of one variety or another. Rare was a country in the Islamic world that did not have several.[18] A majority of the Egyptian groups were small and short lived. A few larger groups such as the Islamic Group and Islamic Jihad affiliated with international jihadists networks such as bin Laden's al Qaeda network or developed their own international branches.

How well do the Muslim Brotherhood and the jihadists cooperate? We'll discuss this in detail in later chapters. For the moment, suffice it to say that there is little consensus on the issue. Some find the inherent tension between the Brotherhood and the jihadists to be a window of opportunity for defeating the jihadists. To strengthen the Brotherhood, they argue, is to weaken the jihadists. Others argue that the Muslim Brotherhood and the jihadists are merely two sides of the same coin: one possesses a seductive ideology of reform and democracy while the other intimidates its opponents with threats of violence and mayhem. The goal, they note, is the same: an Islamic state.

As things currently stand, both the Muslim Brotherhood and the jihadists have branches throughout the Arab and Islamic worlds, including the Muslim communities of Europe and North America. Parallel fundamentalist movements, some violent and some nonviolent, evolved in Pakistan and

Iran, many with a broad international reach. The Iranian-sponsored groups represent the Shi'a branch of Islam and are heavily supported by the government of Iran.

THE SOURCES OF MUSLIM DISCONTENT

Not only has fundamentalist Islam developed a global reach, but it has become the most vibrant political movement in the Islamic world. This is true of the moderate Islamic parties now flexing their muscle in the more democratic countries of the Islamic world, just as it is true of radical reformers such as the Muslim Brotherhood. Above all, it is true of the jihadists.

It could not be otherwise, for the forces that gave rise to Islamic fundamentalism in the early years of the twentieth century have increased exponentially. For more than five decades, the peoples of the Middle East and Islamic worlds have lived in a vortex of social change. Once rural if not tribal, they now seek a better life in megalopolises so polluted that the very act of breathing is dangerous to their health. Except for the wealthy minority, there is little but squalor. The extended families, that massive network of parents, grandparents, brothers, sisters, uncles, aunts, and cousins extending to the fifth degree that once provided the foundation of Middle Eastern society, are beginning to crumble, much as they did in the United States more than a century ago. Families remain the focal point of individual loyalty, with many individuals devoting some 50 percent of their salaries to helping relatives. Life, however, has become too complex and demanding to be sustained by families alone.

Social despair is paralleled by economic despair. Middle Eastern universities are bursting at the seams, but there are few jobs for graduates. Those jobs that are available go to relatives of the influential or are allocated as a form of political payoff. Little of the region's legendary wealth finds its way to the poor countries of the Islamic world, and even the pampered residents of Saudi Arabia and the Gulf States are now being asked to put their shoulders to the wheel.[19] Sadly, they don't know how. Their whole lives have been spent receiving government handouts while guest workers got things done.

With governments as oppressive and ineffective as they are corrupt, it is only natural that many Muslims have sought salvation in their religion. In the parlance of Christian fundamentalism, "they are hurting." They are looking for a savior. Tragically, there are few avenues for peaceful change in the Islamic world. Secularists are condemned as tools of the United States, Muslim reformers as terrorists. Political parties exist here and there as window dressing, but the only voice that counts is that of the regime. The Islamic movement is the only effective opposition to the politics of the Islamic world as presently constituted. The choice, by and large, is between radical reformers such as the Muslim Brotherhood and Hizbullah on one hand, and various strains of the jihadist movement on the other.

Globalization now threatens to accelerate the pace of change and despair to the breaking point.[20] Satellites, DVDs, and the Internet assault this most conservative of regions with seductive and unrealistic images of Western culture. Many are lured by the promise of Westernization. The devout have recoiled in fear that traditional Islamic values are being irrevocably destroyed. Both sides are fearful and frustrated, the former by what they can't have and the latter by what they might lose. The battle is more than a contest between groups. It also rages within individuals torn by diametrically opposed visions of society. Most want both: Westernization and the security of their faith.

If cultural globalization is seductive and subtle, economic globalization has pounded the Islamic world with the force of a sledgehammer. Virtually all Islamic countries had practiced some form of socialism, with most people, aside from peasants, being employed by the government. Huge bureaucracies gave employment to endless streams of college graduates, while most urban workers labored in government-owned factories. Not much was accomplished, but most people had a job, a pension, and rudimentary health care. Wages were abysmally low—a professor in Egypt made about $200 per month, a schoolteacher about half that much—but food, health care, and housing were all subsidized. One got by.

That now has changed. The World Bank, International Monetary Fund (IMF), and the World Trade Organization have decreed that capitalism will do a better job of curing poverty and violence than government welfare programs. This view is whole heartedly seconded by the United States and other major donors of foreign aid. The poor countries of the Islamic world remain skeptical but have little choice. Most cannot survive without loans from the IMF and the World Bank. State-owned industries are being sold off, jobs jettisoned, overblown bureaucracies trimmed, and social safety nets dismantled. This seems to make good economic sense, but it sows panic among populations that have long survived on government handouts. A narrow class of merchants, land speculators, and industrialists has become inordinately wealthy under the new economic order, but the masses have not.[21] Things have gotten worse, not better. This fact is not lost on the poor of the Muslim world. The gaudy lifestyle of the nouveau riche rub their noses in the collective misery of the poor on a daily basis. Are the poor bitter? Absolutely.

Tragically, political globalization has lagged and with it the much bally-hooed promises of democracy and human rights. On the contrary, the United States and its allies are strengthening oppressive regimes in hope of stifling the jihadists. The United States has also begun to extend its military control over the Islamic world, occupying Iraq, boycotting Iran, and stationing its troops on the sacred Islamic soil of Saudi Arabia. Once again, turn about is not fair play, as immigration from the Muslim world has been restricted and Muslim immigrants find themselves blamed for everything from crime and drugs to unemployment. Muslims bear the brunt of globalization, but enjoy few of its positive aspects.

The citizens of the United States and its Western allies have experienced similar economic and social woes over the course of the past centuries, but the pace of change was slower and more graduated. There was time to adjust. For the most part, governments were competent, and, at least in the Anglo world, capable of adapting to changing realities. When large groups of people became upset, democratic procedures, however flawed, adjusted to their demands. There was also the pride of empire and technological superiority. As people demanded more, the industrial economies of the West were able to provide more. Democracy and human rights were built on a bedrock of economic growth.

None of this exists in the Islamic world. Not only are Muslims locked in a vortex of change and economic chaos, but their political systems are abysmal. Rather than offering hope for a better life, they offer little but oppression and despair. There is no democracy in the Western sense of the word. Corruption is endemic, human rights are honored in the breach, and the quality of services is dismal. Health and welfare services for the destitute are provided largely by the Muslim Brotherhood or similar religious organizations. Ironically, the one area in which the leaders of the region excel is their ability to cling to power and pass it on to their sons. As a result of enhanced technologies in intimidation and repression, peaceful change in the region has become a virtual impossibility. Indeed, a region once renowned for their coups d'etat has now become a region renowned for its aging dictators.

For all of the present woes, the peoples of the Middle East have a deep sense of history and are intensely proud of their past. It was they who provided the cradle of civilization. It was also they who once ruled much of the known world and who set the standard for science and enlightenment during the dark ages that descended on Europe following the collapse of Rome.

It is that very pride in their past that makes the humiliation of the present so bitter. Much like Islamic thinkers of an earlier era, Arab and Muslim intellectuals of today relentlessly debate the cause of their malaise, most placing the blame on colonialism that swept the Islamic world during the nineteenth and twentieth centuries. The Islamic world was fragmented, each mini-country, some no larger than a postage stamp, being endowed with a mini-king subservient to the West. The era of independence that came after the end of WWII was merely replaced by a more insidious form of economic and cultural colonialism that threatened to transform the very roots of Arab and Islamic society.[22]

Of all of the insults to Arab and Islamic pride, none was greater than the creation of Israel. The crusaders, from the Islamic view, had returned, laying claim to the third-holiest shrine in Islam and creating a Jewish state that would banish hopes for Arab and Islamic unity. War after war found the Arabs humiliated by a small Jewish state, itself no larger than a postage stamp. How could so few Jews defeat so many Arabs and Muslims? To accept the possibility of Israeli superiority would be to admit that a basic and fundamental flaw existed in the Arab and Islamic view of the world, an admission that would threaten the very foundations of the faith and the Arab psyche.[23]

GAUGING POPULAR SUPPORT FOR MUSLIM EXTREMISTS

If the peoples of the Middle Eastern and Islamic worlds share a common despair, they differ violently over the cure. Some, a minority, have adopted Western secularism with a vengeance. Others, also a minority, seek salvation in religious governments that imposes servitude in the name of Islam. Between this vast and unbridgeable chasm lies the majority of the world's Muslims. Most would prefer a balance between Islamic morality and modernity. Of these, some are moderate in their religious views, while others incline toward extremism. For those concerned with the relationship between Islam and the war on terror, the obvious questions are: (1) Who is who? (2) How many are there of each? Moderates are potential allies of the United States; extremists are potential allies of the jihadists.

Unfortunately, it is difficult to gauge the intensity with which Muslims embrace their faith. Some researchers have attempted to measure the intensity of Islamic religious emotions by monitoring levels of attendance at mosques or observing the number of people who participate in religious celebrations such as the Haj.[24] Whatever the case, the results are awesome. Mosques are overflowing. Millions of Muslims attend the Haj each year and return to joyous celebrations among friends and families. The 2002 celebration of Biswa Ijtema (three days of prayers and teaching on the banks of the Turag River in Bangladesh) drew a reported two million worshipers from some eighty countries.[25]

Other observers have focused on the explosion of Islamic dress that began in late 1970s and early 1980s. Beards, long a symbol of religious piety, became a statement of opposition to the secular regimes of the Islamic world. The late President Sadat of Egypt banned beards, only to see their numbers multiply. He was assassinated by jihadists in 1981. Religious dress among women has become ubiquitous. Billboards in Egypt and elsewhere advertise the latest in Islamic fashions, many designed in Paris. Even some women traffic police in the Middle East have begun to wear Islamic head scarves tucked neatly beneath their military caps.

How does one interpret this phenomenal upsurge in Islamic dress? Is it an expression of piety, a show of support for religious extremists, or a message of defiance to corrupt and oppressive regimes? For many Islamic men, it is some of each. Deciphering the explosion in Islamic dress among women is far more complex, being variously interpreted as a symbol of piety, support for the Islamic revival, a statement of political opposition, a signal of purity to perspective suitors, submission to family pressure, conformity to the latest style, a means of deflecting over-aggressive males, relief from lengthy hairdos and even reverse sex appeal.[26]

Both the American government and leaders of the Islamic world are deeply concerned with the growing number of religiously based protests against American policy in the region. Participating in protests is a far clearer expression of political involvement than praying in a mosque, and such demonstrations are routinely videotaped by the police for future reference. Demonstrations against the U.S. invasion of Iraq and Israeli policies in the Occupied Territories have been particularly emotional. Most participants in anti-American demonstrations are drawn from the region's universities and high schools and do not necessarily reflect the general sentiment of the population. It's also not clear whether the protests are a manifestation of religious zeal or an expression of nationalistic resentment against U.S. policy. Probably some of each. Whatever the case, they are part of the puzzle.

Yet another piece of the puzzle is the results of the region's fraudulent elections. Candidates of the Muslim Brotherhood scored surprising victories in the Egypt's recent parliamentary elections, despite the fact that the organization was banned. They also made strong showings in Turkey, Morocco, Jordan, Pakistan, and other Islamic countries. Are people voting for Islam, or are they protesting against corrupt and oppressive governments? Again, the answer is some of each. President Mubarak of Egypt tends to attribute the growing popularity of Islamic parties to the region's lack of experience with democracy. As he explained to the U.S. Congress:

> This country was under pressure for years and years, and when you open the gate for freedom, you will find many terrible things taking place. If you have a dam and keep the water until it begins to overflow, and then you open the gates, it will drown many people. We have to give a gradual dose so people can swallow it and understand it. The Egyptians are not Americans.[27]

Yet another way to assess levels of Islamic religiosity is to simply ask people how religious they are, a procedure that is routine in the West. Our colleagues and we have experimented with public opinion research in a variety of Middle Eastern countries with varying degrees of success. Respondents in Egypt and Lebanon, countries with long intellectual traditions, were quite forthcoming with their responses, while respondents in Saudi Arabia all responded that they were deeply religious. It is dangerous to be tepid about religion in Saudi Arabia.

Particularly surprising was the willingness of some 50 percent of the Egyptian respondents to indicate support for the Islamic revival, an oblique reference to the Islamic Fundamentalist Movement. Of these, a hard core of around 14 percent indicated very strong support for the revival. The Lebanese results paralleled those of the Egyptian respondents. More than 90 percent of our Egyptian respondents expressed either strong or very strong support for religion in schools, with the latter category exceeding the 65 percent mark.[28] In much the same manner, more than 70 percent of the Egyptian respondents supported religious censorship of the media. Again, the results among Lebanese Muslims were similar.[29]

Particularly alarming from the American perspective, have been the spate of opinion polls that followed the September 11 attacks on the United

States. A *Times of London* poll conducted shortly after September 11, found that approximately 11 percent of Britain's two million Muslims believed that there was some justification for bin Laden's attacks on the United States; some 40 percent of the respondents disagreed with bin Laden's means, but agreed that his war against the United States was justified. Some 68 percent indicated that their faith was more important than "being British." The results were based on interviews with 1,170 Muslims conducted outside British mosques.[30] In the same period, the *New York Times* reported that a classified Saudi intelligence survey found that 95 percent of educated Saudis supported bin Laden's cause.[31] The director of Saudi intelligence reportedly acknowledged the survey, but attributed its results to Saudi anger against the United States for its support of Israeli oppression in the Occupied Territories.[32] Gallup polls in the Islamic world conducted in 2002 and 2003 registered high levels of anti-Americanism among Muslims, as did a parallel survey sponsored by the Saudi-backed Arab Thought Foundation.[33] A congressional study conducted in the summer of 2003 found that "the bottom has indeed fallen out of support for the United States."[34] Similar results were forthcoming from broader cross-national polls such as those conducted by the Pew Research Center for the People and the Press. By and large, hostility toward the United States focused on American policy in the Middle East, particularly U.S. support of Israel. The spread of American culture was also a concern throughout the Islamic world as well as in much of Europe. Only the Japanese, it seems, are particularly fond of American culture. Interestingly, Muslims retain a high regard for American democracy and freedom. A summary of the Pew results relating to the war on terror are presented in table 2.1.

Unfortunately, assessing public opinion in the Islamic world remains more of an art than a science, and the data reviewed above are merely suggestive. Their consistency, however, is a cause for concern. The post–September 11 surveys, in particular, reflect an abiding rejection of American policy in the Middle East, as do the polls and protests accompanying the U.S. war on Iraq. Both reflect a widespread belief that the United States has declared war on Islam

LEVELS OF ISLAMIC RELIGIOSITY

Taken collectively, our surveys and those of our colleagues suggest that the Islamic community or nation, as it is referred to in Islam, might conve-

Table 2.1   Perceived Popular Views of Terrorist Attacks Chart

	U.S. Policy Caused Attacks Percentage	*Good for U.S. to Feel Vulnerable Percentage*
United States	18	n/a
Total Non-U.S.	58	70
Western Europe	36	66
E. Europe/Russia	71	70
Latin America	58	71
Asia	60	76
Mid-East/Conflict Area	81	65
All Islamic States	76	73

Source: The Pew Global Attitudes Project, www.people-press.org/121901rpt.htm

niently be viewed as consisting of six basic levels based on the intensity of their religious beliefs, their vision of an Islamic state, and their predisposition toward violence. These levels are nonbelievers (*kafirs*), minimalists, practicing, devout, publicists, and fanatics.[35]

To be a *kafir* in Islam requires that one disavow the existence of God and the role of the Prophet Mohammed as His messenger. Merely losing interest in one's faith is not grounds for excommunication. There are few avowed nonbelievers in the Islamic world, most being leftist intellectuals who eschew religious violence and are staunch advocates of a secular state.

This said, many Muslims, like many Jews and Christians, are minimalists. They are Muslim in identity and culture, but are lax in the execution of their religious obligations. Those who do attend the mosque often do so in response to social pressures rather than deep conviction. The minimalists also eschew religious violence and are staunch advocates of a secular state. Based on the research discussed above, this group would probably constitute about 15 percent of the world's Muslim population, although that figure may be unduly optimistic. Most are intellectuals, but that is not to say that most intellectuals are secularists. Indeed, many jihadist leaders possess dazzling intellect as do the leaders of more moderate groups such as the Muslim Brotherhood and Hizbullah.

A third major category of Muslims might be called practicing Muslims. They try to fulfill the basic religious obligations as best they can, some being more successful than others. Religious concerns are important but compete with a broad range of social, economic, and political interests. Practicing Muslims worry about the lack of morality in government and society, but are essentially secular in outlook. They reject religious violence. Practicing Muslims probably constitute about 30 percent of the Muslim population.

The next rung in the hierarchy of Islamic religiosity is occupied by concerned Muslims, a group that approximates the moral majority in the United States. Concerned Muslims are far more likely than practicing Muslims to attend religious lectures, participate in study groups, associate with religious societies, and otherwise make religion a major focus of their lives. Most, however, view religion as a personal affair and incline toward moderation in their political views. Morality, however, is high on their political agenda. They, too, condemn religious violence. The research reviewed above also suggests that concerned Muslims constitute nearly 30 percent of the Muslim population.

The fifth category of Muslims we have termed publicists. Unlike concerned Muslims, publicists believe that religion is far more than a personal affair. Islam, in their view, is a public affair. They display their religiosity via Islamic dress and other signs of piety and they actively encourage others to behave in a religious manner. They are doers rather than talkers and openly advocate a religious state. Most do not advocate violence, but they often support doctrines considered inflammatory by the United States. Our limited research in Egypt and Lebanon suggests that the publicists constitute approximately 20 percent of the Muslim population, a large percentage given their propensity for action. Judging by their statements, they would feel quite comfortable in an Islamic theocracy.

Topping the hierarchy of Islamic religiosity are the fanatics. As with fanatics in all faiths, they are driven by a zeal and singleness of purpose that blinds them to all but the narrowest of doctrines. The Islamic fanatics share a common vision of a pristine Islamic state that differs little from the Islamic state established by the Prophet Mohammed in seventh-century Arabia. If anything, it is more extreme, lacking the humanity, flexibility, and enlightenment that characterized the rule of the Prophet. While Prophet Mohammed looked to the future, the Islamic fanatics look to the past.

The fanatics are not of a single mind, however. The jihadists advocate terror to achieve their goals, while other fanatics have turned to asceticism and are minimally concerned with the political affairs of the temporal world. An interesting example of this phenomenon is the al-Abash of Lebanon, a Sufi group that has openly confronted the jihadists, occasionally with violence.[36] As such, they pose an appealing alternative to the jihadists for fanatical Muslims troubled by Islamic injunctions against the killing of Muslims and innocents.

Fanaticism, then, does not of itself lead to violence. In reality, the jihadists represent an infinitesimally small number of the world's more than one billion Muslims. It is their fanaticism that makes them so dangerous. The CIA estimates suggest that al Qaeda can draw on a global base of six to seven million fanatical Muslims. Potential fighters are placed at 120,000.[37] These are roughly in line with our own estimates.

The six groups form a simple curve, the two extremes of which are the nonbelievers and the fanatics. Numbers are larger among the minimalists and the publicists, with the center of the curve being occupied by the practicing and the devout Muslims. This relationship is illustrated in figure 2.1. Percentages are merely suggestive and could easily vary from time to time and country to country. Lebanon and Egypt are world's apart from Yemen and Saudi Arabia. The rural areas of the Islamic world are often centuries behind their urban centers.

The intensity of religious emotions also tends to ebb and flow as Muslims attempt to reconcile their religious upbringing with the seductive allure of Western lifestyles. Make no mistake, the glitzy life portrayed in Western movies and television programs does have strong appeal to Muslims trapped in the bleak existence of the Third World. Indeed, it is not unusual for individuals to vacillate between the two extremes, exuding piety one day and

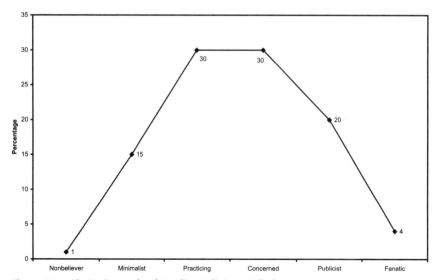

Figure 2.1　Six Basic Levels of Muslim Religious Beliefs

laxity the next. Many of the perpetrators of the September 11 attacks seemed to have experienced similar psychological dilemmas.

The lines separating the different levels of religious intensity are also blurred and shifting. Minimalists merge with practicing Muslims and the latter with concerned Muslims and publicists. Social pressures to display one's faith have increased dramatically over the past few decades and tend to peak during times of crisis. Nevertheless, each of the categories outlined above has a center of gravity and influences how Muslims express their views politically.

As might be expected, support for the extremist groups tends to increase as one ascends the hierarchy of Islamic religiosity. Minimalists and practicing Muslims tend to support the secular political parties of the Islamic world, but are not averse to greater religiosity in education and politics. If they support the extremist parties or groups such as the Muslim Brotherhood, it is largely to protest the ineptness of their own governments. Concerned Muslims are far less opposed to the notion of an enlightened Islamic government, but have little use for the excesses of the fanatics. Many find the views of the Muslim Brotherhood reasonable and far more appealing than the tepid Islam purveyed by government preachers. All in all, concerned Muslims constitute a moderate Islamic voice in the spectrum of Islamic politics. It is they who tend to vote for the moderate Islamic parties and it is they who are increasingly making their voice heard in the political arena of the Muslim world. Publicists, by contrast, openly proclaim their desire for an Islamic state whatever its severity. They are the activists who feel that it is their obligation to prepare the way for an Islamic government. This does not make them terrorists, but it is the publicists who constitute the main support group of the jihadists. The fanatics, in turn, provide the jihadists with their activists and die-hard supporters.

The down slope of the figure 2.1 constitutes what Muslims refer to as the Islamic movement, a broad and somewhat amorphous category that incorporates the full gamut of individuals aspiring for a more Islamic government. The Islamic movement includes concerned Muslims as well as the publicists and the fanatics. All in all, they constitute approximately half of the Muslim population. Few support terror against the United States, but all are deeply concerned that things are not well within the Islamic community and feel they must be changed. Members of the Islamic movement are particularly concerned that the United States has declared war on Islam.

The fit between religiosity and politics, of course, is only approximate. Even minimalists protest the oppressive and inept regimes of the Islamic world by voting for Islamic parties. Indeed, the Islamic Revolution in Iran was supported by confirmed communists who supported the Ayatollah Khomeini in a calculated effort to rid themselves of the Shah. In retrospect, this was a mistake. The clerics continue to rule and most former leftists are either dead, exiled, or rotting in Iran's infamous jails. The converse is also true. Many Muslims with extremist views have turned to prayer rather than politics, believing that personal purity is more relevant to salvation than earthly endeavors. Others have joined *sufi* (religious mystics) groups seeking greater personal communication with God. Most subgroups are apolitical and, as such, represent a threat to the extremists.

SEPARATING ISLAMIC EXTREMISM FROM ANTI-AMERICANISM

Judging by the intensity of their religious behavior, the vast majority of the world's Muslims should be America's allies in its war against terror. This would certainly include those Muslims falling in the minimalist and practicing categories. They fear the extremism of the zealots at least as much as Americans do and they aspire to a quality of political and economic life personified by the United States. Most firmly believe that it is possible to blend science and Islam. Concerned Muslims should also find few complaints with American views on religion. Muslims have prospered in the United States, although some view the security measures put in place following the September 11 attacks with concern.

Unfortunately, the public opinion polls reviewed earlier indicate that hostility toward the United States is not limited to Muslim extremists. On the contrary, it includes just about all Muslims, secularists as well as religious extremists. Being anti-American does not make one a terrorist, but such anti-American attitudes do bolster the jihadists and make it difficult for both the United States and friendly Islamic governments to fight terror. This point was brought home with devastating impact as long-time allies such as Egypt and Turkey, fearing a public backlash, declined to support the Allied invasion of Iraq. Indeed, the media referred to "coalition forces" but that coalition was overwhelmingly dominated by the U.S. and Britain. Saudi Arabia pretended that it was not among them.

Why, then, are Muslims so overwhelmingly opposed to American policy toward the Islamic world? Why has the United States, once a symbol of hope and friendship in the Muslim world, become the enemy? In large part, the answer to these questions is found in the massive gap that separates the way in which Americans and Muslims view the world.

Americans see themselves as a fair and reasonable people who desire nothing more than freedom, justice, and prosperity for all. As the innocent victims of criminal violence, Americans believe that they are fully justified in striking the terrorist with maximum force. In their view, their hands are free of blood.

The image of the United States that prevails in the Islamic world is radically different. Not only is the United States seen as having blood on its hands, but those hands are literally dripping in the blood of Arabs and Muslims. Five widely accepted Muslim perceptions of the United States, in particular, have soured America's relations with the Islamic world and generated support for violence against American targets. The five Muslim perceptions of the United States are listed below.

Muslim Perception 1: The United States controls everything. Perhaps the most widely held of all Middle Eastern perceptions of the United States is the belief that little of importance happens in the region, if not the world, that is not the direct result of American manipulation. Some time ago, by way of illustration, we were discussing events in Baghdad with an Iraqi friend, who pointed with his right hand in the direction of the American Embassy and with his left hand in the direction of the Soviet Embassy. "Whenever anything happens in Iraq," he said with complete conviction, "we ask ourselves was it our friends on the left or our friends on the right?"

Our response to this perception has been to ask if the United States really controls everything, why is the region slipping under the control of the fundamentalists? Why hasn't the Arab-Israeli crisis been resolved? Why did September 11 happen? Why does bin Laden's al Qaeda network remain at large? Why was the Ayatollah Kohmeini victorious in Iran? There can be no doubt that America's military and economic power makes it a major player in the region, but that power has not been exercised with consummate skill. Rather than being a master chess player, the United States is more like a bull in the china shop, lurching from one crisis to another, none of which are ever fully resolved.

Perceptions of American omnipotence in the region reflect the very intrusive role of the United States in the region as well as the tremendous economic and military power that the United States does possess. By the same token, blaming everything on the Americans is a convenient way for the leaders and intellectuals of the region to avoid responsibility for their own ineffectiveness. Whatever the case, blaming the ills of the region on the United States, justified or not, does create intense feelings of animosity toward the American government.

Muslim Perception 2: America is attempting to bring the entire region under its control. This perception reflects a begrudging acknowledgment that the United States does not, at least yet, control everything in the region. Perceptions, however, are emotional rather than rational, and apparent contradictions are part of the psychological game people play to make sense of their world.

The belief that the United States is attempting to take over the world is far more dangerous than the belief that it does control everything, inasmuch as it signals a call to arms. There is still time to act! Every move that the United States makes (or doesn't make) is interpreted as part of an evil scheme to dominate the region and its oil resources. Allowing the Taliban to shelter bin Laden, for example, was seen as a pretext for bombing Afghanistan and putting a regime in power that would be loyal to the United States. An even more insidious view is that the whole Afghan affair was staged by the United States to justify attacks on Iran and other Islamic regimes. Similar flights of fancy saw the United States encouraging Iraq's 1990 attack on Kuwait as a pretext for crippling Iraq and forcing Saudi Arabia, Kuwait, and the other Gulf States to become totally dependent on the United States for their survival. Needless to say, this includes the stationing of U.S. troops on their soil.

Somewhat ironically and with an obvious sense of humor, the Al-Jazeera TV network recently broadcast a debate on whether the United States should be encouraged to take over the region. "At the very least," to paraphrase one participant, "we would have democracy and human rights and would be done with the corrupt and oppressive governments that have been the bane of our existence."[38]

Muslim Perception 3: The United States wants to control and exploit the region, not govern it. The accuracy of this perception is not a matter of much contention. The Middle East is vital to the national interests of the United States, and the United States has historically acted to protect that interest. The United States has also relied heavily on friendly leaders in the region to do its bidding, regardless of how repressive and corrupt they may have been. As might be expected, this policy makes the people of the region feel that their freedoms are being sacrificed for the prosperity of the United States and this fuels long-term resentment. Ruling by proxy, however, saves both lives and money. Occupying territory, as the Israelis have learned to their dismay, is a dangerous and costly business. The United States is now learning the same lesson in Iraq.

Muslim Perception 4: The United States is unabashedly on the side of Israel. This, too, is a difficult perception to dispute as a long series of American presidents have taken office by proclaiming that "Israel has a friend in the White House." Bill Clinton topped Ronald Reagan in his support for Israel, and George W. Bush, in the Muslim view, appears to be topping both. Israel is the largest recipient of U.S. foreign aid and, more often than not, it is a U.S. veto in the Security Council that spares Israel from yet another UN condemnation of its occupation policies. Fortunately for Israel, it is the U.S. vote that counts. Lest there be any doubt about America's sympathies, the United States has begun to arm Israeli submarines with nuclear weapons.[39]

As might be expected, Arabs see themselves being victimized by U.S. policy toward Israel, a view widely shared in Europe and the Islamic world. British Prime Minister Tony Blair has openly criticized George W. Bush for America's one-sided role in attempting to broker a lasting peace in the region, a criticism now subscribed to by the European Union as a whole.[40]

Secular Palestinian leaders have continued to work with the United States in seeking a peaceful solution to the crisis. They have little choice. They can either work with the United States or see power slip to the jihadists.

Muslim Perception 5: The United States has declared war on Islam. This is a profound misperception based on the fact that America's war on terrorism is directed primarily at Muslim groups. It is also fueled by the U.S. occupation of Iraq and its increasingly belligerent policy toward Iran and Syria. It is further rooted in a history of U.S. support for oppressive Muslim regimes, not the least of which are Egypt and Saudi Arabia, the pillars of U.S. policy in the Arab world.

Of all of the above perceptions, the belief that the United States has declared war on Islam is the most lethal. It is lethal in terms of the number of people and countries involved, in terms of the intensity of the motivations inflamed, and in terms of the capacity of the jihadists to build support among Muslim populations by vilifying the United States. As the Saudi ambassador to the United Kingdom commented to a leading British magazine,

> Please don't kick the ambassador out of London for saying this, but if you
> go around the Muslim World, you will find the vast majority of people will

support Osama bin Laden, and this is more tragic than the attack itself. Why would such a crime like this find such support, not just on the streets of Riyadh, but on the streets of Turkey, the streets of Tunis, and the streets of Britain? That comes down to the question of why people hate America.[41]

In the final analysis, it is not the accuracy of Muslim perceptions that is critical, but the fact that they trigger deep emotional responses within the Islamic world. The United States will not be successful in countering terrorists unless we can do a better job of convincing people that America has not declared war on Islam. It would also do well to reconsider its support of oppressive regimes in the Islamic world. All fuel anti-Americanism and anti-Americanism strengthens the jihadists.

NOTES

1. Herbert Busse, *Islam, Judaism and Christianity: Theological and Historical Affiliations* (Princeton, N.J.: Markus Wiener Publishers, 1997).

2. *The Koran: Interpreted.* Translation by A. J. Arberry (New York: Touchstone: Simon & Schuster, 1955), 60–61; Sydney N. Fisher, *The Middle East: A History* (New York: Knopf, 1964).

3. Traditionally, Christians and Jews paid a tax or tribute for the right to live in peace and security among Muslim populations; Philip K. Hitti, *History of the Arabs from the Earliest Times to the Present,* 6th ed. (London: Macmillan, 1956), 204.

4. Majid Khadduri, *War and Peace in the Law of Islam* (Baltimore: Johns Hopkins Press, 1955). Islam divides the world into two, mutually hostile camps: the world of peace (Islam) and the world of war (nonbelievers). Muslims are enjoined to conquer the world of war and bring its subjects into the world of peace. Ideally, this is to be done by conversion. If conversion fails, they must be converted by force. Thus, jihad, in its meaning as a holy war, is both offensive and defensive. Jihad is used to defeat the world of war and defend the world of peace.

5. "Fatwa: What Is Jihad in Islam?" *Islam Online,* 10 Apr. 2002, at http://www.islam online.net/fatwa/english/FatwaDisplay.asp?hFatwaID=18243 (accessed 21 Oct. 2002).

6. Cecil Roth, *History of the Jews* (New York: Schocken Books, 1963). Rather than focusing on a single individual such as Christ or Mohammed, the Jewish faith evolved around a series of key individuals, the foremost of whom are Abraham, the father of the Hebrew people and Moses, the prophet who, upon God's orders, led the Hebrew people to settle in Israel, and Solomon who constructed the Holy Temple that continues to serve as one of the major symbols of the Jewish faith.

7. Yahya Armajani, *Middle East: Past and Present* (Englewood Cliffs, N.J.: Prentice-Hall, 1970), 101.

8. Henry Munson Jr., *Islam and Revolution in the Middle East* (New Haven, Conn.: Yale University Press, 1988) and Farhad Ibrahim, *Confessionalism and Politics in the Arab World: The Shi'a Program in Iraq.* Translated from German into Arabic by the Center for Cultural Studies and Translations (Cairo: Library Madbouli, 1996).

9. For those interested in this topic, see James A. Bill and John Alden Williams,

Roman Catholics and Shi'i Muslims: Prayer, Passion, and Politics (Raleigh: University of North Carolina Press, 2002).

10. Hani A. Z. Yamani, *To Be a Saudi* (London: Janus Publishing, 1998).

11. Related by al-Bukhaaree in Hadith #2652 in Haneef James Oliver, *The "Wahhabi" Myth: Dispelling Prevalent Fallacies and the Fictitious Link with Bin Laden* (*Online Publishing*: Trafford, 2002), 1. Modern jihadists such as bin Laden are often referred to as Salafis on the grounds that they are attempting to impose the pure Salafi interpretation of Islam on the Muslim world. This charge is heatedly denied by Saudi Arabian clerics, who maintain that the Salafi is opposed to terror.

12. Hamdi Rizk, "Egyptian Muslim Brotherhood," *Al-Wasat* 31 (30 Oct. 1999), 31, in Arabic.

13. Oliver, *The 'Wahhabi' Myth.*

14. Robert Lacy, *The Kingdom: Arabia and the House of Sa'ud* (New York: Harcourt, Brace & Javonovich, 1981), 142–143.

15. Stephanie Cronin, *The Army and the Creation of the Pahlavi State in Iran, 1910–1926* (London: IB Tauris, 1997).

16. Andrew Mango, *Ataturk: The Biography of the Founder of Modern Turkey* (New York: The Overlook Press, 2002).

17. Ahmad Moussalli, *Moderate and Radical Islamic Fundamentalism: The Quest for Modernity, Legitimacy, and the Islamic State* (Gainesville: University Press of Florida, 1999).

18. Hala Mustafa, *The Political System and the Islamic Opposition in Egypt* (Cairo: Markaz Al-Mahrusa, 1995), in Arabic.

19. Yamani, *To Be a Saudi.*

20. Benjamin R. Barber, *Jihad VS. McWorld: Terrorism's Challenge to Democracy* (New York: Ballantine Books, 2001); Monte Palmer, *Political Development: Dilemmas and Challenges,* 5th ed. (Itasca, Ill.: Peacock Publishers/Wadsworth, 1997).

21. Gordon Brown and Jim Wolfensohn, "A New Deal for the World's Poor," *Guardian Unlimited-London,* 16 Feb. 2004, at http://www.guardian.co.uk./comment/story/0,3604,1149,00.html (accessed 16 Feb. 2004).

22. Hisham Sharabi, *Neopatriarchy: A Theory of Distorted Change in Arab Society* (New York: Oxford University Press, 1988).

23. F. Ajami, *The Arab Predicament,* 2nd ed. (Cambridge, U.K.: Cambridge University Press, 1992).

24. James A. Bill, "Resurgent Islam in the Persian Gulf," *Foreign Affairs* 63 (Fall 1984):108–127.

25. Anisur Rahman, "Tabligh Jamaat Host Biggest Congregation of Muslims after Hajj," *Islam Online,* 30 Jan. 2000, at www.islamonline.net/completesearch/English/mDetails.asp (accessed 21 Oct. 2002).

26. Pioneering work in this area was conducted by Zeinab Radwan, *Appearance of the Hijab among University Students* (Cairo: National Center for Social and Criminal Research, 1982). Also see Andrea B. Rugh, *Reveal and Conceal* (Cairo: American University of Cairo Press, 1987).

27. *New York Times* (12 Oct. 1993): A3, in Monte Palmer, *Comparative Politics* (Itasca, Ill: Peacock Publishers/Wadsworth, 2001), 434.

28. Monte Palmer, Madiha El Safty, and Earl Sullivan, "The Relationship between Economic and Religious Attitudes in Egypt" (paper presented at the annual meeting of the Middle East Studies Association of North America, Providence, R.I., 1996).

29. Hilal Khashan and Monte Palmer, "The Social and Economic Correlates of Islamic Religiosity" (paper presented at the annual meeting of the Middle East Studies Association for North America, Chicago, December 1998).

30. "The Voice of British Muslims: Divided Loyalties on the Home Front," *Sunday Times-London*, 4 Nov. 2001, at http://www.Sunday-times.co.uk/news/pages/sti/2001/11/04/stiusausa01022.html (accessed 4 Nov. 2001); "British Muslim Support for Terror," *Sunday Times-London*, 4 Nov. 2001, at http://www.Sunday-times.co.uk/news/pes/ sti/2001/11/04/stiusausa01025.html (accessed 4 Nov. 2001).

31. "95 Percent of Saudis Supported bin Laden's Cause," *Arabic News*, 29 Jan. 2002, at http://www.arabicnews.com/ansub/Daily/Day/020129/2002012944.html (accessed 22 Mar. 2002).

32. "95 Percent of Saudis Supported bin Laden's Cause," *Arabic News*, 29 Jan. 2002, at http://www.arabicnews.com/ansub/Daily/Day/020129/2002012944.htm (accessed 6 Feb. 2002).

33. Brian Whitaker, "Polls Apart," *Guardian Unlimited*, 4 Mar. 2002, at www .guardian.co.uk/elsewhere/journalist/story/0,7792,661807,00.html (accessed 4 Mar. 2002); Karen De Young, "Arabs' Opinion of West: Yes and No," *International Herald Tribune*, 8 Oct. 2002, at http://www.iht.com/articles/73099.html (accessed 8 Oct. 2002).

34. Christopher Marquis, "U.S. Image Abroad Will Take Years to Repair, Official Testifies," *New York Times* (5 Feb. 2004). A complete transcript of Tutwiler's prepared remarks can be found at the Bureau of International Information Programs, U.S. Department of State, at http://www.usinfo.state.gov/.

35. We personally have been associated with more than twenty survey research projects in the Middle East over the course of the past thirty years. A few, such as those cited earlier, have focused directly on religiosity. Others examined attachments to traditional values and reluctance to change. Some, such as the Al Ahram survey of bureaucratic behavior, were based on random samples. Others, given the severe restrictions on survey research in the region, were based on quota samples or, in some cases, on snowball samples. We have also made extensive studies of the surveys conducted by others, synopses of which can be found in Madiha El Safty, Monte Palmer, and Mark Kennedy, *An Analytical Index of Survey Research in Egypt* (Cairo: Cairo Papers in Social Science, 1985); Monte Palmer, Hilal Khashan Mima Nedelcovych, and Debra Munro, *Survey Research in the Arab World: An Analytical Index* (London: Menas Press, 1982); Monte Palmer, Ali Leila, and El Sayed Yassin, *The Egyptian Bureaucracy* (Syracuse, N.Y.: Syracuse University Press, 1988); Palmer, El Safty, and Sullivan, "The Relationship between Economic and Religious Attitudes in Egypt"; Khashan and Palmer, "The Social and Economic Correlates of Islamic Religiosity."

36. Nizar Hamzeh and Harir Dekmejian, "A Sufi Response to Political Islamism: Al-Ahbash of Lebanon," *International Journal of Middle East Studies* 28 (1996):217–299.

37. Rohan Gunaratna, *Inside Al-Qaeda: Global Network of Terror* (New York: Columbia University Press, 2002), 95.

38. "Contrary View," Al-Jazeera, 25 Jan. 2002, at http://www.aljazeera.net/programs/op_direction/articles/2002/1/1-23-1.htm (accessed 25 Jan. 2002).

39. Oliver, *The 'Wahhabi' Myth*; Peter Beaumont and Conal Urquhart, "Israel Deploys Nuclear Arms in Submarines," *Guardian Unlimited-London* (12 Oct. 2003).

40. Kamal Ahmed and Ed Vulliamy, "Blair Fears Split with U.S. over Its Support for Israel," *The Guardian*, 16 Dec. 2001, at http://www.observer.co.uk/international/story/0,6903,619515,00.html (accessed 16 Dec. 2001).

41. David Pallister, "Saudis Recall Controversial Ambassador," *The Guardian*, 19 Sept. 2002, at http://www.guardian.co.uk/Saudi/story/0,11599,794579.00.html (accessed 19 Sept. 2002).

3

THE MUSLIM BROTHERHOOD AND HIZBULLAH: RADICAL-MODERATES

Islamic groups devoted to the establishment of Islamic governments in the Muslim world tend to be of two varieties: (1) those willing to seek their goal by peaceful means, and (2) those wedded to the use of violence. The former are typified by the Muslim Brotherhood, Hizbullah, and the emerging Islamic parties that are now reshaping the electoral map of the Islamic world. The latter are the jihadists. The Muslim Brotherhood, Hizbullah, and the emerging Islamic political parties are often referred to as "radical-moderates." They are radical because they are dedicated to the establishment of religious governments in the Islamic world. They are moderate because they would prefer to achieve their goal of an Islamic government by peaceful means. They are also moderate in their vision of an enlightened Islamic state that blends religious morality with the best of modern technology. Indeed, Ayatollah Fadlallah, the spiritual guide of Hizbullah, recently announced his support for cloning, hardly a reactionary position.[1]

One can question just how moderate the Muslim Brotherhood, Hizbullah, and the emerging Islamic parties really are, but their presence as a dominant political force in the Islamic world is indisputable. They draw their support from a broad spectrum of Muslims, including those described earlier as concerned Muslims and publicists. Concerned Muslims tend to view religion as a personal matter but are vitally concerned about the declining of Islamic morality. The publicists are those Muslims who relish displaying their religiosity in public. Even many less devout Muslims find the vision of an enlightened Muslim state an appealing alternative to the political decay that now permeates the Islamic world. The radical-moderates may not be their first preference, but the absence of viable alternatives leaves them little choice.

The Muslim Brotherhood, Hizbullah, and other radical-moderates will have much to say about the success of the United States in its war against jihadist terror. They actively oppose American influence in the Islamic world and they have encouraged popular resistance to both the U.S./British occupation of Iraq and the Israeli occupation of the West Bank and Gaza. It was Hizbullah forces that drove the Israelis from southern Lebanon and it may soon be Hizbullah-type organizations that drive the United States from Iraq.

For their part, the Muslim Brotherhood and Hizbullah maintain that they are not inherently anti-American. Neither has been involved in anti-American attacks for over a decade and a half, and both routinely denounce jihadist attacks against American targets. The problem, they say, is that the United States has declared war on Islam and is unrelenting in its opposition to the establishment of Islamic governments in the Middle East and elsewhere. If the United States would cease its war against Islam and encourage Israel to return the Occupied Territories, they argue, there would be no anti-Americanism in the region.

It is possible that a flexible U.S. strategy toward groups such as the Muslim Brotherhood and Hizbullah would help reduce anti-Americanism in the Islamic world. It would also go a long way toward reducing popular support for the jihadists by providing more moderate Muslims with a nonviolent option for achieving greater morality in government and society. As things currently stand, moderate Muslims face a cruel choice. They can either suffer corrupt and oppressive regimes or they can support groups that advocate violence. There is very little middle ground between the two extremes.

There are, of course, no guarantees that accommodating groups such as the Muslim Brotherhood and Hizbullah will reduce either anti-Americanism or jihadist terror. Many people fear that accommodation will merely be interpreted as a sign of capitulation and increase the power of the jihadists. Advocates of this position argue that the radical-moderates and the jihadists are simply two sides of the same coin, each adopting a different strategy to achieve their common goal of an Islamic state.

The purpose of this chapter is not to resolve this debate, but to clarify the role that the Muslim Brotherhood and Hizbullah play in America's war on terror. Along the way we will examine their organization, operations, strengths, vulnerabilities, and torturous relationship with the jihadists.

THE MUSLIM BROTHERHOOD

The Muslim Brotherhood spans the globe with branches in over seventy countries. The heartland of the Brotherhood is Egypt and neighboring Arab countries with large Sunni populations. Its total membership is difficult to gauge as it often operates under different names and is outlawed in countries such as Saudi Arabia, Syria, and Libya. Joseph Nada, the Brotherhood's commissioner for International Political Affairs, dodged the issue of size, but it is probable that its membership numbers in the millions, with a far larger body of dedicated sympathizers.[2] Whatever the case, the Muslim Brotherhood is the dominant political organization in the Islamic world.

The ultimate goal of the Muslim Brotherhood is the reestablishment of Islamic rule throughout the Middle East and other predominantly Muslim areas of the world. The Brotherhood is not under any illusions that this will happen in the immediate future. Rather, it views the reestablishment of Islamic rule as a long-term process in which secular governments will gradually give way to their Islamic counterparts. As this process gains momentum, the various Islamic governments will come together until a unified Islamic state of some variety emerges.[3] It is not necessary that the Brotherhood rule, merely that the leaders of the country apply Islamic law and govern in the spirit of Islam.

The Brotherhood's objective in the predominantly Christian countries of Europe and North America is to enable Muslim populations to deepen their faith by providing them with a network of mosques, religious schools, and Muslim associations. All, according to the Brotherhood, will help Muslims gain political and economic influence. This process is well underway in Europe, but has lagged in the United States. In France, for example, Muslims have an official religious council that works with the French government to shape government policy toward France's large Muslim minority. Catholics, Jews, and Protestants have similar councils.

Other countries are less convinced of the Muslim Brotherhood's peaceful intent. Russian security officials have uncovered Brotherhood cells throughout the country, accusing them of fermenting rebellion and, in some cases, of supporting al Qaeda. The picture appears to be much the same throughout other areas of the former Soviet Union.[4]

Is the Brotherhood a reformist organization dedicated to the peaceful evolution of an Islamic state or is its commitment to nonviolence merely a stratagem? The testament of Brotherhood is blunt and appears to leave no doubt on the matter.

> Allah is our objective.
> The messenger [The Prophet Mohammed] is our leader.
> Quran is our law.
> Jihad is our way.
> Dying in the way of Allah is our highest hope.[5]

This, however, is not the way that they behave. For more than three decades, the Brotherhood has used persuasion rather than violence to reform Islam from within. Moderation does not apply to the liberation of occupied Islamic lands, the foremost of which are the Israeli-occupied West Bank and Gaza Strip, Russian-occupied Chechnya, and Indian-occupied Kashmir. The only way to liberate the occupied territories, according to the Brotherhood, is jihad.[6] The apparent contradiction between the Brotherhood's moderate face and its testimony glorifying jihad has caused concern that the Brotherhood's present posture is merely a strategic adjustment designed to disguise its true intent. Not so, says the Brotherhood:

> Jihad refers to the holy obligation to declare war upon non-believers [*kafirs*] who encroach upon Muslim lands. That is why we sent 10,000 troops to fight in Palestine in 1948, why we fought against the Soviets in Afghanistan, and why we were active in the predominantly Muslim regions of Central Asia long before the breakup of the former Soviet Union. It is also the same reason that Muslim Brothers play a major role in the liberation of Kashmir and offers their unequivocal support to the Palestinian uprising (intifada). When Muslims are being slaughtered, what choice do we have?[7]

Aside from the holy obligation to liberate Muslim lands, the Brotherhood's argument continues,

> God's law prohibits us from killing either innocent civilians or Muslims. The leaders of the Arab and Islamic World are Muslims because they have testified that, "There is no God but Allah and that Mohammed is his Messenger." We cannot kill them. Make no mistake, they are sinners and will be judged harshly by God. That, however, is His prerogative and not ours. Our job is to lead them back to the true path and to encourage them to apply Islamic law to the best of their ability. We summon, God judges.[8]

This argument is the key to the difference between the jihadists and the Muslim Brotherhood. The jihadists believe that the leaders of the Arab and Islamic world have repudiated Islam through their actions and their cooperation with the enemies of Islam. As such, they are *kafirs* and must be killed. The jihadists also fail to distinguish between military and civilian targets. All *kafirs*, in their view, are potential soldiers.

The Strategies of the Muslim Brotherhood

The Muslim Brotherhood uses three strategies to pursue its goal of reforming the secular regimes of the Islamic world: (1) teaching and preaching, (2) providing welfare to the needy, and (3) political activism. These strategies have been most thoroughly developed in Egypt but find expression in all of the seventy countries in which the Brotherhood operates. We focus on Egypt inasmuch as it remains the nerve center of Brotherhood activities.

TEACHING AND PREACHING

The Muslim Brotherhood was founded as a youth organization designed to strengthen the religious and moral foundation of Egyptian society. Teaching and preaching remain central to the Brotherhood's program. The Brotherhood believes it cannot achieve its objective of an Islamic state without a strong foundation of dedicated believers.

This process, according to the Muslim Brotherhood, begins by "building the Muslim individual: brother or sister with a strong body, high manners, cultured thought, ability to earn, strong faith, correct worship, conscious of time, of benefit to others, organized, and self-struggling character."[9] Strong Muslim individuals, according to the Brotherhood, build strong Muslim families, and strong Muslim families build a strong Muslim society. This accomplished, it is but a small step to the establishment of an Islamic state and the eventual reestablishment of the Islamic nation (*Umma*). Somewhat disconcertingly, the last step in the Brotherhood chain is "mastering the world with Islam."[10]

The Muslim Brotherhood's indoctrination program is carried out in a vast network of mosques, schools, and religious associations. Sermons and lectures stress the need for a moral society and the struggle against the enemies of Islam. The leaders of Muslim countries are seldom attacked directly, but it is not difficult to read between the lines. The United States and Israel are fair game. The Egyptian government denies that it censors Brotherhood sermons, but it watches their content very closely. The censors also pay close attention to the Brotherhood's vast media network that, while heavily religious in content, seldom misses the opportunity to criticize the United States and Israel. This, of itself, is a major source of embarrassment for a Mubarak regime widely believed to have sold out to the United States.

Indoctrination, however, is far more than sermons. It is also the discussions with the faithful that take place before and after the sermons as well as in weekly study groups, monthly meetings of combined study groups, and various trips, camps, courses, workshops, and conferences. The Muslim Brotherhood is very much a "hands-on" organization. Much like Christian fundamentalists, it is in the business of saving souls, and brothers spend endless hours convincing potential converts of the righteousness of their cause. The Brotherhood also attempts to integrate all dimensions of the individual's life within the Brotherhood "family." Prayer and service combine to create the sense of kinship so crucial in Middle Eastern life. Many young people in the Islamic world are bewildered, and the Brotherhood provides them with the sense of belonging and purpose that they so desperately need.

Beyond providing the moral basis for a future Islamic state, the Muslim Brotherhood's indoctrination program provides the foundation for its political and social activities. Numbers are important, but so is zeal. Sympathizers vote and contribute money, but the truly zealous form the cadres of the organization. It is they who get out the vote, volunteer for service in Islamic struggles such as Kashmir and Palestine, and staff the Brotherhood's vast network of schools, welfare centers, and media outlets. The preaching role of the Muslim Brotherhood has other benefits as well. Religious organizations are allowed in most Islamic countries. Political organizations are not. Teaching and preaching provide cover for a broad range of political activities that would otherwise be banned. No one is fooled, but the Brotherhood benefits from the ambiguity.

CHARITY AND WELFARE

The Muslim Brotherhood has long maintained a network of schools and clinics for the poor. Donations from the faithful provide food and clothes, doctors serve without charge in Brotherhood clinics, and Islamic schools combine religious education with instruction in the three "Rs." For students at higher levels, Brotherhood tutors assist with preparation for exams. This is a vital service, for the poor cannot afford to be tutored by their teachers or to buy the notes of their professors. Brotherhood services compare very favorably with the services provided by the government, most of which are dismal.[11] In addition to fulfilling a religious obligation, the Brotherhood's welfare services also play a key role in preparing the groundwork for the emergence of a religious state. Welfare services provide yet another hands-on opportunity for recruiting members and building a positive image of the Muslim Brotherhood as a caring organization capable of meeting the needs of the masses. The governments of the Middle East fail on both counts. Whether or not recipients of Brotherhood services show their gratitude by supporting its political activities is an open question. At the very least, the Brotherhood's welfare programs ensure that poor youth will have some chance of finding jobs in the government and the military, a potential resource should the occasion arise.

POLITICAL ACTIVISM

From a political perspective, the Muslim Brotherhood is best viewed as a very large and powerful pressure group that is engaged in a relentless battle to force the secular governments of the Muslim world to rule in accordance with Islamic law. The Brotherhood's political agenda is most fully developed in Egypt, a country in which it is allowed to operate as a religious organization. The Egyptian constitution prohibits religious organizations from engaging in political activity, but that is a matter of little import. Egypt's elections are a farcical charade, and the Brotherhood merely uses one of Egypt's meaningless opposition parties to serve as a front for its activities. Most Brotherhood candidates run for parliament as independents and, despite government opposition, scored dazzling victories in the first or primary round of Egypt's 2000 parliamentary elections. So dazzling was the Brotherhood's success, in fact, that the police openly prevented supporters of the Brotherhood from casting their ballots in the second round of the elections. The message, however, was clear. If you allow a free vote, the Brotherhood will do very well. This threat is far more than conjecture, for the 1991 elections in Algeria did result in an Islamic victory and was annulled. A decade of turmoil and death has ensued.

The Muslim Brotherhood is under no illusion that it can challenge the Mubarak regime in parliament, but finds the body to be a useful pulpit for airing its views to a national audience. The Brotherhood's representation in parliament also helps it keep an eye on the government and oppose legislation that it considers to be "anti-Islamic." This is a powerful stick, for few of Egypt's parliamentarians want to be branded anti-Islamic. Does this mean that the Brotherhood supports democracy? According to the Brotherhood (Ikhwan):

> This depends on your definition of democracy. If democracy means that people decide who leads them, then the Ikhwan accept it. If it means that people can change the laws of Allah and follow what they wish to follow, then it is not acceptable. Ikhwan only accept to participate in such systems because more benefit will be achieved if they do, and more evil will be avoided. A little help is better than no help at all. . . . Ikhwan accept personal freedom within the limits of Islam. However, if by personal freedom to you means that Muslim women can wear shorts or Muslim men can do *Haram* [forbidden] stuff, then Ikhwan do not approve of that.[12]

The electoral process is merely the tip of the Muslim Brotherhood's political agenda. By the mid-1990s, the Brotherhood was in control of sixteen of Egypt's eighteen main professional associations including those for lawyers, teachers, engineers, and reporters. As Egyptian law allows only one major association for each profession, the Mubarak regime found itself in the embarrassing position of having to negotiate on all aspects of Egypt's professional life with an illegal organization.[13] The Brotherhood used its bargaining power with the government to win unparalleled economic, medical, and personal benefits for its members, victories that have extended its popularity and demonstrated its capacity to get things done. Most members of Egypt's professional associations are not brothers or sisters, but they know a good thing when they see it.

The government often annuls Muslim Brotherhood victories in association elections, but to what avail? Repression only gives credibility to the victim and serves as further testimony to the oppressive nature of the Mubarak regime. Government efforts to purge brothers and sisters from the ranks of Egyptian teachers have had the same result.

Particularly threatening to the Mubarak regime has been the Brotherhood's direct or indirect control of Egypt's student associations. Students in the Islamic world take to the street for the slightest provocation, making them the most volatile actors in the region's politics. If student protests show signs of promise, other groups join in. It is the students, however, who get things started. Mubarak's ruling National Democratic party has increased its efforts to gain a foothold among Egypt's university and high school students, but with minimal success.

Control of Egypt's professional associations, student unions, community organizations, and mosque complexes gives the Brotherhood control of the "street."[14] At a moment's notice, a signal from the Brotherhood can send demonstrators careening thorough the streets of Cairo and Egypt's other major cities. Cairo is the nerve center of Egypt, and to disrupt Cairo is to disrupt Egypt.

Israeli attempts to crush the Palestinian intifada sparked massive demonstrations in Cairo during the spring of 2002, sending hundreds of thousands of demonstrators surging through the streets of Cairo and Egypt's other major cities. Rushing to stay ahead of the demonstrators, pro-American Mubarak intensified his usual tepid condemnations of Israel. The scene would repeat itself in the run-up to the U.S.-British invasion of Iraq when Mubarak briefly condoned the anti-U.S. demonstrations in an effort to boost his flagging popularity but brought in the security forces when the demonstrations turned ugly. Mubarak, a seasoned politician, well understands that anti-Israeli and anti-American demonstrations are seething with anti-government emotions and can turn against the regime without warning. He was not going to take any chances. The demonstrations, however, had made their point. Egypt, a recipient of two billion dollars of U.S. aid on an annual basis, refused to support the invasion of Iraq.

The Muslim Brotherhood is not the only group involved in the anti-American demonstrations, many of which begin as spontaneous explosions of frustration and anger. The Brotherhood, however, has been an active participant in the demonstrations and its ability to inflame the street represents a constant threat to the Mubarak regime.

Less visible are the Brotherhood's relentless efforts to extend its "fifth column" of religious activists within the military and the security services. All pretenses aside, Egypt remains a military regime dependent on military support for its survival. The regime knows that the Brotherhood and the jihadists enjoy broad support in the military, a fact that makes them reluctant to use the regular army against either. Rather, most anti-Brotherhood and anti-jihadist activities are carried out by special security forces in which the Mubarak regime has greater confidence. Be this as it may, the Brotherhood's support within the military provides a measure of security from government repression.

Can the Muslim Brotherhood Be a Source of Stability?

The Muslim Brotherhood considers violence to be counterproductive, arguing that it only serves to kill innocent people and to punish Muslim populations by crippling the economy. The jihadist attacks during the 1980s and 1990s devastated Egypt's tourist industry, leaving tens of thousands without work. The Brotherhood also condemns jihadist violence for giving the Islamic movement a bad name and for giving Islam's enemies a pretext to launch a new crusade against Islam and innocent Muslims. Always pragmatic, the Muslim Brotherhood cautions that governments are more powerful than the Islamic groups. Little, accordingly, is to be gained by fighting a war that will cripple the Islamic movement and ruin its opportunity to achieve an Islamic state by peaceful means. This said, there can be little doubt that the Brotherhood's capacity for violence remains. It can resist the Mubarak regime if forced to do so.

Reflecting its standoff with the Egyptian government, the Brotherhood has offered the Mubarak regime a simple deal: Allow us to promote our religious agenda in a peaceful manner and we will allow you to rule. Government politicians will enjoy all the perks of office and the wealth that accrues to the ruling class; the Brotherhood will help Egypt become a more religious state. The alternative, the Brotherhood implies, is a return to the jihadist violence of the 1980s and 1990s. The deal is a very tempting one. Cooperation with the Brotherhood would allow the Mubarak regime to pretend that it supports Islam. It would also allay accusations that Mubarak is a puppet of the United States. More importantly, giving the Muslim Brotherhood broader scope for its activities would isolate the jihadists by providing more moderate Muslims with a legitimate outlet for their concerns. This, of course is the rub. The Mubarak regime probably fears a broad-based Islamic party more than it fears the jihadists.

The deal that the Brotherhood is offering Mubarak was accepted by King Hussein of Jordan during the 1950s.[15] The young king, then a teenager, used the Brotherhood to counter the leftists and Palestinian radicals intent on overthrowing his shaky monarchy. The king prospered, as did the Muslim Brotherhood. The United States, however, is now putting increasing pressure on Jordan's new king, Abdullah II, to curtail the Brotherhood's support for the intifada in Palestine. This is a tall order, for approximately 70 percent of Jordan's population is of Palestinian origin and support for the Palestinian uprising is a key element in the Brotherhood's program. The line between the Muslim Brotherhood and the jihadists in Jordan is also blurred. The Palestinian resistance group, Hamas, was founded as the military wing of the Jordanian Muslim Brotherhood, and the Brotherhood has been instrumental in brokering tensions between Hamas and the king.

Strong relations were also forged between the Muslim Brotherhood and the government of Yemen during the 1990s, thanks in large part to the Brotherhood's role in easing tensions between Yemen and Saudi Arabia in the aftermath of Iraq's invasion of Kuwait.[16] Much to the irritation of the Saudis, Yemen had supported Saddam Hussein, perhaps believing that the Saudi monarchy would be the next to fall. It did not, and Yemeni workers were expelled from Saudi Arabia. Saudi Arabia also supported a rebellion that erupted in the south of Yemen a few years later. The Brotherhood's intercession eased both crises, and the Brotherhood became a legal political organization operating under the name of the Yemeni Society for Reform.[17] Rather than opposing the government, the Brotherhood became its supporter. The Yemeni government has also mended its ways and is now an ally of the United States in its struggle against the jihadists. Whether it can convince the United States that the Brotherhood is a peaceful organization remains to be seen.

Syria, by contrast, condemns the Muslim Brotherhood as a terrorist organization. The Brotherhood launched a campaign of terror in Syria during the early 1980s that showed signs of becoming a full-scale civil war. The Syrian government unleashed a military assault on the Brotherhood, slaughtering as many as 30,000 of its members. More moderate estimates place the figure at 10,000. Whatever the case, the carnage was horrendous. Membership in the Brotherhood became a crime punishable by death. The leadership of the Brotherhood in Syria fled to Jordan, Germany, and Iraq, as did most of its active members.

The Brotherhood retaliated by launching terrorist strikes into Syria during the mid-1980s, but the Jordan-German branch of the Syrian Brotherhood has since fallen in line with the nonviolent position of the Cairo leadership. Indeed, it has applied to the Syrian regime for permission to return to Syria as a cooperating partner of the ruling Ba'ath party. The Syrian regime has thus far rejected the Brotherhood's offer, the key sticking point being the Brotherhood's refusal to acknowledge its responsibility for the events leading up to the 1982 massacres. In the view of the leadership of the Syrian Brotherhood, it was the government that had created the crisis by attempting to liquidate the Brotherhood.[18]

The Israelis also condemn the Muslim Brotherhood as a terrorist organization. The Israeli position is not difficult to understand, for Hamas, the

Palestinian branch of the Brotherhood, now represents the core of Palestinian resistance to the Israeli occupation of the West Bank and Gaza Strip. Because of the complex relationship between Hamas and the Palestinian jihad, a fuller discussion of Hamas has been delayed until the following chapter. For the moment, suffice it to say that Hamas demonstrates the effectiveness of the Muslim Brotherhood as an armed resistance group.

How the Muslim Brotherhood Is Organized

The far-flung activities of the Brotherhood are guided by an organizational apparatus consisting of a supreme guide, a deputy supreme guide, a thirteen–fifteen member guidance bureau responsible for formulating policy, a larger consultative council, and various specialized committees.[19] The Islamic jurisprudence (*fiqh*) committee consists of trusted Muslim scholars and ensures that the Brotherhood's policies are in line with the Koran and Sunna. Other committees guide the teaching, preaching, welfare, and political activities of the Brotherhood, and a large legal staff defends Brothers who run afoul of the law in the execution of their religious duties. Less visible committees presumably guide the covert activities of the brotherhood, but these are matters of great secrecy.

There is only one supreme guide and he resides in Cairo. Branches of the Brotherhood in other countries are headed by a general secretary and a local consultative council. The Brotherhood reportedly developed an international network in the 1970s, but Joseph Nada, the Muslim Brotherhood's commissioner for international political affairs, debunked suggestions that he headed such an organization and derided its very existence. The fiction of a "network," according to Nada, was fabricated by the international security services in order to link the Brotherhood to the terrorist activities of the jihadists. His six-part interview with the Al-Jazeera television network, however, did note the existence of the Brotherhood representatives for both countries and regions. Regional representatives, according to Nada, meet frequently to ensure that they are pursuing a common policy and to discuss mutual concerns, the most pressing of which are U.S. accusations that the Muslim Brotherhood is a terrorist organization. When the need arises, the country and regional representatives meet on a broader continental basis.[20] Whatever the case, the supreme guide and the guidance bureau shape the key elements of Brotherhood policy from their offices in Cairo, leaving it to branches to work out the details in accordance with their particular needs and circumstances.

Supreme guides have traditionally been elected for life, but Joseph Nada notes that this has now been changed. Incoming supreme guides will be limited to two six-year terms in office.[21] For the moment, the point is largely moot. Ma'moun El-Hodeibi was eighty-three at the time of his election to the position in 2002, having served as deputy supreme guide since 1986. He passed away fourteen months later and was succeeded on January 14, 2004, by Mohammed Mahdi Akef, aged seventy-five. Both were selected by the fifteen or so members of the guidance bureau, most of whom were long-time loyalists of the same generation. Clearly, the Muslim Brotherhood is controlled by a narrow circle of very old men.

Akef, by way of background, joined the Brotherhood in 1950 at age twenty-two. Four years later, he was accused of plotting the assassination of then President Abdul Nasser and spent the ensuing twenty years in prison. On his release, he spent time in Saudi Arabia, Germany, and the United States and was particularly active in establishing youth camps. Returning to Egypt in 1987, Akef gained a seat in Parliament and was placed in charge of the Muslim Brotherhood's youth and professional organizations.[22]

The supreme guide is charismatic (divinely guided) and, according to the Brotherhood's critics, brooks no contradiction. Rather, he serves as a source of imitation and emulation. Bylaws exist, but they give the supreme guide sweeping powers to appoint "commissioners" and initiate policy as he sees fit. Joseph Nada's appointment as commissioner for international political affairs was made by the supreme guide alone and his appointment was not well known within the ranks of the Muslim Brotherhood. Islam Online.com, a major website sympathetic to the Brotherhood, denied that such an appointment had ever been made. Memos of Nada's appointment appeared in 2002, but were unsigned.

Also little known was Nada's peace negotiations with the Mubarak government and his efforts to mediate tensions between Iran and Saudi Arabia following the Iranian Revolution. Similar mediation was carried out between the Iraqis and the Kuwaitis during the Iraqi occupation of Kuwait. Make no mistake, the Brotherhood carries considerable clout within the Islamic world. When an incredulous Al-Jazeera interviewer asked, "You mean that only the supreme guide knew of the missions that you were charged with and that the rest of the Muslim Brotherhood didn't know?" Nada responded, "That is his right according to the bylaws. It is he who deals with issues as they arise and it is often essential that no one knows about it until the appropriate time or that only specific people know about it."[23]

The authoritarian leadership style of the Muslim Brotherhood is typical of secret societies, but it has a price. The dictatorship of the aged has led to accusations that the Brotherhood's leadership, most of which is rooted in the anti-British nationalism of 1940s and 1950s, has lost touch with the demands of the present. Some believe that the supreme guide is too old to carry out his responsibilities effectively. The election of a new supreme guide in 2002 also brought rumors of rebellion by the younger, midlevel leadership of the Brotherhood, most of whom are now well into middle-age.

Generational tensions, however, are more than a matter of age. The younger midlevel leaders were university activists who had played a crucial role in reviving the Muslim Brotherhood in the post-Nasser era. Now well represented in the ranks of doctors, engineers, and other professionals, it is they who claim responsibility for the Brotherhood's recent electoral successes as well as its stunning success in seizing control of Egypt's professional associations.[24] They also feel that they are more in touch with the realities of the modern world than the old guard and that their time for power has come. Rumors of tensions within the Brotherhood are denied by all parties. Nada, clearly one of the old guard, dodged the issue in his Al-Jazeera interviews, suggesting that tensions are part of all large organizations.[25] He also suggested that the younger generation lacked the discipline of its elders.[26]

The ambiguity surrounding the Brotherhood's operations is not difficult to understand. The Brotherhood is a secret organization and most of its activities are technically illegal. The Middle East is a volatile region and a sudden change in the political climate could result in a brutal crackdown on the Brotherhood reminiscent of the purges of the Nasser era. Governmental surveillance of the Brotherhood is pervasive and its lawyers are very busy people. America's war on terror and the attack on Iraq have added a new sense of urgency to the Brotherhood's concern with survival.

Some insight into the Muslim Brotherhood's finances were also provided by Nada, who, in addition to being the Brotherhood's commissioner of international political affairs, is a Swiss industrial magnate and Islamic banker accused by the United States of financing a broad array of radical Islamic groups, including the Muslim Brotherhood. When asked about accusations in *Time* and *Newsweek* that his bank was the "collection box," Nada simply replied that he did not believe that the Brotherhood had any money to deposit. When asked by Al-Jazeera how a group such as the Brotherhood could operate without money, he replied that the organization relied on its members and did not take money from governments or outside sources:

> As I told you before, each member operates independently, doing what he can, maybe spending his money or his energies and the energies of his children. Maybe he travels, organizes meetings, prints books, performs free surgery in a Muslim Brotherhood clinic or tutors students. Giving services is the same as giving money.[27]

This, of course, begged the question, for many Brotherhood members are extremely wealthy, especially those from the Gulf. Nada also failed to mention that the Muslim Brotherhood has its own businesses and that its members have great influence in the region's large benevolent associations that do collect huge amounts of money for religious purposes. This, too, is a gray area in which information is difficult to come by.

The Muslim Brotherhood's Strengths and Vulnerabilities

The "moderate" approach of the Muslim Brotherhood has enabled it to appeal to a broad range of Muslims who, while supporting a strong role for religion in political life, fear the violence and extremism of the jihadists. The moderate face of the Brotherhood also makes it less threatening to protest voters intent on registering their profound displeasure with the corruption and oppression of secular governments in the Muslim world. Protest votes are certainly part of the reason for the dazzling success of Muslim parties in recent years.

Numbers also translate into power, and governments in the region think long and hard before they challenge the Brotherhood. In all probability, serious efforts to uproot the Muslim Brotherhood in Egypt, Jordan, and the Sudan would result in an Algerian-style civil war, a prospect that chills even the boldest of Arab leaders. It certainly chills President Mubarak. The Brotherhood, accordingly, enjoys considerable freedom in pursuing Islamic reform as long as it stops short of challenging the power of the regime. Perhaps justifiably, the Brotherhood and parallel organizations claim victory for the growing strength of the Islamic movement. Secular regimes still reign, but the power of moderate Islamic groups continues to reach new highs throughout the Muslim world. Patience has its rewards.

The Muslim Brotherhood also benefits from its flexibility. Unlike the jihadists, the Brotherhood is not locked into an all or nothing strategy of violence that unnecessarily provokes the animosity of secular governments. Rather, it can adapt its policies to fit the needs of the situation, biding its time while it builds a foundation for eventual victory. In much the same manner, all Muslims, including Shi'a, are welcome to join the organization as long as they are willing to work toward the establishment of an Islamic state within the framework of Brotherhood guidelines. God can deal with the sinners and sort out the sectarian conflicts once the goal of an Islamic state has been achieved.

The jihadists, for their part, are scathing in their critique of the Muslim Brotherhood. Flexibility and patience, from the jihadists' perspective, are merely excuses for doing nothing. Where is the progress toward an Islamic state, the jihadists ask. They can find none. On the contrary, they condemn the Brotherhood's strategy of cooperation for perpetuating secular regimes by "taking the heat off" and making them appear Islamic in the eyes of the public. In the process, corruption and immorality have embedded themselves ever deeper in Islamic society.

The jihadists also scoff at the Muslim Brotherhood's claim that radical Islam is too weak to challenge the military might of the secular regimes. The Shah of Iran, they note, claimed to have the fifth-largest army in the world when his regime collapsed without a whimper in the face of the Ayatollah Khomeini. That army, moreover, was trained by the United States and armed with the latest American weaponry, but to no avail. Military might, the jihadists proclaim, cannot save corrupt apostates who have lost touch with their populations. The Iranian soldiers did not fight to save the Shah, and the soldiers of the Islamic world will not fight to save their corrupt and godless masters. Most soldiers are good Muslims and they will join the revolution.[28]

The jihadist critique of the Brotherhood also contains a number of practical elements. Flexibility, according to the jihadists, equates with a lack of focus. The Brotherhood speaks of guidelines, but the jihadists see few guidelines other than a commitment to cooperate with corrupt regimes in the vain hope of establishing an Islamic state. With everyone doing their own thing, from the jihadist perspective, the goal of an Islamic state gets lost in the shuffle.

The Brotherhood's emphasis on size, from the jihadist perspective, has had the same result. By attempting to gather the vast array of Islamic currents into a single organization, the Brotherhood finds itself in the impossible position of trying to please everyone. The result is stagnation and the defection of the most dedicated members of the organization. The Brotherhood, in the view of the jihadists, has become nothing more than a huge bureaucracy, the zeal of its members being sapped by petty concerns of status and authority.

Perhaps the most telling item in the jihadist critique is its accusation that the Muslim Brotherhood is soft on the Shi'a. By embracing the Shi'a, the jihadists charge, the Brotherhood is giving tacit approval of the Shi'a heresy. The Koran and the Sunna say nothing of Hidden Imams or Ayatollahs. These are all embellishments that have diverted Islam from its true course and cannot conceivably be part of an Islamic state based on the Koran and the Sunna.

In addition to the jihadist critique of the Brotherhood, we would note that the Brotherhood finds itself in competition with the jihadists for the hearts and minds of a large portion of the Middle East's population. Continued moderation threatens defection to the jihadists, while increased radicalism threatens reprisals by the government. The fine line that the Brotherhood has pursued in recent decades is becoming increasingly difficult to walk as the distance between the governments of the Islamic world and their populations continues to broaden.

What is the truth? Is the Muslim Brotherhood a vast octopus that is gradually sapping the will of secular governments to resist the Islamic movement, or is it, as the jihadists maintain, a vast moribund bureaucracy that has lost its capacity for effective action? Is it the militant revolutionary organization proclaimed by its credo, or does it undermine the Islamic movement with false hopes of finding a peaceful road to an Islamic state?

HIZBULLAH: A TALE OF THREE COUNTRIES

Hizbullah (the Party of God) is best known for its activities in Lebanon and particularly its success in driving Israeli forces out of Southern Lebanon. The Lebanese branch of Hizbullah, however, is only one component of a far larger Hizbullah movement. Hizbullah parties also exist among Shi'a populations in the Persian Gulf (Saudi Arabia, Kuwait, and Bahrain), and Hizbullah-type organizations have now emerged to challenge the U.S. occupation of Iraq. All are supported by Iran. Hizbullah also ranks high on the U.S. list of terrorist organizations and has recently become a major focal point of FBI investigations within the United States.

Iran: The Center of the Hizbullah Movement

The saga of Hizbullah begins in 1979 with the victory of the Islamic Revolution in Iran. In one fell swoop, or so it seemed, the Shah of Iran, the king of kings and the key to American strategy in the Middle East, was swept away by a surge of Islamic emotion fired by the Ayatollah Khomeini.[29] Iran had become the first Islamic theocracy of the modern era.

The picture, of course, is far more complex. It was not Islamic emotion alone that had driven the Shah from the Peacock throne, but decades of despotism, megalomania, subservience to the United States, and unbridled corruption. Iranians of all persuasions, secular as well as religious, recoiled from the excesses of the Shah and drifted into the ranks of the revolutionaries. Not all aspired to an Islamic paradise, but it was the fundamentalists who had seized the moment.[30] Others, including nationalists and communists, played along hoping to sort things out once the Shah was gone. Most perished in despair. The mighty army of the Shah, the fifth largest in the world according to his publicists, simply melted away as conscripts returned to their villages.

Flushed with victory, the Ayatollah Khomeini was determined to export his Islamic Revolution throughout the Middle East. It was God's will, and he was the agent of divine intervention. The task would not be easy. The Iranian economy was in shambles, its political system in chaos. Saudi Arabia, Iraq, and the Gulf sheikhdoms, all possessing significant Shi'a populations, plotted their counterattack. The United States, fearing for its domination of the region, blessed their efforts. There could be no compromise. Conflict was inevitable.

The Ayatollah, however, was not without resources. His defeat of the Shah had been the stuff of miracles, inspiring awe throughout the Islamic world. Many Shi'a believed him to be the embodiment of the Hidden Imam.[31] Sunni fundamentalists viewed him as a source of inspiration if not a saint. The Ayatollah's power to sway the masses appeared mightier than the sword. His rhetoric had proven more powerful that the arms of the Shah, and his followers believed that it would be more powerful than the arms of the United States. "God will provide" became his rallying cry to action.

Exporting the Islamic Revolution required more than emotion. It also required a political organization capable of channeling mass emotions into action. Emotions fuel uprisings, but it is organizations that seize power. The Ayatollah's efforts to build an organizational base for his Islamic Revolution were twofold. First, revolutionary organizations were established among Shi'a populations in Lebanon, Iraq, and various Gulf sheikhdoms. They would later become part of a broader Hizbullah movement. Second, the Ayatollah forged alliances with jihadist groups in Egypt, Algeria, and other Sunni countries and provided them with money, weapons, and technical support. He would have preferred to incorporate the Sunni jihadists within the Hizbullah network, but the abiding tensions between the Shi'a and Sunni branches of Islam made that impossible. The Sunni jihadists were willing to accept aid from Iran, but most continued to view the Shi'a as heretics.

Iranian success in inspiring the Sunni jihadists was immediate. The Holy Mosque in Mecca was seized in 1979, Egypt's President Sadat was assassinated in 1981, and the Syrian Brotherhood launched an abortive war against the Syrian regime in 1982. The Islamic Revolution in Iran had been the call to action. Organizing efforts among the Shi'a proved less successful. An abortive 1981 coup in Bahrain was crushed with relative ease, and Saddam Hussein, the newly crowned leader of Iraq, slaughtered Shi'a leaders bold enough to challenge his authority. Clerics suspected of loyalty to Iran topped his list.[32]

Ayatollah Khomeini well understood the threat that his Islamic Revolution posed to the West and feared a counterattack by the United States and its regional allies. It came with a vengeance in September 1980, as Saddam Hussein, encouraged by Saudi Arabia and Kuwait, invaded Iran. The United States, then smarting from Iran's seizure of American hostages, smiled on the venture. The war went poorly for Saddam Hussein, as an Iranian army composed largely of religious zealots held the Iraqis at bay. As described by Mackey:

> The *Basij* [popular militias] operated from nine thousand mosques, enrolling boys below eighteen, men above forty-five, and women. Primarily the zealous products of poor, devout families from rural areas, they volunteered for temporary duty in God's war between school terms or in the interim dividing one season's harvest and the next season's planting. At the front, a *Basij-i* could be identified by his tattered leftover uniform and mismatched boots (often picked up on the battlefield), the bright red or yellow headband stretched across his brow declaring God's or Khomeini's greatness, and the large, imitation brass key, the key to paradise, that hung around his neck. The *basiji-is* gained fame as human minesweepers in the massive assaults that characterized the 1982–1984 phase of the war. Boys as young as twelve, shaped by the fanaticism of the revolution, walked across minefields to clear

the way for the advancing *Pasdaran* [irregular troops], followed by the army.[33]

The war raged for eight years, devastating both countries and blunting the focus of the Islamic Revolution. Iran, alone, may have suffered a million casualties. No one knows for sure. The picture was not much better in Iraq. Rare was the Iraqi family without the loss of a loved one. The economies of both countries were shattered. In one way or another, the United States gave aid to both sides, a policy that led to accusations that it had orchestrated their mutual annihilation. This was inaccurate. The United States feared the Ayatollah's Islamic Revolution, and Saddam Hussein replaced the Shah of Iran as America's ally in the Gulf. Indeed, the United States helped guide Iraqi air strikes on Iran. In retrospect, this was a mistake.[34]

Lebanon: The Crown Jewel of the Hizbullah Movement

In contrast to Iraq and the Gulf, Lebanon proved to be fertile ground for Hizbullah. In the fourth year of a brutal civil war between rival religious groups, this most beautiful of countries had dissolved into chaos. Lebanon's civil war, however, was more than a war among Lebanese. Palestinian militia controlled southern Lebanon, the heartland of Lebanon's Shi'a community. The Syrians, who viewed Lebanon as a breakaway province, used the war as an opportunity to reassert their control over the country and intervened first on one side and then the other. Israel, too, entered the fray, driving the Palestinians from southern Lebanon and occupying Beirut in 1982.

The brutal Israeli occupation of Beirut caused an irate President Reagan to demand an immediate Israeli withdrawal from the Lebanese capital. The Israelis capitulated and retreated to a forty-kilometer "security zone" that included much of predominantly Shi'a southern Lebanon. President Reagan sent U.S. troops to Beirut to stabilize Lebanon and protect Israel from Palestinian attacks. In retrospect, this, too, was a mistake. The Shi'a, for their part, had been liberated from the Palestinians only to find themselves oppressed by the Israelis.

It was in this environment that Mohammed Hassan Fadlallah, a senior Lebanese cleric who now ranks as one of the leading Shi'a scholars in the Islamic world, founded the Lebanese branch of Hizbullah. The Shi'a already possessed a political organization, Amal, but it had lost much of its zeal and its leaders seemed more interested in local politics than revolution.[35] Hizbullah, by contrast, was to be a revolutionary jihadist organization intent on establishing an Iranian-type Islamic republic among Lebanese Shi'a. In 1982, Iran dispatched some 1,500 revolutionary guards (armed religious radicals) to Lebanon to provide organizational support and train Hizbullah's militia.[36] Radical Shi'a deserted Amal in droves, firing the ranks of Hizbullah with their revolutionary zeal. Amal remains the larger of the two organizations, but lacks the dynamism of Hizbullah. Little love is lost between the two organizations, vows of fraternity often dissolving into bloodshed.[37]

The confrontation between Hizbullah and the allied peacekeepers was immediate. The American Embassy in Beirut was bombed in April 1983, resulting in the loss of seventeen American lives. The bombing of the Marine barracks followed six months later, killing 241 U.S. military personnel. Both attacks were attributed to Hizbullah, as was the rampage of kidnapping that would follow. Hassan Nasrallah, the secretary general of Hizbullah, denies Hizbullah's role in the carnage, noting that Hizbullah was not fully developed at the time. "At that time there were hundreds of small groups, and there were guns. The PLO went out of Lebanon, while its stores of weapons remained in Lebanon, stores which contained rockets, explosives, guns, and trained young men. . . . These small groups did not belong to Hizbullah."[38] Whatever the case, the United States withdrew its troops from Lebanon. The Islamic Revolution had scored another victory. Its leaders had also become convinced that the United States would withdraw in the face of terrorist attacks. The Israelis, too, found Hizbullah attacks costly and would soon reduce their security zone to a more manageable twenty-four kilometers. Perhaps reflecting their contempt for Arab military prowess, the Israelis had severely underestimated the zeal of the Hizbullah fighters.

Stability came to Lebanon in 1991, its diverse religious factions agreeing to a political system that would divide power more or less equally between the Christians, the Sunni, and the Shi'a.[39] The diverse militias were to be disarmed and merged into the Lebanese army. The sole exception was Hizbullah. The Party of God would be allowed to keep its militia for the time being. Syria would keep the peace by stationing some 30,000 troops in Lebanon. Israel continued to occupy a twenty-four-kilometer security zone in southern Lebanon and had more or less agreed to Syria's peacekeeping operations in Lebanon. Better Syria than the Palestinians.

The scars of the Lebanese civil war ran deep. On the issue of the Israeli invasion, however, there was little conflict. The Israeli occupation was an affront to Lebanese pride and yet another humiliation of Arab and Islamic sensitivities. The issue, however, was tricky. The Lebanese army was too weak to confront the Israelis, and the Syrians were wary of becoming involved in another losing war with their stronger neighbor. Appeals to the United Nations and the United States had proven futile. The United Nations had condemned the invasion to no avail; the United States ignored it.

The Lebanese answer to the Israelis was Hizbullah. It was Shi'a lands that were under Israeli occupation, and Hizbullah's militia possessed all of the hallmarks of a modern army with the exception of air power. Its fighters were also the most motivated in Lebanon, willing to die for God and their sect. For ten long years, Hizbullah militias pounded Israeli positions with relentless daring, forcing the Israeli Defense Force to take unacceptable casualties. Hizbullah strategists well understood that the main military weakness of Israel was its reluctance to suffer the loss of Jewish life. That weakness was exploited relentlessly.

Volunteers flocked to Hizbullah's ranks as it donned the mantle of "national resistance." It remained a preeminently Shi'a organization, but martyrs came from all of Lebanon's major religions, Christianity included. Syria and Iran cheered from the sidelines, relishing Israeli discomfort as it struggled to extricate itself from what Israeli commentators were calling Israel's Vietnam. Ariel Sharon, then minister of defense, was vilified for getting Israel into the mess in the first place. Israel railed against Syria and Iran for arming Hizbullah and threatened to bomb Damascus if the attacks continued. Syria and Iran pleaded innocence. Hizbullah was Lebanese they said.

The struggle against Israel also enabled Hizbullah to establish a new international persona. Terrorism against peaceful nations, including the United States, was renounced. Hizbullah proclaimed that it was no longer a revolutionary terrorist organization, but a movement of national liberation. Attacks on Israeli troops, they noted, were justified by international law. Israel was an aggressor country occupying Lebanese territory. Europe long recognized this metamorphosis; the United States remained skeptical.

Israelis are not quick to admit defeat, but by 2000, they had had enough. The security zone that Israel had occupied since 1982 was evacuated with the exception of the Sheba Farms, a small area of southern Lebanon that had been controlled by Syria at the time of its occupation by Israeli forces. Israel maintained that it would only relinquish its control of the area as part of a broader peace agreement with Syria. The United Nations supported the Israeli position, but Lebanon did not. The wound remained open.

The moment of Hizbullah's glory was equally a moment of crisis. The cause that had propelled Hizbullah into the limelight of Middle Eastern affairs had now vanished. With Israel defeated, Lebanon's power brokers began to view Hizbullah with suspicion, as did Amal, Hizbullah's competitor within the Shi'a camp. A Lebanon that had stoically accepted Israeli bombing as the price of liberation now saw its resolve weaken. Lebanon's economy was on the verge of collapse and the country needed peace, not another war. Hizbullah's success had also propelled Israel closer to the negotiating table with Syria. The price of peace with Israel would be Syria's clampdown on Hizbullah. Syria had little else to offer. Iran was also becoming problematic. An ever-deepening economic crisis had forced the Islamic Republic to cut back on its financial (not military) support for Hizbullah. Iranian liberals, moreover, had gained control of the presidency and were more interested in rapprochement with the United States than in spreading world revolution. Hardline clerics were still dominant, but change was in the air.

Hizbullah thus faced a triple challenge: (1) It needed a cause that would fire the passion of its adherents; (2) It needed to find a role in the revamped Lebanese political system; and (3) It needed to adjust to the possibility of a Syrian betrayal. A failure in any one of the three areas would have catastrophic effects on the future of the organization, the most immediate threat being that of a peace treaty between Israel and Syria.

Always resilient, Hizbullah would make Israel's assault on the Palestinian intifada the centerpiece of its program. Lebanese TV carried nonstop coverage of maimed Palestinian children and Israeli tanks firing on Palestinian civilians, but none more so than Manara, Hizbullah's television channel. The picture was much the same throughout the Islamic world. Israel made no apologies for the severity of its measures, blaming Palestinian terrorists for threatening the security of the Jewish state. The liberators of Lebanon would now devote themselves to the liberation of Jerusalem. A long record of cooperation with Hamas had already been established, and the Hizbullah strategy for attacking Israeli forces had increasingly become the model adopted by the Palestinians. In many ways, Palestine became a win–win situation for Hizbullah. Palestinian victories became Hizbullah victories; Palestinian losses justified greater militancy on the part of Hizbullah. Israel played into the hands of Hizbullah by continuing to occupy the Sheba Farms. The official position of the Lebanese government is that Lebanon remains under Israeli occupation, all the pretext that Hizbullah needs to continue its attacks on Israeli positions in the Sheba Farms.

Part and parcel of the Hizbullah's Palestinian program is a demand for the return of Lebanon's some 300,000 plus Palestinian refugees to Palestine, a cause deep in the heart of all Lebanese. Only a Palestinian victory, Hizbullah tells a Lebanese leadership nervous about Israeli reprisals, can ensure that the Palestinian refugees will not become permanent residents of Lebanon. As things currently stand, the refugee camps are self-governing units sustained by the United Nations. Their residents are not allowed to buy land, and work permits are difficult to come by.[40] This is not an issue of minor concern for a country that already suffers from a 30 percent unemployment rate. The refugee camps are also well armed and have their own militias, a prospect that could easily destabilize Lebanon's most fragile of political systems.

So fragile is the Lebanese political system, in fact, that recent parliamentary elections were contended by some eighteen different religious and ethnic groups, each being assured of seats in the National Assembly in some semblance to their size and power. The same principle applies to the allocation of positions in the bureaucracy and military, although the command structure of the military inclines toward the Maronite Christians. Even the leadership of the country is a three-way tug of war between Lebanon's three presidents: the president of the country is a Christian Maronite; the president of the government (prime minister) is a Sunni Muslim; and the president (speaker) of the National Assembly is a Shi'a Muslim. None can accomplish anything without the support of the others. This means, in effect, that each of Lebanon's main religious sects can hold the government hostage until its interests have been accommodated. Wags suggest that the most powerful president is the "fourth president," a sarcastic reference to Bashar al-Asad, the president of Syria. The Israelis don't laugh, knowing well that both Syria and Iran could cripple Hizbullah operations if they so desired.

This, then, is the Lebanese government that the United States is pressuring to rein in Hizbullah, an ironic position seeing that Hizbullah is, for all intents and purposes, part of the government. Hizbullah holds six seats in the National Assembly and was offered a position in the cabinet. It declined, perhaps wanting to avoid the stigma of corruption associated with power in Lebanon. Understandably, U.S. efforts to force Lebanon to freeze Hizbullah's bank accounts have met with firm refusals. No one in Lebanon wants another civil war.

But what does Hizbullah do once peace comes to the region and its causes have come to an end? One answer is provided by Nizar Hamzeh, the leading expert on Hizbullah.[41] In his view, Hizbullah is becoming increasingly integrated into the Lebanese political system. With time, militancy will give way to electoral politics as Hizbullah seeks to strengthen Islam via the ballot box. Others remain skeptical. For the present, Hizbullah retains its large military capacity and its stock soared when it forced an exchange of an Israeli reserve intelligence officer and the bodies of three Israeli soldiers for sixty-two Arab war dead and some 430 Arab prisoners in January 2004.[42] It is also Hizbullah that patrols much of the Lebanese-Israeli border. In the summer of 2003 the Lebanese army was poised to replace Hizbullah troops on the Israeli border, but deployment slowed as Hizbullah vowed resistance.[43] At least for the moment, Hizbullah's support of the Palestinians requires a presence on the Israeli border. The threat of rocket attacks against Jewish settlements in northern Israel also offers Hizbullah a measure of protection against Israeli attack.

What Is Hizbullah and How Does It Operate?

First and foremost, Hizbullah is a Shi'a religious organization dedicated to the defense and propagation of Islam. Its ultimate goal is the establishment of Islamic governments in the Middle East and broader reaches of the Islamic world. Hizbullah is also a political party representing the interests of Lebanon's Shi'a, a welfare agency providing a broad array of health and welfare services to Lebanon's poor, and a vast military machine that proved its mettle by breaking the Israeli occupation of southern Lebanon. Israel and the United States note that Hizbullah is also a base for jihadist groups attacking Israel. Hizbullah does not deny these charges, maintaining that liberation is not terrorism. This view was expressed by Ayatollah Sayyed Mohammed Hussein Fadlallah, the spiritual guide of Hizbullah, "Suicide attacks in occupied Palestine are not the craven acts of the morally depraved as they are portrayed by the Western media, but a form of legitimate resistance amid escalating dangers."[44] It is not entirely clear whether the U.S. occupation of Iraq falls in that category.

Hizbullah is, moreover, a business conglomerate replete with gas stations, construction companies, electric utilities, supermarkets, banks, and a television network. It is also probable that Hizbullah's commercial activities include drugs, counterfeiting, money laundering, and gun running, although such charges are heatedly denied by the Hizbullah leadership.[45]

Finally, Hizbullah is a satellite of Iran's Islamic Revolution and an agent of Iranian foreign policy. Far from denying its links with Iran, the home page of Sayyed Hassan Nasrallah, the secretary general of Hizbullah (Lebanon), proclaims that he is "the representative of the Imam Khamenei, the Supreme Guide of Iran, in Lebanon."[46] It could not be otherwise, for Iran remains Hizbullah's chief supplier of money, weapons, and international support.

In reality, Hizbullah is all of the above and more. It is a state within a state that controls territory, defends its territory, and conducts foreign policy independently of the Lebanese government. Indeed, the Lebanese government finds it difficult to conduct its foreign policy without the agreement of Hizbullah. Hizbullah is also widely believed to have established an international network that extends from Europe to North and South America. Hizbullah denies the existence of such a network.

Is Hizbullah a terrorist organization? That depends on whom you ask. For the Israelis, there is no doubt in the matter. Hizbullah's support of the Palestinian jihadists is a matter of record and Hizbullah rockets pose a clear and present danger to Israeli border regions, including the city of Haifa. The United States shares the Israeli assessment, citing the Hizbullah role in the 1983 attacks on the American Embassy and marine barracks. The Islamic world, by contrast, views Hizbullah as a liberation organization whose freedom fighters were instrumental in liberating southern Lebanon from Israeli occupation. The European Union has long distinguished between the military and political wings of Hizbullah, accusing the former of harboring terrorists cells, while accepting the latter as a legitimate political organization. In 2004, the EU began to vacillate on the issue.

Much like the Muslim Brotherhood, then, Hizbullah's activities cover the waterfront. They teach and preach, they provide a vast array of welfare services including hospitals and schools, and they are deeply involved in both domestic and regional politics. All contribute to Hizbullah's power base. The military wing is the foundation of the organization's power in Lebanon, while its schools, mosques, and media outlets fire the zeal of the faithful and provide a ready avenue of recruitment. Hizbullah's welfare agencies highlight both the compassion of the organization and the efficiency of its operations. The Lebanese government fails on both counts. They also provide opportunities for recruitment, although we could find few signs that gratitude led to increased membership in the organization. Hizbullah's commercial activities provide much needed cash as well as employment for its cadres.

Estimates of Hizbullah's strength are difficult to come by, with estimates of its hard-core fighters ranging from a few hundred to thousands. In a recent interview with Al-Jazeera, Hassan Nasrallah, the secretary general of Hizbullah, brushed aside the commentator's suggestion that Hizbullah had 4,000 fighters willing to die for their cause, responding, "God is willing, we have a great number . . . with a martyrdom wish . . . and do not need to mention that number."[47] While estimates of the organization's strength vary, it was sufficient to drive the Israelis from the occupation zone in southern Lebanon. Supporters and sympathizers rank in the tens thousands and probably more.

This vast array of activities is guided by a religious elite headed by Sheik (religious scholar) Hassan Nasrallah, the secretary general of Hizbullah. Nasrallah is assisted by a guidance bureau of some eight to twelve members, each of whom oversees one of the organizations diverse activities. Each of the three regions of Lebanon in which Hizbullah operates also has a director. Most senior officials, in common with the Iranian political system, are clerics. Hassan Fadlallah, the founder of Hizbullah, remains its spiritual guide but, as expressed by a Hizbullah-sponsored website, "remains somewhat distant from running the party."[48]

It is Iran that outlines the broad contours of Hizbullah activities. During the 1980s, Iran urged violence against the United States and its allies in the region. The party line emanating from Iran became far more subdued during the 1990s, as Iran sought to build bridges with the United States and its Arab neighbors. It has become even more quiescent in the aftermath of the U.S. invasion of Iraq. This does not guarantee that Iran's hard-line clerics have had a change of heart, but it does mean that they need time to sort things out. Hassan Nasrallah acknowledged the "guidance" role of Iran in a recent *Time* interview:

> Khamenei is supreme spiritual leader [*vali-e-faqih*], a religious model. As is the duty of this model he does advise Hizballah as well as other Muslims, not just in private meetings but in public speeches. . . . What he told Hizballah is what he always says in his speeches: that the only route to freeing the occupied lands is jihad, that people must awaken and resist, and that the people of Palestine must be helped. . . . Muslims must follow these prescriptions, and we have such a religious belief.[49]

All of this takes money, huge amounts of money. Hizbullah's militia absorbs vast amounts of money, as do its welfare and service programs. Activists also have to be paid and the families of martyrs cared for. Traditionally, Iran supplied Hizbullah with weapons and footed the bill for its social service network. Iran's economic problems have now become so severe that it can no longer play that role. Arms continue to arrive, but Hizbullah has been increasingly forced to rely on its own resources for the remainder of its operations. Indeed, *Al Waton al Arabi*, an Arabic news journal, contained a remarkable article detailing an emergency meeting of the Hizbullah pilot bureau in which new funding strategies were studied. An expansion of business activities was discussed as was greater reliance on drugs, gun-running, and counterfeiting.[50] For its part, the United States Drug Enforcement Agency has accused Hizbullah of having ties with a U.S. drug ring.

Strengths and Vulnerabilities

The success of Hizbullah over the course of the past two decades can be attributed to a variety of factors, not the least of which are the dynamism of the Hizbullah leadership and the zeal of its members. Lebanese of all faiths grudgingly acknowledge that the Hizbullah leadership is outstanding. Hizbullah students at the American University of Beirut are among the most serious in the student body. This is a well-trained, well-organized, and very sophisticated organization. All things considered, it is probably the most efficient organization in Lebanon. It is also a high-tech organization adept at utilizing the latest weapons and communications technologies.

The strength of Hizbullah also finds its roots in a Shi'a culture that lends itself to militancy and sacrifice.[51] Martyrdom is the ultimate sacrifice and assures entry into heaven. Adding to the spirit of sacrifice within Shi'a culture is the tremendous veneration of devout Shi'a for their religious leaders. Ayatollah Fadlallah, the spiritual guide of Hizbullah, is one of the leading religious figures of the Shi'a world. For his followers, and they include Iraqis as well as Lebanese, his pronouncements are much like the pronouncements of the pope if not more so. Hassan Nasrallah, the secretary general of Hizbullah, studied in both Najaf and Qum, the two major centers of Islamic learning. Nasrallah's official biography glories in suffering and sacrifice, noting that, "With high spirits, Sayyed Hassan Nasrallah dealt with the martyrdom of his eldest son Hadi, who was martyred during a clash with the 'Israelis,' as a father who was happy for the martyrdom of his son, for [it is] obtaining the blessing of the martyrdom that opens the gates of the garden [of heaven] for a believer."[52]

Having listened to countless hours of Nasrallah's sermons, we can testify to their power and charisma. U.S. evangelists pale by comparison. The Arabic language is the language of the Koran and lends itself to emotion, but none more so than in Nasrallah's speeches.

Hizbullah takes little for granted, and the zeal of its members is continually reinforced by Hizbullah mosques, media, schools, and welfare agencies. Particularly important is the services that Hizbullah provides to the families of its fallen martyrs. These services include monthly food allowances, education, health care, and resources permitting, housing.[53] All enable Hizbullah fighters to serve their God (and ours) with the confidence that their families will be provided for. Pictures of fallen martyrs adorn billboards and buildings in the predominantly Shi'a areas of Lebanon, assuring that Hizbullah martyrs will be honored by the living and serve as heroes for future generations of Shi'a fighters. Honor, too, is a key element of Arab and Islamic culture.

Hizbullah also thrives because the Lebanese government is too weak and too fragmented by religious bickering to take effective action against this most powerful of organizations. This is all the more the case because Syria, the effective ruler of Lebanon, finds Hizbullah to be a useful weapon in its struggle with Israel. Iran, too, finds Hizbullah a useful tool in its foreign policy and ensures that Hizbullah militias are well armed. Hizbullah will remain a powerful force in the region as long as it has the support of Syria and Iran.

However dazzling its success in driving Israel from southern Lebanon, Hizbullah is probably the most vulnerable of the major Islamic groups linked to the war on terror. There are many problems, not the least of which is that Hizbullah is running out of causes. The Lebanese continue to support the Palestinian uprising, but not with the same zeal that they supported the liberation of Lebanon. Christian and Sunni groups are also losing patience with Hizbullah's continued struggle for the Sheba Farms, viewing it as an unnecessary provocation of Israel. America's growing hostility toward Hizbullah also makes the Lebanese nervous. They can't control Hizbullah, but many would like to.

The struggle between Hizbullah and Amal, the rival Shi'a organization, shows few signs of abating, and rumors are rife of conflicts within Hizbullah itself. Such conflicts will inevitably increase if and when Hizbullah is forced to make the transition from a revolutionary organization to a mainline political party. Electoral politics may appeal to Hizbullah moderates, but not to its hardliners. Particularly problematic would be the decommissioning of what amounts to a standing army. It is the military wing of Hizbullah that is the source of its power.

A far more immediate threat to Hizbullah is the very real possibility of a peace treaty between Syria and Israel, a key feature of which would be the dismantling of Hizbullah's military wing. Hizbullah is mindful of this threat, and as early as 2000, rumors were circulating that Hizbullah had established shipping facilities in Cyprus as an alternative transit route for Iranian arms should Syrian cooperation prove unreliable. The U.S. strike on Iraq has also had an unnerving effect on Syria, with the Asad regime going out of its way to convince Washington that it does not support terror. The first step in this direction was the symbolic closing of Hamas offices in Damascus. It is doubtful that Syria would end its support for Hizbullah without a peace treaty with Israel, but it could well curtail Hizbullah's activities as a gesture of good faith to Washington.

Iran, the godfather of the Lebanese Hizbullah, is also encouraging Hizbullah to modify its radicalism in response to the U.S. attack on Iraq. Israel is calling openly for U.S. attacks on Iran, and both Iran and Syria are firmly convinced that Israel dictates U.S. policy. They also believe that the United States is trigger-happy. Nevertheless, U.S. pressure on Iran could well backfire. Iran's Shi'a clerics are unlikely to accept the defeat of their Islamic Revolution without a fight to the end, and that fight requires an active Hizbullah organization in Lebanon. It also requires an active Hizbullah organization in Iraq. With radical Shi'a clergy in control of Iraq, the pressure on the oilfields of Kuwait and Saudi Arabia could well be insurmountable. It was this fear, along with the nightmare of attempting to occupy Iraq, that dissuaded the United States from toppling Saddam Hussein in 1991.

Hizbullah Iraq

Will there be a Hizbullah movement in Iraq parallel to the Hizbullah movement in Lebanon? Inevitably. A prototype of an Iraqi Hizbullah movement is already in place and operates under the name of the Supreme Council for the Islamic Revolution in Iraq (SCIRI). The real question is not whether a Hizbullah movement will exist in Iraq, but how powerful the movement will become.

The SCIRI was formed in 1981 as a collection of Shi'a opposition groups opposed to Saddam Hussein. The group includes an existing Hizbullah party as well as the Badr Corps, the military wing of the council. All fled to Iran with the outbreak of the Iran-Iraq War (1980–1988), as did other Shi'a opposition groups such as the Dawa (Call) party. The Dawa party had been founded in the early 1950s and represented the major religious challenge to the Iraqi regime prior to the outbreak of its war with Iran. The Badr Corps was active throughout the war fighting on the side of the Iranians. It also responded to the U.S. call for a Shi'a rebellion in the aftermath of 1991 defeat of Saddam Hussein, attempting to occupy the holy cities of Karbala and Najaf. The SCIRI suffered heavy losses when the United States abandoned the Shi'a rebellion, with its more visible members again seeking refuge in Iran. The Badr Corps remained active in Iraq throughout the period, launching attacks against Iraqi positions in remote areas.[54]

Both the SCIRI and its Badr Corps were headed by Ayatollah Mohammed-Baqer Hakim until his assassination in 2003. The leadership of the Corps then passed to his brother. It was their father who had created the Dawa party during the early 1950s, suggesting a strong link between the two movements. Baqer Hakim returned to Iraq in May 2003 protected by guards from the Badr Corps under an agreement worked out with Washington. He vowed moderation and a willingness to work within Iraq's multi-ethnic framework, but rejected a Western-style democracy. There would be justice, tolerance, and freedom, but it would be based on Islamic law. The moral laxity of the West would not be accepted.[55] He was assassinated shortly after his return to Iraq.

The SCIRI was one of several Iraqi opposition groups eligible for U.S. financing under the Iraqi Liberation Act, but it refused to take U.S. money or attend meetings of the Iraqi opposition organized by the United States. This said, the organization does not appear to be short of money, long maintaining a television channel, several radio stations, and a variety of schools and clinics among Iraqi exiles in Iran. All are now entrenched in Iraq. The SCIRI maintains offices in Geneva, London, Vienna, Beirut, and Damascus, with representatives in Canada, the United States, and most countries of Western Europe. This does not constitute an international network, but it does suggest that the SCIRI is in touch with a broad range of Islamic groups and organizations, including those of a radical nature.

The SCIRI states that it is merely an umbrella organization that coordinates the activities of various Shi'a groups including a variety of tribal chiefs. While this may be the case, the transition to a full-fledged organization on the model of Hizbullah-Lebanon is but a step away. The militia (Badr Corps) is already in place, as are the organization's education, welfare, and media facilities. Indeed, the Badr Corps, which has a reputed 13,000 members, took control of the holy city of Najaf for a brief period during 2003. The SCIRI also enjoys the strong support of the leadership in Iran.[56] It is they who have been paying its bills.

Conditions for the growth of a vibrant Hizbullah in Iraq are more than favorable. Some sixteen million Iraqis (60 percent) are Shi'a, and Iraq is the site of Najaf and Karbala, the most sacred of Shi'a shrines.[57] Najaf is the resting place of the Caliph Ali, the patron saint of the Shi'a sect. Karbala is the cite of Caliph Ali's martyred son, Hussein, the second most important figure in Shi'a Islam. Najaf was the world's most revered center of Shi'a learning before Iranian students were forced from its seminaries by Saddam Hussein. The Iranian city of Qum now claims that honor, but as one of Iran's leading clerics acknowledges, Najaf will again have the final say in religious matters once it recovers its past glory.[58] The ferocity of Saddam Hussein's vengeance against Shi'a suspected of supporting Iran is only now coming to light, as occupation forces uncover mass graves of Shi'a victims. One grave alone contained a purported 15,000 corpses.[59] Much like the Israeli response to the Holocaust, Iraq's Shi'a have vowed "never again." Iraqi Shi'a are also adamant in their rejection of Western occupation. It was they who led the charge against the British occupation in the 1920s and it is they who are leading the call for an end to the U.S. occupation of Iraq.

Not only are conditions in Iraq favorable for the emergence of an Iraqi Hizbullah, but Iran is determined to see that it happens. It could not be otherwise. Iran fought a brutal eight-year war with Iraq (1980–1988) and cannot accept an Iraqi regime that is hostile to the Islamic Republic. Far more urgent are Iranian fears that the United States plans to use Iraq as a base for an attack on Iran. Indeed, in the months immediately after the U.S. victory in Iraq in May 2003, Washington accused the Islamic Republic of sheltering terrorists and developing weapons of mass destruction. The script was virtually identical to the script used to justify the war against Iraq, but began to mellow as the costs of occupation mounted.

A strong Hizbullah movement in Iraq would prolong the misery of U.S. occupation forces in Iraq and might well make Washington think twice before attempting the occupation of Iran. It would also enable Iran to increase its pressure on Saudi Arabia and Kuwait, both of which contain significant Shi'a populations. The Shi'a population in Saudi Arabia is not large, but it is centered in Saudi Arabia's oil fields and has long been the target of oppression by the Saudi royal family. As a leading Shi'a website notes, 95 percent of the religious and political prisoners in Saudi jails are Shi'a.[60] Rumors also abound of a Shi'a alliance stretching from Iran to Lebanon. Hizbullah-Lebanon speaks openly of such an alliance, and the early months of the U.S.-led occupation of Iraq found agents of Hizbullah-Lebanon in Iraq. Syria, a longtime ally of Iran, has dodged the issue.[61]

Iran, moreover, will find little difficulty in supporting a vibrant Hizbullah organization in Iraq. The border between the two countries is long and porous. Many of Iraq's Shi'a look to Iran as the protector of the Shi'a sect, a view strengthened by the large number of Iraqi clergy of Iranian origin. Trade, legal and otherwise, is now increasing, and Iranian Shi'a are again flocking to the holy mosque in Najaf. Saddam Hussein had done his best to curtail both.

Obstacles to Hizbullah's Expansion in Iraq

Although Iraq presents fertile ground for the emergence of a powerful Hizbullah movement, obstacles abound. At least for the moment, Iran fears an American attack and, other than calling for a speedy U.S. exit from Iraq, it is unlikely to provoke U.S. anger by rushing the launch of a full-fledged Iraqi Hizbullah. On the contrary, it appears that Iran is attempting to dampen the activities of its Hizbullah allies in Lebanon. The SCIRI is following suit, calling for the rapid end to the U.S. occupation of Iraq and popular elections, but not challenging the United States directly. In the meantime, both are biding their time as they wait for the burden of U.S. casualties to take its toll on U.S. morale. Turkey is also hostile to growing Iranian influence in Iraq, as is Saudi Arabia. Saudi Arabia played a major role in financing Saddam Hussein's war against Iran, and Saudi money will have a long reach among Iraqis attempting to recover from three wars and ten years of economic sanctions.

Hizbullah also faces problems at the domestic level. Iraq, like Lebanon is a mosaic of diverse religious and ethnic groups. The Shi'a are the largest of Iraq's religious groups, but their influence is limited to Baghdad and the southern half of the country. The Kurds, about 20 percent of the population, want autonomy and their share of Iraq's oil, much of which is in the Kurdish areas of northern Iraq. The Shi'a might be willing to give the Kurds autonomy, but not the oil.

There is also the religious problem. Kurds are not Arabs, but they are predominantly Sunni in faith and have little interest in living under the rule of Shi'a mullahs tied to Iran. Iraq's Sunni Arabs are adamant in their rejection of rule by Hizbullah or any other Shi'a group. Religious hostility is part of the problem, but so is Sunni fear of Shi'a reprisals. While only 20 percent of the population, Sunni Arabs have ruled Iraq with an iron hand for some eighty years and well understand the Shi'a desire for vengeance. Rule by an Iranian-backed organization such as Hizbullah would represent a threat to the survival of Iraq's Sunni community and will be resisted by every weapon at their disposal, including the support of Saudi Arabia, Turkey and, in all probability, the United States. Iraq is also home to more than a million Tur-komans (ethnic Turks), who, with the encouragement of Turkey, are demanding a strong voice in the shaping of Iraqi politics. As one might expect given their Turkish background, they are opposed to both Hizbullah and the Kurds. Iraqi Christians fear Muslim extremism of any variety. Welcome to Iraq.

Iran and the SCIRI face other problems as well. Iraq has a long tradition of secularism and many Iraqi's, Shi'a and otherwise, fear rule by the religious extremists. Youth in particular, believe that technical skills are more important to their survival than religious science and enrollment at Iraqi seminaries has long been in decline.[62] *The Economist* reports that "the number of clerics in Najaf is thought to have dropped from about 7,000 to fewer than 1,750.[63] This drop in the number of clerics, plus twenty years of Saddam Hussein's rule, have left the Shi'a clergy a major rebuilding task. Many rural communities are without preachers.

Iran and the SCIRI are also faced with an anti-Iranian bias among Iraqi Shi'a. Iranians are not Arabs, and hostility between the two communities runs deep. Rare, indeed, was the Iraqi family that did not suffer losses during Iraq's bloody eight-year war with Iran. This raises an identity crisis of sorts for many Iraqi Shi'a. Are they primarily Arabs who happen to be Shi'a, or are they primarily Shi'a who happen to be Arabs?[64] How Iraqi Shi'a resolve this question will have much to say about the success of Hizbullah in Iraq. Many Iraqi Shi'a seem inclined to resolve the issue by following ayatollahs of Arab background.

Adding to the SCIRI's woes is an abiding debate over the proper role for Shi'a clerics. Ayatollahs in the Iraqi tradition tend to place preaching and prayer above politics. They comment on politics and provide spiritual guidance to political leaders, but not more. Politics, in their view, is a dirty game that serves only to diminish the dignity of the clergy and its moral effectiveness. Ayatollahs of the Iranian tradition, by contrast, believe that it is both the right and obligation of the ayatollahs to rule. Government, in their view, is the most powerful agency in the Islamic world and its power must be placed in the service of God.

A far greater threat to the emergence of a vibrant Hizbullah movement in Iraq is the bitter power struggle for dominance among Iraq's ayatollahs. Only one can be the grand ayatollah of Iraq and its holy cities, a position that has been vacant since 1992. There is little doubt that Baqer Hakim aspired to the position of grand ayatollah, a position occupied by both his father and grandfather. Perhaps that was a motive for his assassination.

If the SCIRI is to prosper, it must stay in the forefront of efforts to drive the United States from Iraq. To do so, however, it risks a U.S. attack on both itself and its Iranian sponsors. Thus far, the SCIRI has walked a fine line, launching verbal attacks against the United States while allowing other radical groups to do the dirty work of organizing protests and attacking U.S. troops. There is no shortage of protests, each new demonstration bringing a new high in anti-Americanism and increasingly trenchant calls for a Koranic rule. The SCIRI seems almost moderate in comparison, participating in the U.S.-sponsored ruling council calling for elections and cooperation among Iraq's diverse groups, albeit with a proviso that democracy in Iraq would have to conform to Islamic scriptures. In the meantime, the framework for a Lebanese-type Hizbullah is being put in place.

The difficulty with the SCIRI's moderate approach is that it may allow more radical clerics to gain control of the Shi'a masses. The first few months of the occupation, for example, saw the Dawa party open offices in twenty-seven of Iraq's largely Shi'a cities.[65] It is not entirely clear whether Dawa is a competitor or ally of the SCIRI. Both have deep roots in the Hakim clan and both have links to Iran. Press reports suggest that the Dawa, itself, may be divided between those guided by Ayatollah Ali Khamenei, the supreme guide of Iran, and those who follow Ayatollah Mohammed Hussein Fadlallah, the spiritual guide of the Lebanese Hizbullah.[66] Dawa now appears to be more moderate than the SCIRI, but appearances are deceiving. Indeed, the Shi'a faith allows its members to hide their true intentions if it serves God's work. Shi'a have even escaped persecution by claiming to be Sunni.

The most immediate challenge to the SCIRI, aside from the loss of its venerated and charismatic leader, is posed by the as-Sadr movement. The as-Sadr movement consists of supporters of Ayatollah as-Sadr who was assassinated in 1999; it is headed by his son, Muqtada as-Sadr. The son, presumably in his late twenties or early thirties, lacks the experience and religious credentials of the father and has attempted to compensate for both by whipping anti-American sentiment into a frenzy. In the fall of 2003 the young as-Sadr boasted a militia of some 10,000 strong, proclaiming his own government of Iraq. Both moves were condemned by the United States and an aging Shi'a establishment, but for the moment, the younger Sadr has seized the momentum within the Iraqi Shi'a community. Should he be killed, a probable event given the challenge that he poses to the United States, the SCIRI, Iran, and the Shi'a establishment, a raft of equally radical youth are waiting in the wings.

In the meantime, Iran has hedged its bets by inviting Muqtada as-Sadr to Tehran, where he received the royal treatment including a meeting with Supreme Guide Ali Khamenei of Iran. Khamenei reportedly told him, "You are the Hassan Nasrallah of Iraq. You will force the Americans from Iraq just as Nasrallah has forced the Israelis from Lebanon."[67] It is difficult to substantiate the story, but if true, it would appear that Iran is playing both ends of the political spectrum: using the SCIRI to create turmoil within the ruling assembly while simultaneously using as-Sadr to attack the United States from without. Driving the United States out of Iraq is more important for Iran than dominating the Iraqi Shi'a movement in the short run. That can be sorted out later.

Coping with an Iraqi Hizbullah: Strategies and Pitfalls

A seemingly logical U.S. ploy for stopping the emergence of a powerful Hizbullah movement in Iraq would be to allow ascetic (nonpolitical) Shi'a clerics of Arabic origin to play a major role in the governing of the country. This was the cornerstone of Saddam Hussein's Shi'a strategy but, as he found to his dismay, was not without its risks. U.S. policymakers may find Hussein's experience instructive.

The story began in 1992 with the death of Grand Ayatollah Khoui in 1992. Khoui was a profound intellect whose ascetic views had dampened the appeal of Iraq's more radical ayatollah's. The race was for a new grand ayatollah for the Iraqi Shi'a. Much depended on their reputation among senior Iraqi clerics and the breadth of their popular support. Needless to say, Saddam Hussein was anxious to promote the fortunes of an Arab ayatollah of ascetic views. This continued to dampen the appeal of the radical clergy, while blocking Iran's leadership of Iraq's Shi'a community. If it created dissension among the Shi'a ayatollahs, so much the better.

Toward this end, Saddam Hussein lent his support to Mohammed Sadiq as-Sadr, an Iraqi ayatollah renowned for his ascetic, nonpolitical views.[68] Rumors of a deal between Hussein and as-Sadr swept the Shi'a community, while as-Sadr's opponents began referring to him as the "regime ayatollah."[69] Whether or not there was a deal, Saddam Hussein embraced as-Sadr and allowed him to broadcast his sermons over Iraqi radio and television, a privilege denied to his competitors. As-Sadr was also allowed a freedom of movement denied to his competitors and given control of foreign students studying in Najaf.[70] Tensions escalated as rumors circulated that Saddam Hussein had ordered the assassination of all non-Iraqi ayatollahs.[71]

In reality, very little is nonpolitical in Iraq. As-Sadr's sermons struck a responsive chord among Iraqi Shi'a and, intentionally or not, he emerged as a competitor of Saddam Hussein. This danger increased in the early months of 1998, as as-Sadr's sermons grew increasingly critical of the regime and he urged his followers to attend Friday prayers in person rather than watching them on television.[72] Attendance at Friday prayers increased apace, reportedly attracting more than 100,000 worshipers crowded into the Grand Mosque of Najaf and its surrounding courtyards to hear as-Sadr speak.

As-Sadr and his two sons were murdered by unknown assailants in February 18, 1999. Saddam Hussein was accused of the assassinations, but Hussein was not the only party with a motive for eliminating as-Sadr. As-Sadr's supremacy posed a dire threat to the aspirations of his rivals. Lest there be any doubt on the matter, as-Sadr had ordered Iraqi Shi'a to give their religious contributions directly to the poor and needy rather than going through the clergy. In one fell swoop, the coffers of his rivals were put at risk.

Iran's displeasure with as-Sadr was also intense. It could not be otherwise, for as-Sadr's ascendancy had dampened Iranian influence among Iraqi Shi'a, fragmented the Shi'a community, and strengthened the Iraqi city of Najaf as a competitor to the Iranian city of Qum as the spiritual center of Shi'a faith. These were not minor issues, for Iranian dominance of the Shi'a communities in Iraq and Lebanon had become a cardinal principle of Iranian foreign policy. To paraphrase al-Qisi in reference to the four ayatollahs who were assassinated in Iraq during 1998, "It is possible to make two lists of the assassinated ayatollahs: those assassinated by Saddam Hussein and those assassinated by Iran and its agents."[73]

The United States appears to be following Saddam Hussein's strategy in attempting to block the emergence of a strong Hizbullah movement in Iraq. Shortly after the fall of Saddam Hussein, the very moderate Sheikh al-Khoei, head of the al-Khoei Charitable Foundation in London and son of a former grand ayatollah, was flown to Iraq on a U.S. military aircraft and accompanied to the holy city of Najaf by U.S. Special Forces. He was assassinated within days, with speculation on his assassination pointing to the as-Sadr movement. Ayatollah Sestani, another moderate ayatollah, was placed under house arrest by the as-Sadr movement and threatened with assassination if he did not return to Iran. The United States came to the rescue and Sestani's moderate views made him America's new man among Iraqi Shi'a. He is profoundly uncomfortable with the honor, all the more so since the attempted assassination of his deputy in 2003. An abortive attack on Sestani was reported in 2004, but remains unconfirmed.

At the same time that the United States courted moderate Shi'a in an effort to block growing Hizbullah and Iranian influence in Iraq, it also allowed Christian missionaries to play a growing role in the distribution of relief aid. This inflamed Muslim hostility to the United States and placed the missionaries in grave danger if they were to attempt to proselytize Muslims. Medical missionaries have already become the target of assassinations in both Yemen and Lebanon.

The United States must also overcome the legacy of distrust resulting from its treachery in the 1991 war against Iraq. The United States called on Iraqi Shi'a and Kurds to revolt and then abandoned them to Saddam Hussein. It was Saddam Hussein's subsequent slaughter of Shi'a and Kurds that prompted the United States to impose no fly zones in the Kurdish and Shi'a zones respectively. If the Shi'a continue to be wary of the United States, it is not without cause.

CAN THE MUSLIM BROTHERHOOD AND HIZBULLAH SERVE AS A COUNTERWEIGHT TO THE JIHADISTS?

Having surveyed the "middle ground" of the Islamic movement, we now return to one of the most intriguing and critical questions on America's war on terror. Are the Muslim Brotherhood, Hizbullah, and other more moderated Islamic groups potential allies of the United States in its war on terror, or are they merely the deceptive facade of an Islamic movement intent on transforming the Muslim world into an Islamic state?

Attempts to answer this question have been the source of great controversy as well as great confusion. It could not be otherwise, for relations between the jihadists and the more moderate organizations of the Islamic world are a matter of great secrecy. They also tend to ebb and flow with the circumstances of the moment, periods of rapprochement giving way to hostility and then to renewed efforts to forge a common ground.

The Case for Working with the Radical-Moderates

The case for using the Muslim Brotherhood, Hizbullah, and other more moderate groups as a counterweight against the jihadists is a blend of realism, Machiavellianism, and idealism. The realist argument is simple and direct. The radical-moderates find support among a broad segment of the Muslim population and are simply too numerous to crush. The Turks, not shrinking violets when it comes to police brutality, have tried for almost ninety years to stamp out Islamic fundamentalism and have failed. The picture is the same throughout the Islamic world. The American record in the Middle East is dismal, and it is folly for the United States to believe that it can succeed in crushing Islamic fundamentalism when some of the world's most brutal dictators have failed. Attacking the radical-moderates is tantamount to declaring war on Islam and will only serve to push the more moderate segments of the Islamic world into the hands of the jihadists. The jihadists are attacking America, and the United States has enough problems without bolstering their ranks.

Is cooperating with the Muslim Brotherhood and Hizbullah a risky proposition? To be sure. But, the realists ask, does the United States have the capacity to cripple the Brotherhood and Hizbullah? If so, what would be the costs of such an operation? Unlike bin Laden and the Taliban, the Brotherhood cannot be bombed. There is no clear target. The Brotherhood is everywhere. Nor can the United States send in the marines. To do so would be to occupy most of the Islamic world, a chilling task for a country that experienced problems with occupying Iraq. Western laws also make it virtually impossible to close down the Muslim Brotherhood's associations abroad. Unlike the jihadists, they have committed no crime. Hizbullah may be more vulnerable, but it is still a tricky proposition.

The Machiavellians take the argument one step further: divide and conquer. As we have seen in earlier discussions, there is little unity in the Islamic movement. The radical-moderates and the jihadists disagree on just about everything from leadership to the role of the Shi'a in an Islamic world. They are also in competition for control of the Islamic movement. The more the moderate radicals are allowed to play a significant role in their respective countries, so the Machiavellian argument goes, the more the jihadists will be pushed to the margins. If the moderates are given a voice, they will have little need for violence.

The benefits of working with the Muslim Brotherhood and other more moderate groups are also substantial. They understand Muslim culture and Muslim psychology far better than the United States and they know who the jihadists are and where to find them. Such knowledge is of vital importance in America's war on terror. This knowledge is also vital for countering attacks on U.S. troops in Iraq and other areas of the Islamic

world. Always cynics, the Machiavellians bolster their argument by noting
that the radical-moderates are hungry for power and have a long record of
selling out to secular regimes for a share of the spoils. This has been a pervasive jihadist criticism of the Muslim Brotherhood and other more moderate
Islamic groups. True cynics might also suggest that giving the Muslim fundamentalists a taste of power might be the best way to defeat them. If one is
to judge by the Iranian and Taliban experience, people soon tire of Islamic
rule.

The idealists, in turn, are concerned about human rights and religious
freedoms. How does one attack Islamic groups without laying the groundwork for attacks on religion in Europe and North America, both of which
have large Muslim minorities? Muslims, after all, pray to the same God as
Christians and Jews. The picture is much the same in regard to democracy
and human rights. How can one attack the more moderate Islamic groups
without attacking democracy? This is more than a philosophical question.
The United States has recently launched a "democratic initiative" designed
to build peace and stability in the Muslim world. In all probability, promoting democracy in the Islamic world means empowering Islamic groups
intent on creating an Islamic state. The United States cannot have it both
ways. If it wants democracy, it is going to get a large dose of religious influence throughout the Muslim world.

The Case against the Radical-Moderates

The argument of those who urge the United States to attack the Muslim Brotherhood and Hizbullah begins by rejecting the assumption that the
more moderate Islamic groups are indeed moderate. Both the Muslim
Brotherhood and Hizbullah, they recall, had espoused violence in earlier
periods of their history, and, in the case of Hizbullah, that violence was
directed against American targets. Both now disavow violence as a means
of achieving an Islamic state, but they could change their minds. Indeed, a
mid-2003 poll within the Egyptian branch of the Muslim Brotherhood
found that 38 percent of those polled wanted to reinstate the military wing
of the Brotherhood, presumably out of business since the group's change of
heart in the early 1970s. Some 26 percent thought Brotherhood members
should have military training.[74]

Virtually all of the more "moderate" groups, moreover, support violence against countries occupying Muslim lands. Israel has borne the brunt
of this violence, as have Russia and India in their seemingly futile efforts to

crush the jihadist rebellions in Chechnya and Kashmir, respectively. The line between supporting violence to liberate occupied Muslim land and the use of violence for achieving an Islamic state, in the view of the hardliners, is smoke and mirrors. Violence is violence, and the Muslim Brotherhood and other more moderate groups are merely the seductive facade of a unified Islamic movement that shares a common goal of Islamic rule. While the jihadists bludgeon the secular regimes of the Islamic world with violence, the moderate radicals subvert them from within. The Muslim Brotherhood and Hizbullah may appear to be moderate, caution the hardliners, but that is only in comparison with the jihadists.

The hardliners also argue that the line separating the moderates and the jihadists is not all that clear. All Islamic groups possess a broad range of members. Some are true advocates of peaceful change, while others incline toward the jihadist position. Even outwardly peaceful groups, the hardliners warn, are easily converted to the jihadist cause. It all depends on who's in charge. In much the same manner, the hardliners draw a clear line between the Muslim Brotherhood and Hizbullah. The Brotherhood has a long history of moderation; Hizbullah has been in the forefront of attacks on Israel. It may soon be in the forefront of attacks on Allied troops in Iraq. Much the same applies to the Islamic parties that are mushrooming throughout the Muslim world. Some are truly moderate and provide an important avenue of political expression for moderate Muslims concerned about the political and moral decay of their societies. Others, such as those now in control of the frontier provinces of Pakistan, are blatant advocates of the Talibanization of Pakistan including the forced veiling of women. Not unexpectedly, the jihadists have thrived in this environment.

Our own assessment is in line with that of the realists. Much is to be gained by cooperating with the more moderate Islamic groups and efforts to eliminate them will only increase terrorism and push the United States into a war with Islam. Do the hardliners have a point? To be sure, but this is not a war of easy choices. Some suggestions on the topic will be offered in the final chapter.

The American government seems unsure of what to do, preferring to pick and choose on a case-by-case basis. The Muslim Brotherhood is largely ignored. Hizbullah seems doomed to attack. The emerging Islamic parties are a source of bewilderment. This, however, does not address the fundamental question: Is the United States willing to accept rule by Islamic parties dedicated to the establishment of an Islamic state? If the answer is no, America will be at war with Islam.

NOTES

1. Cilina Nasser, "Fadlallah Condones Human Cloning: Cleric Asks 'Why Should Anyone Prohibit Something New?'" *Daily Star-Lebanon.com*, 2 Apr. 2002, at http://www.dailystar.com.lb/04_03_02/art24.htm (accessed 4 Mar. 2002).

2. Nada, "Interview with Joseph Nada," Parts 1–6.

3. Muslim Brotherhood Home page, n.d., at http://www.ummah.org.uk/ikhwan (accessed 12 Apr. 2002).

4. "Russian Security Services Uncover Muslim Brotherhood Operations," *Islam Online*, 18 Oct. 2002, at www.islamonline.com/ (accessed 18 Oct. 2002); Ahmed Rashid, *Jihad: The Rise of Militant Islam in Central Asia* (New York: Penguin Books, 2002).

5. Muslim Brotherhood Home page.

6. Muslim Brotherhood Home page.

7. Paraphrased from Muslim Brotherhood Home page.

8. Paraphrased from various Brotherhood documents.

9. Muslim Brotherhood Home page.

10. Muslim Brotherhood Home page.

11. Saad Eddin Ibrahim, *Egypt, Islam, and Democracy* (Cairo: American University of Cairo Press, 1996).

12. Muslim Brotherhood Home page, Questions Section, some punctuation modified.

13. Joel Campagna, "From Accommodation to Confrontation: The Muslim Brotherhood in the Mubarak Years," *Journal of International Affairs* 50, no.1 (Summer 1996):278–304.

14. Fysal Al-Qassem (moderator), "The Arab Street: Panel Discussion," Al-Jazeera, 16 Apr. 2002, in Arabic, at http://www.aljazeera.net/programs/op_direction/articles/2002/3/4-25-1.htm (accessed 6 May 2002); Abdullah, Mahar, "Will the Islamic Street Explode after the Strike on Afghanistan," Al-Jazeera, 30 Oct. 2001, in Arabic. Interview with Abdullah Al Hamid II Sheikh Mubarak, Royal School of Islamic Jurisprudence, at http://www.aljazeera.net/programs/shareea/articles/2001.10/10_30_1.htm (accessed 5 Nov. 2001).

15. Musa Keilani, *The Islamic Movement in Jordan* (Amman, Jordan: Dar Al Bashir, 1990), in Arabic.

16. Joseph Nada, "Interview with Joseph Nada, Commissioner of International Political Affairs for the Muslim Brotherhood," in Arabic. Part 4 of six interviews by Ahmed Mansour of *Al-Jazeera Online*, 28 Aug. 2002, at http://www.aljazeera.net/programs/century_witness/articles/2002/8/8-28-1.htm (accessed 9 Sept. 2002).

17. Abdul Karim Qassem Saeed, *The Muslim Brotherhood and the Fundamentalist Movement in Yemen* (Cairo: Madbouli, 1995).

18. Ali Sadr Eddin Al-Baiya'nooni, "The Political Future of the Muslim Brotherhood in Syria," Al-Jazeera, 29 Nov. 2001, in Arabic. Interview with Ahmed Mansour.

19. Amr El Choubaki, "Speaking in Tongues," *Al Ahram Weekly Online*, 663 (6–12 Nov. 2003), at http://weekly.ahram.org.eg/print/2003/663//eg1.htm (accessed 8 Nov. 2003). For a more extensive review of the Brotherhood, see "Special File: The Muslim Brotherhood: Where Is It Headed?" Al-Jazeera, 2 Dec. 2002, in Arabic, at http://www.aljazeera.net/in-depth/muslims_brothers/2002/12/12-2-18.htm (accessed 5 Dec. 2002).

20. Nada, "Interview with Joseph Nada," Part 1, 4 Aug. 2002, at http://www.aljazeera.net/programs/century_witness/articles/2002/8/8-7-1.htm (accessed 9 Sept. 2002).

21. Joseph Nada, "Responses to Testimony of Youssef Nada," in Arabic. Part 6 of six interviews by Ahmed Mansour of *Al-Jazeera Online*, 5 Oct. 2002, at http://www.aljazeera.net/programs/no_limites/articles/2002/10/10_5_1.htm (accessed 13 Oct. 2002).

22. "Settling for Small Steps," *Al Ahram Weekly*, 24 Jan. 2004, at http://weekly.ahram.org.eg/2004/674/eg5.htm (accessed 24 Jan. 2004). Dates and activities vary from source to source.

23. Nada, "Responses to Testimony."

24. Amil Khan, "Brotherhood Faces Crisis," *Middle East Times*, No. 45, Nov. 2002, at http://www.metimes.com/2K2/issue2002-45/eg/brotherhood_faces_crisis.htm (accessed 9 Nov. 2002).

25. Nada, "Interview with Joseph Nada," Part 5, 9 Sept. 2002, at http://www.aljazeera.net.programs/century_witness/articles/2002/9/9-5-1.htm (accessed 9 Sept. 2002).

26. Nada, "Responses to Testimony."

27. Nada, "Interview with Joseph Nada," Part 1, 4 Aug.

28. Tarig El Halim, "Views on the Transformation of the Islamic Movement in Egypt: The Muslim Brotherhood in Half a Century," in Arabic, *Al Manar al Jadeed*, no. 15 (Dec. 2001); Ahmed Qauwisi, "The Islamic Movement on the Doorstep of the Twenty-first Century," in Arabic, *Al Manar al Jadeed*, no. 15 (Dec. 2001).

29. James A. Bill, *The Eagle and the Lion: The Tragedy of American-Iranian Relations* (New Haven, Conn.: Yale University Press, 1988); Sandra Mackey, *The Iranians: Persia, Islam and the Soul of a Nation* (New York: Dutton, 1996); Said Amir Arjomand, *The Shadow of God and the Hidden Imam* (Chicago: University of Chicago Press, 1984).

30. Marvin Zonis, *Majestic Failure: The Fall of the Shah* (Chicago: University of Chicago Press, 1991).

31. Marvin Zonis and Cyrus Amir Mokri, "The Islamic Republic of Iran," in *Politics and Government in the Middle East and North Africa*, Tareq Y. Ismael and Jacqueline S. Ismael, eds. (Miami: Florida International University Press, 1991), 114–150.

32. Farhad Ibrahim, *Confessionalism and Politics in the Arab World: The Shi'a Program in Iraq* (Cairo: Library Madbouli, 1996), in Arabic, translated from German by the Center for Cultural Studies and Translations.

33. Mackey, *The Iranians*, 323.

34. Gay Cavender, Nancy C. Jurik, and Albert K. Cohen, "The Baffling Case of the Smoking Gun: The Social Ecology of the Political Accounts in the Iran-Contra Affair," *Social Problems* 40, no. 2 (1993):152–165.

35. Augustus R. Norton, *Amal and the Shi'a: Struggle for the Soul of Lebanon* (Austin: University of Texas Press, 1987).

36. Eyal Zisser, "Hizballah in Lebanon: At the Crossroads," *MERIA* 1, no. 3, (Sept. 1997, at http://www.biu.ac.il/SOC/besa/meria/journal/1997/issue3/jv1n3a1.html (accessed 9 May 2002).

37. Michael Young, "Hizballah outside and in," *MERIA*, 26 Oct. 2002, at http://www.merip.org/pins/pin37.html (accessed 9 May 2002);"Army Comes between Rival Resistance Groups: Dispute over Soccer Field Leads to Several Injuries," *Daily Star-Lebanon*, 2 Feb. 2002, at http://www.dailystar.com.lb/02_02_02/art17.htm (accessed 2 Feb. 2002).

38. "Interview with the Secretary General of Hizbullah Sayyed Hassan Nasrallah," Al-Jazeera, 14 Feb. 2002, 7–8, at http://www.nasrallah.net/English/Hassan/khitabat/khitabat033.htm (accessed 16 Apr. 2003).

39. Farid El Khazen, *The Breakdown of the State of Lebanon, 1967–1976* (London: IB Tauris, 2000).

40. "Lebanon Won't Let Palestinians Buy Land," *Jerusalem Post*, 14 Oct. 2003, at http://www.jpost.com/servlet/Satellite?pagename=JPost/JPArticle/ShowFull&cid=1066113923633&p=1008596981749 (accessed 14 Oct. 2003).

41. Personal communication.

42. Christopher Slaney, "Israeli Prisoner Swap Success," *Middle East Times*, No. 5, Jan. 2004, at http://metimes.com/2K4/issue2004-5/reg/israeli_prisoner_swap.htm (accessed 31 Jan. 2004).

43. Nicholas Blanford, "Goksel: Army Effectively Deployed in South," *Daily Star-Lebanon*, 6 May 2003, at http://www.dailystar.com.lb/06_05_03/art2.asp (accessed 6 May 2002).

44. Ibrahim Mousawi, "Fadlallah Explains Religious Basis for Suicide Attacks," *Daily Star-Lebanon*, 8 June 2002, at http://www.dailystar.com.lb/08_06_02/art5.asp (accessed 8 June 2002).

45. Jihad Salem, "Important Emergency Meeting in the Majlis As Shoura (Hezbullah Lebanon) to Discuss the Disaster of the Decrease in Iranian Support," *Al-Waton Al-Arabi* (9 Apr. 1999), 32–33, in Arabic.

46. "Citation of the Biography of His Eminence Sayyed Hassan Nasrallah," Nasrallah Home page, n.d., at http://www.nasrallah.net/main/moharamf/nasrashora.html (accessed 16 Apr. 2003).

47. Interview with the secretary general of Hizbullah Sayyed Hassan Nasrallah by Al-Jazeera, 14 Feb. 2002, at http://www.nasrallah.net/English/Hassan/khitabat/khitabat 033.htm (accessed 16 Apr. 2003).

48. "Hizbullah—the Party of God: Hizballah—Social Radicals," Hizbullah Home page, n.d., at http://www.almashriq.hiof.no/Lebanon/300/3220/324/324.2/Hizballah (accessed 9 Apr. 2002).

49. "Interview with Hizballah Secretary-General Sheik Hassan Nasrallah" *Time Europe,* 1 Nov. 2000, at http://www.time.com/time/Europe/webonly/mideast/2000/11/Nasrallah.html (accessed 9 May 2002).

50. Salem, "Important Emergency Meeting," 32–33.

51. Manocheht Dorraj, "Symbolic and Utilitarian Political Value of a Tradition: Martyrdom in the Iranian Political Culture," *The Review of Politics* 59, no. 3 (1997):489–521.

52. Nasrallah Home page, n.d., at http://www.nasrallah.net/main/moharamf/nasrashora.html (accessed 16 Apr. 2003).

53. Jacob Qasir, "Report about the Advance and the Help of Emdad Committee for Islamic Charity until Date of 31/3/1997," Hizbullah Home page, 9 May 1998, at http://almashriq.hiof.no/lebanon/300/320/324/324.2/hizballah/emdad/index/html (accessed 15 Apr. 2003).

54. Safauddin Tabraian, "A Glance at the History and Inclination of the Supreme Council for the Islamic Revolution in Iraq," *Hamshahri* (Persian Morning Daily) 11, no. 3023 (15 Apr. 2003), translated by Net Iran, at http://www.netiran.com/Htdocs/Clippings/FPolitics/030415XXFP01.html (accessed 17 Apr. 2003); M. Javad Routh, "Najaf Seminary Following Fall of Dictator," *Hamshahri* 11, no. 3025 (17 Apr. 2003):1, at http://www.netiran.com/Htdocs/Clippings/FPolitics/030417XXFP01.html (accessed 17 May 2003).

55. Safauddin Tabraian, "A Glance at the History and Inclination of the Supreme Council for the Islamic Revolution in Iraq," *Hamshahri* 11, no. 3023 (15 Apr. 2003), translated by Net Iran.

56. Tabraian, "A Glance at the History."

57. Yitzhak Nakash, *The Shi'is of Iraq* (Princeton, N.J.: Princeton University Press, 1994).

58. Routh, "Najaf Seminary Following Fall of Dictator."

59. Stephen Franklin, "Iraq Littered with Mass Graves Stuffed with Untold Number of Victims," Infotrac CJ112422853 (21 Jan. 2004).

60. "Religious Curbs in Saudi Arabia—Report," *Jafariya News*, 30 Jan. 30, 2001, at http://www.jafariyanews.com/dec2k2/13_saudicurbs.htm (accessed 23 May 2003).

61. "Hizbullah Official Says Iraq Will Ally with Lebanon, Syria, Iran," *Daily Star-Lebanon*, 25 Apr. 2003, at http://www.dailystar.com.lb/25_04_03/art26.asp (accessed 25 Apr. 2003).

62. Hanna Batatu, "Iraqi Underground Shi'a Movements: Characteristics, Causes and Prospects," *Middle East Journal* 35, no. 4 (1981):578–594; Mackey, *The Iranians*.

63. "Iraq's Shias Return to the Exile," *The Economist* (7 May 2003):25.

64. Graham F. Fuller, *The Arab Shi'a* (New York: Palgrave, 2001).

65. Beth Potter, "Threat of Islamic Militancy Looms in Iraq," *Middle East Times,* 17 May 2003, at http://www.metimes.com/2k3/issue2003-20/reg/threat-of-Islamic .htm (accessed 17 May 2003).

66. Sami Shaurash, "Muktadar As-Sadr Shuffles the Cards: Shi'a War against Americans or Shi'a War against Shi'a," *Al-Wasat*, no. 612 (20 Oct. 2003):4–6, in Arabic.

67. Shaurash, "Muktadar As-Sadr Shuffles the Cards."

68. Ahmed Al Katib, "The Events in Najaf: Will They Ignite Riots or an Intifada?" *Al-Wasat* (1–7 Mar. 1999), 14–15, in Arabic; Asaad Hidar, "As Sadr in the Week Before," *Al-Wasat* (1–7 Mar. 1999), 13–14, in Arabic.

69. Mustafa Sarour, "Assassination of As-Sadr Preceded by a Deadly Telephone Debate: Preemptive Strike or Provocation to Civil Strife," *Al-Wasat* (1–7 Mar. 1999), 10–12, in Arabic.

70. Al Katib, "The Events in Najaf."

71. Al Katib, "The Events in Najaf."

72. Al Katib, "The Events in Najaf."

73. Saad Al Quisi, "Najaf: City of Slaughter in the War of the Marjaiyat," *Al Waton al Arabi* (5 Mar. 1999), 20–21, in Arabic.

74. Rose El-Youssef, quoted in Omayma Abdel-Latif, "Truth or Dare?" *Al-Ahram Weekly*, 4 June 2003, at http://weekly.ahram.org.eg/print/2003/643/eg8.htm (accessed 21 June 2003).

4

THE JIHADIST MOVEMENT
AND HOW IT EVOLVED

The jihadists are Muslim extremists intent on establishing an Islamic state through violence. In their view, reform is an illusion. Cooperating with secular governments, they say, merely adds to their legitimacy and makes them harder to defeat in the long run. In the meantime, the cancer of Western culture corrupts Muslim youth and undermines the pillars of the Islamic faith. Much as the Prophet Mohammed declared a jihad against the infidels from Mecca, so the jihadists believe it is their task to drive the infidels from the lands of Islam. Who is an infidel? Anyone, Muslim or otherwise, who obstructs the jihadist vision of an Islamic state. It is the jihadists themselves who will make that determination.

Beyond this point, there are so many variations within the jihadist movement that they defy description. Groups form, splinter, and regroup under different names. Some were inspired by Egyptian jihadists. Others find their roots in Iran or Pakistan. Some are large and well organized; others are embryonic. Some network, others prefer to operate independently. Bin Laden's al Qaeda network is the most renowned of the jihadist groups, but it is just one of many. Egypt, alone, had some ninety jihadist groups during the 1980s. Global figures could well reach several hundred. Even al Qaeda is now splintering into a multitude of autonomous groups. How tightly they are linked to al Qaeda is a mystery. Many groups have received support from al Qaeda but do not follow its dictates. Others serve as subcontractors, carrying out specific operations for al Qaeda and then returning to their own agenda. Like most subcontractors, they pick up jobs as they

85

come along. Still others are graduates of Afghanistan who have branched out on their own. This does not make them part of al Qaeda, but it does make them part of the jihadist threat. Even groups distant from bin Laden are inspired by his example. Adding to the confusion is America's tendency to attribute all terrorist attacks to al Qaeda, whatever their origin. This is misleading and suggests that the problem can be solved by the arrest of the al Qaeda leadership. Arrests are made, but the attacks continue.

The present chapter traces the evolution of the jihadist movement from scattered groups of student radicals through the evolution of international networks capable of striking America and its allies. Each step along the way has seen the jihadists respond to adversity by extending their reach and developing new and more deadly strategies for striking their enemies. That evolution continues today.

EGYPT AND THE ORIGINS OF MODERN JIHADISM

The jihadist movement emerged in Egypt as part of the broader Islamic revival spawned by the humiliating defeat of the Arab armies in the Six Day War of 1967.[1] The Egyptian Army, the vanguard of the Arab forces, collapsed in about four days. In its wake came a psychological crisis as Egyptians struggled to understand how a secular regime that had spent twenty years preaching militarization and industrialization could simply crumble in the face of an Israeli attack. The picture was much the same throughout the Arab world. Islam, always a dominant force in Arab culture, filled the psychological emotional vacuum left by the war.

In reality, the jihadist movement in Egypt had begun long before the humiliation of the Arab forces in the Six Day War. Its origins, while difficult to pin down precisely, began as a bitter strategy debate within the Muslim Brotherhood over the use of violence as a political weapon. The strongest voice on the side of violence was that of Sayyed Qutb, a brilliant intellectual who argued that reform was pointless and only served to corrupt Muslims and strengthen the enemies of Islam.[2] Infidels were to be killed, not accommodated.

The debate was largely theoretical as long as the Nasser regime was in power. By the mid-1960s, however, mass frustrations were approaching the breaking point. Egypt had suffered through a long and unpopular war in Yemen and President Nasser himself would later acknowledge that his grand experiment in forced socialism had been a dismal failure.[3] Sensing mass discontent, Qutb's faction within the Brotherhood plotted the violent overthrow of the Nasser regime. The plot failed and Qutb was executed.

Perhaps Qutb's greatest mistake had been impatience. The Six Day War broke out two years later and threw the Egyptian government into chaos. Nasser resigned but recanted in the face of a mass outpouring of popular emotion. Then Field Marshall Abdel Hakim Amer, commander of the Egyptian forces and longtime friend of Nasser, committed suicide following accusations that he had plotted to overthrow the government. His wife suggests that he was assassinated by Nasser.[4] Nasser was terminally ill and died in 1970. One way or another, the regime lost its will to resist the fundamentalists.

Nasser was replaced by Anwar Sadat who, fearful that he would be overthrown by the communists and other leftists, revived the Muslim Brotherhood as a counterweight to his adversaries. In the process, he also opened the door to a virtual explosion of jihadist groups.[5] They, too, were given free reign to attack leftist groups intent on opposing Sadat's rule. It was they, along with the Brotherhood, who transformed the "street" from a bastion of the left into a bastion of Islam.

With leftists crushed and Sadat secure in his presidency, the jihadists demanded that the Egyptian president, a former member of the Muslim Brotherhood, transform Egypt into an Islamic theocracy. Sadat resisted, and the battle was joined. It culminated in the 1981 assassination of Sadat by the Islamic Group, Egypt's largest jihadist group. The word jihadist had entered the world's vocabulary. Buoyed by the assassination of Sadat, the jihadists waged a relentless war against the Egyptian government that showed signs of becoming a civil war before tapering off toward the end of the 1990s.

Most of the ninety some jihadist groups to emerge in Egypt during the 1970s and 1980s were formed by students from middle- and lower-middle-class backgrounds. Largely rural, their conservative traditions clashed with the urban immorality of Cairo and Alexandria. Indeed, youth was the hallmark of the jihadist movement, with the majority of its members being students or recent graduates.[6] Most were trained in technical fields like medicine and engineering rather than the mind-bending fields of politics or philosophy. Such, at least, were the results of Saad Ibrahim's interviews with jihadists imprisoned in the aftermath of Sadat's assassination.[7] Most were also frustrated by the corruption of the Sadat regime and the glaring economic inequities of Egyptian society.

The early years of the jihadist movement were a spontaneous explosion of faith, optimism, frustration, and naivety. There was no organizational network as such, but members of the diverse groups, most of which were little more than small cells, seemed to be aware of each other and interaction between groups was not uncommon. Hala Mustafa suggests that this may have been the results of contacts developed in prison, one of the main breeding grounds of the jihadist movement.[8] Mobility between groups was also common as groups splintered and reformed.

By 1992, Egypt appeared to be on the brink of civil war. As described by Aoude:

> Until July 1992, Islamic forces controlled many villages and small towns in several governorates in Egypt. In some cases they had political power that paralleled the Egyptian state.[9]

The Islamic Jihad

Most of Egypt's smaller groups have now fallen by the wayside or merged with their larger competitors. Of these, two groups, the Egyptian Islamic Jihad and the Islamic Group (Al-Gama'a al-Islamiyya) have developed a broad international reach and are featured on the U.S. list of international terrorist organizations. The Islamic Jihad was formed in the 1970s and gained notoriety with the assassination of President Sadat. In 1998, the group split with Dr. Ayman al Zawahiri, affiliating his wing of the jihad with bin Laden's al Qaeda network. The two groups merged in 2001.

Relations between al Zawahiri and bin Laden apparently developed during the Afghan rebellion against the Soviets, when al Zawahiri fled to Afghanistan to escape prosecution in Egypt. Egyptian "Afghans" were trained in bin Laden's camps and, with the end of the Afghan rebellion in 1989, began to make their way back to Egypt. They were implicated in 1993 plots to assassinate Egypt's prime minister and minister of interior and in a 1995 plot to assassinate President Mubarak. They were also the prime suspects in failed attempts to blow up the American and Israeli embassies in Manila in 1994 as well as the successful 1995 bombing of the Egyptian Embassy in Pakistan. All of the above events occurred before the merging of the Islamic Jihad and al Qaeda, and there can be little doubt that al Zawahiri added much needed muscle to bin Laden's al Qaeda network. Indeed, the Islamic Jihad is widely believed to be the force behind the 1998 bombings of the American embassies in Nairobi, Kenya, and Dar es Salaam, Tanzania. Al Zawahiri's prints also appear large on the 2000 bombing of the

USS *Cole* in Aden, Yemen, and the September 11 attacks on the United States, although this is a matter of speculation. Given this record, one might question who is the greater threat to America: bin Laden or al Zawahiri? Questions remain about bin Laden's health. Al Zawahiri remains at large. He is clearly capable of exploiting the resources of the al Qaeda network. He is equally capable of reestablishing his own network.

The splintering of Islamic Jihad and the merger of its al Zawahiri branch with bin Laden has left the Islamic Jihad in disarray. It has reportedly regrouped under the leadership of Tharwat Salah Shehata (Abu Sama) who was, himself sentenced to death in absentia for his role in the 1995 assassination attempt on President Mubarak.[10] He was part of al Zawahiri's group in Afghanistan but disagreed with the merger of the Islamic Jihad and al Qaeda. As such, Shehata was also positioned to transform his wing of the Islamic Jihad into an international network capable of threatening American and allied targets.

The Islamic Group (Al-Gama'a al-Islamiyya)

The background of the Islamic Group roughly parallels that of the Islamic Jihad. It was founded in 1973 in the very traditional areas of Upper Egypt (southern Egypt) and spread rapidly to student groups in Cairo and Alexandria. It, too, was used by Sadat as a counterweight to his leftist adversaries, but the honeymoon was short lived. Hounded by Sadat's police, the group's leader, Sheikh Omar Abdel al-Rahman, the "blind sheikh," fled to Saudi Arabia where he was welcomed by wealthy Saudi backers. Many of the Islamic Group's members were jailed following Sadat's assassination in 1981. Others fled to Afghanistan where they joined the jihad against the Soviets. Well trained in terrorist tactics by bin Laden and others, they later returned to Egypt to continue their struggle against the Mubarak regime.

The Islamic Group shared the Islamic Jihad's commitment to violence, but its targets differed. While the Islamic Jihad focused on the assassination of key political leaders, the Islamic Group focused on creating domestic turmoil. The 1990s saw the Islamic Group launch a vicious terrorist campaign against foreign tourists, which culminated in the 1997 slaughter of sixty-two tourists in Luxor. U.S. businessmen were also warned to leave Egypt or face the consequences. This was not a minor concern, for more than 10,000 Americans lived in Egypt at the time, us among them. Indeed, Egypt was rapidly becoming an American colony. The government and business community remained, but the tourists, a mainstay of the Egyptian economy, did not. Hotel occupancy collapsed. Banks, theaters, nightclubs, bookstores, and other businesses were also attacked, which compelled the minister of interior to proclaim that Egypt was at war with the jihadists.[11]

Along with its attacks on foreign tourists, the Islamic Group began to inflame tensions between Muslims and Egypt's Coptic community. The Copts, a Christian community that dates to the earliest days of Christianity, constitutes some 10 percent of the Egyptian population and had always lived in relative harmony among Egypt's Muslim majority. Tensions, however, existed and flare-ups had become frequent as the two communities began to encroach on each other's territory. Copts would say the encroachment was one sided. A particularly violent riot erupted when a family in the upper floor of a jointly occupied apartment building hung out their wash to dry on the edge of the balcony. Water dripped on the drying laundry of the family below. We don't remember whether it was Christian water that dripped on the Muslim laundry or vice versa, but the result was a full-scale religious riot. The Islamic Group entered the fray by attacking Christian shopkeepers and calling for the forced application of Sharia law on the Copts. President Mubarak denounced the growing religious violence, but the damage was done.

It was at this point, however, that the tide shifted against the Islamic Group. The attack on Luxor proved to be profoundly unpopular among an Egyptian workforce heavily dependent on tourism. The Islamic Group also suffered heavy losses from government attacks and many of its key members were either jailed or forced into exile. The Islamic Group began to rethink its strategy of violence and key members of the jailed wing of the party called for a truce with the Egyptian government. As might be expected, the truce initiative split the Islamic Group into pro- and anti-truce factions. The truce was initially supported by Sheikh Abdel al-Rahman, who was incarcerated in a U.S. prison for orchestrating the 1993 bombing of the World Trade Center, but he later changed his mind. The truce is holding in Egypt, but the Islamic Group remains active throughout the world. In 1998, the radical wing of the Islamic Group developed close ties with bin Laden's World Islamic Front for Jihad Against the Jews and Crusaders, but was not necessarily under bin Laden's control.

Most published reports find the Islamic Group in disarray and of little threat to either the Egyptian government or the United States. Strangely, the Egyptian government has accepted the truce, hardly the tactic of a government on the brink of victory. There can be little doubt that the Islamic Group possesses the capacity to exploit the Afghan Arabs and forge alliances with other jihadist groups. Much like the Islamic Jihad, it remains a key player in the jihadist war against America.

THE ISLAMIC REVOLUTION

Paralleling the rise of the jihadist movement in Egypt was the evolution of Shi'a jihadism in Iran. Much as in Egypt, religious emotions in Iran had been inflamed by a lethal blend of Westernization, poverty, corruption, oppression, and bizarre leadership. As we have seen in the earlier discussion of Hizbullah, the Ayatollah Khomeini welded this reservoir of mass frustration into an Islamic Revolution that swept the Shah of Iran from his throne. Khomeini, to be sure, was not the only source of opposition to the Shah in Iran. Leftists and nationalists of all varieties, many armed, swelled the ranks of the revolution. Most doubted the capacity of the clerics to rule, believing that it would be they who claimed power. It was Khomeini, however, who captured the imagination of the masses, and it was he who would rule Iran. Secular revolutionaries fortunate enough to escape death or imprisonment fled to the West.

Perhaps the United States could have overlooked the loss of its stellar ally in the Cold War had Khomeini proven humble and compliant. The Shah, after all, had become a bizarre individual whose erratic policies raised eyebrows in Washington.[12] The United States, moreover, had always found Muslim clerics useful allies in its struggle against the godless Soviets. Khomeini, for all of his faults, was an avowed anticommunist. Perhaps there was hope.

Khomeini, however, was not the humble sort. His hatred of the Americans eclipsed his hatred of the Soviets. The United States, Khomeini proclaimed, was a great Satan who controlled the Islamic world by keeping Israel and the likes of the Shah and Saddam Hussein in power. It was not bin Laden who focused jihadist attentions on America, but the Ayatollah Khomeini.

No sooner had he seized power in Iran, than Khomeini proclaimed a grand Islamic Revolution, a jihad to end all jihads—that would drive America and everything American from the Middle East. Israel was to go, as were the secular leaders of the region, most of whom were beholden to the United States.

Khomeini's contribution to the jihadist movement was threefold. First, as mentioned earlier, he created a network of Shi'a jihadist organizations headed by Hizbullah Lebanon. It was these organizations that led the charge in his Islamic Revolution. They may or may not have mellowed, but their origins were in the most violent of jihadist traditions. Second, Khomeini's victory in Iran demonstrated that Islamic groups could smite the most powerful of leaders and humiliate the most powerful of nations. All that was required was faith. The psychological impact of this message on the jihadist movement was incalculable. Everything became possible. Third, Khomeini made sure that it did. Arms and money poured into hands of the Sunni jihadists, many of whom were invited to Iran for training in revolutionary tactics. The jihadist movement now had a national home free from attack by foreign security forces.

For all of Khomeini's impact on the jihadist movement, it would be a mistake to believe that the marriage between Khomeini's Islamic Revolution and the Sunni jihadists was a smooth one. Iranian support was welcomed by the Sunni jihadists, but not the Shi'a doctrine of hidden imams and ayatollahs. Both, in the view of the Sunni jihadists, were embellishments invented by the Shi'a long after the passing of the Prophet Mohammed. Neither had a place in the Sunni vision of an Islamic state. Indeed, many Sunni jihadists considered the Shi'a to be heretics and feared that they were intent on exporting their apostasy to the Sunni world. Their distrust was requited by the Shi'a, long the victims of Sunni oppression. Pakistan would witness open battles between rival Sunni and Shi'a groups, hardly a propitious sign for the future. Cooperation between Iran and Sunni jihadists existed, but not unity.

It is difficult to gauge how far Khomeini's Islamic Revolution would have gone if Saddam Hussein, the leader of Iraq, had not chosen to invade Iran. Iran continues to be a key support base of the jihadist movement. It will certainly have a major role in determining Shi'a attitudes toward the American-led occupation of Iraq.

PAKISTAN: THE JIHADIST GATEWAY TO THE FAR EAST AND CENTRAL ASIA

Yet a third jihadist tradition emerged in the Indian subcontinent, a region that constitutes the countries of India, Pakistan, and Bangladesh. If Egypt nourished the Arab jihadists and Iran their Shi'a counterparts, it was Pakistan that nourished jihadism in India, Afghanistan, Central Asia, and the Far East. The key element in this process was Pakistan's vast network of religious schools. Other culprits included the governments of Pakistan and the United States.

But let us begin at the beginning. India won its independence from Britain in 1947, but rejoicing soon turned to fear as a violent civil war between Hindus and Muslims swept the subcontinent. With reconciliation beyond hope, the predominantly Muslim areas of the subcontinent were hastily patched together into the country of Pakistan. The split was messy, the new nation being little more than a collection of hostile ethnic groups.

Islam, it was hoped, would provide the glue that held the country together. Pakistan was to be an Islamic state; the Koran its constitution. But it was not to be. The more populous eastern provinces seceded from the union in 1971, forming the new country of Bangladesh. What remained of Pakistan was fragmented by splits between Pakistan's Sunni majority (70 percent) and its Shi'a minority (27 percent). Both, in turn, were divided among themselves. The Sunni, by and large, adhered to one of three schools of Islamic interpretation: the Barelvi, Deobandi, and the Ahli Hadith. The Barelvi is both the largest and most tolerant of the three schools, often blending local customs with Islamic practice. The Deobandi, by contrast, advocates the strict application of Islamic law including the establishment of an Islamic state in Pakistan. The Deobandi doctrine was also the doctrine of the Taliban in Afghanistan, the leaders of which were trained in Deobandi schools in Pakistan. The Ahli Hadith, if anything, is more extreme in its interpretation of Islam than the Deobandi and has largely been funded by Saudi Arabia.[13] For all intents and purposes, it has embraced the Wahhabi doctrine of Saudi Arabia.

Each of the three main Sunni doctrines has its own schools and mosques and has generated its own political parties. The parties, it turns out, have spawned radical spin-offs, many of which have been active in jihadist violence.[14] Jane's IntelWeb *Terrorist and Insurgency Groups* lists no less than six Pakistani groups linked to jihadist violence.[15] Jihadist violence has been most closely associated with the Deobandi and Ahli Hadith groups, both of which have seen their influence expand since the mid-1970s. The Deobandi has been favored by the Pakistani government, the Ahli Hadith by Saudi Arabia.

Adding to the religious fervor in Pakistan has been the Tabligi Jamaat, a large Islamic missionary and benevolent society that often attracts a million or more pilgrims to its annual meeting in Rawindi, Bangladesh.[16] It also possesses branches throughout the world, including the United States, Russia, France, and most countries of Central Asia. The Tabligi Jamaat is not a terrorist organization, but the zealousness of its religious teachings have led to accusations that the organization lends itself to jihadism. The Harakat ul-Mujahideen, one of Pakistan's largest jihadist groups, recruits largely from among members of the Tabligi Jamaat.[17]

While space does not allow a full discussion of Pakistani history, suffice it to say that all of the requirements for a jihadist uprising were in place by 1970: a deeply ingrained tradition of religious teaching, incompetent and corrupt secular governments, the dazzling wealth of the few pitted against the grinding poverty of the many, and a political geography characterized by remote areas largely beyond the control of the central government.

In the early 1970s, an embattled Bhutto government wavered from the secular tradition established by earlier Pakistani rulers and curried favor among the country's Islamic groups. This process became a rush in 1977 as General Zia ul-Haq seized power in a military coup and attempted to legitimize his rule by posing as the champion of Islam. While the influence of secular parties faded, the Islamic groups were given broad rein to expand their operations. The extremist Deobandi were favored and grew from a small minority to some 15 percent of the Pakistani population. The Ahli Hadith also prospered, the ul-Haq government being anxious to please his rich Saudi Arabia backers. The schools of both grew dramatically.[18] The jihadist movement grew apace, as Deobandi-Ahli Hadith violence targeted both the Shi'a and the more lax Sunni Barelvi.

Perhaps to ease the sectarian violence precipitated by the jihadists, the ul-Haq regime focused their energies on Kashmir, a predominantly Muslim region on the Pakistani border that had been awarded to India in the frantic efforts to bring the 1947 civil war in India to a close. Pakistan had fought and lost two wars with India over Kashmir and had blamed India for the 1971 secession of Bangladesh. A third war between India and Pakistan erupted in 1972, but lasted only two weeks. The jihadists represented a new front in Pakistan's continuing war with India. While Indian casualties mounted, the Pakistani government feigned innocence. The jihadist struggle for Kashmir continues unabated, symbolic crackdowns by the Pakistani authorities not withstanding. A fourth Indo-Pakistan war could well raise the specter of a nuclear holocaust.

The Pakistani jihadists received a further boost in the early 1980s when they were enlisted in America's jihad against the Soviets in Afghanistan. In retrospect, this was a mistake. The Pakistani jihadists emerged from Afghanistan well trained, well armed, and well connected with other jihadist groups in the region.

Two Pakistani groups, in particular, have been noted for their militancy: the Harakat ul-Mujahedeen (HuM) and the Lashkar-e-Toiba (LT). The HuM is linked to radical elements in the Deobandi school long favored by the Pakistani government and is a mainstay of jihadist violence in Kashmir and India. The LT finds its roots in the Saudi-sponsored Ahli Hadith school of thought and was recently implicated in the downing of an Indian airliner and the bombing of the Indian Parliament. Neither has been in the forefront of anti-American violence, but both have been linked to bin Laden and are mainstays on the U.S. List of Designated Foreign Terrorist Organizations.

As elsewhere, jihadist groups in Pakistan splinter and change their names with great frequency. The HuM, by way of example, first emerged as a splinter group of the Harkat ul-Jihad-i-Islami, a jihadist group created in 1980 to fight the Soviets in Afghanistan. The two groups later merged and formed the Harkat ul-Anasr, which later came full circle and was renamed the Harkat ul-Mujahideen. Along the way it was suspected of establishing al-Faran, a front organization, and the Jaish-e-Mohammed (the Army of Mohammed) and other terrorist groups. The Army of Mohammed duly changed its name to Khudam-u-Islam, proclaiming that its new mission was limited to preaching and welfare. The Lashkar-e-Tayyiba, for its part, was outlawed and subsequently changed its name to Jamaat-ud-Dawa. It, too, now claims that its activities are limited to preaching and welfare. The permutations continue.

In part, this endless sequence of fragmentation and regrouping is the result of personality conflicts and ideological debates within the jihadist movement. It is also a strategic ploy designed to keep the United States at bay. Once a group appears on a U.S. anti-terrorist list, it is closed down by the Pakistani government and reconstitutes itself under a different name. The transformation of the HuM to the Harkat-ul-Ansar, for example, occurred in 1993 and was brought about by U.S. anger over the HuM's refusal to return the American weapons that it had acquired during the war against the Soviets. The United States is mollified and life goes on, as does the war in Kashmir and elsewhere.

Pakistani jihadists have also played a key role in the spread of jihadism to East Asia. As B. Raman, the former head of the counterterrorism division of India's External Intelligence Agency writes:

> Evidence available to date indicates that while the terrorists from Malaysia and possibly Singapore were trained in the headquarters of the Jaish-e-Mohammad (JEM) in the Binori madrasa complex in Karachi, those from

Indonesia were trained in the Muridke complex of the LET, near Lahore. The HUM traditionally trained recruits from the southern Philippines and Myanmar, in addition to those from Xinjiang, Chechnya and the Central Asian Republics. The HUJI trains those from Bangladesh. Before October 7, 2001, the training camps of the HUM and the HUJI were located in eastern Afghanistan. [19]

India, as might be expected, keeps close tabs on Pakistani jihadists. Not only are the jihadists spearheading the violence in Kashmir, but their bombing of the Indian Parliament brought the war to the very heart of India. Other attacks seem to be inevitable. Muslims constitute approximately 11 percent of India's one billion citizens and most are hostile toward an Indian government that they accuse of gross prejudice against its Muslim citizens.[20] Religious flare-ups between Hindus and Muslims are common, but none more so than during the mid-1970s when Indian efforts to control their exploding population focused indiscriminately on the castration of poor Muslims. The program was soon scrapped but symbolizes the abiding tension between the two religious groups. Few Indian Muslims are jihadists, but the long history of conflict between Hindus and Muslims does help explain why some Indian Muslims are sympathetic to the jihadist cause.

The situation in Bangladesh has been largely ignored by a world media constrained by sound bites, but largely parallels that of Pakistan. The Jamaat, an Islamic party, is well represented in the Bangladeshi parliament and its youth organization is active in global organizations such as the International Islamic Federation of Student Organizations and the World Assembly of Muslim Youth. These are not jihadist organizations, but they do provide a venue for communications and recruitment among Muslim students. Litner notes that the Jammat student group dominates the approximately 10,000 Deobandi schools in Bangladesh and maintains close ties with radical groups in Pakistan, Malaysia, Indonesia, and the Middle East.[21] Faziui Rahman, the leader of the jihadist movement in Bangladesh, a coalition of Bangladeshi jihadist groups, signed bin Laden's 1998 declaration of war against America. The government of Bangladesh denounces terror but has been less than stringent in controlling a jihadist movement that enjoys a broad base of popular support.

AFGHANISTAN AND THE MAKING
OF A MUSLIM HERO

The role of the jihadists became even more vital with the 1979 Soviet invasion of Afghanistan, Pakistan's neighbor to north. The Soviets were closely aligned with India, and the presence of a Soviet puppet regime in Kabul raised the very real prospect that India would be in a position to control some two-thirds of Pakistani borders, a terrifying prospect for the Pakistanis.

Iran's Islamic Revolution was also of concern to Pakistani leaders, for Khomeini's inflammatory rhetoric was not lost on Pakistan's Shi'a population. The Pakistanis did not want the Soviets in Afghanistan, nor did they want a Shi'a revolution on their borders. Afghanistan was a predominantly Sunni country and Pakistan wanted to make sure that it stayed that way.

The United States shared Pakistan's concern on both counts. Khomeini's Islamic Revolution threatened to sweep the United States and its allies from the region, not the least of whom was the Saudi royal family and its control of one-fourth of the world's proven oil reserves. Soviet control of Afghanistan would have much the same result, placing it within easy striking power of the Persian Gulf. Neither the Islamic Revolution nor the Soviet invasion of Afghanistan could go unchallenged.

An obvious step toward solving both problems would be a U.S.-sponsored jihad against the Soviets in Afghanistan. A Vietnam-style war would be inflicted on the Soviets, Pakistan would be bolstered in its struggle with India, and the jihadists would be preoccupied in Afghanistan. Better to support indigenous freedom fighters, U.S. officials reasoned, than risk the deployment of American troops in hostile territory.

It may have dawned on the United States that its jihad in Afghanistan was promoting the Islamic Revolution, but no one seemed overly concerned. The Soviet Union was a proven enemy, and no one really expected the mullahs to stay the course in Iran. It now appears that the American-sponsored jihad in Afghanistan was the first step in transforming the jihadist movements of Egypt, Iran, and Pakistan into an international network capable of challenging the United States. A coalescing of the jihadist movement would have occurred with or without Afghanistan, but the Afghan experience accelerated this process by years if not decades.

That, however, was not clear at the time, and it seemed natural for the United States to funnel supplies to the jihadists in Afghanistan via Pakistan. The Afghan operation was placed in the hands of the ISI, the Pakistani intelligence service.[22] The CIA footed the bill and helped with weapons and recruitment but was excluded from the management of the Muslim volunteers who had begun to trickle into Pakistan at the onset of the 1980s. India and Kashmir were of greater concern to the Pakistanis than Afghanistan, but Afghanistan was the ticket to U.S. military aid. It was the ISI who decided who went where and with what arms. The United States may be technically correct when it claims that it did not train bin Laden's al Qaeda fighters. It might have been better if it had.

Why did Afghanistan, a desolate and impenetrable country bypassed by the course of history become the crucible of the world's jihadist movement? The answer is quite simple. The Americans, Pakistanis, Saudis, Iranians, jihadists, and other interested parties could not challenge the Soviet occupation of Afghanistan without creating an elaborate infrastructure of manpower, training, intelligence, supplies, money, communications, and everything else needed to fight a sustained war against a superpower.

Because the war against the Soviets was to be a religious war, that infrastructure had to be profoundly religious in nature. Pakistan became the main point of entry for waves of holy warriors who streamed into Afghanistan from all parts of the Islamic world. Many came from the Arab countries, giving rise to the term "Afghan Arabs" whether they were Arabs or not. The term stuck, and foreign fighters linked to Afghanistan continue to be referred to as Afghan Arabs. Pakistan would give refuge to some two million Afghan refugees and host some seven jihadist groups. The Afghan Arabs were God's soldiers who feared neither death nor hardship. Indeed, they seemed to court death. Men of religion also became key links in the communication and distribution process; mosques became convenient rendezvous points. This is not to denigrate the role of the Afghans in liberating their own country from Soviet rule. It was they who did most of the fighting. It was the Afghan Arabs, however, who transformed the Afghan rebellion into a true jihad.

The rush of men and materiel into Afghanistan created an urgent need for a central base to process recruits and coordinate incoming Islamic aid. The task of establishing this base fell to Dr. Abdullah Azzam, a leading figure in the Jordanian branch of the Muslim Brotherhood and subsequently a professor at the International Islamic University in Islamabad, Pakistan. His second in command was Osama bin Laden, then a young man in his twenties.[23] The choice was logical, for bin Laden had been trained in economics and engineering and possessed a strong practical background in business and construction engineering. Adding to his credentials were his contacts with the Saudi royal family and wealthy Saudi contributors. By and large, he was the Saudi's man in Afghanistan. The processing base bin Laden helped create was simply referred to as "the base" by the Afghan Arabs. "The base" in Arabic is al Qaeda. Much to the chagrin of both the Americans and the Saudis, bin Laden's al Qaeda in Afghanistan would become the embryo for his al Qaeda terrorist network.

The jihadists emerged from the war in Afghanistan with an exhilarating sense of victory and an unshakable faith in their ability to reclaim the Islamic world in the name of Allah. They also emerged from Afghanistan with a cadre of well-trained fighters who numbered in the thousands, if not the tens of thousands. It is premature to speak of an international jihadist network at this point, but fundamental steps had been taken in that direction. Groups from the three major jihadist centers—Egypt, Pakistan, and Iran—had been brought in contact with each other. They had also been brought in contact with bin Laden and his access to rich financier "angels" in Saudi Arabia and the Gulf. The jihadists, moreover, had acquired a new sense of legitimacy. Bin Laden's pictures hung from mosques throughout Saudi Arabia and the Gulf. He was the new Saladin, slaying the invading crusaders. The Soviets had been the enemy of the moment, but jihadists saw little difference between the Soviets and the Americans. Both were godless and both were guilty of usurping Muslim lands. The Soviets oppressed Muslims in Afghanistan and Central Asia; the Americans defiled Islam through their support of Israel and their godless regimes of the region.

Afghanistan gave birth to the Afghan Arabs, that free-floating pool of jihadist fanatics vowing to die in the name of God. Some of the Afghan Arabs returned to their countries of origin where they either strengthened existing jihadist organizations or created their own.[24] Others awaited God's call from the more comfortable environs of the Europe, North America, or promising locations in the Third World. The very breadth of their dispersion assured a future foundation for international action. Those Afghan Arabs with a price on their heads bided their time in Afghanistan.

Bin Laden, for his part, made a triumphant return to Saudi Arabia in 1989 and was lavishly feted by a Saudi royal family anxious to bask in the glow of its illustrious Islamic hero. Not only had the royal family been at the forefront of the Afghan jihad, but it was a Saudi, albeit of Yemeni origin, who had led the charge. This was powerful stuff for a Saudi regime reeling from Khomeini's charges that it was a group of debauched hypocrites who had sold out to the Americans. According to Bodansky, "The praise and media attention made bin Laden a sought-after celebrity. He spoke at countless mosques and private gatherings. Some of his fiery speeches were recorded; well over a quarter of a million official cassettes were sold and countless illegal—and later, underground—copies were also made and distributed."[25]

Bin Laden's speeches avoided criticism of the monarchy, but it was not too difficult to read between the lines. The royal family wanted to bask in bin Laden's glory. It did not want a potential competitor. In traditional Saudi style, the royal family attempted to buy him off with lavish construction contracts, but he refused. Tensions reached the breaking point with Iraq's invasion of Kuwait in 1990. The Saudis feared that they would be next and turned instinctively to the United States for protection. Bin Laden, by contrast, urged the monarch to rely on God.

The jihadists had driven the Soviets from Afghanistan. They could surely protect Saudi Arabia from Sadaam Hussein. As described by a senior U.S. intelligence officer,

> Bin Laden "presented a ten-page paper to Prince Sultan," the Associated Press reported "describing how he and his colleagues could train Saudis to defend themselves and how equipment from his family's large construction firm could be used to dig trenches on the border with Iraq and lay sand traps against potential invaders." Bin Laden told Prince Sultan he could "bring all his supporters and defend the country under his command. And he made all the [guarantees] that his supporters would not give you [the Saudi authorities] a hard time. They would defend the country against the invading Iraqi army. And he said 'You don't need Americans. You don't need any other non-Muslim troops. We will be enough. And I will even convince the Afghanis to come and join us instead of the Americans.'"[26]

The royal family was not persuaded and remained firm in its decision to rely on the United States, the price of which was the stationing of American forces in Saudi Arabia, the heartland of Islam. Bin Laden departed for the Sudan with the blessing of the royal family. He was essentially a businessman, and the Sudan offered dazzling opportunities for those not adverse to risk. He was also a jihadist.

THE SUDAN: AN INTERNATIONAL
TERRORIST NETWORK TAKES SHAPE

Afghanistan had provided the basic building blocks for an international jihadist network. Even with the experience of Afghanistan, however, the jihadist movement remained a series of volcanic eruptions, powerful but uncoordinated. If the jihadist movement were to achieve its goal of establishing Islamic governments in the Muslim world, it would have to transcend the stage of random and uncoordinated violence that had characterized the movement's early decades. Goals had to be agreed on, targets set, strategies developed, command structures established, forces marshaled, weapons procured, recruits processed, finances arranged, intelligence networks established, and safe communications secured. In short, the war machine that the United States had helped the jihadists organize in Afghanistan had to be replicated on a global scale.

Particularly pressing was the need to coordinate the three basic components of the jihadist movement: the Egyptians, the Iranians, and the Pakistanis. This meant bridging the gap between the Shi'a and the Sunni, a task equivalent to squaring the circle. The Egyptians and Pakistanis were also divided by a vast chasm of culture, language, and tradition. The former were overwhelmingly concerned with the Arab world, the latter the Indian subcontinent. Aside from Afghanistan, contact between the diverse branches of the jihadist movement had been minimal.

The hero of the Sudan was not bin Laden, but a Muslim cleric named Hassan Abdallah al-Turabi. Turabi, a brilliant intellectual, received a master's degree in law from the University of London (1957) and a doctorate of law from the Sorbonne (1964). He did not fear the West nor was he awed by it. Rather, Turabi had a sound understanding of both the strengths and weaknesses of Western modernity. He applauded the West's capacity to promote human welfare through science and law but was appalled by its hedonism and moral depravity. Like many true Islamic intellectuals before him, Turabi sought ways of placing the technological advances of the West at the service of Islam. His goal was to bring order and development to the Muslim world without sacrificing the religious values of Islam.

For the moment, however, there were more practical matters. American hostility toward Iran and its Islamic Revolution had demonstrated that neither the United States nor its allies would tolerate an expansion of Islamic rule. It was not enough to attack Western puppets in the Islamic world, Turabi argued. The United States would not relinquish its grip on the Muslim world until it had tasted the sting of battle. This required the creation of an international jihadist network capable of fusing the energies of the Egyptian, Pakistani, and Iranian jihadists. It also required links to the Muslim Brotherhood and other more moderate elements in the Islamic movement. All would have to be mobilized in the service of Islam.

Once the network was complete, Turabi's argument continued, it would attack its adversaries with a three-pronged strategy. First, secular leaders in the Islamic world, most of whom were beholden to the West, would be destabilized and, if possible, overthrown. Second, Islamic lands occupied by the West would be liberated by force. This was a direct reference to Israel, a country the jihadists viewed as a Western outpost in the heart of Islam. Third, jihadist networks would be established throughout the world, particularly in North America and Western Europe. This fifth column would enable the jihadist movement to attack the enemy from within. The West would not be safe until Islam was safe.

Turabi's strategy drew heavily on the experience of the Ayatollah Khomeini's Islamic Revolution, especially its use of Hizbullah groups to drive the United States from Lebanon. The soldiers of Islam had struck and America had recoiled. Turabi had also studied the successes of other terrorist movements, the IRA in particular. When London subways were bombed, the British began to think seriously about withdrawing from Northern Ireland. If the United States were bombed, the Americans would begin to think seriously about withdrawing from the Middle East. All that was missing was the capacity to bring the full resources of the jihadist movement to bear in a coherent and rational manner. This had not been done. It would be Turabi's contribution to the jihadist movement.

The opportunity for decisive action came in June 1989, when General Omar al-Bashir, a devout Muslim and follower of Turabi, seized power in the Sudan. Bashir became president of the country and Turabi was given free reign to transform the Sudan into an Islamic state. Islamic law became the order of the day as the Sudan proclaimed itself the world's second Islamic theocracy. Turabi's main focus, however, was not the Sudan. The Sudan was merely his venue for establishing a global Islamic network capable of challenging the West.

What Turabi Brought to the Jihadist Movement

Turabi possessed a number of attributes that were essential to the development of an international jihadist network. Turabi's writings had established him as the preeminent Sunni theologian of his era, a dazzling intellect who possessed the moral authority to ride herd over a much fragmented jihadist leadership. There could be no network without a head, and it was Turabi, more than any other single individual, who spoke for a deeply divided Islamic movement that included the Muslim Brotherhood as well as the jihadists. All, according to Turabi, would play a vital role in achieving their common goal of an Islamic state. The jihadists would attack the enemies of Islam with violence; the moderates by internal subversion. In much the same manner, Turabi's philosophy opened the door for rapprochement with Shi'a Islam, at least at the operational level. The Iranians could deal with Turabi far more effectively than they could cooperate with Sunni jihadists who viewed the Shi'a as heretics.

Also of key importance to the networking process was the breadth of Turabi's contacts, including a multitude of wealthy benevolent associations. As he later boasted, "I know every Islamic Movement in the world, secret or public."[27] He further boasted, "I also meet Heads of State of Arab countries, Muslim countries and many non-Muslim countries."[28] Two of Turabi's strongest supporters among the Arab heads of state were Muammar Qadaffi and Saddam Hussein. Finally, Turabi provided the jihadist movement with a secure base of operations. Much like Afghanistan, the Sudan was a quagmire of conflict and intrigue, a destitute and bankrupt country torn by civil war and the machinations of its neighbors. If Afghanistan had been impenetrable, the Sudan was just the opposite, sharing common and largely unpatrolled borders with no less than nine different countries. What better environment for the establishment of a jihadist network?

Bin Laden and Iran: The Twin Pillars of Turabi's Network

Turabi possessed the stature, the vision, and the contacts required to guide an international jihadist network. Forging such a network, however, needed more than words. There had to be base camps and training facilities, financiers, weapons experts, document forgers, communications experts, organizers, and intelligence operatives, not to mention a hard core of dedicated soldiers. This was the work of technicians. Turabi was a theologian, a philosopher, and a politician, but he was not a technician. Nor was the destitute country that he controlled in the name of Islam capable of sustaining an international jihadist network. It could provide shelter for the network, but little more.

Fortunately, from Turabi's perspective, he did not have to start from scratch. Many of the technical skills required for an international jihadist network had already been developed, at least in embryonic form, by the Ayatollah Khomeini. Others were provided by the jihadist network developed in Afghanistan. Turabi's task was to bring the existing pieces together in a fertile environment for growth.

The first of these pieces was Osama bin Laden, the hero of Afghanistan. Bin Laden's skills were well known to Turabi and, having exiled himself to the Sudan, he became part of Turabi's inner circle. The relationship between Turabi and bin Laden was straightforward. Turabi was a religious luminary: a model to be followed and emulated. Bin Laden was a jihadist, a businessman and a war hero, but he was not a theologian. Turabi concentrated on the network's grand design; bin Laden made it work. This is not to denigrate bin Laden's role. Bin Laden brought to the network his ties to the Afghan Arabs, many of whom looked to him as a leader. Bin Laden also provided access to rich Saudi and Gulf angels and designed an apparently foolproof financial network, which, by all accounts, continues to befuddle American sleuths. His companies built many of the training camps for the Turabi network, and his foreign offices became links between the network and Islamic groups in Europe and elsewhere. In the process, bin Laden laid the foundation for what he eventually transformed into his al Qaeda network.

Turabi's relationship with Iran was far more complex. Both were dedicated to forging an international jihadist network capable of resisting America and its Western allies. Each, moreover, needed the other. The Iranians needed entry into the Sunni world. Turabi needed the financing and technical expertise that the Iranians could provide, not to mention the resources of their Hizbullah networks in Lebanon and the Gulf. Indeed, visits to Tehran had convinced Turabi that the Iranians were light years ahead of the Sunni jihadists in terms of their revolutionary capacity. Lurking in the shadows, however, was the ever-present tension between the Sunni and Shi'a versions of Islam.

Turabi was willing to work things out with the Shi'a, but this was less the case with the other Sunni jihadists who continued to view the Iranians as dangerous heretics bent on extending their heresies to the remainder of the Islamic world. Also lurking in the shadows was the question of who was using who. Turabi was the head of the jihadist network. It could not be otherwise. Sunni jihadists would not take orders from a Shi'a. There can also be little doubt that Turabi saw himself as the future caliph of the revived Islamic *Umma* or nation. He was not, as his speeches amply demonstrated, a man of small ego. It was the Iranians, however, who footed much of the bill and provided much of the technical infrastructure. Indeed, between 1991 and 1993, Iran literally transformed the landscape of the Sudan by spending millions of dollars on construction projects, many of which were implemented by bin Laden's companies.[29] In the process, jobs were provided for the Afghan Arabs and more recent recruits. In the words of the adage, he who pays the piper calls the tune. The Iranians were not passive bystanders.

The Network Emerges

The international jihadist network that took shape between 1991 and 1993 revolved around a variety of conferences designed to find a common ground that could unite the diverse elements of the Islamic movement, particularly its jihadist wing. The conferences, in turn, led to the establishment of various umbrella organizations designed to facilitate and coordinate the activities of its members. In April 1991, for example, Turabi hosted an Islamic Arab People's Conference, the deliberations of which resulted in the formation of the Popular International Organization (PIO), an organization dedicated to revolutionizing the Sunni Islamic world. A permanent council that represented the fifty countries in which Islamic revolutionary activity took place was duly established in Khartoum, the capital of the Sudan.[30] A variety of jihadist organizations affiliated with the PIO, including groups from Pakistan, Kashmir, Afghanistan, Egypt, Algeria, and elsewhere. Later the same year, Turabi reportedly established a parallel body designed to coordinate relations between the jihadists and the Muslim Brotherhood.[31] Turabi was the spiritual guide of the PIO and its coordinator, but he lacked the power to impose his view on the various affiliate organizations.

By and large, Turabi's PIO was little more than a clearinghouse for channeling support and information to various jihadist groups. Links were strengthened between the Pakistanis and Arabs, and, to a lesser degree, between Iran and the Sunni jihadists. The Egyptians and the Algerians were the particular beneficiaries of this enhanced cooperation and received training in Pakistan and Iran as well as in the Sudan.

Turabi's PIO also possessed a hard-core contingent of Afghan Arabs who were unable to return to their home countries. Again, Turabi's control was less than absolute. Many of the Afghan Arabs looked to bin Laden for leadership. Others inclined toward Pakistan and the infamous ISI. The rift was not a minor one. Pakistan was intent on using the Afghan Arabs in Kashmir, while Turabi was intent on the destabilizing of sub-Saharan Africa, about half of which was predominantly Islamic in character. Islamic Africa, Turabi preached, was in chaos and well-organized Islamic groups could seize power with relative ease. It was, in his view, free for the taking.[32]

No sooner had Turabi's network taken shape than the Muslim world exploded in violence. Algeria dissolved into civil war in 1991 as jihadists threatened to seize control of one of the largest countries in the Arab world. Egypt was not far behind. The same period saw Hamas and the Islamic Jihad challenge the PLO for control of the Palestinian resistance. The Palestinian struggle for independence had long been noted for its violence, but the jihadists added a new weapon to the conflict: the suicide bomber. The same period witnessed the 1993 bombing of the World Trade Towers. The war had reached America.

THE BATTLE FOR ALGERIA

Turabi and his network did not create the jihadist upheavals in Algeria, Egypt, and the Occupied Territories, but they added to their intensity. The Algerian story is of particular interest as it illustrates how rapidly an ostensibly secular state could be subverted by a determined Islamic movement. It also illustrates the dangers inherent in efforts to play the more moderate Islamic groups against the jihadists.

The story began in 1931, some three years after the founding of the Muslim Brotherhood in Egypt, when an association of Algerian *ulema* was founded to fight the French colonization of Algeria. The movement was inspired by the Muslim Brotherhood and eventually opened a liaison office in Cairo to encourage young Algerian students studying in Egypt to adhere to the teachings of the Brotherhood. Most of these students were pursuing their studies at Cairo's renowned Al-Azhar University and it was they, in conjunction with students from other religious universities, who established Algeria's first Islamic party in 1947. The Algerian branch of the Muslim Brotherhood was established in 1953. Algeria's war for independence was to be launched the following year.[33]

The bulk of the fighting was carried out by the National Liberation Front (FLN), a secular leftist movement that advocated the rapid industrialization of Algeria under the twin banners of nationalism and socialism. Once in power, the FLN followed the Egyptian model. Government factories provided employment for urban workers, while government welfare programs attempted to create a socialist paradise. Food and rents were subsidized and education and health care were free to all. Both were failures. State factories and farms were unproductive; cradle to grave welfare schemes became a bureaucratic nightmare. Algeria was broke, and its debtors were unforgiving.

Also unforgiving was Algeria's increasingly restive population. The Muslim Brotherhood and other Islamic groups flourished. Some advocated moderation; others became jihadists. The groups involved were so many and so varied that they defy easy description. Some were small bands, others were full-fledged militias. They fought the government and they fought each other. The more the economic situation deteriorated, the stronger the jihadists became.

In desperation, the Algerian government jettisoned its socialist dreams and turned to capitalism. Privatization became the order of the day as the massive state-owned factories were scaled down and Algeria's social safety net began to fray. Efficiency increased, but so did unemployment and poverty. Students, once confident of a government job, faced the grim prospect of unemployment. According to government figures, 1990 found approximately half of the Algerian population pauperized.[34] Not reformed was a legacy of corruption that permeated all facets of government activity. Government "barons" pushed corruption to new heights as they skimmed 10 percent off sales of divested government properties and staked claim to prime real estate.[35] They were the prime beneficiaries of Algeria's gradual transition to capitalism.

There was, of course, the danger of an explosion. Mass frustrations mounted, but the regime seemed confident that it could keep them in check until capitalism had transformed Algeria into a model of prosperity. The one current of opposition that the regime could not bottle up was the radical Islamists with their clandestine networks that lurked in the shadows of Algeria's mosques.

Mass demonstrations rocked Algeria in 1988 and raised the specter of civil war. The government attempted to buy time by offering Algerians a limited democracy. They hoped that the emergence of moderate political parties would offer a safety valve for mass frustrations and turn the tide against the jihadists. The key element in this gamble was the legalization of the Islamic Salvation Front (FIS).[36] The FIS had emerged in 1989 as a umbrella organization designed to unify Algeria's diverse Islamic groups in what appeared to be their final battle against the Algerian government. The moderates within the FIS argued for participation in elections scheduled for the coming year; the jihadists refused, but found little support for violence as long as an electoral victory was in the offing.[37] Local elections were scheduled for June 12, 1990.

It seemed that the government's strategy of divide and rule had worked. The FIS had split into two factions: moderates versus the jihadists. The moderates, according to government strategy, were to be bought off with high government positions and the perks of office, while the army turned the full force of its power on the jihadists. It was not to be. Cooler heads prevailed and a senior FIS theologian worked out a compromise between the two sides. Elected members of the FIS were "empowered to give orders and be obeyed," but they were not bound by the orders of secular officials. Elected FIS deputies were also to oppose all policies that contradicted Islamic law or that threatened the establishment of an Islamic state.[38]

The FIS captured 55 percent of the vote in the 1990 municipal elections, although it is difficult to say whether the vote was an expression of support for the fundamentalists or a protest vote against a corrupt and oppressive government. Far more frightening was the prospect of an FIS victory in the parliamentary and presidential elections promised for the following year. If the FIS repeated its sweeping victory in the local elections, Algeria would become an Islamic state and the moribund regime of generals, politicians, and bureaucrats that had ruled Algeria since its independence would be swept from office. Presumably, they would be swept into jail.

What to do? The answer was obvious: rig the elections. A new electoral law "concocted by the Ministry of Interior" virtually assured a victory for the regime.[39] The FIS declared a general strike. Algeria's major cities were paralyzed as demonstrators jammed thoroughfares and protesters stormed government buildings.

The government responded by rekindling the split within the FIS. Jihadists were arrested, while the moderates were allowed to operate freely. The general strike was broken and the moderates, then dominant, led the FIS into the legislative elections. This proved to be an empty victory. The moderates controlled the shell of the FIS, but its military wings (there were two, each with different leadership) remained under the control of the jihadists.

The legislative elections scheduled for November 26, 1991, followed a two-stage format. The first stage resembled primary elections in the United States, with any candidate receiving an absolute majority of the votes being declared the winner. If no candidate received a majority, a second or run-off stage was to choose between the two leading candidates. The FIS scored a resounding victory in the first round of the elections. Its ultimate victory in the second round was never in doubt. Algeria's military leaders annulled the electoral process before a second round could be held. It was their only hope of keeping Algeria out of the ranks of the Islamists.

No sooner had the elections been nullified than the FIS went into its "crisis mode," its code word for going underground. A secret meeting of the FIS leadership, dominated by the jihadists, declared a jihad against the government for blocking the establishment of an Islamic state. Posters declaring the jihad appeared in all of the 12,000 registered (legal) mosques controlled by the FIS. Far more important were the thousands of "free mosques" created by the FIS without official approval. While the registered mosques exhorted the faithful to support the jihad, the free mosques became armed camps.[40] The war had begun. To date, it has claimed the lives of more than 100,000 Algerians.

The jihadists broke with the FIS in the fall of 1992, leaving it an empty shell. They also turned on each other. Indeed, the gutting of the FIS resulted in the emergence of four separate jihadist armies, not to mention a multitude of urban gangs loyal only to their leader. All were violent, but none more so than the urban gangs for whom violence became an end in itself.[41] The winner in the gruesome battle, at least for a time, was le Groupe islamique armé or the GIA. This was not surprising, for the groups that had merged to form the GIA had a long history of combat in Algeria. They also had the strongest ties to Turabi's network. The GIA's view of the world was simple: Algeria was to become an Islamic state ruled by the strict interpretation of Islamic law. Anyone who disagreed with this position would be killed.

The power of the GIA reached its zenith in 1995 and declined sharply thereafter. That date also marked the unraveling of Turabi's network. The problems of the GIA, however, were largely homegrown. Leading a jihadist group is risky business, and each disappearance of a GIA emir brought a new round of consultations as sub-emirs set about the tricky task of selecting a new supreme emir to whom they would swear absolute allegiance. For those who failed to make the cut, it was a bitter pill.

It was also a dangerous one, and defections were common. The selection process was itself flawed, with young firebrands buoyed by records of violence being elected over older and more experienced competitors. Each new emir viewed his competitors with a jaundiced eye and feared treachery at every turn. Absolute allegiance was not to be gained by compromise and negotiation. There was also the problem of the other jihadist militias. They, no less than the army and police, had become the enemy. Assaults by the military and police also took their toll on the GIA much as they took an awesome toll on Algeria's citizens.

The level of violence abated after 1998, but a day rarely goes by that is unmarked by carnage of one form or another. Sometimes the targets are rural hamlets obliterated in a hit and run strike. Other times they are police stations, government officials, journalists, or popular singers. In the meantime, the jihadist struggle in Algeria has been exported to a North African community in France that numbers in the millions. Few are terrorists, but the majority of Algerian and North African immigrants in France live in squalor and are blamed by the French authorities for France's epidemic of crime and drugs. Given these circumstances, it is not surprising that France has become fertile ground for the jihadists.

THE PALESTINIAN JIHADISTS:
HAMAS AND HOLY JIHAD

The jihadist movement in Palestine, like its Algerian counterpart, found its origins in Egypt and the Muslim Brotherhood. Both the Algerian and the Palestinian jihadists flourished with support from the Turabi network. The experience of the two movements, however, were radically different. The Algerian jihadists focus on transforming Algeria into an Islamic state. The Palestinian jihadists focus on liberating the Occupied Territories from Israeli rule. If one is to believe their rhetoric, they are also intent on liberating Israel, itself. The Algerians pursue their goals by slaughtering Muslims. The Palestinian jihadists slaughter Jews. The jihadist struggle in Algeria is largely a side-show ignored by the world community. The jihadist struggle in Palestine has dominated world politics for more than a decade. Indeed, Jerusalem has become the rallying cry for both al Qaeda and Hizbullah. The Algerian jihadists have peaked. The Palestinian jihadists grow stronger by the day. It is they who now dominate war against Israel and it is they who, in all likelihood, will determine the fate of the Palestinian struggle for independence. Rumors abound that Hamas, the largest of the Palestinian jihadist groups, is poised to replace the PLO as the standard bearer for the Palestinian resistance.

The Palestinian jihadists have avoided attacks on American and European targets. Their enemy, they proclaim, is Israel, not the United States. The liberation persona of the Palestinian jihadists lends an air of legitimacy to their operations. They are not terrorists, they claim, but freedom fighters. Washington scoffs at this claim, but it is accepted by the Islamic world. It also plays well in Europe.

The influence of the Palestinian jihadists on the evolution of broader jihadist strategy has been formidable. Heretofore, jihadist groups had avoided cooperation with secular revolutionary movements. What was to be gained, they argued, by helping the secularists seize power? Hamas and Holy Jihad, by contrast, demonstrated the relative ease with which well-organized jihadist groups could dominate independence movements by merging the twin passions of nationalism and Islam. It is now they who are the most dynamic force in the Palestinian resistance. The Palestinian jihadists have also demonstrated the benefits of adapting the strategies of Shi'a groups such as Hizbullah Lebanon. Indeed, the success of the Palestinian jihadists is largely attributable to techniques developed by Hizbullah. Foremost among these have been the widespread use of suicide attacks, including the used of suicide attacks against civilian populations.

Hamas

Hamas, the largest of the Palestinian jihadist groups, began as an off-shoot of the Palestinian wing of the Muslim Brotherhood. In the view of many, it is not a jihadist group at all, but merely a branch of the Muslim Brotherhood that has been forced into violence by the Israeli occupation of the West Bank and the Gaza Strip. Israel and the United States disagree. Whatever the case, the Brotherhood had been established in Jerusalem and other major Palestinian cities by 1946, some two years before the 1948 Arab Israeli War that culminated in the establishment of Israel. The Israelis won the war, but Jordanian and Iraqi forces occupied Jerusalem and the central regions of Palestine, an area generally referred to as the West Bank. Egypt would retain the Gaza Strip, a narrow coastal plain adjacent to Egypt's Sinai Peninsula.

The emir of Trans-Jordan annexed the West Bank in 1952 and renamed his small sheikhdom the Kingdom of Jordan. In the process, he annexed a large share of the Palestinian population. Some were the residents of the West Bank. Others were refugees. All became citizens of Jordan, and Jordan became a predominantly Palestinian country. The price of the annexation was the assassination of the Jordanian king, Abdullah I. He was followed in office by his grandson, Hussein, then a youth in his late teens. Attempted coup followed attempted coup, but the young king survived. He had three pillars of support: the British, loyal Jordanian tribes who feared a Palestinian takeover, and the Muslim Brotherhood. The king's alliance with the Brotherhood was a natural fit. Both were wedded to tradition and both feared the leftists.

The situation changed dramatically with the crushing Arab defeat in the Arab-Israeli war of 1967, the Six Day War. The West Bank and Gaza, the remaining parcels of geographic Palestine, were now under Israeli occupation. Palestinians feared that they would be driven from their remaining lands and forced into a stateless diaspora of refugee camps and endless migration. The Arab states supported the Palestinian cause, but they did not want more Palestinian refugees.

To make matters worse, the Palestinians could no longer rely on Egypt or other Arab countries to liberate their land. If Palestine were to be liberated, it would be liberated by Palestinians. But how was this to be achieved?

How were Palestinians to succeed where the Arab armies had failed? Answers to these questions are still being worked out. Suffice it to say that the Palestinians possessed two paths to their quest. The first was the Palestinian Liberation Organization, the PLO, a loose confederation of leftist groups under the leadership of Yasir Arafat. The second choice was the Muslim Brotherhood.

The aftermath of the Six Day War found Arafat and the PLO in the ascendancy. For much of the Arab world, the PLO was the government of the Palestinians. For Israel, the PLO was public enemy #1. Israel feared PLO terror. It also feared that the international community would forcibly establish a PLO-led government in the Occupied Territories. The latter fear was greater than the former. Few Israelis worried much about the Muslim Brotherhood and its imitators. On the contrary: The Israelis would encourage the growth of the Brotherhood as a counterweight to Arafat and the PLO.[42] In retrospect, this was a mistake.

The Palestinian Muslim Brotherhood also feared the ascendance of the very secular PLO. A secular PLO would stifle the Islamic movement in Palestine, much as Nasser had stifled the Muslim Brotherhood in Egypt. Palestine could not be both secular and Islamic. Particularly disconcerting for the Palestinian Brotherhood was the PLO's military capacity. The PLO had its own militias; the Brotherhood did not.

It was this reality that let to the emergence of Hamas as the military wing of the Palestinian Brotherhood.[43] The official date for the founding of Hamas is listed as 1987. In reality, the nucleus of Hamas was established much earlier and was simply called the military wing (*raa el askary*).[44] The original members of Hamas were all members of the Brotherhood, but with time, Hamas developed its own identity and its own membership. Membership in the Muslim Brotherhood was not a prerequisite. Zeal was.

The line between the two movements has always been vague. The 1988 Covenant of the Islamic Resistance Movement, the official name of Hamas, referred to the organization as "one of the wings" of the Muslim Brotherhood in Palestine.[45] Much like the Muslim Brotherhood from which it evolved, Hamas utilizes three distinct strategies to pursue its objectives: preaching (*dawa*), welfare, and politics. Teaching and preaching are the province of Hamas's mosques and schools, while its welfare services are coordinated by the Islamic Association, one of the nonmilitary branches of the organization. The Islamic Association maintains a wide variety of clinics, orphanages, and training centers, all of which are vital to the existence of a population characterized by extreme poverty. Hamas's welfare services also play an active role in caring for the families of martyrs. As we have seen in the case of Hizbullah, a suicide strategy requires that martyrs depart for heaven confident in the knowledge that their loved ones will be cared for. Families of martyrs, according to Israeli sources, receive an estimated $1,000 adjustment allowance, although the exact sum remains a matter of debate.[46] The Israelis claim that much of the money is provided by Saudi Arabia.[47] Politics, for the most part, means terrorist strikes against Israeli targets and the elimination of suspected collaborators. Politics also means preparing for eventual elections if and when a Palestinian state materializes. There can be little question that Hamas would do well in fair elections for a Palestinian government.

Each of Hamas's diverse branches operate in relative independence, a strategy that provides it with maximum flexibility. Hamas's military operations are carried out by covert groups such as the Izz al-Din al-Qassam battalions. The Islamic Association, its principle welfare agency, is officially recognized by the Israeli government. The Israeli government is now moving away from the distinction between welfare and terror and is targeting a variety of nonviolent groups linked to the Hamas organization.

Palestinian Islamic Jihad

Much like Hamas, the founders of the Palestinian Islamic Jihad joined the Muslim Brotherhood while studying in Egypt. Unlike, Hamas, their zeal soon exceeded the moderation of the Brotherhood and they formed the Palestinian Islamic Jihad. The philosophy of the Palestinian Islamic Jihad, much like the other Jihadist groups emerging in Egypt during the mid-1970s, was one of revolutionary violence. Indeed, the Palestinian Islamic Jihad become so close to the Egyptian jihadists that they were implicated in the 1981 assassination of President Sadat and deported to Gaza.[48] After a brief rapprochement with the Palestinian branch of the Muslim Brotherhood, they again branched out on their own, and preached a violent blend of jihadism and Palestinian nationalism. The emphasis was on the latter, for there could be no Islamic state in Palestine until the Israelis had been defeated. That, in the view of the Islamic Jihad, could only be achieved by force. This philosophy is shared by a variety of smaller groups that also operate under the Holy Jihad name. These include the Islamic Jihad-the-Temple and the Islamic Jihad Squad, among others.

The leaders of the Islamic Jihad were profoundly influenced by the 1979 victory of the Ayatollah Khomeini in Iran and viewed it as a sign from

God that overwhelming military force could be overcome by faith and sacrifice.[49] The leader of the Islamic Jihad fled to Beirut toward the end of the 1980s, and ties between Islamic Jihad and Hizbullah increased apace. So did ties to Iran. Hizbullah's influence on both the Islamic Jihad and Hamas can be seen in the unrelenting wave of suicide bombing that began in earnest in the mid-1990s. Suicide attacks were not unknown among Sunni Jihadists, but they had been perfected by Hizbullah and its Iranian sponsors.[50]

Relations between Hamas, Holy Jihad, and the PLO

Hamas and the Holy Jihad cooperate, but not without disagreements over strategy and leadership.[51] The early months of 2004 saw increased rumors of unity discussions between the two groups. Dr. Abdul Sitar, a political scientist at Najah University on the West Bank, suggested that such speculations were premature. He acknowledged growing cooperation in field operations between the two groups, but suggested that they remain far removed from ideological unity. Jihad remained wedded to the violent imposition of an Islamic government in Palestine, while Hamas remained rooted in the more flexible ideology of the Muslim Brotherhood. The growing cooperation between the two organizations is motivated more by Israeli counterterrorist tactics than by a common program and likely will abate if and when the Israeli-Palestinian conflict is resolved.

Jihad and Hamas share a common suspicion of the PLO and the Palestinian Authority that it controls. As the covenant of Hamas states with clarity: "The day the Palestinian Liberation Organization adopts Islam as its way of life, we will become its soldiers, and fuel for its fire that will burn the enemies."[52] Be that as it may, joint attacks between Hamas, Islamic Jihad, and the al-Aksa Martyrs Brigades, an off-shoot of the PLO, are becoming increasingly frequent. Although there are continuing attempts to forge a common strategy between the PLO and the jihadists, to date it has been largely unsuccessful. The PLO wants to call off the suicide attacks in the hope that the Israelis will allow the creation of a Palestinian state on some but not all of the Occupied Territories. The jihadists ask why. The suicide attacks, they note, have been the only things that have worked. They also accuse the PLO of selling out to the Israelis in an effort to keep its control of the Palestinian Authority. Israel and the Palestinian groups did agree to a three-month truce in the summer of 2003, but it was largely stillborn and gave way to escalating violence on both sides. Nevertheless, talks of a truce continue.

The Palestinian Jihadists: Strengths and Vulnerabilities

It is not difficult to understand the growing power of the Palestinian jihadists. The PLO and the Palestinian Authority that it controls are large and unwieldy bureaucracies that operate much like the other governments in the Arab world. They are oppressive, inefficient, and corrupt. The Palestinians could tolerate oppression and corruption if the PLO showed signs of liberating the Occupied Territories. It has not. Israel, for its part, has done little to either meet Palestinian demands or to increase the effectiveness of the Palestinian Authority. On the contrary, Israel has kept the Palestinian Authority on a tight leash. In the meantime, Israeli settlements in the Occupied Territories continue to multiply. The only solution for both problems, in the eyes of many Palestinians, is the jihadists. Polls conducted during the summer of 2003 by the Palestinian Center for Public Opinion indicated that some 57 percent of the Palestinians wanted the intifada to continue.[53] Questions of who will rule Palestine can be sorted out later.

The jihadists are also buoyed by a global network of support that extends from Jordan and Lebanon to Palestinian communities throughout the world. Most Palestinians are not extremists, but they do want a Palestinian state. The jihadists may now represent the best hope for the attainment of that goal. Iran, Syria, and Saudi Arabia are among the strongest supporters of the Palestinian jihadists, topics examined at greater length in subsequent chapters. Bin Laden also has a vested interest in ensuring that Israel is defeated.

This said, the Palestinian jihadists have their own share of problems. Israeli counterterrorist operations, including targeted assassinations of the Hamas and jihad leadership, have exacted an enormous toll on both organizations and their supporters. The United States has also placed enormous pressure on Saudi Arabia, Iran, Syria, and Lebanon to curtail their support of the Palestinian jihadists. This pressure has not stemmed the flow of external support to the jihadists, but it has raised its costs. Syria has closed the Damascus offices of Hamas and Holy Jihad and Iran is nervous. The Palestinian Authority is also under intense pressure from Israel and the United States to bring the jihadists under control. The PLO, for its part, is ambivalent toward the jihadists. They are a useful weapon in forcing Israel to the negotiating table, but they are also competitors for the control of the resistance movement. Efforts to reign in the jihadists could also threaten civil war.

By far the biggest threat to the Palestinian jihadists is the very real possibility that a peace treaty will be signed with Israel. What would be the role of the jihadists in a reborn Palestine? Would they simply become an ordinary political party and attempt to achieve their goal of an Islamic state by the ballot box, or would they resort to violence? Also unresolved is the existence of Israel. The PLO has agreed to accept the existence of Israel. The jihadists, as yet, have not. Both issues could fragment the jihadist movement. It is also probable that outside forces will continue to meddle in their internal affairs, not the least of which are Syria, Iran, and Hizbullah. Ironically, it could well be suicide attacks that force peace between Israel and the Palestinian Authority.

THE JIHADIST WAR COMES TO AMERICA

On February 26, 1993, a van loaded with explosives was detonated in the underground parking garage of the World Trade Center. Six people were killed and more than 1,000 were wounded. The U.S. mainland had remained free from foreign attack during two world wars, but that was no longer the case. The jihadists had struck in the heart of America's largest city. The attacks had been orchestrated by Sheikh Omar Abdul Rahman, a blind sheikh, and the spiritual guide of Egypt's Islamic Group. The Islamic Group, as noted earlier, was one of the world's dominant jihadist movements and one of the jihadist groups accused of assassinating Egyptian President Anwar Sadat in 1981. Abdul Rahman was implicated in the assassination but released from prison on a legal technicality.

This itself is curious, for Egyptian authorities seldom worry about technicalities. Indeed, Egypt's prisons are littered with convicts who have never had a trial, fair or otherwise. The blind Sheikh, however, was not an ordinary prisoner. Egypt was on the verge of a civil war, and little was to be gained by granting Abdul Rahman his wish of martyrdom. All things considered, a dead saint was a greater threat to the Egyptian government than a live spiritual guide. Still, there was no reason to allow the Sheikh to rally his troops from prison. The only choice was exile.

Abdul Rahman migrated to the United States by way of the Sudan. He obviously had contacts with the Turabi network, but Turabi's involvement in the attacks on the World Trade Center remains uncertain. Abdul Rahman was not under Turabi's control, but they did share common goals. Turabi, moreover, was in the business of facilitating attacks on the United States, whatever their origin. Why did the American authorities allow Abdul Rahman to settle in the United States? The only reasonable explanations are laxity and a failure to take the jihadist threat seriously. The man was not an obscure individual and his activities were well known to American officials in the region.

U.S. authorities considered the bombing of the World Trade Center to be an isolated act. Subsequent events proved them wrong. The same year found American forces in Somalia under attack by rival war lords, the dominant one of whom was supported by the Turabi network. The man in charge was Osama bin Laden. In part, the jihadist attacks were the result of a simple misunderstanding. The United States believed that it was on a humanitarian mission. The jihadists believed that the U.S. relief effort was a pretext for establishing a base in the Horn of Africa. This, from Turabi's perspective, could not be allowed. A U.S. base in the Horn of Africa would place his plans of the control of Islamic Africa in jeopardy and enable the United States to strike jihadist bases in the region at will. Of equal importance was Turabi's desire to inflict a defeat on the United States. Jihadist morale would be bolstered and America would think long and hard before challenging jihadist forces in the future.

Somalia was ideally suited for Turabi's venture. Somali warlords did most of the fighting, while Turabi's network supplied weapons and kibitzed from the sidelines. The most bitter fighting occurred in Mogadishu in 1993, where U.S. troops took heavy losses. They left Somalia a few months thereafter. Bin Laden listed Somalia as one of his major victories against the United States. The American withdrawal from Somalia reinforced the jihadist conviction that the United States would withdraw from a country rather than take casualties. It also demonstrated the effectiveness of Turabi's strategy of utilizing civil wars to promote jihadist causes.

This theory was put to the test the following year as Turabi's network supported the Muslim side in the Bosnian Civil War. By 1994, Afghan Arabs were reportedly integrated into Muslim forces, while the Iranians, the paymasters in Turabi's network, provided the Bosnian Muslims with funds and weapons. This, however, did not appear to be a source of major concern to the West. In one of the curious twists of fate so common in the region, America and its European allies found themselves on the side of the Muslims. Both turned a blind eye to the operations of the Turabi network.

The real test of Turabi's belief that the United States could be bullied from the Middle East would be Saudi Arabia. With the Americans put to flight, the fragile Saudi monarchy would collapse of its own weight, and the jihadists would be poised to claim the grand prize of Middle Eastern politics. In one fell swoop, they would lay siege to the holiest cities in Islam and 25 percent of the world's proven oil reserves. Indeed, the region as a whole would be thrown into chaos. The battle for Saudi Arabia began in November 1995 with the bombing of a Saudi National Guard barracks in Riyadh, the capital of Saudi Arabia. Five Americans trainers were killed, scores were wounded. The jihadists had also sent a message that they could strike in the heart of the Saudi kingdom. The scene repeated itself a few months later as jihadists detonated the Khobar Towers, a U.S. Marine facility in the Saudi city of Dhahran, the heart of the Saudi oil fields. A total of 241 Americans were killed.

The attacks had been carried out by local jihadists, but who called the shots: Turabi, bin Laden, the Iranians, or the Iraqis? There was no smoking gun, but all were linked in one way or another with Turabi's Sudanese network. The shadow of bin Laden loomed large, for he was in contact with the Saudi groups and he had become obsessed with driving the United States from the sacred soil of Islam. American troops were not occupying Saudi Arabia, but for bin Laden, their very presence constituted occupation. In the final analysis, bin Laden was implicated in the first attack, while the attack on the Khobar Towers was charged to the Saudi Hizbullah and ipso facto, Iran.

Whatever the case, the Turabi network had to be destroyed. The United States branded Sudan a terrorist state and made menacing moves to overthrow the Bashir regime. The Saudis weighed in by outbidding Iran for the cooperation of the Sudanese leader. Along the way, they promised to use their considerable influence in Washington to ease the U.S. pressure on Khartoum. Bashir, for his part, had tired of both Turabi and Iran. Turabi acted as if he were the ruler of the Sudan and Iran had become lax in its generosity. Turabi would manage what remained of his terrorist network from jail. This was not a difficult task, for his imprisonment was intermittent and largely symbolic. Bashir was not about to risk the killing of a saint to be. The Sudan also remained an Islamic state. Turabi himself complained that the severity of Bashir's draconian laws were excessive and a contravention of democracy.[54] The man who had jailed Turabi could not afford to appear anti-Islamic.

FROM TURABI TO BIN LADEN

With Turabi's Islamic network in remission, the leadership of the jihadist movement shifted from Turabi to bin Laden. Its focus shifted from the

Sudan to Afghanistan. It was in the wilds of Afghanistan, the scene of his earliest triumphs, that bin Laden established the base for his jihad against America.

The defeat of the Soviets in the late 1980s had thrown Afghanistan into chaos, as rival warlords plundered what they could and destroyed much of what remained. Perhaps in desperation, a group of religious students, the Taliban, seized control of city of Kandahar. Order was restored and Islamic rule was imposed.[55] At least for the moment, they were the good guys. The Afghan Arabs who remained after the defeat of the Soviets gravitated to the Taliban, adding to the firepower of their hosts. Bin Laden and Turabi provided financial support to the Taliban, as did wealthy donors from Saudi Arabia and the Gulf. The lifeline of the Taliban, however, was the Pakistani ISI.

Kabul, the capital, was seized in 1996, with much of the country following suit. War continued to range in the largely Shi'a north, but for all intents and purposes, Afghanistan had become the world's third Islamic theocracy. It was also its strictest. Women were completely veiled and only allowed to leave their domiciles in the company of a male relative, preferably a father, brother, or husband. Western music was banned and morality police clubbed doubters into submission. All in all, the Taliban managed to make Iran and Saudi Arabia appear as bastions of liberalism, although such images tax the imagination. The supreme guide of the Taliban was Mullah Omar, the leader of the attack on Kandahar. He had been elected to that position by his fellow students based on "his piety and his unswerving belief in Islam."[56] Some of the students also believed that he had been chosen by God.

It was to Taliban-controlled Afghanistan that bin Laden fled following his expulsion from the Sudan in 1996. It was a logical refuge, for he retained a strong base of support among the Afghan Arabs and had strong bonds with Mullah Omar, the leader of the Taliban. Whether he actually married one of Omar's daughters is a matter of some dispute.[57] Marriage is a common technique for strengthening power alliances in the Middle East and both had a strong motive for maintaining the alliance forged during the Afghan rebellion. Bin Laden needed a refuge and a base for his terrorist network. Omar needed support in his war against the northern warlords, at least some of whom were supported by Iran. The region's legendary hospitality may also have played a role, as did their shared fanaticism. Whatever the case, the bond between bin Laden and Omar was strong enough to survive the 2001 U.S. bombing of Afghanistan.

The bin Laden who returned to Afghanistan in 1996 was a far different individual than the bin Laden who had left the country some eight years earlier. He had gained tremendous experience by helping Turabi build his international network and he was well aware of its weakness. Bin Laden had also forged contacts with jihadist groups worldwide and he now held the keys to Turabi's financial network. It could not be otherwise, for bin Laden had established that network. Finally, Somalia had cast bin Laden in command of a key Turabi operation, a role that he relished and that provided him with direct experience in confronting the United States.

Turabi, however, was but one of several forces that shaped bin Laden's view of the world. The zeal that had propelled him to Afghanistan in the early 1980s had been instilled by the intensity of his Wahhabi indoctrination. Whether this was augmented by messianic personality traits is difficult to ascertain, given the limited information available. Such traits are not uncommon in the Middle East, a region renowned for its saints and holy men. Bin Laden's revolutionary views were later shaped by Dr. Abdullah Azzam, the head of the support organization created to coordinate Islamic aid to the Afghan jihad. Bin Laden became both his deputy and his student. The original plans for al Qaeda were sketched by Azzam in 1987 and 1988 as something akin to an Islamic rapid deployment force. Bin Laden urged the immediate deployment of al Qaeda as part of a global jihad. Azzam insisted that al Qaeda remained focused on Afghanistan. Assam was assassinated in 1989. Bin Laden was implicated in his murder.[58] Bin Laden's views were also shaped by al Zawahiri, the leader of Egypt's Islamic Jihad as well as by a variety of other Muslim intellectuals. Indeed, one of bin Laden's greatest strengths was his ability to surround himself with great intellects and draw on their skills. Al Zawahiri, for example, became bin Laden's second in command.

Arabs are quick to note that the United States also played a role in honing bin Laden's revolutionary zeal. In their view, bin Laden was a devout businessman who had gone to the Sudan to avoid open conflict with the Saudi regime. His goal was to demonstrate that Muslim businesses could develop the Islamic world without dependence on the West. In the best Islamic traditions, Muslims would help Muslims. The Sudan would prosper as would bin Laden's companies. Branded a terrorist and deprived of his Saudi citizenship, bin Laden was forced from the Sudan. It was this turn of events, in the Arab view, that transformed bin Laden into a full-fledged terrorist.[59] Whatever the case, bin Laden's bitterness toward the United States and Saudi Arabia deepened over the course of the 1990s and his avocation as a terrorist became his vocation. His break with the Saudi regime had been slow and torturous, but once made was categorical. He had urged reform on the royal family without success. They had now become *kafirs*. It was for America, however, that bin Laden reserved his greatest hatred. Much like the Ayatollah Khomeini before him, bin Laden viewed America as the "great Satan." He hated America for attacking Islam and he hated America for blocking the success of the jihadists in Egypt and Algeria. Both were on the verge of succumbing to the jihadists, only to be stabilized with Western support. Little, in bin Laden's view, was to be gained from Muslims killing Muslims when the real culprit was America. The battle had to be taken to the United States. There was no other alternative. These thoughts had been the stock and trade of the Turabi network, but it would be bin Laden who brought them to fruition.

It was in the security of Taliban-controlled Afghanistan that bin Laden put together an international terrorist network that built on the strengths of the Turabi network while avoiding its flaws. The Turabi network had suffered from a lack of focus and was torn by internal dissension. This, in bin Laden's view, was the result of Turabi's effort to weld the entire Islamic movement into a unified force: moderates as well as jihadists, Sunni as well as Shi'a. First and foremost, bin Laden's network had a single head capable of issuing and enforcing his orders. Toward this end, he adopted the title of sheikh, a religious title that implied great religious learning and the right to issue religious decrees. He lacked the religious credentials to justify the title of sheikh and its prerogatives, but this was of little concern to his followers. Bin Laden's exploits in Afghanistan, Somalia, and the Sudan spoke for themselves. Unlike Turabi, bin Laden was not a philosopher bogged down in the fine points of Islamic jurisprudence. His philosophy was his faith, and that faith required jihad.

Also avoided was Turabi's error of attempting to integrate the entirety of the Islamic movement within the confines of a single organization. Bin Laden's network was a jihadist network. Unlike the Muslim Brotherhood and Hizbullah, it had little interest in cooperating with secular regimes or their foreign masters. Bin Laden's organization was also a Sunni organization. Cooperation with Shi'a Iran and its Hizbullah network was welcome, but that would be a strategic decision decided on a case-by-case basis. Much the same was true of the Pakistanis, although they required more finesse. Afghanistan was home territory for the Pakistanis and it was Pakistan that became bin Laden's main supply route. Their interests had to be placated.

This said, bin Laden's network was an extension and modification of the Turabi network. Plans for attacks on American targets had already been drafted, although it is not clear precisely who their author had been. Cells in the United States and Europe had also been established, with America and Britain proving to be fertile ground for jihadist operatives fleeing the Middle East. Viewed in this light, al Qaeda was yet another stage in the evolution of a jihadist movement that had found its origins in the student activism of the 1970s. Far more than Turabi's network, bin Laden's al Qaeda network became an international entity free from dependence on a single country. Al Qaeda, the Arabic word for base, became precisely that: a base for training, supplying, financing, and coordinating attacks on the United States and its key allies. Turabi's network could not survive the diplomatic and economic pressure placed on the Sudan by the United States and Saudi Arabia. Bin Laden's al Qaeda network survived the bombing of Afghanistan as well as an international manhunt of unparalleled proportions.

The success of the bin Laden's network speaks for itself. The 1998 bombing of the American embassies in Kenya and Tanzania, the 2000 bombing of the USS *Cole*, and the September 11 bombing of the World Trade Center and the Pentagon all bore bin Laden's stamp. Post–September 11 attacks leave little doubt that the jihadist movement is alive and well. March 2002 witnessed forty people killed when grenades were thrown into the diplomatic chapel in Islamabad, Pakistan. In May of the same year, fourteen people were killed when a car bomb exploded outside of the Sheraton Hotel Karachi, Pakistan. Eleven people were killed and forty wounded the following month when bombs exploded in the vicinity of the U.S. Consulate and Marriot hotel in Karachi. In October 2002, the scene shifted to Bali with the killing of 202 people in the bombing of a popular resort. Three hundred more were wounded. Most of the victims were Australians, but American tourists had been anticipated. May 2003 saw suicide attacks strike the U.S. compound in Riyadh, Saudi Arabia. Twenty people were killed and 194 wounded. The same month would witness Jewish and Spanish deaths in Morocco. The spring of 2004, in turn, saw more than 200 killed in an attack on Madrid rail stations. More than 1000 were wounded. These attacks were merely the most spectacular of a long list of attacks attributed to al Qaeda.

The list of failed attacks now coming to light are even more chilling. In February 2002, Italian police arrested four Moroccans possessing maps of Rome's water system and entrances to the American Embassy. In May of the same year, an al Qaeda member was arrested for planning to detonate a radioactive bomb in the United States. In 2003, Italian police arrested five

Moroccan men for plotting attacks on Italian churches, NATO bases in Italy, and various sites in London. Other 2003 plots included the discovery of British labs for producing ricin, as well as planned attacks on the Washington, D.C., subway system and the Brooklyn Bridge. In 2004, the cancellation of commercial flights between the United States and Europe became commonplace, the French broke up a major chemical attack, and ricin-laced letters were mailed to the U.S. Senate Office buildings, to mention but a few. Rare is the day that a plot of some variety is not attributed to al Qaeda.

The above list only recounts attacks on America and its Western allies. Not listed is the continuing bloodshed in Algeria, Chechnya, Israel, Iraq, Kashmir, the Philippines, and other jihadist battlegrounds. America and its allies live under various levels of alert, with both U.S. and British officials warning that a major jihadist attack against a Western power is imminent.

All of the plots listed above have been blamed on al Qaeda, but what does that mean? No one is precisely sure what the al Qaeda network looks like. According to Gunaratna:

> Al Qaeda pursues its objectives through a network of cells, associate terrorist and guerrilla groups and other affiliated organizations, and shares expertise, transfers resources, discusses strategy and even conducts joint operations with some or all of them. . . .[60]

Gunaratna also cites Western intelligence sources suggesting that between 10,000 and 100,000 recruits graduated from al Qaeda training camps in Afghanistan between 1989 and October 2001. The larger figure is that of the CIA. The CIA similarly suggests that al Qaeda can draw on the support of 6 million plus supporters worldwide. German intelligence places the figure at 70,000.[61] Presumably, one would have to add graduates of camps in Iran, Lebanon, the Sudan, and elsewhere to these figures.

THE CONTINUING EVOLUTION OF THE JIHADIST MOVEMENT

The difficulty with prevailing descriptions of al Qaeda is that they tend to equate al Qaeda with the jihadist movement. There can be no question that al Qaeda is the most dangerous of the jihadist groups confronting the United States, but a variety of other Islamic groups also possess an international reach, not the least of which are Hizbullah, Hamas, the Muslim Brotherhood, Egypt's Islamic Group, and the remnants of Turabi's network. Indeed, the Israelis refer to Hizbullah as the "A-Team" of terror.[62] All may interact with al Qaeda when it suits their purpose, but they are not controlled by bin Laden. Much the same is true of the innumerable local jihadist groups that exist throughout the world, some no larger than a handful of thugs masquerading as holy men. They may contract with al Qaeda, but they are equally capable of contracting with any other jihadist group, present or evolving. The same applies to the some 100,000 recruits that the CIA believes to have graduated from bin Laden's training camps. They are a resource for bin Laden. They are equally a resource for other jihadist networks. Members of bin Laden's International Islamic Front, an assembly of jihadist groups associated with his 1998 declaration of war against America, are now asserting their independence and strengthening their own international networks replete with recruitment, training, and financing operations. They also continue to avoid past mistakes and find new ways to attack America and its allies. That, after all, is the process of evolution.

NOTES

1. F. Ajami, *The Arab Predicament, 2nd ed.* (Cambridge, U.K.: Cambridge University Press, 1992); Sadiq Jallal Al Azm, *Self-Criticism after the Defeat* (Beirut, Dar Al-Taliah, 1969), in Arabic; Adeed Dawish, "Requiem for Arab Nationalism," *The Middle East Quarterly* 10 (Winter 2003), at http://www.meforum.org/article/518 (accessed 3 Nov. 2003).

2. Ahmad Moussalli, *Moderate and Radical Islamic Fundamentalism: The Quest for Modernity, Legitimacy, and the Islamic State* (Gainesville: University Press of Florida, 1999).

3. Abdel Majid Farid, *Nasser: The Final Years* (Reading, U.K.: Ithaca Press, 1994); Salah Addin A.-Hadidi, *Witness to the Yemen War* (Cairo: Madbouli, 1984), in Arabic.

4. Berlinti Abdul Al Hamid, *The Marshall and I* (Cairo: Madbouli, 1992), in Arabic.

5. Mohammed H. Heikal, *Autumn of Fury: The Assassination of Sadat* (London: Andre Deutsch, 1983).

6. Kemal Khalid, *They Killed Sadat: Secrets of the Legal Proceedings in the Case of the Jihad Organization* (Cairo: Preservation House, Dar I'tisam, 1988), in Arabic.

7. Saad Eddin Ibrahim, "Anatomy of Egypt's Militant Islamic Groups: Methodological Note and Preliminary Findings," *International Journal of Middle East Studies* 12, no. 4 (1980):423–453.

8. Hala Mustafa, *The Political System and the Islamic Opposition in Egypt* (Cairo: Markaz Al-Mahrusa, 1995), in Arabic.

9. Ibrahim G. Aoude, "From National Bourgeois Development to Infitah: Cairo 1952–1992," *Arab Studies Quarterly* 16, no. 1 (1994):19.

10. Charlene Gubash, "Egyptian Militant Group in Disarray: New Boss to Resume

Mission: Bringing Down the Government," *MSNBC News*, 2 June 2003, at http://msnbc.com/news/692862.asp (accessed 2 June 2003).

11. *New York Times.com* (28 Nov. 1993), 8(N) cited in Monte Palmer, *Comparative Politics* (Itasca, Ill.: Peacock Publishers/Wadsworth, 2001), 434.

12. Marvin Zonis, *Majestic Failure: The Fall of the Shah* (Chicago: University of Chicago Press, 1991); James A. Bill, *The Eagle and the Lion: The Tragedy of American-Iranian Relations* (New Haven, Conn.: Yale University Press, 1988).

13. Mandavi Mehta and Ambassador Teresita C. Schaffer, "Islam in Pakistan: Unity and Contradictions" (a report from the CSIS Project Pakistan's Future and U.S. Policy Options, 7 Oct. 2002).

14. "Terrorist Organization Profiles," *Kashmir Herald*, 2, no. 5 (5 Oct. 2002), at http://kashmirherald.com/profiles/Harkat%20ul-Jihad-i-Islami.html (accessed 5 Oct. 2002).

15. "Terrorist and Insurgency Groups," *Jane's IntelWeb*, Nov. 23, 1998, at http://intelweb.janes.com/resource/Groups_table5.htm (accessed 24 Oct. 2001).

16. B. Raman, "Islamic Jihad and the United States," SAPRA, 2000, at http://www.subcontinent.com/sapra/terrorism/terrorism20001029a.html (accessed 5 June 2002).

17. B. Raman, "Harkat-ul-Mujahideen: An Update," ICT.org , 20 Mar. 1999, at http://www.ict.org.il/articles/articledet.cfm?articleid=85 (accessed 4 Feb. 2004).

18. Mehta and Schaffer, "Islam in Pakistan."

19. B. Raman "The Prodigal Sons Return," *Asian Times*, 2, 15 Oct. 2001, at http://www.atimes.com/atimes/Southeast_Asia/DJ15Ae03.html (20 June 2003).

20. V. S. Naipaul, *A Million Mutinies Now* (New York: Viking, 1990).

21. Bertil Lintner, "Religious Extremism and Nationalism in Bangladesh" (paper presented at the international workshop on Religion and Security in South Asia at the Asia Pacific Center for Security Studies in Honolulu, Aug. 2002).

22. Rohan Gunaratna, *Inside Al-Qaeda: Global Network of Terror* (New York: Columbia, 2002), 24.

23. Gunaratna, *Inside Al-Qaeda*, 18–22.

24. Sami Haddad (moderator), Panel discussion: The Future of the Afghan Arabs after the Defeat of the Taliban, 25 Nov. 2001, at http://www.aljazeera.net/programs/opinions/articles/2001/11/11-25-1.htm (accessed 1 Dec. 2001).

25. Yossef Bodansky, *Bin Laden: The Man Who Declared War on America* (Roseville, Calif.: Prima Publishing, 2001), 28.

26. Anonymous, *Through Our Enemies' Eyes: Osama Bin Laden, Radical Islam, and the Future of America* (Washington, D.C.: Brassey's, 2002), 114.

27. Hassan Al-Turabi, "Islamic Fundamentalism in the Sunna and Shi'a Worlds," *Sudan Foundation Religious File Number 6* (London 1997), at http://www.sufo.demon.co.uk/reli006.htm (accessed 26 June 2002).

28. Al-Turabi, "Islamic Fundamentalism."

29. Bodansky, *Bin Laden*.

30. Bodansky, *Bin Laden*.

31. Bodansky, *Bin Laden*.

32. Bodansky, *Bin Laden*.

33. Liess Boukra, *Algérie la terreur sacrée* (SA Lausanne: FAVRE, 2002), 194.

34. Boukra, *Algérie la terreur sacrée*, 74–75.

35. Boukra, *Algérie la terreur sacrée*, 73.

36. Rachid Boudjedra, *FIS do la haine* (Paris: Donoel, 1992).

37. Boukra, *Algérie la terreur sacrée*, 83.

38. Boukra, *Algérie la terreur sacrée*, 212.

39. Boukra, *Algérie la terreur sacrée*, 214.

40. Boukra, *Algérie la terreur sacrée*, 106–107.

41. Boukra, *Algérie la terreur sacrée*, 236.

42. Emile Sahliyeh, *In Search of Leadership* (Washington, D.C.: The Brookings Institution, 1988).

43. Hamas is an acronym for Islamic Resistance Movement (in Arabic).

44. Interviews with Monte Palmer, Jordan, 2000.

45. The Covenant of the Islamic Resistance Movement (Hamas), 18 Aug. 1988, at http://www.mideastweb.org/hamas.htm. (accessed 6 May 2002).

46. This is according to documents seized in an Israeli raid on Palestinian headquarters relating to the payment to Fatah activists. Fatah is the main group in the PLO. No mention is made of payments to Hamas or jihad activitists. "Fuad Shoubaki's Office's Handling of the 'Al Aqsa Martyrs Brigades' Request for Financial Aid," Arab Terrorism website, n.d., at http://www.arabterrorism.tripod.com/documents2.html (accessed 6 May 2002).

47. Janine Zacharia, "Hamas Funding is 50% Saudi, God Tells Congressmen," *Jerusalem Post*, 16 July 2003, at http://www.jpost.com/ (accessed 16 July 2003).

48. Muhammed Muslih, *The Foreign Policy of Hamas* (New York: Council on Foreign Relations, 1999).

49. Beverly Milton-Edwards, *Islamic Politics in Palestine* (London: IB Tauris Academic Studies, 1999).

50. Meir Hatina, *Islam and Salvation in Palestine: The Islamic Jihad Movement* (New York: Syracuse University Press, 2001).

51. Hatina, *Islam and Salvation in Palestine*.

52. Cited in Awad Ar Rajoob, "Hamas and Al-Jehad Certify Coordination and Endeavors Toward Unity," Al-Jazeera (18 Jan. 2004).

53. The polls were conducted by the Palestine Center for Public Opinion and Public Opinion Research of Israel organizations. Sample size was not provided. Janine Zacharia, "Poll: 59% of Palestinians Support Continuation of Terror after State Is Created," *Jerusalem Post*, 22 Oct. 2003, at http://www.jpost.com/ (accessed Oct. 22, 2003).

54. Hisham Aldiwan, "No Comeback in the Cards for Sudan's Former Islamist Strongman," *Daily Star-Lebanon*, 18 June 2002, at http://www.dailystar.com.lb/18_06_02/art21.asp (accessed 18 June 2002).

55. Peter L. Bergen, *Holy War, Inc.: Inside the Secret World of Osama bin Laden* (New York: The Free Press 2001).

56. Ahmed Rashid, *Taliban: Militant Islam, Oil and Fundamentalism in Central Asia* (New Haven, Conn.: Yale University Press, 2001), 23.

57. Bergen, *Holy War, Inc.*

58. Gunaratna, *Inside Al-Qaeda*.

59. Mohammed Kharishan, "First War of the Century: Organization of Al Qaeda and Its Relation with the Taliban," Al-Jazeera (29 Oct. 2001), in Arabic. This view is shared by Jason Burke (I. B. Tauris, 2003) in his book *Al-Qaeda: Casting a Shadow of Terror*.

60. Gunaratna, *Inside Al-Qaeda*, 95

61. Gunaratna, *Inside Al-Qaeda*, 8, 243.

62. David Rudge, "Hizbullah: 'A-Team' of International Terror?" *Jerusalem Post*, 23 May 2003, at http://www.jpost.com/ (accessed 23 May 2003).

5

THE JIHADIST WAR PLAN

The first step in defeating the jihadists is to understand their war plan for reconquering the Islamic world. The more the United States and its allies understand this plan, the easier it will be for them to thwart the jihadists' next move. At the very least, there will be fewer surprises. Speaking of a war plan may seem unduly dramatic, but it is not. The jihadists spend endless hours debating their strategy for reconquering the Islamic world. That debate is never ending. Each victory brings new opportunities; each defeat demands new adjustments. As we have seen in the preceding chapter, the jihadists have had their share of both. The jihadist war plan, like the jihadist movement, itself, is evolving.

The essence of a good war plan is a thing of many parts. It starts with a well-defined goal. What precisely is the organization attempting to accomplish? Without a clear goal, everyone is spinning off in a different direction. More than likely, they are at each other's throats. A clear goal, however, is only the beginning. Resources have to be mobilized and focused on the target. This requires recruitment, training, motivation, coordination, communication, logistics, and everything else that goes into the war effort. A good war plan also seeks allies and garners mass support. Both are critical to victory. Even this is not enough. An effective war plan also requires an understanding of the obstacles to be overcome. What does the enemy look like and what are his strengths and weaknesses? Where are the opportunities and the minefields? It is this assessment that guides strategies for attacking the enemy. Finally, a good war plan is flexible. Errors are corrected; the adjustments of the enemy countered.

The early war plans of the jihadists suffered on all counts. Their goal was an Islamic state, but there was little agreement on precisely what that meant. Who was to be in charge and how was it to be organized? Was it to be based on the rigid interpretation of Koranic scriptures, or was it to be an enlightened Islamic state that expressed the compassion and innovative teachings of the Prophet Mohammed? Was it to embrace the Shi'a, or were they to be tortured as heretics? These questions fragmented the fundamentalist movement, as did personality conflicts and turf wars. Most jihadists preached fire and brimstone, placing themselves on the fringe of the broader Islamic movement. Resources were wasted and a lack of coordination prevented the jihadists from seizing the initiative when secular governments were reeling from their attacks. Jihadist strategy focused on violence, but they seemed unsure of the enemy. Some attacked government officials, while others turned on secular Muslims or, in the case of Pakistan, the Shi'a. Few turned on the West.

By and large, the early jihadists viewed themselves as a historic vanguard whose role was to ignite an Islamic revolution. Moved more by zeal than experience, they assumed that a wave of violence would spark a mass revolt and topple unpopular governments.[1] This turned out to be the case in Iran, but not elsewhere. The governments of the Islamic world were unexpectedly resilient, as were their Western supporters. Muslims were also frightened by jihadist violence and put off by the hell-fire content of their sermons. Big on zeal, jihadists had few practical solutions for the problems besetting the Islamic world.

For all of their errors, the early jihadists transformed the political landscape of the Islamic world. The Islamic Revolution succeeded in Iran because the Iranian jihadists were better organized and could draw on the hierarchal structure of the Shi'a faith. It might have succeeded in the Sunni world if the Sunni jihadists had been able to capitalize on the euphoria that swept the Islamic world in the aftermath of Iran's Islamic Revolution. Fortunately for the United States and its allies, they lacked the war plan to do so. Attacks escalated, but there was little coordination or follow through. Weak governments had time to regroup and the advantage was lost.

Jihadist planning improved dramatically during the Turabi era and more so with the establishment of al Qaeda. The success of the jihadist movement has increased apace. The Islamic world is threatened with chaos, the might of the Israeli army has been defied, and the United States mainland has suffered the most devastating attack in its history. Each day, or so it seems, brings new alerts. Nevertheless, the record of the jihadists remains a mixed bag. America took bin Laden's best shot and survived. Its stability was never in doubt. Bin Laden and al Qaeda, moreover, had no plans for capitalizing on their victory. They expected the United States to collapse like a deck of cards and with it, the opposition to jihadist rule in the Muslim world. They were stunned when it did not. All in all, the dream of a jihadist revolution is little closer to achievement today than it was when the Ayatollah Khomeini seized power in Iran in 1979.

The success of bin Laden's September 11 attacks, much like the earlier successes of the jihadists, was a combination of cunning, zeal, surprise, and laxity. The cunning and zeal remain, but surprise and laxity have decreased. The picture is far from adequate, but the jihadists will find coming attacks more challenging than those of the past. The jihadist movement, for its part, is now experiencing a painful period of self-criticism and reevaluation.[2]

This is not to minimize the threat of the jihadist attacks. The jihadists are lethal and will remain so for decades to come. They do, however, have vulnerabilities that must be exploited if America is to win its war on terror. Some jihadist vulnerabilities are inherent in their plan for attacking the United States and its allies. Others involve their capacity to execute their war plan. The present chapter examines the current jihadist war plan as well as probable adjustments that will be forthcoming in the next few years. The next chapter analyzes the capacity of the jihadists to execute their war plans, present and future.

JIHADIST STRATEGY: THE PSYCHOLOGY OF TERROR

The basic axiom of jihadist strategy is the belief that an Islamic state cannot be achieved by peaceful means. As we have seen in their critique of the Muslim Brotherhood, the jihadists believe that peaceful change is an illusion and that cooperation with secular governments strengthens them while corrupting the jihadists. The only choice, accordingly, is violence. The jihadists would prefer to launch massed armies against their opponents, much as the forces of the Prophet Mohammed swept all before them. But, as things currently stand, that is impossible. The jihadists simply lack the military capacity to seize and hold territory for a sustained period of time. Their only option, accordingly, is to terrorize the infidels into submission; to destroy their will to resist.

In reality, then, the jihadist war plan is overwhelmingly psychological. Terror is the jihadist instrument of choice for creating fear and chaos among their adversaries, be they Americans or errant Muslims. All fear death, all but the jihadists.

Terror has other psychological uses as well. Terrorist victories keep the jihadists in the public eye, making them appear larger than life. Bin Laden and al Qaeda have become household words. Victories also bolster the spirits of cadres, supporters, contributors, and potential recruits. This is vital, for few people want to bet on a loser. Victories also convey an image of power and inevitability to the millions of Muslims sitting on the fence in the vain hope of picking a winner in the war on terror. One has to survive, the most perilous of tasks in the Islamic world.

Terror may provide the jihadists the means of achieving their goal of an Islamic state, but it also has a down side. It scares Muslims and deprives the jihadists of much-needed popular support. Jihadist violence, particularly the killing of Muslims, has created theological furor within the Muslim community. The jihadists, accordingly, have gone to great lengths to convince the world's Muslims that they are on the side of the angels. This, as we shall see shortly, has not been an easy task. The jihadist commitment to violence also makes their strategy inflexible. It is violence or nothing. As such, they have lost ground to the moderate-radicals who stress peaceful change while maintaining the threat of violence.

The role of violence in the jihadist war plan has also created bitter strategic debates within the jihadist movement itself. The Islamic Group, Egypt's largest jihadist group, declared a truce in the late 1990s. No one is quite sure what that means or how long it will last, but violence, at least for now, has stopped. It is possible that the Islamic Group has abandoned violence as a strategy and is shifting to a strategy of nonviolence. It is also possible that the Islamic Group is merely licking its wounds and regrouping. Hamas and the Palestinian Holy Jihad also declared a truce in 2003, but it soon folded. The topic continues to be discussed. This fundamental conflict over strategy hinders cooperation within the jihadist movement and makes it difficult for jihadists to mobilize their resources to the maximum degree. It also calls the entire persona of the jihadists into question. Without violence, they differ little from the Muslim Brotherhood. For the moment, however, the jihadist faithful are buoyed by the operation of al Qaeda and its spin-offs. Violence remains the cardinal principle of jihadist strategy.

The debate over violence, it should be noted, does not apply to terror against America. The jihadists are not attempting to forge an Islamic state within in the United States, nor are they attempting to curry the favor of the American public. Their goal is to drive the United States out of the

Islamic world. This requires violence against Americans in the Islamic world and attacks on the United States itself. The psychological nature of the jihadist war plan does not make it any less deadly. Indeed, efforts to terrorize people into submission requires ever larger doses of terror.

THE COMPONENTS OF TERROR

The terrorist operations of the jihadists fall into six broad categories: random terror, political terror, economic terror, cultural terror, revolutionary terror, and cataclysmic terror. We examine the advantages and disadvantages of each. This accomplished, we turn to the propaganda war and jihadist efforts to convince Muslims that terror is ordained by God. This, too, is a vital part of jihadist strategy. It is also a hard sell.

Random Terror

Random terror is the indiscriminate killing of civilian populations. Targets are less important than the number of casualties. The more the better. Major urban centers are preferred locations in as much as they are politically sensitive and will garner maximum media attention. The objective of random terror is to destabilize governments by sowing panic among civilian populations. Mass resolve may be strengthened in the short run, but governments that lose the capacity to protect their citizens over a sustained period of time lose their capacity to rule. Random terror brought both Algeria and Egypt to the brink of civil war, and random terror in Israel continues to confront the Jewish state with one of the greatest challenges of its modern history. Saudi Arabia appears to be next on the list of the jihadists. America witnessed the ultimate in random jihadist violence on September 11, 2001, with the destruction of the World Trade Center. We are witnessing it again in Iraq.

Even when random terror fails to destabilize a country, the costs of survival are themselves terrifying. Egypt, Algeria, and Israel have all survived by mass arrests, military trials, and collective punishments (blowing up houses and neighborhoods). In the process, innocent people are punished for crimes that they have not committed. Some blame the jihadists for their misery. Others take revenge by joining the jihadists.

Random terror also keeps the jihadists in the public eye and exaggerates their power. Both play a critical role in maintaining the élan of their supporters in this most psychological of wars. Concessions from nervous governments merely add to the élan, as does the flight of nervous foreigners.

Aside from events such as Stepmber 11, the techniques for executing random violence are virtually limitless. They range from simple pipe bombs to the suicide attacks the Israelis now refer to as the H-bomb. Other items in the list would certainly include hijacking, kidnapping, arson, car bombing, and other acts of random violence that now dominant the daily press. Instructions for most can be found on the Internet, with one of the best manuals for random terror produced by the U.S. Army for use in Latin America. It was updated for use against the Soviets in Afghanistan and appears to have been incorporated in al Qaeda training programs. As a specialist on ABC News commented, "In fact, a visit to the U.S. Army's website offers scores of publicly available field manuals on everything from conducting psychological operations to sniper training."[3]

The advantage of random terror, from the jihadist perspective, is that it is cheap, easy, requires few people, needs minimal technology, and, with the exception of the suicide bombers, is relatively safe. Individuals carry out their deadly tasks and then fade into the woodwork. Bombs detonated by cell phones are now making random terror far less risky. Bombs can be planted days in advance and detonated from miles away. Stolen phones are preferable. The Middle East is also one of the most heavily armed regions of the world, making weapons and explosives readily available. Some Lebanese have their own rocket launchers, Kalashnikovs, and hand grenades. All are mementos from the Lebanon's long and bitter civil war. Israeli settlers are probably the most heavily armed population in the world. All things considered, random terror is virtually unstoppable if the jihadists possess a broad base of support within the target community.

For all its ease of operation, random terror is essentially a psychological softening-up process. To be effective, it must be supported by an organization capable of seizing power once a government has been weakened. The jihadists continue to lack this capacity. Random violence against innocent civilians is also a flagrant violation of all but the most extreme interpretations of Islamic law. So, too, is the killing of Muslims.[4] Indeed, the very heart of the Prophet Mohammed's message was the demand that Muslims put aside their tribal hatreds and unify for the greater good of God. Koranic injunctions against violence continue to inhibit jihadist efforts to build the base of popular support on which their success will ultimately depend.

Terrorizing civilian populations, moreover, is a two-way street. It may destabilize secular governments, but it also sows fear among the Muslim community.[5] Rather than being the saviors, the jihadists have become the villains. Early jihadists successes were based on quick and dirty attacks that assumed that victory would be swift. Victory has not been swift, and tolerance of the jihadist violence has worn thin. For the most part, Muslims fail to understand why the goal of an Islamic state requires the killing of Muslims. This is all the more so because Muslims find themselves doubly cursed. They are cursed by the random violence of the jihadists and they are cursed by the brutality of government repression. They just want the violence to stop.

Finally, it should be noted that random terror in the Middle East is losing its shock value. Jihadist attacks against Muslims are rarely reported in the world press and receive minimal coverage in the regional press. Random terror against Americans gets more bang for the buck.

Political Terror

Political terror focuses its wrath directly on the symbols of secular power. Innocents are spared, but political officials of every stripe and nationality are fair game. Presidents, prime ministers, generals, judges, diplomats, bureaucrats, soldiers, rural gendarmes, and everyone in between have felt the sting of jihadist terror. Some have been felled by an assassin's bullet. Others have perished in the rubble of buildings gutted by terrorist bombs or have been the victims of hijackings.

The logic of political violence is compelling. The political regimes of the Islamic world are illegitimate and despised by their populations. In any case, none is willing to test its popularity in free presidential elections. The assassination of a tyrant promises to throw many countries of the Islamic world into chaos. Whether it would lead to an Islamic state is an open question. The military would decide. This, from the jihadist perspective, is not without its advantages. It was a military coup in the Sudan, it will be recalled, that paved the way for the emergence of the Turabi network. The 1977 Zia ul-Haq coup in Pakistan had also seen the jihadists flourish.

Much the same logic applies to jihadist attacks on American political targets. The jihadists firmly believe that the United States will withdraw in the face of sustained casualties, much as U.S. forces withdrew from Lebanon in 1983 and Somalia in 1993. Scholars in the Middle East refer to the American reluctance to sustain casualties as the "Vietnam complex." Those who studied in the United States are convinced that American public opinion will prevent any U.S. government from staying the course in a prolonged conflict. America can bomb Iraq, in their view, but it cannot endure sustained terrorist attacks against U.S. troops now occupying the country. If their views are correct, Iraq will provide a critical showdown between the United States and the jihadists. If the United States and Britain succeed in pacifying Iraq, secular governments throughout the Islamic world will attack the jihadists with renewed vigor, as will the Israelis, the Russians, and the Indians. Potential supporters of the jihadists will also cut their losses. If the United States runs, the jihadists will have a field day. Everyone in the Islamic world is watching Iraq and they like what they see.

By the same token, there can be little doubt that bin Laden believed that the September 11 attacks on the Pentagon and those planned for the White House would throw the United States into chaos. This did not happen, but the jihadists were buoyed by the success of their attacks. The governments of the Islamic world are far less fortunate, especially those of Saudi Arabia and Pakistan. The jihadists also relish the shock value of political assassinations. Random violence may have become less newsworthy, but political assassinations are still front-page news.

For all its advantages, political terror has failed to topple the secular regimes of the Islamic world. Indeed, political survival in the Middle East has become an art form. A region that epitomized instability and chaos during the 1950s and 1960s now boasts an honor roll of aging tyrants. Hafez al-Asad ruled Syria with a hand of steel from 1970 to 2000, succumbing to old age and passing the torch of power to a son. Husni Mubarak, the president of Egypt came to power with the jihadist assassination of Sadat in 1981 and has ruled for well over twenty years without challenge. His son, too, is now waiting in the wings.[6] Even Saddam Hussein, perhaps the most hated man in the world, survived several U.S. presidents before his ouster by American troops. Qadaffi has set the record for survival and hopes to extend his longevity by becoming the ally of the U.S.

Political assassinations are high-risk operations that require extraordinary planning and coordination. They also invite violent counterattacks by the government. The repression that follows political attacks is invariably more brutal than that occasioned by random violence against civilians. The political regimes of the Islamic world may not be overly concerned about their citizens, but they are concerned about their own survival. The attempted assassination of Nasser in 1954 resulted in the near destruction of the Muslim Brotherhood, and a Brotherhood uprising against President Asad of Syria in 1982 resulted in the slaughter of thousands of people, many being innocent bystanders. The merest suspicion of political malice provides an immediate ticket to prison in most countries of the Islamic world.

For one reason or another, high-profile assassinations in the Islamic world have decreased. This does not mean that political violence has become a thing of a past, but it is clearly a tool that is used with discretion. Low-level political terror, by contrast, appears to be increasing, particularly terror against foreign nationals working in the Islamic world. Killing foreigners creates an international crisis and is manifestly political. This will not place the jihadists in power, but it will make it far more difficult for the United States and its allies to work effectively in the region. The recent nervousness of Westerners in Saudi Arabia is a case in point. Indeed, a debate is now swirling over the ability of the Saudi regime to survive the barrage of political terror without dramatic reforms.[7] It also provides the jihadist with key psychological victories. Killing Americans electrifies the media. It also sends shock waves through the American community in the region. The temporary closing of American embassies has now become routine in the Islamic world.

Economic Terror: The Oil Weapon and Beyond

Also lethal are jihadist attacks on the economic foundations of secular states. Attacks on tourists in Egypt, the Philippines, Indonesia, and elsewhere have crippled key tourist industries and placed inordinate pressure on the citizens of countries already wracked by poverty and unemployment. The economy of Algeria has been virtually destroyed. Throughout history, political collapse has been preceded by economic collapse.

Economic terror is not limited to the Islamic world, but now threatens to engulf North America and Europe as well. High on the jihadist agenda is the oil weapon. The industrial economies of the world run on oil, and any sustained disruption in Middle Eastern oil supplies could wreak devastation in the industrial world. The mere mention of a crisis in the Middle East sends oil prices rocketing.

To date, the oil weapon has only been used once, that being in the turmoil of the Arab-Israeli War of 1973. Oil shipments to the United States and its allies were curtailed, sending the price of oil spiraling from approximately $3 per barrel in 1973 to some $40 per barrel in the early 1980s. The price of industrial goods skyrocketed, and the economies of the Third World were sent into a free fall, as the cost of borrowing money became insupportable.[8]

Flooded with fabulous wealth and dependent on the United States for their survival, the Saudis and other oil producers have renounced the oil weapon, pretending that it's possible to separate politics from economics.[9] The brutality of Israeli counterterrorist measures has met with new calls for an oil embargo, but has produced little more than an embarrassed wringing of hands by the leaders of the oil states. The Saudis bitterly condemned the U.S. invasion of Iraq but privately assured Washington that oil prices would remain stable.

The jihadists, by contrast, are more than willing to use the oil weapon against the United States and its allies. Their goal is salvation rather than survival, and many feel that the Middle East might be a more religious place without the corrupting influences of oil. Oil pipelines stretch for thousands of miles and make inviting targets, as do the oil platforms and refineries of the region. Iraqi pipelines have become prime targets in resistance efforts to force the U.S. evacuation of Iraq. They will be more so if the United States carries out its plans to export Iraqi oil via Israel. Also vulnerable are the massive tankers that transverse the narrow straits of the Persian Gulf. The jihadists signaled their ability to attack tankers with their attack on the USS *Cole* in 2000. In 2002, a Yemeni terrorist group called the Islamic Army of Aden-Abyane claimed responsibility for an attack on a French supertanker. This group is presumed to have been acting under contract with al Qaeda.

The oil weapon is not merely a matter of pipelines and refineries. It also manifests itself in the fabulous wealth that pours into the coffers of the oil kingdoms, at least some of which finds its way into the hands of the jihadists. It was that wealth that financed the bin Laden's jihad against the Soviets, and the United States believes that Saudi oil money helped to finance the September 11 attacks on America. The Israelis maintain that half of Hamas's revenues come from Saudi Arabia.[10]

Other economic targets also abound in Europe and North America. The security of atomic generating plants and water supplies has been called into question. The economic impact of the September 11 attacks is being measured in the billions of dollars and has thrown a pall of despair over a world economic system. Indeed, the very cost of America's war on terror has imposed phenomenal strains on the United States and its allies, with Israel recently requesting an additional 10 billion dollars in U.S. aid to keep the Israeli economy afloat.[11] In retrospect, the economic impact of the September 11 attacks was far greater than its political impact, a message unlikely to be lost on the jihadists. The jihadists are also well aware that much of

America's fabled industrial plant is largely unguarded. For the moment, they are focused on high-profile targets but this could change.

Cyber-warfare is now entering the jihadist vocabulary as they see ways to exploit the West's dependence on computers. The director of Britain's National Infrastructure Security Coordination Center cautions: "For terrorist groups like al-Qaida with limited resources, it would be 'a very attractive method' of attack, that would cause 'huge damage.'"[12] American officials have also reportedly concluded that al Qaeda is poised to use the Internet as a lethal weapon. Examples include using the Internet to unleash the floodgates of dams or to cause damaging power surges.[13]

The main disadvantage of economic terrorism is that it punishes innocent Muslims, including supporters of the jihadists. A wedge is thus driven between the jihadists and their support base, a liability that the jihadists can ill afford if they are to be effective. This liability does not apply to economic terrorism against America and its First World allies.

Cultural Terror

Cultural terror attacks the symbols of Western culture and all other cultural influences that violate the jihadist vision of Islamic purity. Girls' schools have been attacked in Afghanistan and Saudi Arabia, journalists and pop singers have been assassinated in Algeria, and Western classics have been forced from Middle Eastern libraries. A university in Pakistan, for example, recently banned Ernest Hemingway's *The Sun Also Rises* and Jonathan Swift's *Gulliver's Travels*. Both were deemed vulgar.[14] Similar bans have been imposed at the American University of Cairo. Efforts are increasing to purge vulgarity from the Internet and satellite networks, both of which now penetrate the remotest regions of the Islamic world.[15]

But to what end? Cultural terrorism is not going to overthrow secular governments or send shock waves through the West. To expect that is to miss the point. Western pop-culture, in the eyes of the jihadists, is more than a testimony to bad taste. It is viewed by the jihadists as the main weapon in America's psychological war against Islam. Some jihadists fear the cultural offensive of the United States more than they fear its weapons. The latter brings salvation; the former destroys the Muslim soul from within and paves the way to hell. Lest further evidence be needed on the matter, the American government has recently launched new radio and television stations designed to flood the Islamic world with yet a larger dose of pop music. Radio Monte Carlo and Radio Sharq (East) had already filled this void in much of the region. Islamic stations counter with a steady diet of fire and brimstone mixed with strident anti-Americanisms. The end result will probably be a generation of schizophrenic Muslims.

The jihadists are under no illusion that they can change the message of Western culture. Their hope is to slow down the perversion of Islamic minds by killing the messenger. This is a thankless task as well as one that paints the jihadists with an extremist brush. Nevertheless, cultural terrorism seems doomed to continue. It is too central to the jihadist war plan to be ignored.

Revolutionary Terror

Although less visible to American audiences, the jihadists have scored major victories by aligning themselves with ethnic and religious conflicts throughout the Islamic world. The jihadists play the leading role in the Palestinian, Kashmiri, and Chechnyan conflicts, bringing new zeal to secular liberation movements that had showed signs of stalling. They also remain very active in Kosovo, Bosnia, Afghanistan, and Somalia and have fueled the growing wave of religious violence now sweeping Africa and Asia. In Indonesia, for example, the jihadists are accused of fueling religious violence that has displaced more than 600,000 Christians.[16] The more Muslims find themselves in conflict with other religious groups, the more the jihadists prosper. The prospect of a civil war also looms large in Iraq, a country in which the jihadists are becoming increasingly active.

In the process, the jihadists are making their jihad a global reality, bolstering the morale of supporters and investors while stretching the Western capacity for intervention to the breaking point. The Russians are bogged down in Chechnya with no end in sight, Israel is under siege, the United States and Britain are attempting to extricate themselves from Afghanistan, and UN security forces continue to patrol Kosovo and Bosnia. Afghanistan is dissolving into chaos and the Taliban are returning. Lessons learned by the jihadists in Chechnya, the Occupied Territories, Kashmir, and elsewhere are now being applied in Iraq as U.S. authorities encounter a growing number of Afghan Arabs willing to die in the latest of jihadist causes.

Catastrophic Terror

This leads us to the final key element in the jihadist war plan: the acquisition of weapons of mass destruction (WMD). WMD are the ultimate weapon of terror, striking fear in the heart of millions and leveling the playing field between superpowers and the jihadists. During the 1950s and 1960s, fear of a Soviet nuclear attack prompted the slogan "Better red than dead." The "green bomb," the unfortunate name attached to Pakistan's recently developed nuclear bomb, could well have the same effect, prompting Western public opinion to press for a withdrawal from the Islamic world.

The jihadists appear to have made little progress to date, but captured al Qaeda documents indicate that efforts to acquire WMD, including nuclear weapons, were on the drawing board. According to British sources, there is evidence that bin Laden has built a crude dirty bomb that can make an area uninhabitable for ten years.[17] Nuclear scientists from Pakistan were arrested for "cooperating" with al Qaeda but later cleared, or so it seems. Far more likely is the ability of the jihadists to acquire some of the former Soviet Union's 600 tons of weapon-grade nuclear material that sits virtually unguarded since the collapse of the USSR in 1990. The scariest scenario is that suitcase bombs developed by the Soviets will find their way into the hands of the jihadists. A popular French spy novel, *Djihad*, by Gerard de Villiers, traces the journey of a Russian nuclear pocket bomb from Chechnya to New York.[18] In the book, the bomb was sold to Afghan Arabs in Chechnya by a Russian commander for several million dollars and was then carried to Istanbul in the dilapidated van of an Islamic charity caring for the Chechnyan wounded. The van's trips were routine, as were bribes paid to the diverse border guards. From Istanbul, the bomb was shipped in a container of cheap artifacts to a dealer in Montreal and from there was smuggled into the United States via an obscure border crossing. Fortunately, this is the stuff of fiction.

Postwar Iraq saw frequent looting of nuclear plants.[19] The North Koreans, part of the axis of evil, have now developed nuclear weapons, reportedly with assistance from Pakistan, an ally in America's war on terror. Iranian cooperation with China and Russia has led to U.S. accusations that the Islamic Republic is developing nuclear weapons. It already possesses delivery systems capable of reaching Israel. The Iranians deny U.S. charges but say that their national interest forces them to counter Israel's nuclear weapons. To make matters worse, the dismantling of Libya's nuclear program has revealed the existence of a brisk black market in nuclear materials.[20]

Far more accessible are chemical and biological weapons such as ricin, salmonella, cyanide, anthrax, and smallpox. Some biological and chemical attacks have been prevented, but others have not. London officials inter-cepted a plot to release cyanide gas in the London Underground, and in 2004 the French thwarted a major chemical attack in Paris. Ricin, the dead-liest of the chemical agents, has been found in Britain, France, and the United States. Captured al Qaeda computers indicate that the jihadists also have easy access to the materials required for the manufacture of botulinum, salmonella, cyanide, anthrax, and other chemical agents.[21]

The jihadist drive for WMD is insatiable. It is those weapons, more than any other, that provide the best opportunity for the jihadists to defeat the United States and Israel. Of course, Muslims would also be put at risk. A nuclear attack on America would probably trigger a massive U.S. strike against any Muslim country plausibly associated with the jihadists. The reported 6,000 deaths caused by the U.S./British invasion of Iraq would pale by comparison. President Bush, it should be noted, has not ruled out using nuclear weapons in the war on terror.

Would the jihadists actually resort to using WMD against America and its allies knowing that it would put millions of Muslims at risk? More than likely. Those committed to dying in the cause of God can hardly be con-cerned with the sacrifice of others. The question is, can they be stopped in time?

TERROR AND THE PROPAGANDA WAR

While terror constitutes the heart of the jihadist war plan, their goals cannot be achieved without the support of a critical mass of the world's Muslim population. The jihadists need Muslim support to sustain their ranks and to aid and abet their operations: to provide shelter, communications, money, and information on the activities of their adversaries. They also need an out-pouring of Islamic emotions to place secular governments on the defensive and make them wary of supporting America's war on terror.

A second key dimension of the jihadist war plan, accordingly, is propa-ganda. If the purpose of terror is to frighten people into submission, the goal of jihadist propaganda is to convince Muslims that they, the jihadists, have God's blessing. This is vital, for it is God's blessing that assures the jihadists that they will have an honored place in heaven. Without that blessing, the jihadist would be nothing but a gang of thugs. To join their ranks would be to offend God and court damnation, hardly a recipe for success.

The hardest part of this sell is convincing jihadist cadres and supporters that God's blessing gives them the right to kill all who stand in their way: Muslims as well as non-Muslims, innocents as well as combatants. The killing of innocents and Muslims flies in the face of most interpretations of Islamic law and is not an issue that can be easily skirted.[22] Jihadist propagandists have addressed this issue with great skill in a step-by-step process that begins by citing Islamic texts that call on Muslims to defend their faith against attacks by infidels. This is scripture and is not subject to argument.

Muslim scriptures calling for jihad against the enemies of Islam, in turn, are used to justify attacks on the military personnel of Israel, a country that occupies Muslim lands, including Jerusalem, the third holiest site in Islam. Added to the mix are Israeli counterterrorist measures, graphic pictures of which have become the standard fare of news telecasts in the Islamic world. The pictures are not pretty and rare is the Muslim who questions the right of the Palestinians to defend themselves.

Now comes the tricky part of the jihadist argument. What constitutes military personnel? Is it merely soldiers and police, or is it also the politicians and bureaucrats who give the orders? Or is it the broader civilian populations that support Israel's war against Islam by toiling in defense industries and paying the taxes that sustain the government? Can one truly win a war without defeating a country? Indeed, the jihadists ask, are not children the oppressors of the next generation?

These arguments have enabled the jihadists to win the propaganda battle in the struggle against Israel. Even main-line establishment preachers have now declared suicide attacks against Israeli civilians to be within the pale of Islamic law, albeit with hedges suggesting that civilians should not be the prime target of the attack.[23] This has been a propaganda victory for the jihadists. The legitimacy of killing innocent civilians has been forced into the public consciousness by *fatwas* issued by a broad range of Islamic scholars. Most have limited their justification of suicide attacks to the special circumstances of the Palestinian struggle, pointedly condemning bin Laden's attacks on the United States.

But "Ah," say the jihadists, "where is the difference? Why does Islamic law justify the killing of Israeli civilians but not the killing of U.S. citizens? It is the Americans who are supporting the Israelis. It is the Americans who are killing innocent Iraqis. It is the Americans who are threatening Syria and Iran with attack. It is the Americans who are stationing their forces in Saudi Arabia with the intent of killing Muslims. What is the distinction? If one is legitimate, why not the other?"

The same principle applies to the killing of Muslim political leaders. If the leaders of the Islamic world serve the enemies of Islam, the jihadists ask, have they not repudiated their faith and become *kafirs*, subject to death under Islam law? Killing Muslim officials who support the United States, according to the jihadists propagandists, is justified under Islamic law because these officials have ceased to be Muslims. Their deeds have repudiated their faith and they have joined the forces of Satan. It is at this point, that the jihadist part company with the main body of Islamic jurisprudence, but not necessarily public opinion. Thinly disguised in this argument is a blatant appeal to the vast majority of the world's Muslims, most mired in poverty, who suffer the oppression of secular leadership on a daily basis. The jihadist message is simple and direct: God has sent us to rid you of this scourge. Violence is your only hope. Islam is the solution.

The most difficult task faced by jihadist propagandists is justifying the killing of innocent Muslims, be they opponents of the jihadists or innocent victims of random violence. How far does Islamic law stretch? Muslims who have strayed from the true path according the jihadists, strengthen the enemies of Islam and stand in the way of the resurrection of an Islamic state. They deserve death. As for innocent Muslims killed by terror, the means justify the ends. Everything must be sacrificed for the resurrection of an Islamic state. The innocent will receive their reward in heaven. It is this logic that has resulted in more than 100,000 deaths in Algeria during the past decade.

In sum, the jihadist message of an Islamic paradise on Earth is packaged with the promise of eternal salvation for Muslims willing to sacrifice their all for the glory of Islam. This package has intense appeal among a narrow spectrum of the world's most zealous Muslims. For those of a less cataclysmic temperament, the jihadist message offers escape from the deprivation, despair, and humiliation that is the lot of the vast majority of the world's Muslims. Added to the mix are heavy doses of anti-Americanism and anti-Zionism, both of which strike a vibrant chord throughout the Islamic world. The jihadists have also been skilled in casting their message of violence within Islamic scripture and are quick to note that the only real victories of the Islamic and Palestinian movements have been the products of violence. The experience of Iraq has strengthened this view.

While clever, the jihadists' propaganda war has been going poorly. There are many reasons for this. The vast majority of jihadist victims are Muslims. This sows fear of jihadist violence among potential supporters and justifies counterviolence by Middle Eastern governments. Another problem is the needless excesses of the jihadists. As jihadists' self-analyses candidly admit, killing in both Algeria and Egypt became an end in itself, a senseless pageant of violence for which there could be no Islamic justification.[24]

The jihadists have also been forced to confront the reality that most of the world's Muslims don't want to revert to seventh-century Arabia. The jihadist message has simply been too intolerant for most Muslims. Even those who may have found the tranquil and serene image of seventh-century Arabia appealing have been appalled by the performance of those Islamic states that do exist. The goal of the Prophet Mohammed was to enlighten the masses, not suppress them. The spirit of Islam that produced the dazzling science and art of the golden years of Islam is not the spirit that the jihadists have brought to Afghanistan, Iran, and the Sudan. A more moral society, yes; rule by religious police, no.

Further, the jihadists have suffered from the vagueness of their message. "God is the Solution" targets the frustration of Muslim populations but offers potential supporters nothing of a concrete nature. The jihadists don't have an economic plan, and it is not clear that their vision of education extends beyond religious education. Everything is fuzzy. Indeed, the economic performance of Iran, the world's Islamic theocracy, has been dismal, with 41 percent of Iranians with a better-than-high-school education being unemployed. The unemployment figure among the less educated is 23 percent.[25] Islam has not solved Iran's economic problems, and the mass frustrations that once fueled the Islamic Revolution are now turning on the Islamic leaders of Iran. Far from providing economic solutions, jihadist attacks on Western tourists and other economic targets have deprived millions of Muslims of their livelihoods. Governments are not falling, but Muslims are suffering.

The jihadist message, in sum, has been adequate to keep them in business, but lacks the broad appeal to propel them into power. The moderate Islamic groups, by contrast, have made marked improvement in sharpening their message by placing themselves on the side of the poor, democracy, and economic reform. The jihadists have not kept pace. The strongest weapons in their propaganda arsenal remain condemnation of Israel and anti-Americanism.

THE JIHADIST WAR PLAN OF THE FUTURE: COMPELLING LOGIC FOR ATTACKING AMERICA

The jihadist war plan has succeeded in propelling them onto the global stage, but all is not well. Fears of a jihadist takeover in Algeria and Egypt are fading. Terror shook the secular governments of the Islamic world, but most have survived. America suffered the pain of attack, but the stability of the United States was not called into question. On the contrary, the attacks unleashed a massive and unforeseen display of national solidarity.

The jihadists thus find themselves in a dilemma. They must either alter their war plan or find themselves alienated from the support base on which they depend for a continuance of their jihad. As things currently stand, they can punish, but they cannot win.

As a result, the jihadists now have three basic choices: to continue a path of anti-Muslim violence that has become counterproductive, to shift to a strategy of nonviolence that would leave them virtually indistinguishable from the Muslim Brotherhood and Hizbullah, or to shift to a war plan that limits violence to American, European, and Israeli targets. Violence against Muslims would be avoided.

Of the three choices, only the option of limiting terrorist attacks to America, Israel and Europe—the axis of evil according to the Islamic movement—possess all of the advantages of the current jihadist strategy with none of the disadvantages. The logic of this position is compelling.

Limiting terrorist attacks to the enemies of Islam allows the jihadists to retain their persona of violence without running afoul of Islamic law or sowing fear and economic despair among much needed supporters. As noted earlier, even establishment preachers support violence against Israel. They cannot, of course, condone violence against the United States, but it is not too hard to read between the lines.

With the stigma of killing Muslims gone, jihadists become heroes, firing the zeal of supporters and exploiting the full range of frustrations and nationalistic emotions that seethe throughout the Islamic world. Jihadist rule is not popular, but attacks on the United States and Israel are. By stressing the latter, mass concerns about the harshness of jihadist rule are swept into the background and lose their immediacy. If increased attacks on Americans bring reprisals, so much the better. Muslims would be pushed into the jihadist camp.

Other potential benefits also abound. The end of jihadist violence against Muslims would facilitate cooperation with the Muslim Brotherhood and other more moderate groups in the Islamic world and would quell accusations that the jihadists have given the Islamic movement a bad name. This, in turn, would force the governments of the region to ease their pressure on the jihadists and create an environment conducive to their foreign operations. The United States would complain, but would be unlikely to receive more than the usual symbolic gestures of compliance. Should this drive a further wedge between the United States and the secular governments of the Islamic world, the jihadists would praise God.

In much the same manner, the jihadists would no longer be judged by their ability to overthrow the secular governments of the Islamic world. This was long the stated goal of the jihadist movement, and their failure to do so has had a depressing effect on the movement as a whole. Victories against American, European, and Israeli targets would be much easier to come by. Americans, Jews, and Europeans are everywhere. They can't hide and they can't withdraw from their global activities without enormous political and economic sacrifice. All of this buys time for the jihadists while they regroup in the aftermath of September 11 and adjust to the realities of a much harsher world.

Given the above logic, it is very probable that jihadist strategy during the coming decade will focus increasingly on America and its allies. With the United States in retreat, as bin Laden assures his colleagues it will be, everything else will fall into place. Secular governments in the Islamic world will collapse and the jihadists will seize power. The emerging jihadist war plan will also place increased emphasis on psychological warfare as it taunts the United States with an unending stream of cryptic threats and its perpetual game of "where in the world is Osama bin Laden?" Finally, the new jihadist war plan places greater emphasis on working within the broader confines of the Islamic movement. Rather than fighting the Muslim Brotherhood and other moderate Islamic Groups, the jihadists will use the growing popularity of the moderates to extend their own activities.

ONE WAR PLAN OR SEVERAL?

The war plan described above evolved over the course of the past three decades as zeal was tempered by experience. There was no proclamation of a grand plan, but merely the reality of what was possible and what was not. Each jihadist group embraced that part of the war plan most compatible with its capabilities and philosophy. The Islamic Group targeted civilians and tourists; the Holy Jihad specialized in political assassination. The Pakistani jihadists focused on India and Kashmir, Turabi looked to Africa, and bin Laden was obsessed with America and his Saudi homeland. Some groups cooperated with the Shi'a, others did not. Turabi attempted to weave all of the plan's diverse components into his international network, but with mixed results.

The logic of bin Laden's strategy to kill Americans, however compelling, continues to be undermined by deep divisions within the jihadist movement. Hamas and the Palestinian Holy Jihad have gone out of their way to convince Washington that they are not anti-American. They are trying to blunt America's support of Israel, not increase it. Hizbullah, too, remains unconvinced of America's vulnerability and is attempting to avoid an American strike. Egypt's Islamic Group has declared a truce and appears to be retreating from violence. Hamas and the Palestinian Holy Jihad have also been flirting with a truce, hoping to enhance their position in a final settlement with Israel. Still other jihadist groups remain obsessed with local violence. Sunni and Shi'a jihadists continue their internecine conflict in Pakistan. Algerian jihadists are unrelenting in the slaughter of innocent civilians, often destroying complete villages. Watching Algerian television is depressing.

Cooperation within the jihadist movement exists, but on an ad hoc basis and often takes place at the lower levels of the jihadist organizations rather than at the top. There is no giant super-structure of which bin Laden is the commander in chief, but a multitude of diverse groups that cooperate and contract with bin Laden. These divisions impair the mobilization of jihadists resources, as does continuing hostility toward the jihadists within the Islamic world. Muslims are not fond of the United States, but neither are they crazy about the jihadists.

Does this mean that bin Laden has ceased to be a threat to America and its allies? Not at all. It just means that things could be worse. Bin Laden remains a lethal threat to America and that threat will increase if he is able to force a common war plan on the jihadist movement. For the moment, that appears unlikely. There is not a single war plan, but several, each jihadist group picking and choosing from the menu of strategic options that best suits its circumstances. This, in bin Laden's view, is an error.

There can be little doubt that bin Laden's war plan offers the jihadists an intriguing solution to their lagging fortunes within the Islamic world. The pressing questions for both the jihadists and the United States are: Can they do it? Do they have the organizational capacity and support to make this shift in strategy a reality? It is to these topics that we turn next.

NOTES

1. Hala Mustafa, *The Political System and the Islamic Opposition in Egypt* (Cairo: Markaz Al-Mahrusa, 1995), in Arabic; Kemal As-Said Habib, "The Experience of the

Islamic Movement in Egypt," *Al-Manara*, no. 12 (2000), at http://www.almanar.net/issues/12/121.htm (accessed 13 Dec. 2001).

2. Kemal As-Said Habib, "The Experience of the Islamic Movement in Egypt," *Al Manar*, no. 21 (n.d.) http://www.almanar.net/ussues/12/121.htm (accessed 13 Dec. 2001); Mansour Al Zaiyat, "Sharia and Life Series: Islamic Groups and Violence," Al-Jazeera (11 Aug. 2002), in Arabic. Interviewed by Mahir Abdullah.

3. John Pike, interviewee, ABC News, 20 Dec. 2002, at http://www.abc news.go.com/sectons/world/Daily_News/binladenterror_000918.html (accessed 20 Dec. 2002).

4. Yousef Qaradawi, "Violence and the Islamic Groups, Part 1," Al-Jazeera, 7 July 2001. Interviewed by Hamid Al Ansari, in Arabic, at http://www.aljazeera.net/programs/shareea/articles/2001/7/7-7-1.htm (accessed 7 July 2001).

5. Habib, "The Experience of the Islamic Movement in Egypt.

6. After three years of persistent rumors, President Mubarak has officially stated that his son will not succeed him in office. The rumors continue. Gamal Essam El-Din, "It Won't Happen Here," *Al-Ahram Weekly*, 8–14 Jan. 2004, at http://weekly.ahram .org.eg/2004/672/eg2.htm (accessed 9 Jan. 2004).

7. Michael Scott Doran, "The Saudi Paradox," *Foreign Affairs*, Jan/Feb. 2004, at http://www.foreignaffairs.org/ (accessed 1 Jan. 2004).

8. Monte Palmer, *Politics of the Middle East* (Itasca, Ill.: Peacock Publishers/Wadsworth, 2002).

9. Charlotte Denny, "Opec Pledges Flood of Oil in Event of Conflict," *Guardian Unlimited*, 18 Feb. 2003, at http://www.guardian.co.uk/international/story/0,3604,897752,00.html (accessed 18 Feb. 2003).

10. Dore Gold, *Hatred's Kingdom: How Saudi Arabia Supports the New Global Terrorism* (Washington, D.C.: Regnery Publishing, 2003).

11. Herb Keinon, "Israel Gets Smaller Aid Package than Requested," *Jerusalem Post*, 21 Mar. 2003, at http://www.jpost.com/ (accessed 21 Mar. 2003).

12. Barton Gellman, "Cyber-Attacks by Al Qaeda Feared," *Washington Post*, 27 June 2002, at http://www.washingtonpost.com/ac2/wp_dyn/A50765-2002Jun26 (accessed 4 July 2003).

13. "U.S. Officials Poised to Use the Internet as a Lethal Weapon," *al Wasat*, 618 (1 Dec. 2003):1–2.

14. Rory McCarthy, "Professors Fight to Keep Swift on Syllabus as Pakistan's Islamists Target 'Vulgar' Classics," *Guardian Unlimited*, 10 July 2003, at http://www.guardian .co.uk/Pakistan/Story/0,2763,995166,00.html (accessed 10 July 2003).

15. Berween Shoreh, "Another AUC Book Slashed by the Censor," *The Middle East Times* 49 (7 Dec. 1998), 402; Gabrielle Menezes, "The Art of the Ban," *Cairo Times* 7, no. 42 (Jan. 2004).

16. Jef M. Sellers, "Religious Cleansing," *Christianity Today*, 15 Apr. 2003, at http://www.christianitytoday.com/ct/2003/004/27.98.html (accessed 18 July 2003).

17. Nick Fielding and Joe Laurier, "Bin Laden 'Almost Had Uranium Bomb,'" *Times Online-London*, 3 Mar. 2002, at http://www.Sunday-times.co.uk/article/0,1782238 94,00.html (accessed 3 Mar. 2002).

18. Gerard DeVilliers, *Djihad* (Paris: Malko Productions, 2000).

19. Abdel Azim Ramadan, "Fundamentalist Influence in Egypt: The Strategies of the Muslim Brotherhood and the Takfir Groups," in *Fundamentalisms and the State: Remaking Polities, Economies, and Militance, The Fundamentalism Project,* Vol. 3, Martin E. Marty and Scott Appleby, eds. (Chicago: University of Chicago Press, 1993), 152–183.

20. Ian Traynor, "Nuclear Watchdog Fears Terrorist Dirty Bomb after Looting at al-

Tuwaitha," *Guardian Unlimited*, 14 May 2003, at http://www.guardian.co.uk/inter national/story/0,3604,955374,00.html (accessed 15 May 2003).

21. George Jahn, "AP: Nuclear Black Market Is Small, Covert," *Yahoo News*, 2 Feb. 2004, at http://story.news.yahoo.com/news?tmpl + story&cid = 514&e + 5&u = /ap/ 20040202 /ap_on_re_eu/nuclear_black_market.html (accessed 2 Feb. 2002).

22. Barton Gellman, "Al Qaeda Near Biological, Chemical Arms Production," *Washington Post*, 23 Mar. 2003, at http://www.washingtonpost.com/wp-dyn/articles/ A12187-2003Mar22.html (23 Mar. 2003).

23. Yousef Qaradawi, "Violence and the Islamic Groups, Part 1," Al-Jazeera, 2001. Interviewed by Hamid Al Ansari, in Arabic, at http://www.aljazeera.net/programs/ shareea/articles/2001/7/7-7-1.htm (accessed 24 Aug. 2002).

24. The legitimacy of attacks on Israeli civilians has prompted extensive debate within the mainstream Islamic community. The mufti of Egypt issued a *fatwa* saying that the actions of the Palestinian resistance were justified by the severity of Israeli repression. This contradicted an earlier *fatwa* by the grand sheikh of Al-Azhar, the foremost Islamic university in the Muslim world. Both the mufti and the grand sheikh of Al-Azhar, it is interesting to note, are appointed by the Egyptian government. "Mufti of Egypt: Suicide Attacks against Israel Are Legitimate," *Middle East Online*, 6 Dec. 2001, at http://www .middle-east-online.com/ (accessed 7 Dec. 2001), in Arabic; "Islam Allows Jihad with Conditions, Bans Terrorism," *Arabic News*, 12 Dec. 2001, at http://www.arabicnews .com/ansub/Daily/Day/011212/2001121240.html (accessed 22 Mar. 2002).

25. Mansour Al Zaiyat, "Sharia and Life Series: Islamic Groups and Violence," Al-Jazeera (11 Aug. 2002), in Arabic. Interviewed by Mahir Abdullah.

26. Steve Fairbanks and Bill Samii, "Iran: Weak Economy and High Unemployment Worry Tehran," *IPR Strategic Business Information Database*, 30 Apr. 2003, Info-Prod, Middle East Ltd., at http://infotrac-college.thomsonlearning.com/itw/ (accessed 6 Feb. 2004).

6

THE JIHADIST WAR MACHINE

A sound war plan, however well conceived, is not enough to claim victory. The future success of the jihadists will depend to a large degree on their ability to execute their war plan in an effective manner: to recruit and train soldiers; to establish communication and logistic networks; to maintain base camps, weapons depots, and media outlets; and to plant sleeper cells in the heart of enemy territory. This is the stuff of organizations. Bin Laden made his mark in the jihadist world precisely because he was able to create an organization capable of executing his deadly schemes.

The objective of the present chapter, accordingly, is to examine the jihadist war machine. How good is it? What are its strengths and weaknesses? How are these weaknesses best exploited?

ORGANIZING THE JIHADISTS:
THE PYRAMID OF TERROR

How good are the jihadist organizations? Do they have the organizational muscle to carry out their deadly threats against America and the industrialized world? Questions beget questions. How are the jihadists organized? What about their leadership? How skilled and dedicated are their cadres? Can they sustain a prolonged confrontation with the United States, or will they fold under the pressure of an American onslaught? These questions are foremost on the minds of the individuals, groups, and countries that support the jihadists. The jihadists are playing a dangerous game, and no one wants to be on the losing side. These questions are also being asked by the opponents and competitors of the jihadists, for the fate of the jihadists will have much to say about their own futures.

The typical jihadist group is a unique hybrid that blends the organizational structure of a modern bureaucracy with the authority patterns of the priesthood, the opaqueness of an oriental secret society, the cell network of a communist underground, and the honor code of the Mafia. All jihadist organizations are headed by an emir (prince of the believers) or sheikh (learned religious scholar). Titles are important because they establish the right to religious leadership. The emir heads a consultative council consisting of sub-emirs who, in turn, head the various administrative departments required to achieve the mission of the organization. The consultative councils are often large and may have fifty or more members depending on the size of the organization. In such cases, a handful of senior sub-emirs serve as a powerful executive committee or politburo. The consultative council, as the name suggests, is not an exercise in democracy. Opinions are aired and suggestions made, but there are no votes. The voices of powerful sub-emirs, those with a large following within the organization, carry more weight than sub-emirs of lesser stature. The wise emir listens carefully to the views of his sub-emirs and spends a great deal of time assessing the mood of the council. It would be foolhardy to fly in the face of broad opposition, but that is his prerogative.[1] A rough sketch of our view of the typical jihadist organization is provided in figure 6.1.

While the organizational chart of jihadist organizations may resemble that of a modern bureaucracy, the functions of its units reflect their deadly mission and the shadowy environment in which they operate. The religious unit (Council of Islamic Jurisprudence), for example, consists of religious scholars and ensures that the activities of the organization are in conformity with the Koran and Sunna. As noted in the preceding chapter, this is vital. Fighters being asked to sacrifice their lives must be absolutely convinced that their actions are sanctioned by Islamic law. Barring this, they will not reap their reward in heaven. Koranic justification is also vital to convince supporters at all levels that the jihadist cause is just and that the ends justify the most brutal of means, including the slaughter of innocent civilians. This is a difficult task that requires stretching Islamic law to the breaking point.[2]

The military branch is the heart of jihadist groups and is responsible for terrorist operations. In a few cases, they also maintain standing militias. During its prime in the mid-1990s, Algeria's le Groupe islamique armé (GIA), one of the largest and most brutal of jihadist organizations in the Islamic

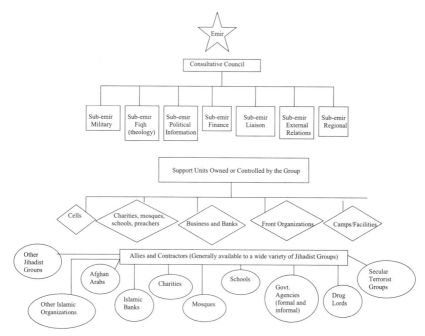

Figure 6.1   Typical Jihadist Organization

world, openly challenged the government on the battlefield. The military wing of the GIA was headed by the national military emir with the support of a variety of advisors and a council of *mujahedeen* (holy warriors). The national command gave way to regional and various local commands, each headed by an emir, and they to a variety of armored patrols, shock units, and suicide squads.[3] In times of crisis, the local units would dissolve into the population while the leadership of the higher units would take to mountain base camps. The Abu Sayyaf group in the Philippines also maintains a standing militia, as does Hizbullah in Lebanon.

With few exceptions, however, the jihadists are unable to match government forces in either numbers or firepower. Rather, the term military is a code word that designates combat as opposed to negotiation. The weapon of choice for the jihadists is terror. The Afghan Arabs enabled bin Laden's al Qaeda network to develop a formidable militia replete with heavy armor and advanced weaponry. Even in this instance, however, the al Qaeda forces merely supplemented the Taliban forces. They were not, of themselves, capable of defeating Afghanistan's heavily armed warlords.[4] The picture is much the same in Chechnya, with Afghan Arabs supporting the indigenous militias. With the collapse of his Afghan base, bin Laden's military wing, including the Afghan Arabs, has reverted to its terrorist strategy.

The political units of jihadist organizations study the political realities of their respective countries and assess the impact of their attacks on both governments and public opinion. They also search for weakness to be exploited, help in the selection of targets, and otherwise serve as an intelligence-gathering agency. The units for external relations and liaisons, in turn, maintain ties with local jihadist groups, foreign branches, exile groups, international networks, and a wide variety of religious organizations and support groups. The latter would certainly include Hizbullah, the Muslim Brotherhood, and friendly charitable organizations. This does not mean that relations are cordial, but they do keep in touch. Jihadist ties with al Qaeda and Hizbullah are particularly important inasmuch as they are a potential source of funding, weapons, and training. Indeed, it is the ability to provide funding, weapons, and training that enables international networks to enlist the support of local groups. The role of the finance unit requires little elaboration. Fund raising is an all-consuming occupation of all jihadist organizations. Cadres have to be supported, the families of martyrs cared for, weapons purchased, bribes paid, base camps established, and vehicles maintained, to mention only the obvious.

Specialized units such as finance and political affairs are paralleled by a regional hierarchy, with each area of operation being headed by a sub-emir. During its heyday in the early 1990s, for example, the GIA divided Algeria into zones, with each zone giving way to provinces and they to armies, phalanges, sections, and finally to groups or local emirates (princedoms). Emirs at each level reported to the emir above them, suggesting that little was left to chance.[5] In case of crisis, emirs at all levels had the capacity to operate independently, presumably following coded messages leaked to the media. The labels may change from organization to organization and country to country, but the principle remains the same.

Al Qaeda: Variations on a Theme

The organization of bin Laden's al Qaeda network followed a similar pattern, albeit on a more complex scale, with zones and regions being allocated on a global rather than a regional scale. As described by Rohan Gunaratna, a former principle investigator of the UN's Terrorism Prevention Branch:

Immediately below the Emir-General in Al Qaeda's structure stands the *shura majlis*, or consultative council, which consists of very experienced members. . . .

Immediately below the *shura majlis* and reporting to it are four operational committees: military; finance and business; *fatwa* and Islamic study; and media and publicity, which ensure the smooth day-to-day running of Al Qaeda, each being headed by an Emir. While the Emir and Deputy Emir have responsibility for each committee, its members also form compartmentalized working groups for special assignments. At times handpicked members of these committees, especially the military conduct special assignments for Osama or for his designated operational commanders. Some members serve in more than one committee or are rotated between them.[6]

Al Qaeda's liaison and logistics were similar to those of a multinational organizations, and it now seems clear that bin Laden's military branch possessed separate units for the development of weapons of mass destruction. Some of bin Laden's chief sub-emirs had their own networks that they affiliated with al Qaeda, much as modern corporations "take over" their smaller competitors. Zawahiri's branch of Egypt's Islamic Jihad, for example, merged with al Qaeda in 2001. A far larger number of groups allied themselves with al Qaeda but retained their own identities and their independence of action. Fazul Rahman, the leader of a coalition of jihadist groups in Bangladesh signed bin Laden's 1998 declaration of war against the United States, as did Zawahiri's branch of the Islamic Jihad, a branch of Egypt's Islamic Group, and Jamiat ul Ulema in Pakistan. Other groups declined the honor, suggesting that they were inclined to keep a distance between themselves and bin Laden. Cooperation yes; subservience no.

Much like modern corporations, bin Laden outsourced much of his work to independent contractors. The 1995 car bomb attack on the National Guard Barracks in Riyadh, Saudi Arabia, that killed seven people, including five Americans, was apparently contracted to the Islamic Movement of Change.[7] The subsequent 1996 attack on the Khobar Towers, according to a five-year investigation by U.S. authorities, was carried out by a Saudi branch of Hizbullah, with technical guidance by representatives of Hizbullah-Lebanon. Fingers were pointed to Iran as the godfather of the Hizbullah movement, but ties to al Qaeda remain a matter of conjecture.[8] The bombing of the USS *Cole* in 2000 was apparently committed by three Yemeni groups enlisted by close aides to bin Laden: the Islamic Army of Aden-Abyan and two previously unknown groups, the Army of Mohammed and the Islamic Deterrence Forces.[9] The Yemenis did the detail work:

setting up living quarters for the al Qaeda advisors, acquiring the boat and trailer used in the bombing, and even planning to film the event from a hillside.[10] The actual planning of the USS *Cole* bombing is attributed to Tawfiq bin Attash (and various aliases), a Yemeni man linked to al Qaeda. He is suspected of playing a role in planning the September 11 attacks. The bombing of the *Cole* itself was attributed to supporters of al Qaeda.[11] In much the same manner, the Islamic Army for the Liberation of the Holy Places claimed responsibility for the 1998 bombings of the American embassies in Kenya and Tanzania. A man who claimed bin Laden was his leader admitted to providing technical and logistical support to the bombers.[12]

The same pattern continues to repeat itself in the post–September 11 era. In Bali, the group Jemaah Islamiya claimed responsibility for the 2002 bombing that killed more than 200 people. The Imam Samudra of the Jemaah Islamiya claimed his group robbed jewelry stores to finance the bombings. It was reported that he spent time in Afghanistan in the 1990s where he learned bomb-making skills.[13] He probably had al Qaeda contacts, but the Pakistani group HuM also had extensive training camps in the region and was one of the main jihadist groups funded by the CIA.[14] Credit for the 2003 Moroccan bombings has been shared between the Islamist group Assirat al Moustaquim (The Religious Path) and the extremist group Salafia Jihadia. All fifty suspects arrested had ties with the Salafist movement, which reportedly has ties with al Qaeda. Initial reports indicated that the perpetrators of the attack were recently formed slum groups who resembled thugs more than religious devotees. Later reports seemed to implicate bin Laden, but his role may have been inspiration rather than guidance.[15] The mujahedeen in the Arabian Peninsula claimed responsibility for the 2003 bombing of the housing compound in Saudi Arabia. Saudi officials claim the terrorists were receiving orders from bin Laden, but to date the details remain fuzzy.[16]

Except for the September 11 attacks on America, then, al Qaeda provided funds and technical support, but local groups carried out the attacks. This pattern of loose affiliations and outsourcing makes it difficult to attribute blame with any degree of accuracy. After summarizing a long history of jihadist attacks on American and allied targets, a senior U.S. intelligence officer acknowledges that in most cases it is difficult to trace a clear line of responsibility to bin Laden. This, he continues, misses the point. "What is important is that the attacks fit the thematic parameters bin Laden has set for the 'guerrilla' war he is waging and inciting against the Crusaders and 'apostate' Muslim regimes. At a minimum, the attacks . . . suggest bin Laden's views and aspirations are shared by Islamists in many areas of the world."[17]

This loose pattern of affiliations, outsourcing, and inspiration also makes it difficult to give a precise description of what al Qaeda, as presently constituted, looks like. In the view of Rohan Gunaratna, a former principle investigator of the UN's Terrorism Prevention Branch, al Qaeda was forged from 3,000 of the best and brightest of the 10,000 to 100,000 jihadists who passed through al Qaeda training camps in the decade preceding the September 11 attacks on America.[18] They are distributed on a global basis and even with arrests, remain an ever-present threat to the United States and its allies. Jason Burke, the chief reporter of *The Observer* (London), views al Qaeda as a tight group of associates who have been with bin Laden since the early 1980s. They plan and pay, but operations are carried out by "scores of other militant Islamic groups around the world which have, or had, some kind of relationship with bin Laden or figures connected to him. But imagining that all these groups were all created or run by bin Laden is to denigrate the particular local factors that led to their emergence."[19] It is this pattern of affiliations and outsourcing, in his view, that provides the al Qaeda with the image of being a grand international network. Peter Bergen, a journalist and author of the book *Holy War, Inc.*, likens al Qaeda to a large holding company, with units being added and spun off as the need of the moment dictate.

Like all analogies, the comparison of jihadist groups to a modern corporation is both insightful and deceptive. The organizational chart of the typical jihadist group does, indeed, resemble that of a modern corporation with its CEOs and layers of executives. This modern organizational framework provides the jihadists with the specialization they require to confront the power of modern governments, be they the secular regimes of the region or the United States and its allies.

There are, however, differences. The organizational structure of the jihadists reflects an all-consuming concern for secrecy and security, with few individuals in a position to identify more than a minor part of the organization. The structure of jihadist organizations also anticipates massive reprisals and can readily convert into a crisis mode until the pressure eases.

The essence of the jihadist organization, however, lies elsewhere. It is not the organizational framework of the jihadists that make them a lethal threat to America, but their patterns of leadership and the zeal of their employees. Neither follows the normal corporate pattern. Few Western

CEOs court martyrdom by fire; few employees work for peanuts, endure excruciating hardships, and are willing to die for the firm. The jihadists are not about profits. They are about conversion, conquest, and destruction. But, above all, they are about personal salvation. A modern organizational structure is merely a means to an end. To focus on outward appearances is to profoundly miss the point.

LEADERSHIP IN JIHADIST ORGANIZATIONS

The authority that a jihadist emir exercises over his followers is a combination of religious authority and charismatic authority. Simple religious authority is based on the desire of individuals to gain salvation by following the rules of their religion be it Islam, Christianity, or any other faith. Clergy are obeyed because of their superior knowledge of the faith and their ability to guide believers along the path of salvation. Many people, however, want more than guidance. They want a religious leader who possesses a clear sign of God's blessing, a leader who can work miracles and lead them to salvation. Leaders who possess God's blessing are said to be charismatic. They possess the gift of grace. When such a religious leader appears, the zealous follow him slavishly. This is most assuredly the case of the jihadists and their supporters.

Of course, one does not have to be a holy man to have the gift of grace. Indeed, people under stress or living in unsettled times have always sought a hero or savior to lead them to salvation. More often than not, the desire for a savior has led to myth building, as people created heroes to provide them with a sense of security. Max Weber, one of the founding fathers of modern social science, thus coined the word charisma.

> Charisma refers to a certain quality of individual's personality by which he is set apart from ordinary men and treated as endowed with supernatural, superhuman or at least specifically exceptional powers and qualities. . . . In primitive circumstances this peculiar kind of deference is paid to prophets, to people with a reputation for therapeutic or legal wisdom, to leaders of the hunt, and heroes in war. It is very often thought of as resting on magical powers.[20]

Hitler's mass rallies demonstrated the phenomenal power of a charismatic leader to guide a nation on the verge of collapse. People followed a maniac because they were desperate. As Hans Gerth sets the scene:

Persons whose career expectations are frustrated or who suffer losses in status or income in the intensive vocational competition of modern capitalism should be especially likely to accept the belief in the charismatic leader. Those placed on the disadvantaged side of life always tend to be interested in some sort of salvation which breaks through the routines associated with their deprivation. Such "unsuccessful" persons were to be found in every stratum of German society. Princes without thrones, indebted and subsidized landlords, indebted farmers, virtually bankrupt industrialists, impoverished shopkeepers and artisans, doctors without patients, lawyers without clients, writers without readers, unemployed teachers, and unemployed manual and white-collar workers joined the movement. National Socialism as salvationary movement exercised an especially strong attraction on the "old" and "new" middle classes, especially in those strata where substantive rationality is least developed, and will be most highly represented among those seeking salvation by quasi-miraculous means—or at least by methods which break through the routines which account for their deprivation.[21]

The people of the Islamic world are equally distraught. Most are poor and oppressed and have little hope for a better future. It is only natural for them to seek salvation in their religion. That, after all, is the message of Christianity as well as Islam. It is also natural for them to seek a charismatic religious leader capable of leading them to the Promised Land. This is particularly true of the jihadists. Jihadists and their supporters are "true believers" who have an abiding need to identify with a charismatic religious leader capable of promising salvation. Perhaps this is due to the intensity of their religious training. It would also seem to have a great deal to do with the fears and anxieties that permeate the region as well as a culture that stresses blind obedience to the father.[22] In a recent al-Jazeera interview, Mansour Zayat, perhaps the most famous of Egypt's Islamic lawyers, did his best to explain the relationship between the emir of a jihadist group and his followers. The emir in question was Abdul Rahman, the blind sheikh now incarcerated in a U.S. prison for his role in the 1993 bombing of the World Trade Center.

Interviewer: What did the Grand Sheikh Abdul Rahman have to say about the truce declared in June of 1997?

Zayat: He learned of the initiative in prison in the U.S. He supported it a few days later saying, "They are youth who believe in who raised them." Only the Sheikhs of the Islamic Group can initiate actions. That is because of the deep esteem in which they are held by their sons [disciples], supporters and admirers. It is much like a military commander gives orders to his soldiers. Only the sheikhs have that power. No one else. . . .

Interviewer: I didn't ask about the qualities of a leader, but about the military nature of the organization. . . . This relationship that makes an ordinary individual give his absolute loyalty—I don't want to say blind loyalty—to a man who is not a political leader. Isn't this dangerous even at the level of an Islamic state? Doesn't it create a problem when youth become so religious that they will consciously obey any order unto death? . . .

Zayat: No it is not a military relationship. . . . It is spiritual. Maybe it is a relationship of love. It is a relationship of confidence. There are so many non-military considerations in the relationship.[23]

It was the fusion of religious authority and charisma that enabled the Ayatollah Khomeini to mobilize the Iranian people against the Shah of Iran, and it was the same power that enabled his Islamic Revolution to inflame the Middle East. Far from being a mere grand ayatollah, the most exalted of religious ranks in Shi'a Islam, the Ayatollah Khomeini was viewed by many of his followers as the living embodiment of the Hidden Imam, or *marja-i-taqlid uzma*. This vision was justified by his smiting of the Shah, that most venerable of American allies. Lest more miracles be needed, U.S. helicopters sent to rescue American hostages captured by overzealous revolutionaries were mystically felled by sand in their engines, the stuff of miracles indeed.

The power of charismatic leaders such as Khomeini to sway the masses can only be understood with the realization that the relationship between a leader and his followers is a two-way street.[24] Khomeini's religious credentials had established him as an agent of the Hidden Imam and object of emulation, while his years of revolutionary struggle had transformed him into a folk hero most assuredly blessed by God. This, however, was only part of the equation. The second part of the equation was that the Iranian masses were searching for a divinely inspired leader to lead them from the social, economic, and political decay of the Shah's regime. Many were willing to obey Khomeini's orders unto death because they believed in his mystical powers. Indeed, mass folklore elevated Khomeini to the stature of a minor deity precisely because they wanted a hero to believe in.[25] Twenty-five years later, his heirs perpetuate the myth of his sainthood in the hope that his charisma will shore up their flagging popularity. They have little choice. The Ayatollah Khomeini's successor, Ayatollah Khamenei, is neither charismatic nor a gifted religious scholar.[26] On the contrary, he was a lesser cleric rushed to the position of supreme guide in haste and compromise. There is no magic, and the Islamic Revolution has suffered accordingly.

Khomeini is the model that other jihadist leaders aspire to. Bin Laden has become a mythical folk hero of gigantic proportions, but lacks the religious profundity of Khomeini. He has adopted the title of sheikh, but he is not a religious scholar. This fine point has been lost in the shuffle. The myth of bin Laden has become larger than life and fuels the jihadist movement of today much as the myth of Khomeini fueled the Islamic Revolution of the 1980s. Even his ability to escape the power of the United States has become the stuff of miracles. Everyone, including the Americans, is waiting for the next blow. In the meantime, psychological warfare has reached new levels. Each new terrorist alert in the United States and Europe has become a psychological victory in this most vicious game of cat and mouse.

Charismatic leadership, however, is only part of the jihadists' story. Religious authority is equally important. It is the religious authority of jihadist leaders that enables them to issue *fatwas* about what is or is not permissible in Islamic law. These *fatwas* are binding on the members of the group and are a key element in the power of the emir. As there are lots of religious leaders, there are lots of *fatwas,* many of which are contradictory. Some senior religious leaders have issued *fatwas* decrying the killing of innocent civilians. Others have embraced the jihadist position, decreeing that the killing of civilians is justified as long as it is necessary to protect the Islamic faith. The authority of *fatwas,* as the above example suggests, is binding only on the followers of the religious leader who issued it. The more popular the religious leader, the more powerful his *fatwas.* The *fatwas* of Ayatollah Khomeini became law in Iran and much of the Shi'a world.

Bin Laden has issued a variety of *fatwas* supporting his war against the United States, but even senior religious leaders who support his quest suggest that he lacks sufficient religious credentials to do so. Some have resolved the matter by issuing parallel *fatwas* of their own.[27] For bin Laden, however, it is his followers that count. In their view, bin Laden's successes are clear proof that he is divinely inspired. A sign of God's blessing supercedes theology.

Possessing mystical religious credentials also enables jihadist leaders to promise entry to paradise for those willing to risk their lives in the service to their faith. It is this power, more than any other that enables the jihadists to recruit suicide bombers. Jihadist emirs have picked up this practice from the Shi'a despite the fact that Sunni Islam rejects the notion that high priests possess such mystical powers. The end, in their view, justifies the means.

In much the same manner, mystical religious credentials give jihadist leaders the power to excommunicate their opponents by branding them as *kafirs*. Thus, the leader of the Algerian GIA, that most bloody of jihadist organizations, used this principle to justify the mass killing of innocent Algerians.[28] By declaring them nonbelievers, he had signed their death warrant.

The jihadist style of leadership clearly has its advantages. CEOs and generals can praise, encourage, and bully, but they cannot guarantee a place in heaven nor can they dispatch errant employees to hell. Profit seeking is based on greed and status, while success is reflected in the ostentatious display of wealth. Jihadism, in contrast, is based on the desire for salvation; status is gained by sacrifice and death. It's a whole different ball game.

The Downside of Jihadist Authority Patterns

Do the greater motivational advantages of jihadist leaders give them an insurmountable advantage in dealing with the West? Not at all. Jihadists simply have a different set of problems, many of which can easily be exploited in the war on terror. The effectiveness of a jihadist leader is proportional to his ability to establish absolute spiritual and psychological dominance over his followers. To be effective, he must convince them that he is, indeed, a divinely inspired vicar of the Prophet Mohammed. Barring this, his orders will be debated and his ranks depleted with defections as erstwhile followers seek a more inspired guide.

The founding fathers of jihadist organizations were invariably individuals of intense zeal and spirituality who, in the best biblical traditions, attracted a small group of disciples. As their movements grew, they consolidated their spiritual authority by launching ever-bolder raids against the infidel, trials by fire that demonstrated their prowess as generals and conveyed the impression of divine guidance. Mullah Omar, the leader of the Taliban, had established his intellectual and spiritual leadership among his student followers and consolidated that authority by leading the Taliban to victory after victory in the Afghan war against the Soviets.[29] To avoid any doubt, he symbolized his authority by wrapping himself in the cloak of the Prophet Mohammed, the most venerable of Afghanistan religious treasures.[30]

In the case of bin Laden, the struggle for supremacy did not appear to be in issue. He was the hero of Afghanistan and Somalia and the probable author of the attacks on the American troops in Saudi Arabia. Impeccable credentials indeed. He had also chosen his subordinates with great care, most of whom he had become acquainted with in Afghanistan or during his apprenticeship under Turabi. Bin Laden was influenced by his lieutenants, many of whom were renowned for their intellect and depth of religious knowledge, but it was he who brought all of the pieces together.[31] It was also he alone who had total knowledge of the al Qaeda network. As such, he could listen without being outflanked. But what happens when bin Laden is gone? He may become a saint in the eyes of his followers, but who will pick up the pieces?

The leadership of jihadist organizations also has its practical problems. The emir is the pope. He serves for life and remains inviolable. The doctrine of the organization is the religiously inspired vision of the founder. Apostasies cannot be tolerated, and those prone to sedition have to be purged. To avoid potential misunderstandings, disciples are kept at arms length lest they steal the glory of the leader. Bin Laden has become a household word, but few people can name even one of his lieutenants. Information is carefully guarded and shared with subordinates selectively and sparingly. Only the leader has the full picture, and even information shared with subordinates may be of questionable quality or explicitly designed to create insecurities within the command structure. The practice of keeping potential competitors at arm's length is not unique to the jihadists but pervades all Arab organizations.[32]

All of the flaws inherent in the charismatic style of leadership are amplified by the process of succession. It is not easy to transfer God's special blessing, the gift of grace, to a subordinate who has been kept at arms length. Technically, selection of a new leader is accomplished by a vote of some sort among the dominant sub-emirs sitting as the *shura* (consultative) council. The aura, however, is gone. There is also the prickly matter of ideological conflict (for example, moderates versus conservatives), personal jealousies, and turf wars, all of which had been kept under control, if not encouraged, by the supreme guide. All now burst into the open, with the losers either defecting with their personal entourage or biding their time while they wait for the opportunity to seize control of the movement. The primary goal of the newly proclaimed emir, for his part, is to consolidate his authority, a task best achieved by putting his own people in key positions. The position of the losers is further threatened, as is the potential for defections.

The selection process often finds the nod going to the more zealous of the fallen leaders' lieutenants, for zeal is the foundation of jihadist organizations.[33] Indeed, the jihadist movement was born out of impatience with the caution of the Muslim Brotherhood. The very concept of jihad implies action.

All signs suggest that al Qaeda may be going through a similar process.

Bin Laden may or may not be alive, but al Qaeda has gone to great lengths to assure the world that he is. In part, this is psychological warfare. Myth building buoys supporters, keeps al Qaeda in the public eye, and even sparks imitators. All drive Western security agencies crazy. What happens if he is dead? He has disappeared from view, and the authenticity of bin Laden tapes promising new attacks is a matter of great controversy.

Zawahiri is often cited as being bin Laden's second in command, but this, too, is a matter of speculation. Zawahiri is bin Laden's personal physician and, by all accounts, played a major role in shaping bin Laden's philosophy of jihad.[34] These, however, are personal ties and do not convey the power to control other emirs once bin Laden has disappeared. Each emir has his own power base and each, in all probability, aspires for dominance. It is also unlikely that Zawahiri possesses the keys to bin Laden's financial network, the complexities of which are mind boggling. He can control his own faction within al Qaeda, but probably not much more. This is a question of jealously. It is also a question of Zawahiri's prosaic religious credentials and relative invisibility. It is bin Laden who has taken the credit for his reputed genius. It is more than likely, accordingly, that the loss of bin Laden will have a depressing effect on the jihadist movement, much as the loss of the Ayatollah Khomeini led to confusion in Iran and the Shi'a world. Bin Laden will continue to inspire, but he will not continue to lead.

Other leadership problems abound. Security forces have exacted a heavy toll on the jihadist leadership. Some have been killed, while others have been arrested or forced into exile. This has disrupted the chain of command within jihadist organizations, spawned turf wars, and raised serious questions concerning precisely who is in charge.[35] In the case of the Islamic Group and Egyptian Jihad, Egypt's two largest jihadist organizations, the leadership is split three ways between the troops on the ground, those imprisoned, and those in exile, each with differing concepts of the strategy to be pursued.[36] While those in exile tend toward theoretical reflection born of isolation and experience, the troops are taking the risks and making battleground decisions based on the realities of the moment.

The problem, however, is deeper. The culture of Islamic countries places a premium on age, with the older jihadist leaders demanding deference due to age, experience, and prior sacrifice. The younger leaders, having tasted power, are anxious to set the world on fire, both literally and figuratively. Many of the younger jihadist leaders simply find the orders of their superiors, presumably smuggled from the jail via Islamic lawyers, to be out of touch with the realities on the ground. The younger leaders also want more power. The veterans are reluctant to grant it.

While generational tensions within the jihadist organizations have been noted for some time, the crisis came to a head in 2002, when the imprisoned leaders of the Islamic Group formally renounced violence. The younger jihadist leadership as well as many exiles slammed the decision and vowed to continue their jihad. This gave the appearance that the older leadership, while respected, had lost control of their organizations.[37] Up to now, however, the truce has held.

The core of the jihadists' leadership problems, then, is the intense personalization of relationships between leaders and followers. Unlike modern corporations or armies in which reasonably similar cogs can be moved from one position to the next based on education and experience, authority patterns among the jihadists are overwhelmingly dependent on emotion, zeal, and psychological dominance. Individuals are not subservient to the institution. They are subservient to a particular leader. Replacements are found, but it takes time to establish new patterns of trust and loyalty. In the meantime, the strength of the organization is weakened. Also weakened are the complex communication systems of the jihadists, most of which rely heavily on personal contacts. Leadership transitions in the West are often difficult, but not to the same degree.

Decision Making in Jihadist Organizations

The personalization of leadership, in turn, influences the ways in which jihadist organizations make decisions. Wise and perceptive leaders can act with speed and alacrity to seize the moment and strike with force at their enemies. Indeed, pressure to demonstrate their *baraka* (divine blessing) forces action, lest cadres and supporters become impatient and shift their loyalties to new and more dynamic emirs. Ironically, the aura of bin Laden has enabled him to play a waiting game, abetted by propaganda victories and a steady stream of strikes against isolated Western targets.[38] Pressure for a major strike, however, is mounting. Charisma requires that the hero remain active. Followers are looking for signs of God's continued blessing, not laurels.

This is just the beginning of the jihadists' problems. The wisdom of emirs is not guaranteed, and few checks exist to curb errant whims. Emirs who speak with the inspiration of God are not easily defied. They also make poor listeners, inspiration surpassing experience and advice. In much the same manner, self-critiques of the jihadists' problems have stressed their reluctance to build on the experience of others. This problem is now being alleviated by the greater communication with the jihadist movement and finds expression in the wholesale adoption of Shi'a tactics by the Sunni jihadists. Nevertheless, many jihadist groups continue to go their own way, ignoring the pitfalls of others. The best example of this is the continuing attacks on Muslims in Algeria and elsewhere.

Emirs, like princes throughout history, have also found cooperation difficult. They meet and negotiate, but they are reluctant to relinquish sovereignty to competitors. Alliances are made, but are fragile. Fear and distrust characterizes all Middle Eastern organizations, and the jihadists are no exception. Allies are essential, but few are trusted. Exceptional leaders such as the Ayatollah Khomeini and bin Laden can forge broad alliances, but they are few and their alliances seldom survive their passing. Indeed, even moderate voices in the Islamic movement are now praying for the emergence of a charismatic Sunni cleric similar to the Ayatollah Khomeini to galvanize the Islamic movement.[39] Given the above array of problems, charismatic decision making often results in ill-conceived projects that squander resources and alienate public support. Even the Ayatollah Khomeini made errors of judgment, the most cataclysmic of which was his refusal of Saddam Hussein's 1982 offer of peace in the Iran/Iraq War. The Iraqis were in retreat, and acceptance of Hussein's peace offer would have enabled the Ayatollah to bilk Saudi Arabia and Kuwait for billions of dollars in war reparations. Both Saudi Arabia and Kuwait had helped finance the war and had little option but to buy their way out of a venture that had gone terribly wrong. Similarly, it was errors by the jihadist emirs, particularly their excessive use of violence against Muslims, that alienated their supporters and placed them on the defensive. These same errors have kept the jihadists from developing a strong follow-up capacity that would enable them to better capitalize on their victories. Indeed, the whole pattern of jihadist history has been one of daring attacks with little follow-up. This will not achieve their goal.

The vulnerabilities inherent in the jihadist leadership style suggest that the easiest way to deal with their organizations may be to target their leaders at all levels. The arrest of senior leaders disrupts decision making; the arrest of midlevel leaders disrupts operations. Unlike modern organizations, jihadist organizations do not just keep on going. They revive, but it is an agonizing and debilitating process that seriously depletes the destructive capacity of the organization. Al Qaeda now shows signs of going through this process.

THE JIHADIST SOLDIERS: WHO ARE THEY, WHAT MOTIVATES THEM, AND HOW GOOD ARE THEY?

In the final analysis, it is the cadres who are the core of any organization. Leaders plan; cadres execute. Elegant organizational structures and gifted generals go for naught if the troops can't get the job done. Are cadres the strength of jihadist organizations or a source of weakness to be exploited by America in its war on terror? Again, questions beget questions. Where do the jihadist cadres come from? What drives them? How are they trained and recruited? How good is their discipline and morale?

Where do jihadist cadres come from? The answer is simple: everywhere. Most are Muslims of Middle Eastern or Pakistani origin, but the Islamic populations of Bangladesh, Indonesia, and Malaysia are all well represented, as are Muslims from sub-Saharan Africa, Central Asia (the former USSR), Europe, and North America.

One reason that it is so difficult to establish a jihadist profile is that individuals migrate to the jihadist cause for different reasons. The ranks of jihadists who ignited the jihadist movement in Egypt included doctors, engineers, and other professionals. Many of the perpetrators of September 11 were the scions of wealthy Saudi families, albeit families of Yemeni or Palestinian origin. Some seethed with frustration about a corrupt regime; others appeared to be seeking greater meaning for otherwise hollow lives. Many of the jihadists who fueled the reign of terror in Algeria were little more than street thugs organized into religious gangs by local emirs.[40] Richard Reid, the infamous shoe bomber, was a lonesome drifter who sought belonging within the confines of a jihadist mosque.[41] Much of the same appears to be true of Americans fighting with bin Laden in Afghanistan. The jihadists have also crossed the gender line, vastly expanding the size of the terrorist pool with female suicide bombers. If the leaders are well educated, most of the rank and file is drawn from the poor and destitute. Death in the name of God is their path to salvation.

Jihadists are recruited in a wide variety of venues, including Islamic student associations, mosques, cafes, prisons, and Islamic welfare centers. Those displaying the requisite zeal are gradually introduced into the rituals of the jihadists. The poor are provided with books and clothes, the lonely with belonging, the sinners with the hope of redemption, and the angry with outlets for their wrath. Algerian police psychologists suggest that many recruits are attempting to escape the scorn of low social status by establishing a new identity. Others yearn for power and view themselves as heroes of Islam or movie stars. Weapons and killing accentuate the thrill of power. In a few cases, the jihadists have simply been kidnapped and forced into service. Most accentuate their new identity by assuming a heroic name or referring to themselves as the father of a male child. Even unmarried jihadists assume this practice, which has the added advantage of confusing the police.[42] Jihadist recruiters are superb psychologists who spend hours ministering to the psychological needs of their recruits and assessing their psychological vulnerabilities.

In reality, the job of the jihadist recruiter is probably not that difficult. Incidental evidence suggests that most recruits already lean toward an authoritarian environment if not violence. Many recruits, inflamed by the Soviet attack on Islamic Afghanistan and the lure of everlasting salvation, sought out jihadist organizations and flocked to the ranks of the Afghan Arabs. Others were ferried to Afghanistan by the Muslim Brotherhood, Hizbullah or, as in the case of Saudi Arabia, by establishment mosques. Still other recruits have been introduced to the jihadists by friends or family. Many of the female jihadists are the wives or daughters of jihadists. Whatever the case, we could find no evidence suggesting that the supply of potential recruits was diminishing.

Once they have entered the ranks of the jihadists, recruits undergo an intense blend of religious indoctrination and technical training, much of the latter focusing on their role in terrorist operations. Of the two, religious indoctrination is probably the most important, for it is religious zeal and the promise of eternal salvation that drives the jihadist cadre. All doubts about the sanctity of their mission must be banished from their minds. To question that their mission has been ordained by God is to vacillate in the face of duty. It is also to question the authority of the emir and to jeopardize discipline within the jihadist organization. Doubt breeds disaster. Faith must also weld individuals from diverse backgrounds into a cohesive force, surmounting the fears, jealousies, and personality conflicts that are the bane of all organizations in the Middle East.

Skill training is more prosaic and resembles training traditionally received by terrorists and guerilla groups throughout the modern era. Bin Laden's training manuals differed little from U.S. intelligence manuals provided for use in the Afghan war against the Soviets. Indeed, Western security experts seized an eleven-volume encyclopedia of terror in the sweep of suspected al Qaeda sites in the aftermath of the September 11 attacks. Some 6,000 plus pages in length, the encyclopedia is a self-help guide to the construction of everything from pipe-bombs and booby traps to demolition of bridges and stadiums.[43] Also covered are first aid, map reading, weapons repair, construction of mines and mine fields, interrogation, sabotage, and the principles of war, including psychological warfare. Particularly frightening was the volume discussing the use of biochemical agents, including anthrax and ricin, both of which have been used by jihadist groups in the post–September 11 era. Ricin is a highly toxic chemical that, according to the *London Times*, was "used on the tip of an umbrella by a Bulgarian secret service agent to kill the dissident Georgy Markov in London in 1978."[44] Few areas of the jihadist war plan described in chapter 5 are left untouched.

The encyclopedia was disseminated in both book and CD format and was dedicated to bin-Laden and Abdullah Azzam, bin-Laden's mentor in Afghanistan. A shorter training guide, entitled *Military Studies in the Jihad against Tyrants*, was seized in London in May 2000. Along with instructions on explosives, it advises potential terrorists on ways to assimilate in Western culture. The *New York Times* describes the volume, some 180 pages in length, as "part philosophical treatise, part training guide, part 'Spy vs. Spy' from a back issue of *Mad Magazine*."[45] The manual, with "Do Not Remove" stamped on the cover, was seized in a jihadist guesthouse.

Western experts have played down the significance of the training manuals, suggesting all of the materials that they contain are freely available on the Internet. One U.S. expert notes that "a visit to the U.S. Army's website offers scores of publicly available field manuals on everything from conducting psychological operations to sniper training and how to install Claymore anti-personnel mines.[46] The web also provides instructions for building rockets for under $3,000 and once contained instructions for building an atomic bomb. The latter instructions were provided by a college student and are now no longer available online.

Prosaic as it may be, the training manuals speak volumes about the capacity of al Qaeda and other jihadist groups to inflict devastating damage on America and its allies. Brighter recruits are also sent abroad for more specialized training, the United States and Britain long being the venue of choice. That now is proving more difficult.

How Good Are the Jihadist Cadres?

The strength of jihadist cadres is their zeal. Indeed, it is doubtful that the personnel of any other organization on earth can match the dedication and zeal of the jihadist cadres. They are ready to die for their cause and may actively court death. The jihadists are also easily motivated. They are look-ing for salvation and openly seek the reassurance of their emirs. Secular organizations spend millions on motivational consultants with far less suc-cess. Jihadists want to succeed in their deadly task and are presumably anx-ious to acquire the necessary skills.

The jihadists also benefit from the diversity of their personnel. Aside from a rarity of blue eyes and blanched skin, the jihadists do not fit a com-mon profile, a problem compounded by the growing number of East Asian, African, and female jihadists. A broad mix of skin colors, gender, training, and socioeconomic backgrounds makes it increasingly easy for the jihadist leadership to match personnel to the country and task at hand.

For all their zeal and sacrifice, the attitudes and work habits of the jihadists personnel are seriously flawed. In part, the problems besetting the jihadists are those that beset virtually all Middle Eastern organizations. Other problems reflect the venality of human nature, and still others are unique to the jihadist venture.

In the first category of problems is the general malaise that pervades virtually all Middle Eastern organizations: Fear, loathing, and distrust are everywhere. Similar organizational tensions are illustrated in the somewhat humorous description of life in an Egyptian office. For those of serious pur-pose, the pervasiveness of this behavior is not a laughing matter.

> No sooner is an official promoted to the post of manager than he ceases to accomplish any constructive work. His primary concern is to receive the compliments indiscriminately leveled at him from every quarter, and to smile with condescending magnanimity at the servile flattery lavished at him by his former colleagues.
>
> Such a state of affairs has naturally developed out of a corrupt system of bureaucracy fostered and consolidated over the years, as a result of a deeply-rooted fear in the hearts of juniors towards their superiors. Managers have actually capitalized on this fear in order to force more submission and humility on already humble juniors and to extort from them every possible kind of service and every conceivable kind of flattery.
>
> With such material and moral accouterments adorning the post of manager, it is only natural that officials should be vying with one another to attain this post through all the means available, not excluding hypocrisy, bribery, backbiting, double-dealing and deception.[47]

Tensions within Middle Eastern organizations are eased by friendship rituals, the most prominent of which is the cigarette ritual. Colleagues sit around, sipping coffee or strong tea laced with sugar, offering each other cigarettes. There is seldom a need to exchange cigarettes, for everyone has some. The need is for an act of sharing. No one is fooled, but things go easier, at least until someone leaves the room and the gossip starts. The principle is not that different in the United States, but the bite is in the degree.

To survive in this environment, employees attach themselves to a patron or sub-emir capable of looking after their interests. The deal is a simple one: They support the sub-emir and the sub-emir looks after their interests and facilitates their advancement. The patron needs people in critical places. They are his people and support him in his turf wars with other sub-emirs. If he wins, they win. If he bolts the organization in a test of wills, most of his supporters will also bolt, for their position in the parent organization has been compromised. If the sub-emir falls by the wayside, his clients have to scramble for a new patron, not a pleasant task for those who have bet on the wrong horse. This is not to suggest that patron-client networks are forged in iron, for an emir with fading power may find that his supplicants have gone elsewhere. One has to survive.

The result of this situation is that jihadist organizations tend to represent a mosaic of personal networks that reach their apogee in the grand emir. Loyalty to the organization tends to become secondary to the loyalty of the network. Clashes of policy and personality among the sub-emirs reverberate throughout the organization, sapping its cohesiveness. In some instances, conflict among rival patron-client networks leads to open violence.

This brings us to a second category of personnel problem decried by the jihadists in their self-analyses, that of the human failings of their cadres. Jihadists may be purer of heart than the average individual but, for all of their religious indoctrination, they remain human. Jealousy, greed, pride, and the lust for power pervades jihadist organizations much as it pervades most human organizations.[48] Even one of bin Laden's key lieutenants was caught with his hand in the till. The jihadists, however, can less afford the consequences of human frailty than most other organizations. Secrecy requires they run a tight ship, and even minor glitches can spell disaster for a jihadist cell.

If the above problems apply to virtually all Middle Eastern organizations, the jihadists also have their own unique cross to bear, that of the overzealousness of their cadres. The same zeal that propelled the jihadists into the world arena possessed a cruel underside that saw killing become an end in itself. The excesses of the jihadists rank and file have pushed potential supporters away from the jihadists, and, in the eyes of many, justified gov-

ernmental efforts to crush them. It was the jihadists, rather than the government, who had become the danger. Indeed, the entire Islamic movement
was in danger of becoming discredited.

The zeal of the rank and file has also made it difficult for the leadership
to bide its time and play a waiting game. The troops demand action. Emirs
who preach moderation find their ranks depleted as zealots flock to their
more animated competitors. This has led to hasty and unwise decisions as
divinely inspired emirs have found themselves running to keep ahead of
their troops.

In much the same manner, the zeal of cadres defies compromise or
even a willingness to adapt to the new realities imposed by the war on terror. The jihadist creed is founded on the fundamental belief that God will
provide. There is no need for compromise. Recklessness and daring become
substitutes for prudence and rational behavior.

It would also be a mistake to assume that zeal is uniformly intense
across the spectrum of jihadist organizations. An infinitesimal number of
jihadists have actually sacrificed everything to join the ranks of the Afghan
Arabs or have willingly sacrificed their lives in suicide attacks. Both the
Egyptian and the Palestinian jihadists are now experimenting with truces
while they search for a strategy that fits the new realities imposed on them
by the war on terror. It also appears that many of the September 11 hijackers
did not fully understand that they had embarked on a suicide mission. A
dangerous mission, yes; suicide no. Mohammed al'Owhali, a member of the
al Qaeda team sent to destroy the American Embassy in Nairobi, got cold
feet at the last moment and started running. He survived the bombing and
is now in a U.S. prison serving a life sentence without parole.[49] Suicide
bombers, the ultimate weapon of the jihadists, are very scarce resources who
must be carefully nourished and allocated with care.

Collectively, the above mix of personnel problems has created a debilitating crisis of morale within the jihadist organizations. Many jihadists are
dispirited, especially those who lack the zeal and tenacity of the Afghan
Arabs. Again, the problems are many. In part, the morale problems besetting
the jihadists are merely the product of a daunting lifestyle. The hunters have
become the hunted, cut off from their families and living in fear as they run
from camp to camp. A few camps are elegant, most are severe. Security
forces also target relatives, adding to the anguish of the troops. These bur-
dens were easier to bear during the heyday of the jihadist movement, but
victories are no longer easy to come by and losses are high. The test of faith
has become arduous, especially for those past the prime of youth. The

authors of the jihadist truce in Egypt, for example, had spent long years in prison. The prime opponents of the truce were to be found in the ranks of youth and the exiles.

The core of the morale problems, however, lies within the internal dynamics of the jihadist organization. Distrust and insecurity among emirs and sub-emirs has led to purges and witch-hunts, most fueled by innuendo and the all-pervasive rumor. Hard information is a rare commodity in the jihadist world, and one can never be too sure of one's colleagues. Adding to the tension is the pervasive conflict among patron networks and the ever-present fear of a defector or government spy. The intensity of Islamic indoctrination has not put an end to human venality.

Insecurity breeds harsh discipline, with the more severe infractions punished by flogging or other penalties common in early Arabia.[50] Indeed, the Taliban and al Qaeda troops opened fire on their colleagues when discipline wavered in the face of U.S. attacks.[51] Also severe are the loyalty rituals that, in extreme cases in Algeria, called for the murder of family members.[52] Little wonder that idealists committed to an Islamic paradise of peace and prayer find themselves dismayed by the realities of jihadist organizational life.

The organizational environment of the jihadists, then, is essentially negative and conflictual. Zeal drives the jihadist during the attack mode, but internal dissensions sap the strength of jihadist organizations once the attack mode has passed. Like most emotional highs, the zeal of the jihadists has been difficult to maintain over long periods of time. Many simply drift back to a more conventional lifestyle or revert to a less demanding form of religious expression. Others lose focus, uncomfortable with the waiting game. The jihadist mentality is better suited to creating environments of chaos than to carrying out the mundane bureaucratic tasks required to transform the fruits of their violence into a broad base mass organization. Conventional employees may be less zealous than the jihadists warriors, but they are far better suited to the routine tasks required to sustain the organization over the long haul.

Finally, it should be noted that the jihadists are not the James Bonds they appeared to be in the aftermath of the September 11 attacks. The hijackers often bragged of planned exploits, perhaps feeling a need to bolster their spirits. In retrospect, their operations appeared clumsy, creating gross security breaches and littering the countryside with clear signs of their intentions. Unfortunately, U.S. security procedures were equally flawed. It is hoped that this will change and that the jihadists will have to get better if they are to succeed in their new war plan of concentrating their efforts on America and its allies.

THE PHYSICAL PLANT

Even the most dedicated jihadist organizations require a physical infrastructure of training camps, shelters, weapons depots, and supply lines if they are to carry out their bloody operations effectively. Early jihadist organizations were simple affairs, centered in friendly mosques, squalid slums, and sparse base camps secreted in remote hideouts. As jihadist ambitions increased, the infrastructure requirements increased proportionally. In the case of the larger jihadist organizations such as al Qaeda, physical plants now rival those of an army or multinational corporation. They have recruiting centers, training camps, supply networks, communications centers, sleeper cells, weapon dumps, laboratories, safe houses, and a secure headquarters for the leadership. They also maintain a variety of front organizations for contracting with suppliers, coordinating with sympathetic religious organizations, disseminating propaganda, dealing with outsourcers, and meeting with representatives of friendly governments. The task of describing the physical facilities of al Qaeda would, itself, require a book of several hundred pages and has been the stuff of minute investigations of al Qaeda camps in Afghanistan and elsewhere.

The advantage of the smaller jihadist groups is the ability of their members to live off the land, take the bus to work, and remain indistinguishable from their neighbors. Most sport beards or wear the *hijab* (Islam dress) as the case may be, but that is now the norm in the Middle East and merely enhances their cover in poorer neighborhoods. Many work for the government, including the police and the army. This is not exceptional, for most people in the Islamic world work for the government. Their jobs are usually not auspicious, but they do have access to sensitive areas and useful information. Other infrastructure demands are relatively minor. Most jihadists have their own military-type weapons, not a rarity in the Middle East, and materials for rudimentary explosives are not too difficult to come by. They are also easy to obtain in the United States.

The disadvantage of the smaller groups is their lack of size and reach. The disadvantage of larger networks such as al Qaeda and Hizbullah is the size and complexity of their physical plant. Facilities are identified by security agencies and destroyed. They are rebuilt, but that takes time and money.

Bin Laden has attempted to minimize his exposure to U.S. anti-terrorist measures by placing much of his infrastructure in areas of chaos and decentralizing his leadership structure. Hizbullah is far more visible and far more vulnerable.

Much like the smaller jihadist groups, sleeper cells and front organizations are expected to be innocuous and self-supporting, with members of the sleeper cells often behaving in most non-Islamic ways to avoid suspicion: indulging in sex and booze in the name of God. The practice of disguising their true religious beliefs was perfected by Shi'a to avoid the persecution of the Sunni majority and suits the needs of the jihadists admirably. Actually, it is remarkable how much the Sunni jihadists have adopted the tactics of the Shi'a.

Although the shift to the sleeper cells and the decentralization of leadership has kept al Qaeda and its spinoffs active while it reassembles, its infrastructure is contracting and its dynamism has been blunted. This may be of little solace to America and its allies, for much of the jihadist infrastructure remains in place and is likely to remain so for some time.

In sum, the main organizational strengths of the jihadists war machine are (1) leadership styles that inspire total devotion; (2) a cadre of fanatic followers who willingly sacrifice their lives in defense of Islam; (3) technological sophistication; and (4) a physical plant that provides for training, weapons, communications, logistics, and funding on a global basis. These strengths are balanced by (1) the highly personalized authority patterns that are disrupted by the loss of an emir; (2) the excessive zeal of cadres and lapses in morale that accrue during setbacks or periods of inactivity; (3) tensions and conflicts within and between competing jihadist organizations; and (4) the vulnerability of their physical plant to attack.

The most effective manner of combating the strengths of the jihadist war machine, accordingly, is to target jihadist leaders at all levels, to demoralize the jihadists by forcing them to suffer highly publicized defeats, and to constantly disrupt their physical plant. The more energy they expend on running and rebuilding, the less remains to attack America and its allies. Attacking the allies of the jihadists is equally important, a topic we turn to next.

NOTES

1. The model of a typical jihadist organization was pieced together from a wide variety of sources as well as extensive personal experience in working with Middle Eastern

organizations. The exact pattern may vary from group to group, but the basic format is the same.

2. Yousef Qaradawi, "Violence and the Islamic Groups, Part 1," Al-Jazeera (7 July 2001), in Arabic. Interviewed by Hamid Al Ansari.

3. Liess Boukra, *Algérie la terreur sacrée* (SA Lausanne: FAVRE, 2002).

4. Ahmed Rashid, *Taliban: Militant Islam, Oil and Fundamentalism in Central Asia* (New Haven, Conn.: Yale University Press, 2001).

5. Boukra, *Algérie la terreur sacrée.*

6. Rohan Gunaratna, *Inside Al-Qaeda: Global Network of Terror* (New York: Columbia University Press, 2002), 57.

7. Adnan Malik, "91 Killed in Saudi Arabia Terror Blasts," *Common Dreams News Center*, 13 May 2003, at http://www.commondreams.org/headlines03/0513-08.htm (accessed 24 Feb. 2004).

8. U.S. Dept. of Justice, "Press Release: Khobar Towers," 21 June 2001, at http://www.fbi.gov/pressrel/pressre101/Khobar.htm (accessed 19 July 2003).

9. Sheila Carapico, "Yemen and the Aden-Abyan Islamic Army," *Middle East Report Online*, 18 Oct. 2000, at http://www.merip.org/mero/mero101800.html (accessed 19 July 2003); "The Suspects," *Yemen Gateway*, 12 Dec. 2000, at http://www.al-bab.com./yemen/cole7.htm (accessed 19 July 2003).

10. Daniel Klardman, Michael Isikoff, and Mark Hosenball, "Investigators Link Last Week's Attacks, Embassy Bombings in Africa and USS *Cole*," *Newsweek Web Exclusive*, 20 Sept. 2001, at http://ww.msnbc.msn.com/id/3066931 (accessed 24 Feb. 2004).

11. "Alleged *Cole*, Sept. 11 Suspect Nabbed," CBS News, 30 Apr. 2003, at http://www.cbsnews.com/stories/2003/05/15/attack/main553982.shtml (2 Aug. 2003).

12. "The U.S. Embassy Bombings in Kenya & Tanzania," *Terrorism Update*, Fall 1998, at http://www.adl.org/terror/focus/15_focus.asp (accessed 27 July 2003).

13. "Imam on Trial for Bali Bombings," *The Guardian-London*, 2 June 2003, at http://www.guardian.co.uk/Print/0,3858,4681917,00.html (accessed 27 July 2003).

14. B. Rahman, "Harkat-ul-Mujahideen: An Update," International Policy Institute for Counter Terrorism, 20 Mar. 1999, at http://www.ict.org.il/articles/articledet.cfm?-articleid=85 (accessed 20 Mar. 20 1999).

15. "Moroccan Bombers Linked to Global Terrorism," *Newsaustralia*, 21 May 2003, at http://www.newsaustralia.com/Moroco-V-Spain/Moroccan_bombers_linked_to_globa.htm (accessed 15 July 2003); Nicolas Marmie, "Morocco Arrests 19 Suicide Bomb Suspects," *Washington Post*, 6 June 2003, at http://www.washingtonpost.com/wp-dyn/articles/A24422-2003Jun6.html (accessed 6 June 2003).

16. Al-Rais Saud, "Saudi Arabia: Lifting the Veil on Implicit Sympathy with the Extremists," *al Wasat* (22 Dec. 2003), 11.

17. Anonymous, *Through Our Enemies' Eyes: Osama Bin Laden, Radical Islam, and the Future of America* (Washington, D.C.: Brassey's, 2002).

18. Gunaratna, *Inside Al-Qaeda*, 8.

19. Jason Burke, *Al Qaeda: Casting a Shadow of Terror* (London: IB Tauris, 2003).

20. Max Weber, *The Theory of Social and Economic Organization* (New York: Macmillan, 1947), 328, 358–359.

21. Hans Gerth, "The Nazi Party: Its Leadership and Composition," *The American Journal of Sociology* 45 (Jan. 1940):526–527.

22. All are discussed at length by our colleague Michel Nehme, in *Fear and Anxiety in the Arab World* (Gainesville, Fla.: University Press of Florida, 2003).

23. Mansour Al Zaiyat, "Sharia and Life Series: Islamic Groups and Violence," Al-Jazeera (11 Aug. 2002), in Arabic. Interviewed by Mahir Abdullah.

24. For an extensive discussion of the charismatic relationship, see Monte Palmer, *Dilemmas of Political Development, 4th ed.* (Itasca, Ill.: Peacock Publishers, 1989), 155–197.

25. Marvin Zonis and Cyrus Amir Mokri, "The Islamic Republic of Iran," in *Politics and Government in the Middle East and North Africa*, Tareq Y. Ismael and Jacqueline S. Ismael, eds. (Miami: Florida International University Press, 1991).

26. Ali Banuazizi and Myron Weiner, eds., *The State, Religion and Ethnic Politics* (Syracuse, N.Y.: Syracuse University Press, 1986); Saskia Gieling, The Marja'iya in Iran and the Nomination of Khamanei in December 1994," *Middle Eastern Studies* 44, no. 4 (Dec. 1997):777–787.

27. Peter L. Bergen, *Holy War, Inc.: Inside the Secret World of Osama bin Laden* (New York: The Free Press, 2001).

28. Boukra, *Algérie la terreur sacrée.*

29. Rashid, *Taliban.*

30. Bergen, *Holy War, Inc.*

31. Rashid, *Taliban.*

32. Monte Palmer, Ali Leila, and El Sayed Yassin, *The Egyptian Bureaucracy* (Syracuse, N.Y.: Syracuse University Press, 1988).

33. Boukra, *Algérie la terreur sacrée.*

34. Lawrence Wright, "The Man behind bin Laden," *New Yorker*, 78, no. 27 (16 Sept. 2002):1–46 (Infotrac 7 Feb. 2004).

35. Boukra, *Algérie la terreur sacrée.*

36. Al Zaiyat, "Sharia and Life Series."

37. For conflict between sheiks who signed the truce and the exiles, see Jailan Halawi, "Rethinking Militancy," *Al Ahram Weekly* 653, 28 Aug. 2003, at http://weekly.ahram.org.eg/print/2003/653/eg6.htm (accessed 30 Aug. 2003); For younger groups, see the emergence of a new Islamic Group branch reported in the *Middle East Times*, 35, 30 Aug. 2003, at http://www.metimes.com/2k3/issue2003-35/eg/ government_clamps_down.htm (accessed 30 Aug. 2003).

38. Anonymous, *Through Our Enemies' Eyes.*

39. Qaradawi, "Violence and the Islamic Groups."

40. Boukra, *Algérie la terreur sacrée.*

41. Stegano Allievi, "Converts and the Making of European Islam," *The Netherlands ISIM Newsletter*, no. 11 (Dec. 2002), 25–26.

42. Hassan Awad, "Jihad Names for Armed Groups," *Al-Wasat*, no. 622 (29 Dec. 2003), 10–11, in Arabic.

43. Nick Fielding, "Encyclopedia of Terror: Revealed: The Bloody Pages of Al-Qaeda's Killing Manual," *Sunday Times-London*, 4 Nov. 2001, at http://www.sundaytimes.co.uk/news/pages/sti/2001/11/04/stiusausa02023.html (accessed 4 Nov. 2001).

44. No Author. "Bulgaria Closes Markov Investigation." BBC News Online, 20 Sept. 2000, at http://www.news.bbc.co.uk/2/hi/world/Europe/934326.stm (accessed 8 May 2004).

45. Alan Feuer and Benjamin Weiser, "Translation: The How to Book of Terrorism," *New York Times*, 1, 5 Apr. 2001, at http://www.library.cornell.edu/colldev/mideast/trmanx.htm (accessed 12 Feb. 2002).

46. John Pike, interviewed by ABC News, 21 Dec. 2001, at http://www.abcnews.com/ (accessed 21 Dec. 2001).

47. *Egyptian Gazette*, 24 Mar. 1982, cited in Palmer, Leila, and Yassin, *The Egyptian Bureaucracy*, 34.

48. Azaam Al-Tamimi, "Failures of the Islamic Movement," Al-Jazeera (11 Nov. 2001), in Arabic. Interviewed by Mahir Abdullah.

49. "Dead Man Walking," *Guardian Unlimited*, 5 Aug. 2001, at http://www.guardian .com .uk/ (accessed 5 Aug. 2001).

50. Boukra, *Algérie la terreur sacrée*.

51. Jonathan Steele, "Stand and Fight, Fleeing Taliban Told," *Guardian Unlimited*, 14 Nov. 2001, at http://www.guardian.co.uk/waronterror/story/0,1361,59306,00.html (accessed 14 Nov. 2001).

52. Boukra, *Algérie la terreur sacrée*.

7

THE ALLIES OF THE JIHADISTS:
THOSE WHO MAKE
TERROR POSSIBLE

America's war on terror is not merely a war against the jihadists. If only it were. It is also a war against those individuals, groups, organizations, and governments that support and finance jihadist operations. It is the allies of the jihadists who facilitate virtually every dimension of the jihadist war effort. This would certainly include recruitment, indoctrination (schools), training, logistics, communications, intelligence, shelter, protection (military), money laundering, documentation, and *wasta*, the Arabic word for connections. Little, if anything, gets done in the Islamic world without connections.

Without their allies, the jihadists would be no more effective than America's home-grown terrorists, be they neo-Nazis holed up in their rural hideouts, leftist Weathermen, or violent religious cults such as the Branch Davidians. All remained isolated because they lacked a base of support sufficient to carry out their demented plans. The jihadists, however, do have allies. That's the rub. They have powerful allies who wittingly or unwittingly enable them to challenge the most powerful nation that the world has ever known. The allies of the jihadists are seldom combatants, but it is they who make terror possible.

The allies of the jihadists can be categorized into three groups: the holy allies, the unholy allies, and the governmental allies. The holy allies include the legitimate institutions of Islam that have been infiltrated by religious extremists. They also include the Muslim Brotherhood, Hizbullah, and other less radical Islamic groups that maintain a complex love-hate relationship with the jihadists. The unholy allies are the broad array of non-Islamic groups ranging from secular terrorist groups to drug lords and weapons dealers. The governmental allies are the governments of the world that support terrorist operations. Some of that support is overt, some covert, some misguided, some inadvertent, and some simply the result of weakness.

In the present chapter, we take a closer look at the allies of the jihadists, their motivations, and the services they perform. We begin by examining the struggle to control the institutions of Islam and then move to an examination of the unholy allies of the jihadists. Finally, we turn to the governmental supporters of terror. They are the most dangerous of the jihadists' allies.

HOLY ALLIES: THE STRUGGLE FOR CONTROL OF ISLAM

The clergy of Islam, much like the clergy of Christianity and Judaism, exhort the faithful to prayer and good works, inspire them to walk in the path of righteousness, and offer guidance in their personal affairs. It is also the clergy who alert the faithful to the dangers confronting their religion and who vilify its enemies. When danger lurks, it is they who suggest appropriate action and decide if and when terror is acceptable within Islamic law. How they decide these issues is critical to America's war on terror.

The clergy in Islam are collectively referred to as the *ulema*, or religious scholars. They are also referred to in the Arabic press as men of religion. Many are graduates of illustrious schools of religious education such as Cairo's Al-Azhar University, a venerable institution that traces its history to the tenth century. Others emerge as lay preachers, guided largely by their faith in God. They lead by zeal and inspiration rather than by the depth of their religious knowledge. The graduates of Al-Azhar preside over the elegant mosques that grace the skylines of Islamic cities, their minarets pointing heavenward in praise of God. The clergy of these glorious structures are government employees and their sermons are closely watched by government censors. The popular men of religion often preach in mosques no larger than a garage or storefront converted into a place of worship. Quantity and zeal compensate for size and elegance. They are everywhere. Islam has also developed its own Billy Grahams, with Islamic tele-preachers becoming the stars of the region's many satellite networks. By and large, the tele-preachers adopt the same tenor as the Muslim Brotherhood and other radical reformers. Zeal sells, but the censor is watching.

Fortunately or unfortunately for America's war on terror, the clergy of Islam are not of one mind on the most pressing issues of the day. Sunni clergy differ from the Shi'a counterparts over the most fundamental points of doctrine. Both, in turn, are also divided into pro-government and anti-government camps, with each camp being further divided between conservatives, moderates, and liberals and they, by interminable personality conflicts and power struggles. Debates over the role of terror as a legitimate weapon in the defense of Islam are particularly bitter. Whatever their conflicts, virtually all preach that America has declared war on Islam.[1]

How does this play out for America's war on terror? The senior religious leaders of the Islamic world were virtually unanimous in their condemnation of the September 11 attacks on the United States. They have been almost as unanimous in their condemnation of the U.S. invasion of Iraq and in their support of the Palestinian cause. This said, the Islamic clergy have been sharply divided over the legality of Palestinian suicide attacks against Israeli civilians. The mufti (chief religious judge) of Mecca declared that attacks on innocent civilians are prohibited by Islamic law, a view echoed by the grand mufti of Saudi Arabia. Other Saudi clerics, however, were less certain on the issue.[2] The grand sheikh of the Al-Azhar Mosque in Cairo, the senior religious authority in Egypt, sharply condemned the suicide attacks against Israeli citizens, stating that Islam forbade ''aggression against innocent civilians of any place, faith or nation.''[3] He later changed his view to say that suicide attacks against Israelis that do not specifically target civilians are allowable in Islam. In the latter case, they are merely the victims of war.

The charge against this point of view was led by Qatar's Sheikh Qaradawi, a leading television figure on Arab cable networks. In Qaradawi's view, Israel is a military society without civilians. There are no innocents in Israel. Similar views were expressed by Lebanon's Mohammed Hussein Fadlallah, one of the most revered figures in Shi'a Islam and the spiritual guide of Lebanon's Hizbullah.[4] The same logic was used by bin Laden to justify the September 11 attacks on the United States.

The role of the Islamic clergy in the war on terror far exceeds the battle for the hearts and minds of the Muslim world. Clergy sympathetic to the jihadists actively recruit members for jihadist organizations. They also raise funds for jihadist activities, serve as a nexus for communications, disseminate jihadist propaganda, and may even establish jihadist training centers. The prime example of the role played by jihadist clergy is provided by Abu Hamza al-Misri, the outspoken leader of the Finsbury Park Mosque in London. The police maintain that the mosque has become a center for recruiting jihadists. Al-Misri has no formal religious training, but his sermons attract a wide audience.

Pro-jihadist clergy in the Islamic world are not protected by democratic freedoms, but their numbers and obscurity make them difficult to track. Most are found among the ranks of the popular "store front" preachers who operate in relative freedom from governmental control. As the Egyptian security forces lament, "We don't have enough certified preachers to go around."[5]

The role of the establishment clergy, by contrast, is to counteract the influence of the jihadists among the masses, a thankless task at best. Most are too closely associated with corrupt regimes to be taken very seriously.[6] The clergy associated with the Muslim Brotherhood and other radical reform groups are a potential obstacle to the jihadists inasmuch as they offer political reform and religious salvation in a more moderate package. There is still plenty of fire and brimstone to go around, probably too much for most Americans. It would also be naive to believe that the jihadists are without supporters in the ranks of the government preachers. The Muslim Brotherhood most assuredly does.

The clergy guide the faithful through millions of the mosques that grace the Islamic world. Egypt alone has more than 50,000 mosques, about 32,000 of which are government mosques.[7] The remainder are popular mosques, many of which are controlled by either the Muslim Brotherhood or the jihadists. The message presented depends largely on the views of the clergy. Passivist and establishment clergy stress prayer and submission to the greater reason of God; jihadist clergy sound the call to battle. Clergy associated with the Muslim Brotherhood and other radical reformers stake out a fiery middle ground, urging vigilance against Islam's enemies and nonviolence in their pursuit of an Islamic state.

Islamic Education: Schools for Terror?

The mosque was long been the center of both religion and science, there being little distinction between the two. Religion was the foundation of all knowledge, scientific and otherwise. Members of the clergy of Islam were referred to as scholars or *ulema* in deference to their education. Much the same was true in the churches and monasteries of medieval Europe, although Muslim scholars made spectacular advances in mathematics and science far in advance of their European counterparts.

The principle remains the same today, although education in the mosque is largely restricted to the study of the Arabic language and religious texts. In the minds of the Arabs, their language is the language of God. Governments, not the clergy, are responsible for public education. Even here, however, the line between church and state is blurred. Cairo's Al-Azhar Mosque has expanded into a vast network of parochial schools, primary through Ph.D., with branches throughout Egypt. All are part of Egypt's system of public education, with Al-Azhar itself boasting the same faculties as any other university, including a large medical school. Students in the Al-Azhar network receive a larger dose of religious training than students in other Egyptian schools, but not without close supervision from the government.

Saudi Arabian students receive a far larger dose of religious instruction. Indeed, approximately one-third of the curriculum of elementary schools is devoted to Islamic topics. This ratio is more or less reflected throughout the Saudi education system, with approximately one-third of Saudi university students majoring in Islamic Studies.[8] Unlike Egypt, Saudi Arabia has an over-supply of certified religious scholars, many finding jobs with the religious police or filling the ranks of the unemployed.[9]

Pakistan, long an ally of the United States, possesses 5,000 to 10,000 plus religious schools or *madrasas*, up from less than 150 just five years ago, although these numbers vary from source to source.[10] All are funded by religious charities, many from Saudi Arabian groups intent on expanding the reach of the ultra-conservative Wahhabi doctrine of Islam. Shi'a schools, a minority, receive indirect funding from Iran. The sharp rise in Islamic schools has been paralleled by an equally sharp rise in violent confrontations between Pakistan's Sunnis and its Shi'a minority.[11]

The role of religious schools in stimulating violence has been widely debated in the Middle East, with a recent debate on the Al-Jazeera television network examining the topic in detail.[12] The debate covered all sides of the issue, with the participants agreeing that all religions, Christianity and Judaism as well as Islam, teach the superiority of their faith and view nonadherents with a degree of suspicion. Until very recently, they recalled, Jews were condemned by the Vatican as the killers of Christ. It was also generally agreed that most holy works, including those of Islam, contain passages that could be interpreted to justify violence.

The problem, according to the debaters, is not Islam, but a perverted interpretation of Islam practiced by a minority of misguided zealots. There was little agreement on how widespread or severe the misguided teaching of Islamic principles had become, but there was recognition that the problem existed.[13]

Sheikh Qaradawi joined the fray by blaming both so-called government sheikhs and the young jihadist sheikhs for the perversion of Islamic doctrine. He referred to the *fatwas* of the jihadist sheikhs as "twisted jurisprudence" and suggested that they still had "soft bones," the Arab equivalent of being green behind the ears.[14]

Whatever the case, the United States is placing intense pressure on Egypt, Pakistan, Saudi Arabia, and other countries of the Islamic world to purge their educational curriculum of materials supportive of terrorism and anti-America attitudes. This is probably a mistake. Tampering with Islamic education deepens the impression that American has declared war on Islam. It is also an extremely sensitive issue that smacks of both crusades and colonialism.

Merely forcing a politically correct curriculum on the countries of the Islamic world, moreover, will not solve the problem. Teachers supportive of the jihadist will preach terror and anti-Americanism regardless of the contents of the government curriculum. The Egyptian government has struggled to purge its education system of teachers sympathetic to the jihadists, but it is not clear that they are succeeding. As long as jihadists maintain a base of popular support, their message will find expression in the educational institutions of the Islamic world. Most of the hard-core indoctrination in the Islamic world, moreover, takes place in jihadists' schools that operate on the fringes of public education systems. Supervision is minimal. Pakistan's 10,000 religious schools are matched by an equal number in Bangladesh, and secret intelligence reports put the number of Islamic *madrasas* in India at 30,000.[15] In Saudi Arabia, the entire education system is controlled by Wahhabi clerics and they have been harshly criticized for stimulating violence, anti-Americanism, and hostility toward the Shi'a.[16] These charges prompted a Saudi survey of text materials with the Saudi foreign minister concluding that "5 percent of the material was considered 'horrible' and 10 percent questionable, while 85 percent called for understanding with other religious faiths."[17]

One must also question whether the act of attending an Islamic school dooms one to becoming a terrorist. Many members of all faiths have received religious educations, only to emerge as agnostics or atheists. Some individuals, particularly those with strong authoritarian tendencies, will undoubtedly be swayed toward violence by religious indoctrination. Others will either become better Muslims or be pushed away from religion altogether. In a curious twist of irony, some Egyptian jihadists blame many of their mistakes on an inadequate understanding of Islam.[18] Most, it seems, were the product of secular education systems.

Finally, one must question the ability of the United States to force a politically correct curriculum on the countries of the Islamic world. Few countries of the Islamic world are willing to risk pushing moderate Muslims into the hands of the jihadists by meddling with Islamic teachings based on the Koran and Sunna. The issue is simply too inflammatory in the wake of a growing wave of Islamic electoral victories. This is all the more the case when the educational reforms are being forced on them by the United States, a country increasingly viewed as the Great Satan. The political leaders of the Islamic world are experts at survival and will not commit political suicide by capitulating to American pressure on an issue of this sensitivity. There will be lots of smoke and mirrors designed to please the United States, but there will be minimal hard action.[19] Even under the best of circumstances, altering Islamic education would be an arduous struggle that would take generations. Hopefully, the war on terror will be over by then.

The Money Trail of the Jihadist Allies: Islamic Charities, Islamic Banks, and Islamic Businesses

Pre-Islamic Arabia, the era of ignorance in Muslim parlance, had degenerated into a society not far removed from Hobbes's state of nature: "All men," or so it seemed "maketh war upon all men." Islam brought humanity a message of peace. It also sought to limit human turmoil by reducing its causes, not the least of which were social inequality and money gouging. Social inequality was to be addressed by obliging Muslims to give generously to the poor, and money gouging was dealt with by forbidding interest on loans.

Lest there be any doubt on the matter, the Koran imposes a 2.5 percent income tax, *zakat*, on all believers. Muslims are also required to pay an additional *zakat* to mark the ending of Ramadan, the holy month of fasting. *Zakat* is one of the five cardinal principles of the Islamic faith, and those who dodge this most holy of obligations may anticipate the wrath of their maker.

Judging from the sums collected, few Muslims are willing to take this risk. The annual *zakat* in Egypt, one of the world's poorest countries, is estimated by Egypt's mufti to have reached $500,000,000 on an annual basis, with an additional $100,000,000 being donated to mark the end of Ramadan in 2002. In Indonesia, another poor country, donations marking the end of Ramadan were expected to reach a billion dollars.[20] "Just think what the *zakat* of 1.4 billion Muslims worldwide could do," said the Egyptian mufti.[21] Many mosques and clergy also receive informal donations from the pious, the sums of which can be quite generous. It is particularly common for Shi'a Muslims to contribute as much as one fifth, or *kums*, of their wealth to senior religious scholars.

In earlier times, *zakat* was simply given to the needy on an impromptu basis or deposited in the *zakat* box at the local mosque. Most mosques have a *zakat* committee and it determines how the charity funds will be allocated.

More recent Islamic history has seen charitable contributions channeled through organized charities that minister to the Muslim poor. The Red Crescent Society is the Muslim counterpart of the Red Cross, the two organizations often cooperating to alleviate human suffering. Some of the larger charitable organizations such as the Society for the Cooperation of the Devotees of the Koran and Sunna have membership in the millions.[22] They also possess branches throughout the world and play a key role in channeling aid from the rich countries of the Persian Gulf to Islam's poor. It is hard to say how many Islamic benevolent associations exist, many being small and localized. The Saudis estimate that there are thousands of such charities in the Middle East, many operating with minimal supervision.[23] Online giving has also made its appearance, a process that will make it easier for the devout to give to the charity of their choice.

It is the benevolent associations and the Islamic banks in which they deposit their funds that have become the focal point of America's war on terror. According to *Islam Online*, a Islamic website reflective of the Muslim Brotherhood, the *zakat* can be spent on anything that serves the cause of God.[24] This includes charity for the poor, salaries of clergy and instructors in Islamic schools, and the maintenance of mosques, Islamic schools, hospitals, and shrines. *Zakat* can also be used for jihads to protect the faith and to defend oppressed Muslims.

This point was made patently clear by prominent Islamic theologian Sheikh Yusuf Al-Qaradawi in response to a question asking if *zakat* funds could be used to pay for transportation to a jihad. He answered:

> If war is waged anywhere to achieve this goal, namely to free the occupied lands of the laws and the tyranny of disbelievers, it is undoubtedly a case of

jihad for the sake of Allah. It thus needs to be financed from the money of *Zakat* the amount of which is to be decided based on the total sum of the charity, the requirements of jihad as well as the degree of the need of other potential recipients of charity. This is all to be decided by reliable scholars, if they are to be found.[25]

The grand mufti of Egypt, a key member of Egypt's government-appointed religious elite, openly urged Egyptian Muslims to send their *zakat* to aid Muslims in Chechnya. His reasoning follows.

Ramadan is supposed to be a blessed month, one of mercy and victory, but the enemies of Islam have turned it into the month of defeats and regression. At the beginning of last Ramadan, Iraq was bombed. In the beginning of this Ramadan, Chechnya was bombed. The Muslim nation must move before its borders totally deteriorate.[26]

These and a spate of *fatwas* from moderate Islamic leaders were issued well before the September 11 attacks on the United States and undoubtedly helped legitimize financial contributions to bin Laden's al Qaeda network. The fact that few have been repudiated remains a source of grave concern to the American government. How is financial support for the jihadists to be dried up when the most moderate of religious leaders openly urge support for jihadist activities? The Israelis have far greater cause for concern, for Palestine is the most symbolic of all Islamic jihads.

As always, much depends on who's in charge of collecting and administering charitable funds. If people sympathetic to the jihadists are in key positions, at least some funds are likely to find their way to jihadist hands. Do the jihadist attempt to infiltrate Islamic charities? Absolutely. It is a major source of their funding. A few charities exist specifically for channeling funds to the jihadists. British investigators, for example, suspect that the North London Central Mosque's Trust falls in this category, but they have no proof.[27] The United States has put at least nine Islamic charities on its list of organizations that fund terrorism, including American branches of the Benevolence International Foundation.[28]

Even the most reputable charities may find that certain branches have fallen under the control of the jihadists. As a recent Saudi Arabian report on jihadist terrorism noted:

In March 2002, the U.S. Treasury Department and Saudi Arabia blocked the accounts of the Somalia and Bosnia branches of the Saudi Arabia-based Al-

Haramain Islamic Foundation. While the Saudi headquarters for this private charitable entity is dedicated to helping those in need, the US and Saudi Arabia determined that the Somalia and Bosnia branches supported terrorist activities and terrorist organizations such as Al Qaeda, AIAI (al-Itihaad al-Islamiya) Islamic Union, and others.[29]

Despite Saudi Arabian protestations of cooperation, the U.S. investigators remain skeptical. The charities of the Saudi Arabia and the Gulf are far wealthier than those of the West and appear to enjoy protection from within their respective governments. The United States accuses; the charities deny.

A few Islamic charities may be blatant in their support of the jihadists, but most are far more subtle. Grants are not made to jihadist groups per se, but to legal front organizations maintained by supporters of the jihadists or to mosques that espouse the jihadist cause. The United States, for example, has accused the Pakistani branch of Kuwait's Revival of Islamic Heritage Society of being a front organization for al Qaeda. The charity denies the accusations, presenting the Kuwaiti government with the names of some 2,870 orphans of the Afghan wars being supported by the charity.[30]

Many charitable organizations are also "networked," with "clean" organizations making grants to less scrupulous counterparts and those to more opaque charities directly linked to the jihadists. The money trail goes up in smoke, and neither the original charity nor its donors are aware of how their monies are being used. At the very least, they cannot be implicated. As the Saudi Arabian spokesman lamented when the wife of the Saudi ambassador to the United States was accused of funding terrorist organizations, "In the past, we may have been naive in our giving and did not have adequate controls over all of our donations. As a consequence, some may have taken advantage of our charity and generosity. . . . This is now changing."[31]

Many charities, moreover, are the blameless victims of jihadist sympathizers who skim funds from legitimate projects and shift them to the jihadists through one mechanism or another. Accounting mechanisms in the Middle Eastern financial institutions are known for their flexibility, and a little skimming is not unusual under the best of circumstances.

It is probable that Islamic charities help the jihadist cause in other ways as well. The larger charities are international in scope and might well provide vital communication links between jihadist groups. Whether they help in logistics and the shifting of key personnel is difficult to ascertain. Their easy access to areas of conflict enables them to so. The prodigious sums that flow through the hands of the Islamic charities also raises suspicion of money laundering. As the U.S. Drug Enforcement Agency (DEA) has learned to its dismay, mingling good money with bad is not that difficult. The point is not to attack the charities themselves, but jihadist allies within those organizations.

The picture becomes even more complex when one adds legitimate businesses to the fray. The business empire of Joseph Nada, foreign minister of the Muslim Brotherhood empire, included a multitude of business that literally spanned the globe and earned him the title of "cement king" of the Mediterranean.[32] Bin Laden's business empire included a daily newspaper, the al-Shamal Islamic Bank in Khartoum, and the Temar al-Mubaraka and Wadi al-Aqiq companies that traded extensively in machinery and agricultural produce—corn, sugar, sesame seed, and fruit. To these were added various construction companies and a reported interest in Afghanistan's opium trade. Proceeds from these and other businesses found their way into accounts in Barclay's Bank in London, Girocredit in Vienna, and various other banks in Hong Kong, Kuala Lumpur, and Dubai.[33] It was these legitimate businesses, in combination with friendly charities and cooperating banks, Islamic and otherwise, that constituted a financial network that spanned some twenty-five countries. This network has now been damaged, but it still exists.

Beyond helping fund the jihadists, legitimate businesses provide jobs for idle jihadists, launder money, ship it around the globe, and provide cover for operatives moving from country to country. Bin Laden's organization even had its own travel agency. Legitimate businesses also fuel jihadist supply lines, purchasing and storing materials until needed, and then shipping them on demand. Some businesses are more legitimate than others; the unsavory ones deal in drugs, arms, and stolen property. If a business is closed down, it simply reopens under a new name.

Islamic banks, as the name suggests, honor the letter of Islamic law by avoiding interest on loans and deposits. Depositors are rewarded by profit sharing or other techniques allowed by Islamic law. According to some estimates, Islamic banks have attracted approximately one-half of the individual savings of the Islamic world and their total assets were expected to reach $400 billion in 2002, up from $150 billion in 1989.[34] Islamic banking is a growth industry.

It is the Islamic banks, according to the U.S. security agencies, that gather charity funds from individuals and organizations and distribute them though surreptitious channels to various jihadist groups. The Islamic banks are also accused of providing the jihadists and their allies with a full range of financial services, including the laundering of illegal money.

Joseph Nada, mentioned above, was once the world's leading Islamic banker. He staunchly denies that such transfers take place. His banks have been closed, but no charges have been brought against him. Depositors have reputedly lost large sums of money, a fact that probably adds to their resentment toward the United States.[35] Once again, there is no smoking gun. Even the non-Islamic banks of the region have a reputation for looseness, with the United States accusing some banks in the United Arab Emirates (UAE) of being the paymaster for bin Laden. Lebanon has also drawn its share of U.S. criticism, as has Israel. Ironically, many of the funds supporting terrorist groups in Israel are channeled through Israeli banks, raising a hue and cry for the reform of one of the world's looser banking systems.[36] Whatever the case, loose financial institutions ranging from banks to money changers are a major component of money-laundering operations estimated to range from $800 billion to as much as $2 trillion on an annual basis.[37]

The latest twist in Islamic banking has been the introduction of the Islamic dinar. Guaranteed by the Dubai Islamic Bank and the Thomas Cook-Al Rostameni Exchange Company, more than 100,000 golden Islamic dinars were in circulation by 2002, with some four tons of gold being traded in e-dinars, the electronic equivalent of the gold dinar coins. While the Islamic dinar is unlikely to replace the U.S. dollar as the international currency of choice, yet another layer of complexity has been added to the money trail.[38] The link-up between the Dubai Islamic Bank and Thomas Cook, the venerable British travel and financial services company, illustrates just how effective the Islamic banks have become in penetrating the world's banking system.

In addition to exploiting Islamic banks and the looser elements of the world banking system, the jihadists have also honed the traditional *hawala* or *hundi* systems for transferring and laundering money.[39] The process is not complex and is often based on verbal commitments among trusted relatives. Your cousin, for example, might deposit $10,000 in a business account of one of my friends in Pakistan. He later transfers it to one of my business accounts in the United States and, in turn, I write a check for $10,000 to a bogus jihadist firm in Chicago. The transfer is virtually untraceable because no records are kept and the names of the bogus businesses keep changing.

The U.S. accusation that some charity funds find their ways into the hands of jihadists is incontestable. Precisely how much money finds its way into the hands of the jihadists is difficult to estimate. No one knows, but even a small percentage of the billions given charity each year is a substantial amount. Wealthy Gulf "angels" also funnel money to the jihadists through Islamic banks. Recent estimates by a consulting firm called Safron Advisors suggest that wealthy individuals in the Gulf region alone, possess some 1.4 trillion dollars, much of which is dispersed around the globe.[40] With this amount of money, even a few "angels" can go a long way.

What to do? Once again, the United States is in a quandary. Because charitable giving is so central to the Islamic faith, attacks on charitable organizations reinforce the impression that the United States has declared war on Islam. Why else, Muslims ask, would the United States deprive the Muslim poor of much needed aid?

It is also a profoundly difficult task to track the money. No international enforcement agencies exist, and cooperation with the countries of the region has produced more smoke than fire. Some simply lack the capacity to keep their banks and charitable organizations in check. Others have blood on their hands or fear the uproar that would follow. Most also resent American intrusion into their internal affairs, perhaps fearing that the revelations might prove embarrassing to members of the ruling elite. Most multinational corporations, moreover, are wary of regulations that would curtain their own financial operations, banking or otherwise.

Finally, there is the question of religious freedom. How does one impose draconian restrictions on Islamic charities, but not on Christian and Jewish charities? One way or the other, the political and social costs of closing down Islamic charities is profound and will inevitably hamper efforts to shut down the jihadist financial network.

UNHOLY ALLIES: DRUG LORDS, MAFIOSO, AND OTHER KINDRED SOULS

Wars and revolution produce an insatiable need for weapons and war materiel, and the jihadist war against America is no exception. Charitable contributions and legitimate business activities help foot the bill, but they are only part of the money trail. Huge sums of money, no one knows how much for sure, result from the cultivation of opium and other drugs. In 2000, Afghanistan, then the stronghold of bin Laden's al Qaeda network, supplied about 70 percent of the world's opium. The *Wall Street Journal* reported that bin Laden's cut was 15 percent.[41] Lebanon, the base of the dominant Hizbullah network, has long been known as a major drug producer. Lebanese discuss the presence of drug cultivation in the Bekaa Valley as a matter of course. Many of the larger drug producers are reputed to be members of the Lebanese parliament or other major politicians. Just as drugs fueled the rebellion in Afghanistan, so did they fuel the fifteen-year civil war in Lebanon. The Lebanese government has made a number of highly publicized raids on drug producers, but most Lebanese remain skeptical.

Beyond funding terrorist activities, drugs are bartered for arms with few intermediaries. In the fall of 2002, for example, two Pakistanis and an American were arrested for attempting to trade five metric tons and 600 kilograms of heroin for four Stinger anti-aircraft missiles.[42] Al Qaeda was presumably the group involved, but it could just as well have been some other terrorist group.

Without users, of course, drugs would be worthless. Alas, the DEA estimates that Americans are spending some $64 billion on illegal drugs annually. With figures this large, it is not clear what the DEA is enforcing. President Bush has called on Americans to do their part in the war on terror by foregoing drugs.

The jihadists also acquire funds from the sale of illicit gems purchased from Sierra Leone, Angola, Liberia, the Democratic Republic of the Congo, and other gem-producing areas of Africa, most of which are threatened by civil war. The African rebels, too, are in urgent need of weapons, and raw gems mined outside of the De Beers cartel is what they have to sell. In the cases of Liberia and Burkina Faso, it was reportedly the presidents of the countries themselves who protected the terrorist agents. The former president of Liberia, Charles Taylor, reportedly received a $1 million bribe for his services.[43] Once acquired, the gems are processed by allied businesses in Antwerp and other processing centers. Some 10 million dollars' worth of gems were processed in the run up to September 11, according to sources in Antwerp.[44] Given estimates that the September 11 attacks cost bin Laden's al Qaeda network something in the range of $500,000, a few million dollars can go a long way.[45]

Gems also provide the jihadists with a safe haven for their funds. Bank accounts can be frozen, but gems simply increase in value. They also are immune from airport metal detectors, easily shipped from place to place without detection, readily convertible to cash, and provide a ready-made avenue for laundering drug money. How does one trace the trail of gems sold for cash? Prices are cheap and entice willing buyers. The situation is the same throughout much of the Islamic world.

Gold has also become a favorite of the jihadists, finding easy outlets in discount centers and providing a hedge against banking sleuths and frozen accounts. In retrospect, it now appears that bin Laden converted many of his financial assets into gold in the days before the September 11 attacks on the United States.

Inevitably, these activities bring the jihadists in league with drug lords and other criminal networks. In the elegant phrasing of Asa Hutchinson, director of the DEA, "drug traffickers and terrorists work out of the same jungle, they plan in the same cave, and they train in the same desert."[46]

The Russian Mafia appears to top the list of jihadist allies in the criminal world. Among other things, they process the jihadists' raw opium, distribute it in Europe and the United States, and provide them with weapons of all varieties. Foreign intelligence sources suggest the list may also include the production of a small nuclear device, but details remain sketchy. What is not sketchy, however, is the fact that the collapse of the Soviet Union opened a vast black market in weapons and weapons technology of all varieties.[47]

Criminal elements, unfortunately, are not the only unholy allies of the jihadists. Limited contacts have long existed among the world's terrorists organization. Reports, for example, have circulated about IRA assistance to the PLO. Both the IRA and the PLO have now renounced violence, but extremist splinter groups in both camps appear to be in limited contact. Links between the Provisional IRA and rebel groups in Colombia have been firmly established. The latter, flush with cash from the cocaine trade, buy IRA expertise for use in their on-going conflict with Colombia's pro-American government.[48] Introductions were presumably made by ETA, the Spanish Basque terrorist group. Links with the jihadists are more speculative. As senior officials in the U.S. Department of State note:

> Relationships between drug traffickers and terrorists benefit both. Drug traffickers benefit from the terrorists' military skills, weapons supply, and access to clandestine organizations. Terrorists gain a source of revenue and expertise in illicit transfer and laundering of proceeds from illicit transactions. Both groups bring corrupt officials whose services provide mutual benefits, such as greater access to fraudulent documents, including passports and customs papers. Drug traffickers may also gain considerable freedom of movement when they operate in conjunction with terrorists who control large amounts of territory.[49]

In addition to facilitating the flow of money and weapons, the unholy allies of the jihadists often provide them with logistics, shelter, training, intelligence, and most other services required for covert operations. This is all the more possible because the Mafia and drug rings are international in scope and operate with relative impunity in their home territories. They are also adept at building networks in the West and in avoiding detection. Could they assist is smuggling operatives and weapons into the United States? Of course, although, the jihadists have not had much difficulty in this area.

Not only is the link between the jihadist and organized crime frightening, but, if America's uphill war against drugs is any indicator, it may be impossible to stop. Billions of dollars are involved and the complexity of the linkages between the terrorists and the criminals defy the imagination. In one recent case, for example, an Israeli arms dealer in Panama sent an e-mail message to a Russian arms dealer in Guatemala saying his customers needed everything from assault rifles to rockets and rocket launchers. The weapons, presumably paid for with drug money, were to be supplied by the Nicaraguan army. The target country was Liberia, with officials speculating that their final destination "was somewhere else."[50]

GOVERNMENTS AS ALLIES OF TERROR

Of all of the allies of the jihadists, none are more vital to their cause than the governments of the world that, directly or indirectly, support terrorism. It is governments of the world that fund, shelter, train, arm, and encourage the terrorist at every turn, even to the point of assisting with the recruitment of jihadist cadres. It is also the governments of the world that allow the allies of the jihadists to operate with relative impunity, be they firebrand preachers, friendly charities, Islamic banks and businesses, criminal organizations, or other symbiotic terrorist organizations. Not all governments do everything, but most, including the United States and Britain, do their part. Few things in the war on terror are certain, but one thing is: The war on terror will not be won unless state support for the jihadists is sharply curtailed. We would like to say eliminated, but that is probably an impossibility.

Which countries support terrorism? The answer is devastatingly simple. Virtually all the countries in the world have supported terrorism in one form or another, not the least of which is the United States. The United States made little secret of its support for bin Laden in the struggle to liberate Afghanistan from Soviet rule. The United States had always looked to Islam as a bulwark against the spread of communism, and Afghanistan was no different. Both feared the Soviets. U.S. support for bin Laden in Afghanistan also differed little from earlier American support for the Contra's in Nicaragua's long and bloody civil war and a host of similar "interventions" in the affairs of Latin America. All were part of America's war against communism. The trouble with Afghanistan was that things went terribly wrong. With the Islamic world free of the communist threat, the jihadists turned against their former ally and launched a new jihad to rid the Islamic world of American domination.

The United States recruited, trained, and armed opposition (terrorist) groups in Iraq in the hope of overthrowing Saddam Hussein and establishing a moderate Iraqi government compliant with the wishes of the United States. The term democracy was bantered about, but few people familiar with the history of Iraq or the ninety some opposition groups quarreling over Saddam's carcass had little hope in the matter. No sooner had Saddam Hussein been put to flight than the United States began arming the Mujahedeen Kalq, the MKO, an anti-Iranian terrorist group sheltered by Saddam Hussein, as a weapon against Iran.

The story of the MKO well illustrates the murky relationships between the West and terrorist groups in the Middle East. The MKO emerged in 1965 as one of a spate of leftist groups opposed to the Shah's rule. A brief flirtation with Ayatollah Khomeini's government ended in 1981 when Khomeini, then firmly in power, turned on the leftist groups that had supported the revolution. Key leaders of the MKO, including Massoud Rajavi, fled to Paris where the organization reconstituted itself as a terrorist group dedicated to overthrow the Islamic regime in Iran. France, however, was more interested in developing economic ties with Iran than in fighting the mullahs, and in 1986 Saddam Hussein became Rajavi's new patron. Iraq was still in the throes of its bloody war with Iran and Saddam Hussein needed all the help he could get. The MKO, some 5,000–10,000 strong, fought the Iranians and, following Iraq's defeat in the first Gulf war (1991), helped Saddam Hussein crush uprisings by the Kurds and the Shi'a. The MKO also unleashed a bloody war of terror against Iranian targets in Iran and abroad.[51]

With Saddam scuttled, Washington again embraced the MKO as a key weapon in its undeclared war against Iran. This venture, however, was short lived. The MKO was a powerful weapon against Iran, but its presence on the U.S. list of terrorist organizations proved embarrassing. Washington backed off, but the use of MKO against Iran continues to be debated in administration circles.[52] In the meantime, the French launched massive raids on the MKO's facilities in the Paris area, claiming that the MKO was intent on making France the center of the European terrorist operations. Indeed, the raid was carried out by no less than 1,300 French security agents.[53] The raids coincided with a sudden Iranian willingness to deliver members of al Qaeda being held in Iran. This has led to speculation that a deal was done between Paris and Tehran to crush their mutual enemies. Was the United States involved? Who knows?

As a practical matter, it is not a question of who is using terror, but of who's ox is being gored. The United States feels that it is justified in using all means at its disposal, including terrorism, to protect itself and the free world from the jihadists and all other threats to the stability of the world. Heading the list of other threats are pariah states intent on developing weapons of mass destruction. The jihadists feel equally justified in opposing U.S. domination of the region, including Israeli occupation of Palestinian territories. This view has few dissenters in the Muslim world.

Why Governments in the Islamic World Are Allies of Jihadist Terror

Why do many countries in the Islamic world aid and abet anti-American terrorism? Why does Lebanon give Hizbullah free reign to control most of its border with Israel? Why does Pakistan's ISI play a key role in supporting jihadists groups in Kashmir? Why do Saudi Arabia and sheikdoms of the Persian Gulf turn a blind eye to charities that are the taproot of the jihadist money tree? Why does Israel continue to expand settlements in the Occupied Territories when they constitute a major stimulus for Palestinian terror? These are vital questions in America's war on terror, for it is hard to cure a problem without understanding its cause. Unfortunately, there are probably as many reasons for resisting America's war on terror as there are countries in the region. The following reasons are among the most prominent.

1. Public Opinion. As a general principle, anti-American sentiment in the Islamic world is so intense that the leaders of the region are reluctant to give their full support to America's war on terror. The Islamic world may not be democratic, but its leaders do fear the masses. This became evident in the run up to the invasion of Iraq, when even staunch allies such as Egypt, Turkey, and Saudi Arabia opposed the U.S./British strike against Iraq. It was not Saddam Hussein that their leaders were worried about, but their own thrones.

2. Religious Pressures. Supporting America's war on terror also places

the leaders of the Islamic world in direct conflict with the Islamic movement in all of its various incarnations. Most Muslims have little difficulty with the United States hunting down the jihadists who committed the September 11 attacks, but they are deeply offended by U.S. pressure to reform Islamic education and curtail the activities of Islamic charitable organizations. It is truly difficult for the leaders of the Islamic world to give full cooperation to America's war on terror when most of their subjects believe that America has declared war on Islam. Indeed, the leaders of the Sudan, Bangladesh, and Saudi Arabia, among others, openly curry mass popularity by supporting the Islamic movement.

3. Differing National Interests. Even countries that firmly support America's war on terror may find that American demands conflict with their own national interests. When President Reagan vowed to get the Israelis out of Beirut in 1982, for example, Prime Minister Menachem Begin of Israel responded, "Jews do not kneel but to God."[54] Ariel Sharon has been equally contentious in his determination to expand Jewish settlements in the Occupied Territories. The struggle between Washington and Tel Aviv over settlements continues and is far from being resolved. Washington believes that the settlements fuel anti-Americanism and serve as a provocation for terror. Sharon believes that they are a vital step in the building of Greater Israel.

4. Terror as Foreign Policy. Beyond having national interests that differ from those of the United States, many countries in the Islamic world find terrorist organizations to be powerful weapons in their foreign policy. Syria, for example, has long supported Hamas and the Palestinian Islamic Jihad in the hope of forcing Israel to make peace with Syria on equitable terms. The deal is a simple one: Withdraw from what remains of occupied Syrian territory and we will withdraw our support for Hamas and Islamic Jihad. Added to the deal is Syrian curtailment of Hizbullah activities in Lebanon, a country under the de facto control of the Syrians. Pakistan similarly relies on jihadists in Kashmir to liberate what it claims to be a Pakistani province.

5. Business Is Business. One of the hardest nuts to crack in America's war on terror has been clamping down on the business and financial centers that launder jihadist money and filter funds to the terrorists. The biggest offenders, according to American sources, are Dubai,

Sharjah, the UAE, Lebanon, and Israel.[55] Israel has subsequently been removed from the list. The United States also accuses the UAE as being a major center for criminal gangs involved in drug and gun running, presumably in cahoots with the jihadists. All protest their innocence but resist altering banking practices in the name of free-market economics and economic survival.

6. Terrorists Are Part of the Power Structure. In some parts of the Islamic world, terrorist organizations are so powerful that they actually constitute part of the ruling power structure. This was very much the case of the Sudan during Turabi's heyday and is very much the case in Lebanon today. Hizbullah is one of the major actors in Lebanese politics and it is the only group in Lebanon allowed to maintain its own militia. Attempts to close down Hizbullah would threaten a renewal of Lebanon's long and bloody civil war, a prospect that is simply unacceptable to the vast majority of Lebanese.

Perhaps the most interesting case of government agencies supporting terror is that of the Pakistani ISI. The ISI, the Pakistani equivalent to the CIA and FBI, possesses a long history of orchestrating jihadist activities in Afghanistan and Kashmir. It has also defied control by Pakistan's political leaders and is variously describe as Pakistan's "invisible government," "kingdom within a state," and "our secret godfathers." During periods of civilian rule, about half of Pakistan's history as an independent state, the ISI was used by Pakistan's generals to keep tabs on civilian politicians. In some cases, it may have plotted their removal from office. It was the ISI that channeled American aid to bin Laden and the Taliban during the Afghan rebellion against the Soviets. It is the ISI that stands accused of funneling weapons and money to the jihadists in Kashmir and setting up spy networks in India. Other charges against this most complex of organizations focus on its complicity in the development of Pakistan's nuclear weapons and its ties with North Korea. General Musharaf has removed the director of the ISI, a former ally, and has attempted to bring the "invisible government" under his control. This will not be an easy task. The ISI has a reported 10,000 members including a massive core of informers.[56] Its tentacles also penetrate all sectors of Pakistan's political life. While blackmail may be too strong a word, the capacity of the ISI to embarrass Pakistan's elite is virtually unlimited.

The U.S. case against Pakistan does not differ markedly from the its case against Iraq and Iran, the main distinction being Pakistan's willingness to allow U.S. Special Forces to operate in Pakistan. Pakistan has also promised to terminate state support for the jihadists and bring Islamic schools and charitable organizations under control. The United States has praised these efforts but notes that Pakistan must stop being a "platform for terrorism."[57]

7. States Are Too Weak to Stop Terrorism. Americans intuitively assume that governments are in control of their people and territory. This is not the case in most areas of the Islamic world. The frontier regions of Pakistan are under the control of tribal sheiks, who rule much as they see fit. They are openly supportive of the jihadists and are now imposing Taliban-style rule on the region. According to some reports, bin Laden t-shirts are a big hit.[58] This stands in sharp contradiction to General Musharaf's pro-U.S. policy, but there is little he can do about it. The territories are simply too mountainous and too remote to be effectively patrolled by the army. Pakistan also lacks the resources to do so. The situation is much the same in Yemen, a mountainous country whose remote tribes have historically been in various degrees of revolt against the central government. The government controls the cities and the flat lands. The mountain tribes are best controlled by bribes. Yemen has allowed U.S. Special Forces to operate in its territory, but the sledding is tough.

8. Collusion with Government Officials. Jihadist sympathizers exist in all strata of society including senior government officials and leading members of the clergy. Some are open in expressing their views; most are not. Some work in the government bureaucracy; others are members of the army and police. Still others are wealthy businessmen well skilled in the art of bribing venal government officials. We asked a well-placed official if he ever accepted bribes. "My family doesn't take bribes," he said with contempt, "we give them." The numbers of jihadist supporters increase as one descends the hierarchy of power. So do their invisibility and the ability to apprehend them. One way or another, officials are shifting resources to the jihadists and turning a blind eye to their activities. People in high positions also provide a modicum of protection to those at lower levels.

9. Delusions of Grandeur. We add megalomania to the list of reasons for supporting terror because it is difficult to find another explana-

tion for Colonel Qadaffi's long history of terrorist operations. Qadaffi believes that he inherited the mantle of Arab leadership from Abdul Nasser and has spared no efforts to portray himself as the champion of Arab causes. This has included support for a variety of terrorists, including the infamous Abu Nidal. No sooner did the world's media ignore the Libyan leader than a new crisis began brewing. Sometimes it was terror, other times it was a renewed drive to unite the Arabs or the sedition of one of his neighbors. During the 1970s, he even sent money to America's Black Muslims in the hope that it would trigger a revolution in the United States. Always believing himself to be something of a religious saint, he sparked outrage among Muslim clerics when he changed the beginning date of the Muslim calendar from the death of Prophet Mohammed to the date of the Prophet's birth. Even in his youth he had organized revolutionary cells, shaving the heads of disciples who disobeyed his orders.[59] Qadaffi's zeal calmed precipitously following the U.S. bombing of Libya in 1986, and the Libyan dictator eventually acknowledged that Libyan agents had been involved in the bombing of Pan American Flight 103 over Lockerbie, Scotland. Qadaffi himself denied knowledge of the affair, but has agreed to pay reparations to the families of the victims. Always unpredictable in his search for notoriety, he has joined the war on terror and embarrassed former friends by revealing the aid they provided to his nuclear weapons program. Of these, none was more embarrassed than Pakistan, a core state in America's war on terror.

There can also be little doubt that Saddam Hussein suffered from bouts of megalomania. Indeed, the role of the Iraq media was to transform Saddam Hussein into a living god. Cults of personality are not rare in the Middle East, but few could match those of the Iraqi dictator. The opponents of the Ayatollah Khomeini also claimed that he had deluded himself into believing that his actions were divinely inspired.

Delusions of grandeur are dangerous. Rational politicians back down in the face of overwhelming odds. They are also willing to negotiate for the best deal. Those suffering from the delusions of invincibility do neither. The only solution is defeat.

Countries with More than One Reason for Supporting Terror

Countries with a single reason for supporting terror are relatively easy to deal with. Syria's support of terrorism, for example, is overwhelmingly motivated by a desire to keep Israel at bay and regain the Golan Heights. Washington has largely accepted this rationale, assuming that Syria's support of anti-Israeli terror will go away once a comprehensive Arab-Israeli peace settlement is in place. At the very least, Washington has been reluctant to attack Syria for fear of igniting a regional conflagration. Rhetoric from the Bush administration suggests that this attitude may be changing, but Syria has made concessions and Washington's energies are focused on its problems in Iraq.

The picture is much different for countries with multiple reasons for supporting terror. As a general principle, the more reasons a country has for supporting terror, the more it will defy America's efforts to stamp out the jihadists. This applies to friends of the United States as well as to its enemies. This point is well illustrated by Saudi Arabia and Iran, two key countries in America's war on terror.

The case against Saudi Arabia is threefold. First, Saudi Arabia sponsors a broad network of religious schools throughout the Islamic world. These schools, by and large, adhere to a Wahhabi doctrine known for its hard-core fundamentalism. It is also a xenophobic doctrine that lends itself to anti-Americanism. Both, in the view of the United States, promote jihadism. Second, the Saudis contribute generously to Islamic charities linked to fundamentalist groups. Some contributions are direct. Some are inadvertent. The result, according to Washington, is the same. The jihadists receive the funds they need to carry out terrorist attacks against America and its allies. Third, Saudi Arabia funds jihadist groups attacking Israel. Israel sources claim that 50 percent of Hamas's funds come from Saudi Arabia.[60] Saudi Arabia has also been the major financial backer of Yasir Arafat and the PLO.

None of the above points are a matter of much dispute. The pertinent question is why does Saudi Arabia, a long-time ally of the United States, continue to pursue policies that undermine America's war on terror? The answer, in a nutshell, is that most of the motives for supporting terror reviewed above are applicable to Saudi Arabia. To begin with, Saudi Arabia is a tribal monarchy whose main claim to legitimacy lies in its support of Islam. Indeed, the title of the Saudi king is "his majesty, the custodian of the two sacred holy places." Supporting Islam has always been and continues to be a cardinal principle of Saudi foreign policy. Saudi sponsorship of Islamic schools symbolized that policy, as did Saudi-sponsored Islamic alliances designed to serve as a counterweight to Arab nationalism.

The legitimacy of the Saudi regime has also been purchased by providing Saudi citizens with a cradle-to-grave welfare system. Schooling is free and home loans, seldom repaid, are available for the asking. All are funded from the kingdom's lavish oil revenues.

Both pillars of Saudi rule have now begun to fray. Well educated and increasingly vocal, Saudi citizens are demanding that a royal family known for its corruption and lax morals clean up its act. Bin Laden, a friend of the royal family before his exile in the Sudan, was one of its foremost critics.[61] His message was basically reform or perish. Even government clerics have become critical of the corruption and ineptitude of the family.[62] Incomes have also started to decline, causing grumbling among a population long accustomed to a free ride.

More than ever, accordingly, the royal family feels compelled to stress its Islamic credentials and support Islamic causes. This involves charity giving of all varieties, much of which is collected by charities that operate with minimal supervision. It also means supporting the Palestinian struggle, the most visible of Arab and Islamic causes. This is all the more the case because Saudi cooperation in the strike against Saddam Hussein was profoundly unpopular in Saudi Arabia. It will be recalled that a Saudi intelligence survey of popular attitudes toward the war against Iraq found that 95 percent of the respondents opposed it.

In much the same manner, strident anti-Americanism in Saudi Arabia makes it difficult for the Saudi government to grant U.S. agents free reign in investigating jihadists attacks on American sites in the kingdom. Part of this reluctance is the pervasive fear and distrust that pervades all areas of life in the kingdom. The royal family, estimated to be between 5,000 and 30,000 in all, also fears that these investigations might produce unpleasant surprises. Many of the family members have been known for their sympathy for Islamic causes, including the jihadists. As the royal family controls almost everything worth controlling in Saudi Arabia, some collusion is inevitable. All things considered, it is probably impossible for the United States to dry up Saudi support for Palestine, fundamentalist education, and Islamic charities without jeopardizing the Saudi regime itself. That might also mean jeopardizing Saudi oil resources. If the royal family goes, it could well be the jihadists who come next.

The American case against Iran returns to 1979 and the Ayatollah Khomeini's overthrow of the Shah of Iran. Proclaiming an Islamic Revolution against the United States and everything American, the hand of Ayatollah Khomeini was seen everywhere: in the seizing of U.S. diplomats in Tehran, in attempted coups in Bahrain, in the attack on the holy mosque in Mecca, in the attacks on the American Embassy and marine barracks in Beirut, in the development of Hizbullah organizations throughout the Shi'a world, and in the funding of Sunni jihadists everywhere. The Islamic Revolution lost some of its steam with the death of Ayatollah Khomeini, but support of terror continued unabated. Iran was a key player in Turabi's network and continues to provide funding and arms to Hizbullah, Hamas, and the Palestinian Jihad. Iran's connections with bin Laden remain more conjectural, but there can be little doubt of Iran's role in resisting the U.S. occupation of Iraq.

Iran denies malice toward the United States but is motivated to support terror against America and its allies for most of the reasons outlined above. Public opinion in Iran continues to be anti-American, and a shaky Islamic government feels compelled to convince its population that it's not backing down in the face of U.S. threats. Iranians, it appears, see little hope for a rapprochement with the United States and are preparing for the worst. This was certainly one of reasons for the shattering defeat of Iran's liberals in its 2003 municipal elections. The liberals had swept previous elections, but their popularity has declined in proportion to American pressure on Tehran. Perceived U.S. attacks on Islam have merely added fuel to the fire. Subsequent elections have also strengthened the hardliners, but the procedures were so flawed that they serve as a poor barometer of public opinion.

Iranian foreign policy continues to oppose a strong U.S. presence in Iraq, Saudi Arabia, and the sheikhdoms of the Persian Gulf. It is in Iran's national interest to do so. All serve as an obstacle to expansion of the Iranian Revolution. All could also be used as a springboard for an American attack against Iran. President Bush has openly discussed the possibility of such a strike, and the Israelis have urged him to do so. Iran's inability to match the U.S. militarily leaves it with two basic choices: (1) It can capitulate to U.S. demands that it dismantle its nuclear facilities and Hizbullah networks or (2) It can attempt to drive the United States from the region by means of terror. The first choice would humiliate the Islamic regime and call its survival into question. The alternative is dangerous, but may be necessary for the survival of the regime. For the moment, Iran is showing signs of cooperation while waiting for the U.S. to recoil from its occupation of Iraq. The SCIRI, Iran's main ally in Iraq, has even joined the ruling council pieced together by the United States. What better way to deflect American anger? It also places a pro-Iranian group on the ground floor of efforts to shape a new political system for Iraq.

Advocates of terror are also well represented in the Iranian power structure. In many ways, Iran possesses two separate political systems: one dominated by Supreme Guide Ali Khamenei and a circle of religious hard-liners intent on revolution and a second centering on President Khatami and liberal reformers anxious to stress economic development and normalized relations with the United States. Agencies supporting terror are under the direct control of the hardliners and cannot be countermanded by Khatami. Collusion with the supporters of the Islamic Revolution occurs at all levels.

In sum, the war against jihadist terror has three components: (1) the jihadist groups that perpetuate the terror, (2) the mass frustration and despair that spawn jihadists and sustain jihadist groups, and (3) the allies who facilitate all dimensions of their activities. To be successful, America's war on terror must address all three. Merely focusing on the jihadists is not enough.

It is the efforts to defeat the jihadists, their supporters, and their allies, that we turn to next.

NOTES

1. This assessment is based on many years of watching a variety of Muslim tele-preachers on diverse Arabic television channels.

2. "Saudi Grand Mufti Condemns Killing of Non-Muslims," *Middle East News*, 25 Oct. 2001, at http://www.middleeastwire.com/Saudi/stories/20011025_meno.shtml (accessed 25 Oct. 2001).

3. "Egyptian Cleric Clarifies Words on Suicide Attacks," *Ha'aretz*, 15 Apr. 2002, at http://www.haaretzdaily.com/hasen/pages/ShArt.jhtml (accessed 15 Apr. 2002).

4. "Qaradawi Launches Sharp Attack on Sheik Al-Azhar," *Middle East Online*, 4 Dec. 2001, at http://www.middle-east-online.com/ArabicNews/Palestine/Dec2001/Qardawi_azhar.html (accessed 5 Dec. 2001).

5. Hamdi D. Zaqzuq, "Interview with the Minister of Wafqs," *Al-Wasat* (4 Jan. 1999), 23–25, in Arabic.

6. Francis Cabrini Mullaney, *The Role of Islam in the Hegemonic Strategy of Egypt's Military Rulers 1952–1990* (Ann Arbor, Mich.: UMI Dissertation Information Service, 1995).

7. Diana Digges, "All Preachers Meek and Mild," *Cairo Times* 1, no. 15, 18 Sept. 1997, at http://www.cairotimes.com/content/issues/Islists/preach 15.html (accessed 21 July 2003).

8. Joseph Nevo, "Religion and National Identity in Saudi Arabia," *Middle Eastern Studies*, 34 (July 1998).

9. Hani A.Z. Yamani, *To Be a Saudi* (London: Janus Publishing, 1998).

10. Febe Armanios, "Islamic Religious Schools, Madrasas: Background," Congressional Research Service, Library of Congress (29 Oct. 2003), 4.

11. "Unfulfilled Promises: Pakistan's Failure to Tackle Extremism," *International Crisis Group Asia Report* 73 (16 Jan. 2004): 1–21.

12. Mohammad Kharishan, "First War of the Century: Organization of Al Qaeda and Its Relation with the Taliban," Al-Jazeera, 29 Oct. 2001, at http://www.aljazeera.net/programs/first_Cent_wars/articles/2001/11/11-1-1.htm (accessed 5 Nov. 2001).

13. Joseph Nada, "Dimensions of the American Attack of Islamic Financing," Al-

Jazeera, 29 Nov. 2001, at http://www.aljazeera.com/programs/no_limits/articles/ 2001/ 11/11-19-1.htm (accessed 23 Nov. 2001).

14. Yousef Qaradawi, "Violence and the Islamic Groups, Part 1," Al-Jazeera, 7 July 2001, 2–3, in Arabic. Interviewed by Hamid Al Ansari, at http://www.aljazeera.net/ programs/shareea/articles/2001/7/7-7-1.htm (accessed 24 Aug 2002).

15. S. Gurumurthy, "Madrasas and Jihad," *Papers Online*, 1 May 2002, at http:// sathyavaadi.triod.com/truthisgod/papers/020501.htm (accessed 20 June 2003).

16. Michael A. Prokop, "Saudi Arabia: The Politics of Education," *International Affairs* 79, no.1 (2003):78–79.

17. John Duke Anthony, "The American-Saudi Relationship: A Briefing by HRH Prince Saud al-Faisal," *Gulfwire Newsletter* (13 Oct. 2002), in "Islamic Religious Schools, Madrasas: Background," Febe Armanios, Congressional Research Service, Library of Congress (29 Oct. 2003), 4.

18. Kemal As-Said Habib, "The Experience of the Islamic Movement in Egypt," *Al-Manara*, 12 (2000), in Arabic, at http://www.almanar.net/issues/12/121.htm (accessed 13 Dec. 2001).

19. Faye Bowers, "On a Dagger's Edge: Saudi Students Face a Changing System," *Christian Science Monitor* (12 Jan. 2004), downloaded from Saudi-U.S. Relations Information Service, at http://www.saudi-us = relations.org/newsletter2004 (accessed 14 Jan. 2004); Mohammed Kharishan (moderator), "Changing the Arab Educational Program at the Request of the United States," panel discussion, Al-Jazeera, 22 Dec. 2001, in Arabic, at http://www.aljazeera.net/programs/first_Cent_wars/articles/2001/12/12-22-1. htm (accessed 29 Dec. 2001).

20. "Indonesia Expected to Collect a Billion Dollars of Zakat Fitr," *Islam Online*, 4 Dec. 2002, at http://www.islamonline.net/completesearch/English/mDetails.asp (accessed 21 Dec. 2002).

21. "Indonesia Expected to Collect a Billion Dollars."

22. Hala Mustafa, *The Political System and the Islamic Opposition in Egypt* (Cairo: Markaz Al-Mahrusa, 1995), in Arabic.

23. "Saudi Arabia Announces Counter-Terrorism Measures," Saudi Arabian press release cited in *Gulfwire*, 9 Dec. 2002, at http://www.gulfwire.com (accessed 9 Dec. 2002).

24. "Fatwa Bank: Salaries to Imams from Zakat," *Islam Online*, 1 Dec. 1999, at http://www.islamonline.net/fatwa/English/FatwaDisplay.asp (accessed 1 Dec. 1999).

25. "Fatwa: Spending Zakah Money on Jihad," *Islam Online*, 11 Apr. 2002, at http:// www.islamonline.net/completesearch/English/FatwaDisplay.asp (accessed 11 Apr. 2002).

26. Mujahid Mleiji, "Mufti of Egypt Calls on Muslims to Send Zakat to Chechnya," *Islam Online*, 12 Dec. 1999, at http://www.islamonline.net/completesearch/English/ mDetails.asp (accessed 12 Dec. 1999).

27. Patrick Butler, "Muslim Cleric Banned from Charity Role," *Guardian Unlimited*, 16 Dec. 2002, at http://society.guardian.co.uk/charitymanagement/story/0,8150, 861057,00.html(accessed 16 Dec. 2002).

28. "Terrorist Finance: Follow the Money," *Economist*, 1 June 2002, 67.

29. "Saudi Arabia Announces Counter-Terrorism Measures."

30. "Kuwaiti Islamic Charity Denies U.S. Terrorist Charges," *Middle East News*, 11 Jan. 2002, at http://www.middleeastwire.com/Kuwait/stories/20020111_meno.shtml (accessed 13 Jan. 2002).

31. "Saudi Arabia Announces Counter-Terrorism Measures."

32. Nada, "Dimensions of the American Attack."

33. Borzou Daragahi, "Financing Terror," *Money*, 30, (1 Nov. 2001):120 (Infotrac A79304052, accessed Sept. 2001).

34. Gamal Essam El-Din, "A Financial Jihad," *Al-Ahram Weekly*, 21–27 Nov. 2002, at http://www.alahram.org.eg/weekly/2002/613/ec2.htm (accessed 21 Nov. 2002).

35. Nada, "Dimensions of the American Attack."

36. Amos Harel, "Israel Does Little to Stop Money Flow to Terror; Shin Bet Sets up New Unit," *Ha'aretz*, 20 Dec. 2003, at http://www.haaretz.com/hasen/spages/377358 .html (accessed 30 Dec. 2003).

37. James Anderson, "International Terrorism and Crime: Trends and Linkages" (Harrisonburg, Va.: William R. Nelson Institute for Public Affairs: James Madison University, n.d.), at http://www.jmu.edu/orgs/wrni/it.htm (accessed 4 Jan. 2003).

38. "Islamic Dinar Gathers Momentun," *Middle East Times*, 2002, at http://www .metimes.com/2K2/issue2002-45/bus/Islamic_dinar_gathers.htm (accessed 9 Nov. 2002).

39. Douglas Farah, "Al Qaeda's Road Paved with Gold: Secret Shipments Traced through a Lax System in the United Arab Emirates," *Washington Post*, 17 Feb. 2002, at http://www.washingtonpost.com/wp-dyn/articles/A22303-2002Feb16.html (accessed 17 Feb. 2002).

40. UAE Ministry of Information & Culture, "Rich Investors from UAE 'Park $266b Abroad,'" *Emirates Bulletin*, 25, 5 Feb. 2002 at http://www.columbia.edu/sec-cgi/gulf/ dataplug.p1.htm (accessed 21 Feb. 2004).

41. "Al Qaeda's Balkan Links," *Wall Street Journal*, 1 Nov. 2001, at http://www.wall-streetjournal.com (accessed 1 Nov. 2001).

42. Eric Lichtblau, "U.S. Raids Foil Plots to Send Arms to Al Qaeda and Others," *New York Times*, 6 Nov. 2002, at http://www.nytimes.com/2002/11/07/international/ asia/07HOMG.html (accessed 7 Nov. 2002).

43. Douglas Farah, "Report Says Africans Harbored Al Qaeda: Terror Assets Hidden in Gem-Buying Spree," *Washington Post*, 29 Dec. 2002, at http://www.washingtonpost .com/wp-dyn/articles/A48929-2002Dec28.html (accessed 29 Dec. 2002).

44. Amelia Hill, "Bin Laden's $20m African 'Blood Diamond' Deals," *Guardian Unlimited*, 20 Oct. 2002, at http://www.observer.co.uk/international/story/0,6903 ,815450,00 .html (accessed 10 Oct. 2002).

45. Hill, "Bin Laden's $20m African 'Blood Diamond' Deals."

46. Lichtblau, "U.S. Raids Foil Plots."

47. Bill Gertz, "Al Qaeda Appears to Have Links with Russian Mafia," *Middle East Times*, reprinted from the *Washington Times*, 10 Oct. 2001, at http://www.metimes.com/ 2k/issue2001-40)/reg/al)qaeda_appears.htm (accessed 10 Oct. 2001).

48. Sandra Jordan, Henry McDonald, and Ed Vullamy, "Sinn Fein's Big Blunder," *The Observer*, 28 Apr. 2002, at http://www.observer.co.uk/focus/sotry/0.6903 .706367.00 .html (accessed 28 April 2002).

49. Senate testimony, Rand Beers, assistant secretary for International Narcotics and Law Enforcement Affairs; Francis X. Taylor, ambassador-at-large for Counter-Terrorism, 13 Mar. 2002.

50. Farah, "Report Says Africans Harbored Al Qaeda."

51. "US-MKO Deal a Breach of Bush's Anti-Terrorism Campaign," *Payvand's Iran News*, 26 Apr. 26, 2003, at http://www.payvand.com/news/03apr/1126.html (accessed 26 Apr. 2003).

52. Elizabeth Rubin, "The Cult of Rajavi," *New York Times Magazine*, 5 (13 July 2003).

53. Elaine Sciolino, "French Arrest 150 from Iranian Opposition Group," *New York Times*, 19 June 2003, at http://www.nytimes.com/2003/06/18/international/europe/ 18FRAN.html (accessed 18 June 2003).

54. Time, 16 Aug. 1982, cited in Monte Palmer, *Politics of the Middle East* (Itasca, Ill.: Peacock Publishers/Wadsworth), 132.

55. Judy Pasternak and Stephen Braun, "Emirates Looked Other Way while Al Qaeda Funds Flowed," *Los Angeles Times*, 20 Jan. 2002, at http://www.latimes.com/news/nationworld/world/la-012002uae.story (accessed 26 July 2002).

56. Tim McGirk, "Has Pakistan Tamed Its Spies?" *Time*, 28 Apr. 2002, at http://www.time.com/time/world/printout/0,8816,233902,00.html (accessed 30 Dec. 2002).

57. "U.S. Envoy Thanks Islamabad for Support against Militants but Asks for More," *Daily Star-Lebanon*, 24 Jan. 2003, at http://www.dailystar.com.lb/24_01_03/art22.asp (accessed 24 Jan. 2003).

58. Pepe Escobar, "The Roving Eye: Get Osama! Now! Or else . . . ," *Asia Times*, 30 Aug. 2001, at http://www.atimes.com/ind-pak/CH30Df01.html (accessed 20 June 2001).

59. Omar Fathaly and Monte Palmer, "Change Resistance among Rural Libyan Elites," *International Journal of Middle East Studies* (1980): 247–261.

60. Dore Gold, *Hatred's Kingdom: How Saudi Arabia Supports the New Global Terrorism* (Washington, D.C.: Regnery Publishing, 2003).

61. Anonymous, *Through Our Enemies' Eyes: Osama Bin Laden, Radical Islam, and the Future of America* (Washington, D.C.: Brassey's, 2002).

62. F. Gregory Gause, *Oil Monarchies: Domestic and Security Challenges in the Arab Gulf States* (New York: Council on Foreign Relations Press, 1994).

8

HOW ISRAEL AND ITS MIDDLE EASTERN NEIGHBORS FIGHT TERROR

Israel has been fighting terror for most of its brief history, but none more so than during the onslaught of jihadist suicide bombings that began in the early 1990s. The countries of the Islamic world also have a long history of fighting jihadist terror. It is they, for the most part, who have been the primary victims of the jihadists. Both Israel and the countries of the Islamic world have scored dramatic successes against the jihadists. Neither, however, has been able to defeat them.

The United States has a great deal to learn from the experience of Israel and the Islamic world in fighting jihadist terror. They are, after all, closer to the problem than anyone else. The objective of the present chapter is to examine the anti-terrorist strategies of Israel and the Islamic world, noting both their strengths and their weaknesses. We begin with Israel, the world's acknowledged leader in fighting terror and then turn to the experience of the Islamic world. It will be noted that Israeli strategy bears a marked resemblance to America's strategy in its war on terror. It could not be otherwise, for the United States regularly seeks Israeli advice on a broad range of terrorist issues, including the best way to quell resistance to the U.S. occupation of Iraq.[1]

THE ISRAELI EXPERIENCE IN FIGHTING TERROR

Aside from serving as a source of national pride, the ancient history of most countries is of little relevance to their modern politics. However, in the case in Israel, it is everything. It is the Jewish kingdoms of ancient Israel that provide the birthright for the modern state of Israel. Israel is the Promised Land, the patrimony of God. Indeed, some Israelis argue that the present state of Israel should incorporate all of the lands of ancient Israel, an area that could well include portions of Lebanon, Jordan, and Syria.[2]

The Jewish kingdoms of ancient Israel were crushed by the Romans in 135 B.C., dispersing Jews throughout Europe and the Middle East. The Jewish Diaspora found life in Christian Europe to be harsh and often violent. Many converted to Christianity. For those who remained true to their faith, Jerusalem, the capital of ancient Israel (Zion) and the site of the holy Temple, became a focal point of hope. All would be well with their return to Zion. Anti-Semitism increased dramatically in the eighteenth and nineteenth centuries as the monarchies of continental Europe sought to ease threats of revolution by blaming Jews for the woes of their subjects.[3] Pogroms, the sanctioned slaughter of Jews, became commonplace in Russia and Eastern Europe.

It was in this environment that Theodor Herzl founded the Zionist movement in the final years of the eighteenth century. The only solution to the persecution of Jews, Herzl argued, was the creation of a Jewish state in which Jews would be able to live without persecution and be free to practice their religion as they saw fit.[4]

The Zionist movement scored its first major victory in 1917, when Britain, having seized control of Palestine from the Turks in World War I, issued the Balfour Declaration, a vaguely worded document designed to placate Jewish demands for a homeland without angering the Arabs. The declaration says: "His Majesty's Government views with favour the establishment in Palestine of a national home for the Jewish people . . . it being clearly understood that nothing shall be done which may prejudice the civil and religious rights of existing non-Jewish communities in Palestine.[5]

The difficulty, of course, was that Palestine was not vacant territory. Geographic Palestine had been incorporated into the Islamic Empire in the period between 632 and 661 A.D. and soon acquired its Arab Islamic character. The origins of the modern Palestinian population can be traced to this era, if not earlier.

A situation thus evolved in which both Jews and Arabs could rightfully claim to be the legitimate heirs of geographic Palestine. The Jewish claim was based on history and religion; the Arab claim on some 1,500 years of continuous occupation. Palestine also had profound religious significance for the world's Muslims, Jerusalem being the third holiest site in Islam. Jews and Arabs both revolted against the British, each hoping to consolidate its claim to Palestine. In the final analysis, it was the Jewish terrorist attacks against the British that forced a British withdrawal from Palestine in 1948. War between the Jews and the Arabs erupted immediately thereafter.[6]

The second Zionist victory came with the War of Independence in 1948, a conflict that saw Jewish forces seize most but not all of geographic Palestine. The Arab armies retained a large enclave neighboring the West Bank of the Jordan River as well as the Gaza Strip, a narrow coastal strip bordering Egypt's Sinai Peninsula. The modern state of Israel had been born. A Palestinian Diaspora had also been born, with many Palestinians living in refugee camps in Jordan, Syria, and Lebanon. Palestinians with marketable skills found positions in the Gulf States or the West. A minority of the Palestinians remained in Israel, becoming Israeli Arabs.

The third Zionist victory came with Israel's lightning victory in the Arab-Israeli War of 1967, also known as the Six Day War. All of the remaining areas of historic Palestine were seized, as were Egypt's Sinai Peninsula and much of Syria's Golan Heights.

The euphoria of victory had yet to settle when the Jewish state was confronted with the knotty and divisive question of what to do with the Occupied Territories. Should they be returned to the Arabs in exchange for a lasting peace or should they be retained by Israel as a defensive shield against future attack or even incorporated into Israel? The disposition of the West Bank and the Gaza Strip were particularly sensitive, for they constituted part of ancient Israel and were of vital significance to religious Israelis. This was especially true of the West Bank, which incorporated the ancient Jewish kingdoms of Judea and Samaria.

The issue appeared to be resolved in 1969 when Israel signed UN Security Council Resolution 242, a document calling for Israeli withdrawal from the Occupied Territories in return for Arab recognition of Israel. Israel signed the document under pressure from an American government fearful that continued hostilities between Israel and its Arab neighbors would bring further Soviet penetration into this most fragile of regions.

Little in the Arab-Israeli conflict remains resolved for very long. The Palestinians refused to recognize Israeli's right to exist and Israel showed little interest in withdrawing from the Occupied Territories. A few religious and security settlements were built in the Occupied Territories, but they were rudimentary affairs and few in number.

All this changed with the 1977 election of Menachem Begin as Israel's prime minister. Begin's Irgun had played a key role in the terrorist campaign that drove the British from Palestine, and he was equally zealous in dealing with the Occupied Territories.[7] The Sinai Peninsula, never part of ancient Israel, would be traded for peace. The West Bank and Gaza, in Begin's view, constituted part of ancient Israel and would never be returned. Rather, they would be settled en route to their eventual incorporation into Israel.

Peace was made with Egypt in 1979. The Arabs' largest army was neutralized and any pretense of Arab unity was shattered. The Peace Accords, brokered by President Carter, also called for the gradual return of Palestinian sovereignty over the Occupied Territories. Anwar Sadat and Menachem Begin, signers of the accords, were awarded the Nobel Peace Prize.

The ink was hardly dry on the peace treaty with Egypt when Begin launched his campaign to settle the Occupied Territories. As the Occupied Territories became increasingly Jewish, they subtly or not so subtly became part of Israel. To underscore the point, Jerusalem was proclaimed the capital of Israel, a claim yet to be recognized by the majority of the rest of the world, including the United States. Settlers, in Begin's view, also meant security. Settlers would control Palestinian terrorists and provide a first line of defense against foreign attack. The Palestinians could have sovereignty over the Palestinian population, but the land belonged to Israel. This, of course, was a contravention of international law, Israel having committed itself to the return of the Occupied Territories by signing UN242 and subsequent documents.[8] It also raised grievous questions about the fate of the Palestinians. Begin had plans for the land but had no intention of incorporating the Palestinians into Israel. Not only would they be a security threat, but Israel's Jewish character would be compromised. The Palestinian birth rate was among the highest in the world; Israel's birthrate among the lowest. It would just be a matter of time before the Palestinians could vote themselves into office.

Begin's settlement policies were extended by his successors, sowing panic among a Palestinian population fearing that they would be driven from the last remaining vestiges of their homeland. Terror and counterterror increased proportionally, exploding in the Palestinian intifada of 1987–1989. The presence of a large settler population living in the midst of Arabs merely served to increase friction and opportunities for terror. The intifada marked a dramatic escalation in Palestinian resistance to the Israeli occupation. It also marked the entrance of Hamas and other jihadist groups into the fray.

The cycle of violence and counterviolence resulted in yet another U.S. effort to reconcile the two sides. Much publicized negotiations were initiated in Madrid in 1991and dragged on through 1993. They were abandoned in 1993 with the stunning news that Yasir Arafat, head of the PLO, and Yitzhak Rabin, the recently elected prime minister of Israel, had been holding secret negotiations in Oslo, Norway. The foundation of the Oslo Accords was the principle that land would be exchanged for peace. Once again, there had been a stark reversal in Israeli policy.

No one had ever accused the hard-line Rabin, one of Israel's most decorated generals, of being soft on Arabs. The forces pushing him toward peace, however, were compelling. The peace treaty with Egypt had effectively deprived the Arab countries of the capacity to fight a war with Israel. The collapse of the Soviet Union in 1990 had further eased Israel's security by depriving Syria and Iraq, the most serious remaining Arab threats to Israel, of cheap weapons and diplomatic support. Iraq had been devastated by the Gulf War of 1991, and Syria, with a keen ear to world realities, was attempting to ingratiate itself with Washington. Syria had also given every indication that it was willing to trade land for peace. The United States was now the dominant power in the world and had pledged to protect Israel from future attacks by its Arab neighbors.

Rabin also came to grips with hard realities of the Palestinian situation. The Palestinians could not be incorporated into Israel and they would not go away. Israel's anti-terrorist measures, moreover, had failed to stem Palestinian violence and the growing influence of Hamas and other jihadist groups in the Palestinian resistance promised more to come.[9] Finally, peace brought new opportunities. Israel would reap a huge peace dividend as it scaled back its mammoth defense budget and extricated itself from the nightmarish occupation of the Occupied Territories and southern Lebanon. The Jewish settlements, the main source of tension between the United States and Israel, would be removed and Israel would be well positioned to become the financial and technological center of the region.

In retrospect the optimism swept the region as the Israeli forces withdrew from predominantly Palestinian areas of the Occupied Territories. These were governed by a newly created Palestinian Authority, while the remainder of the Occupied Territories were patrolled jointly by Israeli and Palestinian forces or remained under Israeli control. The process was to be extended over a period of years until the Palestinians had established a Palestinian state that controlled a large portion of the Occupied Territories consistent with the needs of Israeli security.

The optimism that accompanied the Oslo negotiations was misplaced. All of the key issues were left to be resolved by negotiations, not the least of which were the final boundaries of Israel; the right of Palestinians who had fled in 1948 to return to Israel if they so desired; Jerusalem; the disposition of existing settlements; security measures to be imposed on the new Palestinian state; and the allocation of extremely scarce water resources. There was also a law of physics that states that two objects cannot occupy the same place at the same time. Both communities had grown, and the territory was not large enough for both. The Palestinians would have a state, but it could only accommodate a fraction of the Palestinian population. The economic viability of the new state was also questionable. With few natural resources and less water, its survival would be dependent on international donations and economic arrangements with Israel. Above all, there remained the religious nature of the Occupied Territories. While Rabin, a secular Jew, was willing to trade land for peace, a large segment of the Israeli population was not.

Violence escalated as extremists on both sides attempted to scuttle the Oslo Accords. Rabin was assassinated by a Jewish fanatic in 1996. The peace process continued after Rabin's assassination, but so did the building of settlements and the terror, each side blaming the other for the breakdown in negotiations. The Palestinian Authority was also ineffective in controlling Palestinian violence, scuttling the confidence of an always-nervous Israeli population. A new and far more violent intifada erupted in September 2000, unleashing a cycle of violence and counterviolence that devastated both communities. Ariel Sharon was elected prime minister in 2001 by vowing to crush the violence by force. Sharon elevated the brutality of Israeli anti-terrorist operations to unparalleled levels. He also escalated the building of settlements. Violence continued to escalate, but Sharon was elected for a second term in 2003. The Oslo Accords, for all intents and purposes, were dead.

THE BASIC PRINCIPLES OF ISRAELI ANTI-TERRORIST STRATEGY

The basic principles of Israeli anti-terrorist strategy have evolved over the course of the Jewish state's tortured history. As almost everything else in Israel, they are debated on a daily basis in the Israeli press. Readers wanting more detail have only to sign on to the websites of the *Jerusalem Post*[10] and the English version of *Ha'aretz*.[11] Both are brutally frank in their coverage of Israel's anti-terrorist operations, albeit from an Israeli perspective. Palestinian coverage of Israeli anti-terrorist operations can be found on the Palestine-Net.com website.

Defense

Israeli anti-terrorist strategy begins with defense. Israeli civil defense measures are the most draconian in the world and make a mockery of the domestic security measures put in place by the United States in the aftermath of the September 11 attacks. Boarding an El Al aircraft for Israel guarantees a lengthy security check that leaves nothing to chance. El Al flights are seldom listed on departure screens, passengers being summoned at the last minute and ferried by bus to an El Al aircraft parked on a remote runway. Passengers boarding an El Al aircraft from Egypt are subject to minute searches and an exhausting interrogation about their reasons for visiting Israel. This is particularly the case for passengers carrying passports littered with Arab visa stamps. Controversial passengers are either delayed or denied boarding passes. All of this is annoying, but the hijacking of El Al flights has been virtually eliminated and Israeli internal security agencies have been spared the effort of keeping track of potential troublemakers.

Israelis are also concerned about people leaving Israel. Security agents want to know where you have been, what you did, who you talked to, and what errands Palestinian friends asked you to carry out for them. The interviews are polite but thorough. If concerns arise, supervisors are called in for assistance.

Airport security pales in comparison to the searches and interrogations that await travelers entering Israel via Jordan's Allenby Bridge. Israeli security officials are concerned about gold and jewelry being smuggled to Palestinian friends, but more so about weapons and communications. The Israeli's x-rayed the heels of shoes decades before the September 11 attacks on the United States.

Palestinian laborers crossing into Israel transverse numerous checkpoints where searches are made for arms, explosives, and suspected terrorists. The Occupied Territories are often "sealed" during Jewish and Islamic holy days as well as on emotional anniversaries likely to trigger terrorist attacks. Curfews in the Occupied Territories are frequent and pervasive. Were it not for their dependence on cheap Palestinian labor, the Israelis would probably close the borders permanently.[12] Steps in this direction may soon be in the offing, as the Israeli government is constructing a massive security fence between Israel and the Occupied Territories. The fence is being built on the Palestinian side of the border separating Israel from the Occupied Territories and often involves the demolition of Palestinian homes and businesses. There are negative reactions to the fence on both sides. The Palestinians are irate. The settlers fear that they are being cut off from Israel proper and may be sacrificed as part of a "final solution" being forced on Israel by the United States. Security fences are also being constructed around Jewish settlements in the Occupied Territories, including Syria's Golan Heights. President Bush has condemned the fences, but Prime Minister Sharon has held firm, noting that even the best of friends often disagree.[13]

As things currently stand, Jewish settlements in the Occupied Territories play an integral role in Israeli defenses against terror. Huge blocks of Jewish settlements ring Palestinian-controlled areas of the Occupied Territories, creating Palestinian reservations not unlike the Indian reservations in the United States. Roads, built on land claimed by the Palestinians, link the settlements but these are defensive in nature and are not accessible to the Palestinians. Palestinian areas, by contrast, are linked via circuitous routes that offer Israeli forces ample opportunity to establish checkpoints and otherwise monitor the flow of Palestinian activity.

Settlers also serve in the military reserve, assist border guards and other security units, and often form vigilante groups that enforce frontier justice. Terrorist acts by Jewish settlers embarrass the Israeli government, but generally go unpunished.[14] Those who are punished usually get what amounts to little more than a slap on the wrist. Jail sentences, when imposed, are soon commuted. The Palestinians are the enemy, and the settler presence is viewed as a vital step in controlling the Occupied Territories. Indeed, settlement activity has increased under all recent Israeli governments with the possible exception of Rabin. The Sharon government has consistently advocated the acceleration of settlements, and settlements have increased 16 percent since his reign as prime minister began.[15] Much like Begin, Sharon believes that Israel's claim to the Occupied Territories depends on settlers outnumbering Palestinians.

Settlement activity has not slowed markedly during recent U.S. efforts to broker a lasting peace between the Israelis and the Palestinians. Israel has agreed not to start new settlements, and Washington has agreed that Israel can expand old ones.[16] Discussions continue.

Attack Suspected Terrorists with Maximum Force: No Smoking Gun Required

Israel believes that it is in a war for its survival and acts accordingly. As most terrorist attacks emanate from the Occupied Territories and it is they who bear the brunt of Israeli security measures. Terrorist attacks are followed by sweeps through Palestinian cities and often involve the reoccupation of lands under the control of the Palestinian Authority. Facilities, including the headquarters of the Palestinian Authority, have been searched, weapons and documents seized, and suspected terrorists arrested. Arafat's compound was virtually destroyed. Criteria for arrest are flexible, often being little more than a hunch. Mistakes will be sorted out later. In the meantime, Israeli lives may be saved. Palestinian demonstrators are frequently met with live ammunition or rubber-coated steel bullets.

Known terrorists, many identified by traitors and infiltrators, are targeted for assassination, usually by aircraft. Sheikh Yassir, the leader of Hamas, was assassinated as was his successor.[17] Cars are strafed; buildings bombed. Collateral damage, in the Israeli view, is the price of war. Ground attacks often involve the use of human shields. Terrorists living abroad are targeted by Mossad, the external branch of Israeli intelligence.

In addition to eliminating terrorists, the severity of Israeli anti-terrorist measures serves as a warning to future terrorists and their supporters. Each escalation in the severity of terrorist attacks has been matched by escalation in the severity of the Israeli response and vice versa. The cycle of terror and counterterror goes on, pausing for an occasional truce.

Collective Punishment: Dry up the Swamp

The swamp, in Israeli jargon, refers to popular Palestinian support for the terrorists and their activities. If it were not for popular support, so the Israeli argument goes, the terrorists would have neither the means to attack nor places to hide. This is not a minor consideration, for more than one million of Israel's 6.4 million citizens are Palestinians.[18] The most recent census conducted by the Central Statistics Department in the Palestinian Government stated that the Palestinian population in the Occupied Territories totaled 2.9 million. The Palestinian population of the West Bank alone was nearly 2.3 million people. An additional 1.3 million Palestinians were living in the Gaza Strip.[19]

Collective support for terror, in Israeli logic, warrants the collective punishment of the Palestinian community. The relatives of terrorists have their homes demolished and are often deported from the West Bank. Palestinian families are tightly knit, and Israeli punishments make it very clear to potential terrorists that their relatives will pay for their sins. The same principle applies to the Palestinian community at large. Borders are closed, leaving Palestinian families with little visible means of support. Food shipments are also blocked or delayed, as are medical supplies. Universities are closed for extended periods, sometimes months at a time, leaving future generations without a skill base on which to build their future. Most young boys have been interrogated by security police, a terrifying experience in itself. More terrorizing is the collateral damage that routinely accompanies Israeli sweeps into the Occupied Territories and its targeted assassinations. An April 2002 attack on the Palestinian city of Jenin was labeled a massacre by the Arab media; UN investigators rejected this claim, but called it "horrifying."[20] Collective punishments are designed to place a wedge between the terrorists and the Palestinian community. No terror, say the Israelis, no collective punishment.

The swamp also includes mosques, charitable organizations, and schools that lend support to terrorist activities. Those institutions with suspected links to Hamas or the Holy Jihad, the major jihadist groups operating in the Occupied Territories, are particularly high on the Israeli "watch" list. Both groups deploy suicide bombers within Israel, and Hamas reportedly aspires to the leadership of the Palestinian movement.[21] Hamas denies these rumors, but the Israelis find them chilling. The Palestinian Authority has recognized Israel's right to exist; Hamas and the Palestinian Holy Jihad have not.

Drive a Wedge between the Terrorists and Their Base of Popular Support

Many Israeli analysts stress the need to drive a wedge between the terrorists and the Palestinian population by easing the hardships on the Palestinians and working with moderate Palestinian leaders.[22] Both measures, they argue, will accentuate the tension between the terrorists and the Palestinian population and ease the flow of new recruits to the terrorist camp. Palestinian workers are allowed into Israel and relief funds are channeled to Palestinian welfare organizations despite fears that some may find their way into the hands of the terrorists. Humanitarian strategies, by and large, lack the immediacy of government efforts to stamp out the terrorists.

Destroy the Foreign Base Camps of the Terrorists

The stringency of Israeli counterterrorist measures has forced Palestinian terrorist organizations to rely heavily on base camps in surrounding countries. Egypt, Jordan, Syria, and Lebanon all hosted such groups during the 1960s and 1970s and were the subject of frequent Israeli incursions. Lebanon was invaded in 1982 and Israel maintained a 24-kilometer security zone in southern Lebanon until being driven out by Hizbullah forces in May 2000. Peace between Israel and Egypt has limited overt Egyptian support for Palestinian resistance groups, but the Israelis continue to press Cairo to stem the smuggling of money and weapons across the Egyptian-Israeli border, much of it coming from Islamic groups in Egypt. The picture in Jordan is much the same. Lebanon and Syria remain active supporters of the Palestinian resistance, as does Hizbullah. Israeli aircraft pound Hizbullah positions on a routine basis and Israel attempts to intimidate the Lebanese government by overflights of Beirut and occasional bombings of Lebanese power stations. The Lebanese military, lacking the capacity to challenge Israel, responds to the bombings with anti-aircraft fire, usually for hours after the planes have departed. The overflights are duly reported to the United Nations. Syria is threatened with attack unless it reins in Hizbullah and Palestinian groups in Lebanon, but little has happened to date other than the October 2003 bombing of a suspected training camp for terrorists. The Syrians walk a fine line, allowing enough activity to pressure an Israeli withdrawal from the Israeli-occupied Golan Heights while stopping short of overt provocation. The Damascus offices of Hamas and Holy Jihad have been closed down under U.S. pressure, but it is hard to believe that their presence has disappeared. Hamas and Holy Jihad also receive strong support from Iran as does Hizbullah. Saudi Arabia and the Gulf States offer generous welfare aid to the Palestinian community, a significant portion of which presumably finds its way into the hands of terrorist organizations. Israeli sources claim that the Saudis provide 50 percent of Hamas's funding.[23] The Saudis deny the charge.

Destroy Governments that Support Terrorists and Replace Them with Cooperative Regimes

The ultimate solution to the problem of foreign support, from the Israeli perspective, is the forced replacement of hostile Middle Eastern regimes with leaders of a more cooperative mien. This was the objective of Israel's 1956 war with Egypt and, to a lesser extent, the Arab-Israeli War of 1967. The 1967 war, often referred to as the Six Day War, humiliated the Arab forces and, for all intents and purposes, spelled the end of the Nasser regime in Egypt. Nasser, the major threat to Israel's existence was neutralized and he passed away three years later. His successors have been of a distinctly more cooperative demeanor, making peace with the Jewish state in

1979. Israel's 1982 invasion of Lebanon was designed to dislodge the Palestinians from their base camps. It was also designed to establish a friendly Christian government in Lebanon. Peace was supposed to be made between the two countries and Christian forces were to prevent a return of Palestinian terror. The plan ultimately failed, and Lebanon's civil war dragged on for another decade.

Israel's most recent efforts to place a cooperative government in power focuses on the removal of Yasir Arafat, the elected president of the Palestinian Authority, and his replacement by a government more effective in controlling terrorism. Israeli tactics have been less than subtle. Frequent shelling of Arafat's compound gave way to house arrest and eventually to invasion. The Israelis have justified their attack on Arafat's headquarters by seizing documents reportedly linking the Palestinian Authority to anti-Israeli terrorism. In the fall of 2003, Israel's vice premier suggested that Arafat might have to be killed. "Killing him is definitely one of the options," Ehud Olmert told Israel Radio. "We are attempting to eliminate all of the heads of terror and Arafat is one of the heads of terror."[24] Israel backed down following a hue and cry in the United Nations, but admitted that plans to snatch Arafat had been in the works since 2002.[25] Threats to assassinate Arafat have also continued.

The Israeli prime minister was also an ardent supporter of America's war against Iraq. So much so, in fact, that the Israeli government began issuing statements saying that the decision on the matter rested with President Bush and that Israel was not trying to drag the United States into a war with Iraq.[26] Be this as it may, Sharon is now openly lobbying Bush to forcibly change the regimes of Iran and Syria.

Alliance and Self-Reliance

Israeli efforts to build alliances in its war on terror have focused largely on the United States, Turkey, and Iran. Turkey and Iran, powerful non-Arab countries that surround the Middle East's Arab core, share Israel's antipathy toward the Arabs and have traditionally supported a strong U.S. presence in the region. Iran dropped out of the triangle with the overthrow of the Iranian monarchy in 1979, with the Ayatollah Khomeini subsequently denouncing Israel as an American plot to subvert Islam. Arms trade continues to exist between Israel and Iran, but Iranian support for Hizbullah and the Palestinian jihadists has strained relations to the breaking point. Particularly worrying to the Israelis is the Islamic Republic's acquisition of rockets capable of reaching Israel as well as its on going effort to develop weapons of mass destruction. Israel has announced it will strike Iran if the threat continues.[27] Relations with Turkey have also been dampened by the advent of a fundamentalist prime minister. Nevertheless, joint maneuvers between Israel, Turkey, and the United States took place in 2003.

In the final analysis, the United States remains Israel's staunchest ally, providing the Jewish state with massive amounts of military assistance and countering condemnations of Israeli anti-terrorist measures in the United Nations. As close as Israel and the United States may be, however, they are not of one mind on the disposition of the Occupied Territories. The United States has repeatedly condemned Israeli settlements and pressured the Jewish state to return the Occupied Territories in hopes of bringing stability to this most fragile of regions. The Israelis keep evading the issue.

STRATEGIC TRAPS THE ISRAELIS TRY TO AVOID

Israel's anti-terrorist strategy also focuses on avoiding traps that will reduce its effectiveness. Most are self-evident and require little elaboration.

1. Do not be deterred by fear of civilian casualties. Civilian casualties (collateral damage) are an inevitable product of war, and Israel is at war. This is unfortunate, but the blame rests with terrorist groups who hide among civilian populations.

2. Do not allow the terrorists to hide behind civil-rights legislation. Civil rights are for the peaceful citizens of Israel, not their enemies. Freedoms of the press must give way to the needs of Israeli security. Civil-rights reports, including those of the U.S. government are scathing in their criticism of Israel anti-terrorist policy.[28] Peace activists are particularly unwelcome. A few have been shot.[29]

3. Do not allow the creation of a Palestinian state that is capable of threatening the security of Israel. It is probable that a symbolic Palestinian state will evolve on some portions of the Occupied Territories, but it cannot be a state that supports terrorism or forms alliances with the enemies of Israel.

4. Do not allow international law and the resolutions of the United Nations to hamper anti-terrorist operations. Israel's security takes precedence over UN resolutions, most of which are orchestrated by Israel's enemies. Under no circumstances is a UN security force

such as that deployed in the Balkans to be allowed into the Occupied Territories. A UN force would interfere with Israel's fight against terror. It would also create a de facto Palestinian state over which Israel had little control.

5. Do not bend to external pressure. Europe and the United Nations can be ignored as long as American support remains firm. American pressure can be managed via public relations campaigns, APAIC (the main Israeli lobby in Washington), and Israeli support in Congress.

6. Don't wait for the terrorists to act. If you can see the smoking gun, it's too late.

7. Don't be afraid to go it alone. Alliances are useful in fighting terror but cannot be allowed to shape Israeli policy. Negotiations are slow and result in half-way measures. Neither, in the Israeli view, is conducive to fighting terror.

ASSESSMENTS: CONSEQUENCES AND EFFECTIVENESS

The Sharon government makes no apologies for the severity of its anti-terrorist strategy, bluntly stating that Israel is in a war for its survival. The severity of Israeli counterterrorist measures is also designed to reassure a nervous population weary of living under the constant threat of terror. Israeli leaders believe that a growing population is vital to the security of Israel and "reverse immigration" has always been a problem during times of crisis. Israelis, like people worldwide, want to pursue their careers and raise their families in a secure environment. It is no longer clear that Israel can provide that environment. Security issues have also slowed immigration from abroad. In a curious twist of fate, Jews migrating from the countries of the former Soviet Union prefer Germany to Israel. Security is their greatest concern.[30]

American papers are reluctant to discuss the severity of Israel's anti-terrorist measures, perhaps fearing to embarrass an American ally. The State Department has been less timid, its annual report on civil rights condemning virtually all aspects of Israel's anti-terrorist strategy. The Israeli government routinely protests the report, but life goes on.

The Israeli press is neither reluctant nor restrained in its reporting of the government's anti-terrorist measures. Terror is part of the Israeli existence, and the struggle against terror is of vital concern to all Israeli citizens.

There is no embarrassment, merely debates about effectiveness and repercussions.

Severe questions exist in both regards. Many Israelis fear that the severity of their counterterror measures will erode Jewish values. They are also tired of living in a garrison state in which military convoys and terrorist alerts are a way of life. Adding to feelings of isolation is global criticism of Israel's anti-terrorist policies. Condemnations of the Israeli policies in the United Nations have become routine and easily ignored. It is more difficult to deal with the growing criticism from within the Jewish community. The New Israel Fund, for example, has been sponsoring ads in the *New York Times* and elsewhere calling on American Jews to protect Israel's democratic values. These values, the organization suggests, have been severely eroded since the beginning of the second intifada.[31]

There are also concerns that Israel's anti-terrorist policies will cause a rift between the United States and Israel. A long succession of American presidents has criticized Israel's occupation of the Occupied Territories, finding it to be an obstacle to lasting peace in the region. U.S. concerns have acquired greater urgency in the post–September 11 era; Secretary of State Powell has pointedly warned Prime Minister Sharon not to declare war on the Palestinians. "If you declare war against the Palestinians thinking that you can solve the problem by seeing how many Palestinians can be killed, I don't know that that leads us anywhere."[32] President Bush, a devoted supporter of Israel, has been harsh in his criticism of Israel's security fence, noting that it is being built on expropriated Palestinian land.[33]

Of far greater concern to Israeli citizens is the fact that Israeli counterterrorist measures have not stopped the terror. Senior Israeli police officials describe 2001 as "the year of terror" and add that the number of terrorist attacks in 2001 was greater than the combined total of terrorist attacks for the three preceding years."[34] A total of 1,794 terrorist attacks were recorded in 2001, of which thirty-one were suicide bombings. A reported 208 Israelis were killed in the attacks and more than 1,500 wounded. By mid-2003, the 1,000th day of terror (the second intifada), the IDF estimates that 810 Israelis and non-Arabs had been killed in terrorist attacks, of whom 567 were civilians and 243 were soldiers.[35] The number of wounded was a staggering 5,600. These figures pale in comparison to Palestinian losses during the same period: 2,330 killed, 14,000 injured. Palestinian sources suggest that the Israeli estimates of Palestinian losses have been deflated. They were bitterly critical of IDF estimates that only 18 percent of the Palestinian dead were innocent civilians.[36] The International Committee of the Red Cross took a middle position, expressing "alarm and dismay" at the number of civilians being killed by both sides.[37]

Not only have terrorist attacks persisted, but there has been a marked increase in their severity. Civilians have now become the target of choice and the war has moved from the Occupied Territories to Israel proper and the world at large. Each rise in Israeli security measures has brought a corresponding rise in the sophistication of the terrorist attacks that now feature rockets and suicide bombers. The threat of chemical and biologic weapons is anticipated. Danny Rubinstein, a leading Israeli commentator, simply states that past strategies no longer work. Assassinations have not brought calm and have often triggered more terror.[38] Security officials claim to have prevented 80 percent of the terrorist attacks and that there were only 3,838 attacks in 2003 as opposed to 5,301 in 2002.[39] Neither figure is terribly reassuring to the Israeli population. To them, a 20 percent success rate for the terrorists is unacceptable.

The summer of 2003 brought a lull in the violence, as both Israel and the Palestinians paused to take stock of the carnage. Sharon acknowledged that there would have to be a Palestinian state and issued an insightful statement on the woes of occupation.[40] Approximately 450 of Israel's 5,600 Palestinian prisoners were ordered released from Israeli prisons.[41] Hamas, Holy Jihad, and the al-Aqsa Brigades declared a three-month truce and the near dictatorial authority of Arafat was balanced with the addition of a prime minister to the Palestinian power structure.

There had been no clear winner. Both sides were reeling from the horrendous toll of the violence and it was not clear that either could sustain the cycle of violence much longer. In the final analysis, it was probably American pressure on Israel and Arab pressure on the Palestinians that forced the halt in hostilities. The Bush administration was reluctant to rein in its Israeli ally, but could not ignore the devastating impact of Israeli counterterror measures on American support in the Islamic world. This message was hand carried to Washington by the leaders of Egypt, Saudi Arabia, and Jordan, who all warned of a regional conflagration if things did not change. It was not just a matter of America's war on terror. It was also a matter of survival for these leaders.

Tragically, the truce collapsed in a wave of violence and counterviolence. As usual, each side blamed the other, with neither side showing much enthusiasm for the "road map for peace" cobbled together by the United States, the European Union, and Russia. The Israeli Knesset weighed in by passing a resolution saying that the Occupied Territories weren't occupied.[42]

None of the key issues separating the Israelis and the Palestinians were resolved. Jerusalem, the right of Palestinian refugees to return to Israel, water, Israeli security, the fate of the settlements, and the nature the Palestinian state were all to be worked out by negotiations over the course of the next few years. Even the precise number of prisoners to be released by Israel was unresolved. Still, the United States believes that there is a "realistic" chance for a Palestinian state by 2005.[43]

Is Israel's Anti-Terrorist Strategy Failing?

What, then, explains this cruel paradox: Why have escalations in the severity and sophistication of Israeli anti-terrorist measures produced little more than a stalemate? Every lull in terror, every claim of victory, or so it seems, gives way to new attacks of increased horror. Stones have given way to rockets, and violence in the territories has moved to violence in Israel. Few people believe that the present lull in violence can be sustained. Debates over the reasons for the declining effectiveness of Israeli anti-terror measures have been standard fare in the Israeli press for the past several years. Even Prime Minister Sharon advocated at least a partial withdrawal from the Occupied Territories. Reasons are summarized below.

The core of the paradox begins with motivation. Individuals do not fight bullets with stones or throw themselves at tanks without an intensity of motivation that borders on desperation. In a 2002 interview, Ben-Eliezer, then minister of Defense, acknowledged that the lack of hope among Palestinians encouraged suicide bombers.[44]

The primary component in the desperation of the Palestinians is the loss of land. The Palestinians are attached to their land with the same intensity as the Israelis, Americans, and all other nationalities are attached to theirs. This is not difficult to understand. Historical Palestine is the land of their ancestors and their ancestors before them. Land is also economic and psychological security. Each new expropriation of Palestinian territory for roads, security fences, national parks, and strategic military areas represents a further diminution of what remains of the historical Palestine. To put Palestinian fear in perspective, it is necessary to understand that the Occupied Territories are an infinitesimally small area of land. One can drive from one end of Israel to the other in about six hours on the diagonal; crosswise in less than forty minutes. The Occupied Territories constitute about one-fourth of that.

According to the Israeli human rights group B'Tselem, there were 135 settlements and 380,000 settlers in West Bank and Jerusalem at the end of 2002.[45] Israeli government figures place the number of Jews in all of the Occupied Territories for the same period at 218,862. The number of settlements increased dramatically following the signing of the Oslo Peace Accords as the Israeli government staked its claim to ever-larger segments of the Occupied Territories in preparation for "final negotiations." *Ha'aretz*, one of Israel's leading newspapers, notes that the settler movement is now attempting to "capture" as much land as possible via the "construction of industrial zones, gas stations, landscaped parks, motels, and water towers."[46] The construction of "outposts" has also become prominent in recent years, each manned by a handful of settlers. The outposts are then linked to the main settlement by roads constructed through Palestinian territory or expanded into new settlements. According to *Ha'aretz*, the expansion process is coordinated with Prime Minister Sharon and top IDF officers. Most outposts lack permits, making them illegal according to Israeli law. Some have been closed down; others have been legalized retroactively. The process continues.[47]

Adding to the Palestinian's sense of crisis is the lack of viable alternatives. They simply have no place to go. The Israelis do not want to incorporate the Palestinians within Israel proper, and most Arab governments view them as a security threat. Poorer Arab countries also fear that Palestinians will compete with local workers, aggravating unemployment levels that hover in the 30 percent range. Palestinians, for their part, are vocal about their poor treatment at the hands of their Arab neighbors. The Arab world supports the Palestinian cause, but it does not want Palestinian immigrants or refugees.

Land, of course, is not the only source of Palestinian desperation. Water is sparse and tightly regulated by the Israelis. The Palestinian economy has also been battered by closures and land confiscations. Unemployment rates among the Palestinians average 40 percent, but in some areas approach 80 percent. A Swiss expert on the Right to Food commissioned by the United Nations to study poverty in the Occupied Territories cited a World Bank report indicating that almost one child in ten is suffering from severe malnutrition. The same report indicated that 15 percent of the children under the age of five are acutely anemic. The Swiss expert noted that, "Markets don't function, peasants don't go to the field, and they are humiliated in a very, very shocking way."[48]

Desperation Leads to Radicalism

The Palestinian resistance has long been led by the PLO, a loose umbrella of Palestinian resistance groups under the leadership of Yasir Arafat. Arafat managed to keep the Palestinian resistance in the public eye, but made little progress in regaining control of the Occupied Territory. This led to the first intifada (1987) and the entry of the jihadists into the mix of Palestinian opposition groups. The more the PLO stumbled, the more powerful the jihadists became. The Oslo Accords of 1993 led to the establishment of the Palestinian Authority, a quasi government that controlled some areas of the Occupied Territories. Others remained under Israeli control or were administered jointly by the Israelis and the Palestinians. Negotiations were to result in the return of most of the Occupied Territories, but went poorly. Each side blamed the other. Both blamed Arafat and the Palestinian Authority. The Palestinians found the Palestinian Authority to be ineffective, autocratic, and corrupt. Israelis condemned it for being unable to control jihadist terror. Settlements increased apace, as did jihadist terror. It was the jihadists who introduced the suicide bombers and it was the jihadists who launched suicide attacks in the heart of Israel. The al-Aqsa Brigades, an offshoot of Arafat's al-Fatha movement, followed suit. Not to have done so would have been to see the leadership of the resistance slip into the hands of the jihadists. It was the jihadists who led the charge in the second intifada that erupted in September 2000 and it is they who are biding their time as they wait for the latest U.S. peace initiative to flounder. Jewish extremists are also biding their time.

Israel May Be Creating More Terrorists than It Is Eliminating

Yet another reason Israel may be losing its war on terror is that its antiterrorist measures are producing more terrorists than they are eliminating. The closing of Palestinian universities for months on end has created generations of students with few skills and little future. The destruction of houses and land grabs are creating waves of homeless Palestinians that the Israeli papers now refer to as "lost children."[49] Prisons are bulging with youths suspected of terrorism. Refugee camps, many in existence since the 1948 war, are bastions of hatred. All are the breeding ground for new terrorists, and Israeli security officials warn that the supply of terrorists, including suicide bombers, may be inexhaustible.[50] Danny Rubinstein, a leading Israeli analyst, argues that past strategies such as assassinations cannot work because there are too many terrorists. "The army is no longer chasing down a handful of activists. . . . Hamas has masses of supporters who give forth thousands of activists, and they can easily enlist terrorists. And dozens, if not hundreds, are ready to be suicide bomber *shaheeds* [martyrs]."[51] It is now the terrorists who are becoming the heroes of young kids. Some even swap terrorist trading cards.[52]

The IDF repeatedly denies charges of excessive force and stresses that it does everything in its power to avoid civilian casualties. When a recent F-16 attack on an apartment complex housing suspected terrorists caused a multitude of civilian casualties, the generals said that they would never have approved the attack had they known that there would be civilian casualties. This statement caused a commentator in the hawkish *Jerusalem Post* to comment "Come on! Really? This is the same IDF that has been praised for the excellence of its intelligence."[53]

TACTICAL ADVANTAGE TO THE JIHADISTS

The success of the jihadists is also built on a variety of tactical advantages that the Israelis have found difficult to counter. Of these, none is greater than their continued support among the Palestinian population. Desperation and anger are not limited to a small layer of radicals, but now pervade much of the Palestinian population. Opinion polls conducted in 2002 by the Jerusalem Media and Communication Center, a Palestinian think tank, suggest that some 80 percent of the Palestinians in the Occupied Territories support a continuation of the intifada, with some 64 percent supporting continued suicide attacks within Israel.[54] Figures mellowed during the truce forged during the spring of 2003, but support for the Intifada still remained substantial.[55]

Few Palestinians are gun-toters, but resistance groups do receive funding and shelter from a broad base of the Palestinian population. Terrorists strike and disappear undetected into the throngs of peaceful Palestinians. They are flushed out, but only at a tremendous cost in terms of innocent lives and adverse publicity. The Palestinian support for the intifada, moreover, has not collapsed in the face of Israeli tanks and aircraft. They fear death, but many believe that resistance is their only hope of retaining the Occupied Territories. Global media attention and vacillation on the part of the Israeli government have sustained their hope that violence will succeed.

The jihadists also benefit from the close proximity of the Jewish and Palestinian populations. Settlements in the Occupied Territories are surrounded by Palestinian communities, and 15 percent of the Israeli population is of Palestinian origin. Long docile, Israeli Palestinians have increasingly been accused of abetting terrorist attacks within Israel. Also adding to the difficulty of Israeli security forces is the similarity in the features of the Palestinians and Israelis. Infiltration and disguises are difficult to detect. Indeed, many terrorists have dressed in uniforms of the IDF. One Israeli scientist has gone so far as to suggest that Israelis and Palestinians share a common gene pool.[56]

Israeli security forces have similarly been forced to confront the growing sophistication of Palestinian tactics. Stones and Molotov cocktails have given way to rockets and suicide bombers. Rather than fearing death, the suicide bombers welcome it. Women have enlisted as suicide bombers, doubling the burden on security forces and adding a new layer of cultural sensitivities to relations between the Palestinians and the Israelis. Nothing excites Arab anger quite as quickly as the harassment of an Arab woman.

In much the same manner, the close proximity of jihadist support groups in Lebanon, Jordan, Saudi Arabia, Syria, Egypt, and Iran (via Hizbullah) ensures that an adequate supply of weapons and money make their way through Israeli patrols. Hizbullah Lebanon serves as a virtual base camp for the Palestinian jihadists and has even hinted that it may open a "second front" in northern Israel. This is unlikely, but the threat cannot be ignored and places a further strain on Israeli security forces.

The jihadists have also adopted the Hizbullah tactic of forcing the Israelis to take casualties. Israel finds it very difficult to suffer the loss of Jewish life and has often traded hundreds of prisoners to gain the freedom of a downed pilot or captured spy.[57] Mounting casualties, more than any other factor, forced the Israeli withdrawal from southern Lebanon. The Palestinian jihadists are betting that mounting casualties will force an Israeli withdrawal from the Occupied Territories. In the process, attacks against Israeli soldiers have given way to attacks on Israeli civilians, with Israelis fearing suicide bombings far more than the threat of foreign attacks.[58]

DECLINING MORALE

The regenerative powers of the terrorists and their broad base of popular support has placed an inordinate strain on Israeli security forces, who are far more comfortable killing foreign enemies than fighting civilians.[59] Desertion rates in the IDF are increasing, and the military complains that closures designed to prevent arms smuggling and the infiltration of suicide terrorists often collapse within days due to a lack of manpower.[60] Resistance to serving in the Occupied Territories has also increased, with some 40 percent of eligible reservists avoiding the IDF.[61] A highly publicized group of reservists has similarly issued a public statement stating, "We will not continue to fight beyond the Green Line[62] in order to rule, to expel, to destroy, to blockade, to assassinate, to starve, and to humiliate an entire people."[63] This was followed in September 2003 by a petition signed by twenty-seven reserve pilots that said that they refused to participate in "illegal and immoral" strikes in Palestinian areas in the West Bank and Gaza Strip.[64]

In the meantime, the prolonged reoccupation of territories under the control of the Palestinian Authority has resulted in increased IDF casualties. Foot soldiers are forced to search Palestinian areas with light weapons, making them easy prey to rooftop snipers and ambushes. Tanks entering congested areas are destroyed by mines, and routine patrols come under fire from hidden adversaries. Adding insult to injury, Israeli security forces complain of decreasing resources. The IDF lacks money to provide its soldiers with bullet-proof vests. Senior police officials note that Israel now has only 2.1 policemen per 1,000 residents, as opposed to 3.5 some fifteen years ago.[65] Parallel cuts in the IDF budget are threatened. Occupation is very expensive business.

Further compounding the IDF's woes has been a profound lack of cooperation from the Palestinian Authority. Indeed, Sharon has long accused Arafat and the Palestinian Authority of supporting terror, documenting his argument with items captured in raids on Arafat's offices. The addition of a prime minister to the framework of the Palestinian Authority has brought greater cooperation, but not a willingness to use force against suspected terrorists. Rather, Palestinian prime ministers have chosen to ease the violence via a policy of negotiations and accommodation. Toward this end, Hamas was offered a role in the Palestinian Authority.[66]

LIFE IN A FISH BOWL: EXTERNAL CONSTRAINTS
ON ISRAELI TERRORIST POLICY

Israel probably garners more coverage in the world press than any other country on earth, with the exception of the United States. Every Israeli action is subject to minute examination and relentless criticism. It is not easy to fight a war against terror in a fish bowl, and international pressure has impeded Israel's struggle against terrorism. The United States forced an Israeli withdrawal from the Sinai Peninsula in 1956, bringing the war of that year to a close. Israeli victories in the Six Day War of 1967 were similarly muted by U.S. pressure on Israel to sign UN Resolution 242, a document that places Israeli occupation of the Occupied Territories in contravention of international law. The principle of exchanging land for peace embodied in the UN Security Council Resolution 242 was reinforced at the end of the 1973 Arab-Israeli War by UN Resolution 338. This was a Security Council resolution that called on all parties to implement UN Resolution 242. Again, Israel accepted the resolution under pressure from the United States, much as it capitulated to U.S. pressure in its 1982 withdrawal from Beirut. Rare, too, has been the U.S. president who has not sponsored a peace initiative designed to stabilize the region by forcing a resolution of the Palestinian crisis. Israel has "managed" most of these initiatives, but cannot risk alienation of its major ally. That risk once again came to the fore as Sharon's antiterrorist policies impaired U.S. efforts to build a Muslim coalition against Saddam Hussein.

It is easier for the Israelis to ignore Europe, but that, too, is problematic. Europe has been far more aggressive than the United States in arguing for the interposition of a peace-keeping force to separate the Israelis and the Palestinians, something that the Israelis fear would give the terrorists a chance to recover from recent sweeps and impose a de facto Palestinian state over which Israel would have no control. European countries have also supported stringent UN condemnations of Israel's anti-terrorist policies, most of which have been vetoed by the United States. All of this encourages the Palestinians by creating the hope that an external settlement of the Arab-Israeli conflict will be imposed on Israel. Israel, in turn, accuses the Europeans, with the possible exception of Britain, of being pro-Palestinian. This is not without cause, for a 2003 poll commissioned by the European Commission of the European Union found Israel to be the #1 threat to world peace.[67]

Israel is particularly sensitive to the position of American Jews, often sending high officials to explain the logic of Israeli policy and otherwise maintain a high level of Jewish support for Israel. The Jewish population in the United States is only slightly smaller than that of Israel and is often critical of Israeli policy. A 2003 poll of American Jews indicated that 82 percent of the respondents feared that the Arabs were intent on the destruction of

Israel, but a smaller majority (65 percent) supported the full or partial evacuation of the settlements as a step toward peace.[68] Most, however, are reluctant to take measures that might weaken Israel, fearing that the collapse of the Israeli state would threaten to unleash a new torrent of anti-Semitism and perhaps the survival of a Jewish faith that now numbers less than 13 million worldwide. Both Israel and the American Jewish community well understand that it is the efforts of American Jews that make the United States Israel's most reliable ally.

ISRAEL DIVIDED

To make matters worse, Israelis themselves are not of one mind about the propriety and effectiveness of their counterterrorist strategies. The last two decades have seen dramatic shifts in policy as the hard-line polices put in place by Begin and his successor, Shamir, gave way to the Oslo Accords and Rabin's decision to trade land for peace. This gave way to a most confusing reign of Barak, in which lavish promises to return land for peace were paired with escalating violence and continued settlement of Palestinian lands. The advent of Sharon returned Israel to the Begin era: talks of land for peace giving way to accelerated settlement of the Occupied Territories and an all-out effort to crush the terrorists and their supporters. Sharon blames the Palestinians, saying that repression will stop when the terror stops. The U.S. government has supported this position to a large degree, but also notes that the accelerated settlement of the Occupied Territories is part of the problem. Sharon refuses to acknowledge the connection.

Yet Sharon himself has admitted that there will have to be a Palestinian state. Such statements infuriate the extreme right. Even former Prime Minister Netanyahu has chastised Sharon for being too soft on the Arabs. Former Prime Minister Shimon Peres, by contrast, called on the government to pull out of the Occupied Territories and Sharon, himself, called for the evacuation of the Gaza Strip.[69] All of this creates confusion among the Israeli populous, with a large percentage of Israelis doubting that Sharon has a clear plan to end the violence.[70] Israeli citizens may not believe that Sharon has a plan for ending the violence, but the hard-line policies of "the bulldozer," Sharon's military nickname, offer security in a time of crisis.

Proposed Alternatives to Israeli Anti-Terrorist Strategy

Ariel Sharon's efforts to bludgeon the Palestinians into submission has resulted in a stalemate, raising questions about where Israel's anti-terrorist strategy goes from here. Prior to a September 2003 cabinet meeting on the security situation, a *Ha'aretz* reporter asked a minister what he thought the government could do against suicide bombings. His response was, "No one has a solution."[71]

Four options are widely discussed in the Israeli press. The first option is to revisit the Oslo Accords, a solution that would result in the creation of a Palestinian state on much of the Occupied Territories. The Palestinian state would be nominally independent but linked to Israel by a variety of economic and security ties. This proposal is supported by the Israeli left and the United States but opposed by the Israel's right-wing government. A second option is a forced settlement of the conflict by the international community. The European Union and the Palestinians favor this solution, but Israel and the United States oppose it. The third option is separation. Israel would simply withdraw from those areas of the West Bank and Gaza that are not vital to its security interests and seal off the rest. The settlements would go, but so would the provocations for terror and the burden of occupation. The Palestinians could then fend for themselves and any attacks on Israel emanating from the Palestinian areas would be treated as an act of war by an independent state. The separation solution is championed by the Council for Peace and Security, a group of 1,000 top-level reserve generals, colonels, and Shin Bet and Mossad officials.[72] It is opposed by Sharon and the parties of the right, but the construction of Israel's security fence would seem to be a step in this direction, government disclaimers not withstanding. The final option being widely discussed is transfer. The Israeli government goes to great length explaining that transfer is not ethnic cleansing, but the slogan of Israel's extreme right is less subtle: "No Arabs—no terror."[73] Sharon has long claimed that the Palestinians already possess a state. Its name is Jordan, an allusion to the fact that Palestinians constitute approximately 70 percent of the Jordanian population. Exact percentages are vague and vary from 60 to 80 percent. In the run up to the war on Iraq, the king of Jordan asked Sharon to issue a public statement saying that he would not use a war with Iraq as a pretext for transferring Palestinians to Jordan. Sharon refused.

THE STRUGGLE AGAINST JIHADIST TERROR IN THE ISLAMIC WORLD

The struggle against the jihadist terror in the Islamic world shares much in common with Israel's war on terror. There are, however, important differences. The war in Israel is a struggle for land between two rival claimants: one Jewish and the other predominantly Muslim. Many on both sides believe that it is a struggle for survival. The war against terror within the Islamic world is a civil war between people of the same country and the same religion. It is a war motivated by faith rather than a struggle for national independence. Unlike Israel's struggle with the Palestinians, land cannot be exchanged for peace. The Israelis can close off the territories. The governments of the Islamic world cannot. Israel does not have to worry about sedition within the ranks of its officials and security forces. In many Islamic countries, the jihadist supporters are embedded within the government itself. Israeli politicians can win elections by promising a hard line against the terrorists. Islamic countries fear that elections will lead to victories by Islamic parties, if not the jihadists themselves.

Attack the Terrorists with Maximum Force

Make no mistake, the brutality of anti-terrorist measure in Islamic countries such as Egypt, Syria, Iraq, and Algeria has matched that of the Israelis. Sweeps of slums and rural villages suspected of harboring terrorist have become routine, as have military attacks on secluded base camps. These measures pale in comparison to Syria's slaughter of from 10,000 to 30,000 Muslim Brothers in the Hama uprising of 1982. The exact number is a matter of conjecture. Kidnapping and assassinations (disappearances) are also part and parcel of the struggle against jihadist terror in the Islamic world. Saddam Hussein refined assassination and torture to an art form in his efforts to quell rebellions among the Kurds and Shi'a. Saudi Arabia routinely tortures suspects accused of terror, including citizens of the West.[74] Unfortunately, few countries in the Islamic world limit their anti-terrorism measures to terrorists. Peaceful opponents of the regime also tend to disappear or are thrown into jail without trial or notification of their relatives.[75]

INTERNATIONAL REACH

Security forces in Islamic countries also "track" opponents of the regime living abroad, many of whom are jihadists. This process was facilitated by U.S. efforts to improve cooperation between the security agencies of friendly regimes in Islamic world in the aftermath of the attacks on U.S. forces in Saudi Arabia and the attacks on the American embassies in Tanzania and Kenya. Egyptian jihadists seeking refuge in Albania have been returned to Cairo under American urging, and both Kuwait and Saudi Arabia have taken measures to stem the flow of money into the hands of Egyptian charities suspected of supporting the terrorists. Egypt has also signed anti-terrorists treaties with countries as diverse as Russia, Albania, and Panama.[76] American-sponsored cooperation among its Islamic allies has taken on a whole new dimension since the September 11 attacks.

DEFENSE

Defensive measures have also been strengthened. Airport and border security is far more sophisticated than in years past, as are efforts to protect embassies and tourists. Egypt, for example, has created a Rapid Reaction Force specifically designed to protect its vital tourist industry. The American Embassy in Cairo was already guarded by Egyptian security vans not so discretely parked in adjoining alleys. The suspension of civil rights has also been the norm in the Islamic world, elegant constitutions notwithstanding. Egyptian regimes, for example, have been operating under the "emergency" provisions of the Egyptian constitution for forty-six of the last fifty or so years. They were extended for an additional three years in 2003. Suspects are either thrown into prison without trial or tried in military courts that are exempt from the due process guarantees of the constitution. The 2002 Amnesty International Report accused the Mubarak regime of "generalized and systematic" torture including whipping, electric shocks, and sustained beatings."[77] Amnesty International's assessments were seconded by the UN's concerns over the unusual number of deaths among detainees. Hopes for change are minimal, the torture of political prisoners being more or less endemic in the Islamic world. The Egyptian government does not deny the charges; an Egyptian court recently awarded some $1,000,000 in damages to 1,124 prisoners tortured between 1981 and 2001, about $900 per torture victim.

BRING THE ALLIES OF THE JIHADISTS
UNDER STATE CONTROL

Egypt has also been a leader in efforts to control jihadist mosques and their links to charity organizations. As the policy was described by the minister of *waqfs* (religious endowments), "We do not order preachers to discuss specific subjects and we do not send them written sermons. . . . Individuals who undertake to give sermons or religious lessons in a mosque must obtain prior permission . . . from one of the 27 regional offices of the Ministry."[78] He added that the government was making progress in "nationalizing" Egypt's 27,000 private mosques. Past efforts to control private mosques had failed for a lack of certified preachers, but the minister noted that efforts in this area have been redoubled. By 2003, the government claimed that 20,000 mosques remained to be nationalized. Summer refresher courses have also been instituted for the imams[79] of nationalized mosques to ensure that they are in tune with government policy. The head of one of the summer programs quipped, "They [the trainees] think that Islam will triumph, will spread throughout the world. We teach them that yes, it will, but not in violence. It will spread by evidence and logic."[80]

The government of Malaysia has also begun to crack down on preachers who deviate from the official text approved by the state (provincial) governments. Other Malaysian measures include requiring provincial governments to appoint mosque committees to "ensure that they are run properly" and assigning government tax collectors the responsibility of collecting *zakat*.[81] Kuwait, Saudi Arabia, and Egypt have increased their supervision of Islamic charities, many of which have been accused of channeling millions of dollars to bin Laden and other terrorist groups. In similar moves, both Egypt and Turkey have purged teachers suspected of jihadist leanings, and Turkey has fired teachers who received their education at Egypt's Al Azhar University, claiming that religious education was incompatible with Turkey's secular principles.[82] Purges on suspected jihadists in the government and the military have also been frequent and occasionally have reached to key figures in the regime.

MAKING SECULAR STATES MORE ISLAMIC

Governments throughout the Islamic world have attempted to steal the thunder of the jihadists by polishing the image of establishment Islam. Lavish new "government" mosques dot the landscape of the Islamic world, and Islamic programming has increased on government radio and television stations as have the number of stations themselves.

Far more dramatic have been changes in the content of sermons and religious programs. Once focusing on good works and the nonviolent message of Islam, Egypt's senior religious leaders have become pro-active, condemning the brutality of Israeli efforts to crush the Palestinian uprising, calling for charity donations to be channeled to Muslim forces in Chechnya, and calling for a jihad against the American attack on Iraq.[83]

The picture was much the same in Saudi Arabia, with a senior Islamic cleric issuing a *fatwa* from Mecca, Islam's holiest city, forbidding Saudi Muslims from participating in a strike on Iraq: "Not by word and not by deed, not by guidance and not by gesture, not with supply and not with support."[84] Both occurred in the tense days leading up to the U.S. attack on Iraq and neither statement could have been made without at least the passive agreement of the Egyptian and Saudi governments. The anti-war *fatwas* did not prohibit a U.S. presence for defensive purposes. The United States was not pleased with these statements, but both Egypt and Saudi Arabia faced a critical choice. They could allow government clergy to oppose the war or they could leave the field open to more radical groups, including the jihadists. The situation was much the same throughout the Islamic world.

FIGHTING TERROR BY BECOMING ANTI-AMERICAN

The leeway given to establishment clergy in Egypt and other areas of the Islamic world is symptomatic of a broader effort by the secular governments of the regions to fight terror by distancing themselves from American and Israeli policy. Egypt's President Mubarak has been strident in his verbal attacks on Israeli suppression of the Palestinians and has led the charge in leading Arab condemnation of the U.S. occupation of Iraq. The leaders throughout the Islamic world have followed suit. In their view, American policy toward Iraq and Israel is fueling terrorism and little is to be gained by deepening the chasm between themselves and their populations.

PSYCHOLOGICAL WARFARE

The psychological propaganda offensive against the jihadists has a variety of dimensions. Most Islamic countries are now allowing greater political participation in the hope of empowering secular groups in the struggle against the jihadists. Even Saudi Arabia has acknowledged the need for political reform. Political prisoners, including jihadists, are also being released as a show of good will and, more subtly, as a sign of government confidence in its ability to defeat the jihadists.[85] Whether this message is coming across remains to be seen.

Simultaneously, the media in the Islamic world portrays the jihadists as criminals and thugs in the hope of depriving them of their status as religious martyrs. Names are often withheld for the same reason, publicity and martyrdom being key elements in the jihadist psyche. Egyptian propaganda also gives wide publicity to the violence in Algeria, a clear warning of Egypt's future if the jihadists are not stopped.

MONEY TALKS

The jihadists thrive in mountains and other remote regions where government control is weak at best. Countries such as Yemen, Somalia, Iraq, Nepal, Afghanistan, and Pakistan have a long tradition of maintaining order in remote regions by bribing tribal leaders, a practice that has been extended to the struggle against the jihadists. The only other option is to assault the tribes directly, a dangerous strategy that threatens transforming the war against the jihadists into a civil war.

DIVIDE AND CONQUER: PLAYING THE MODERATES AGAINST THE JIHADISTS

A growing number of Islamic countries are attempting to weaken the jihadists by strengthening the more moderate groups within the Islamic movement. Moderate Islamic political parties in Morocco, Kuwait, Pakistan, and Turkey have been allowed new scope in an effort to give more devout Muslims a peaceful alternative to the jihadists.

Egypt has been ambivalent on the strategy of accommodation, vacillating between attempts to use the Muslim Brotherhood as a counterweight to the jihadists and fears that an unrestrained Brotherhood would prove too popular to control. Recent experiments with moderate Islamic parties in Turkey, Morocco, Kuwait, and Pakistan have justified Egypt's apprehensions. All have seen Islamic parties emerge as a dominant political force in their respective parliaments, and Islamic parties have claimed the premiership in Turkey. In the meantime, the Muslim Brotherhood and Hizbullah follow the strategy of championing democracy and criticizing the obvious failings of their respective governments.

Egypt's posture toward the jihadists has also acquired a degree of ambivalence. The Egyptian government has more or less honored a truce declared by the Islamic Jihad and allied groups. The truce has sharply reduced jihadist violence in Egypt but it hasn't ended the jihadist capacity for terror. On the contrary, it has allowed the jihadists to regroup and shed the terrorist image that had cost them much of their support among the Egyptian populace. They are now rebuilding their mass support by casting themselves as pious preachers victimized by an oppressive government. The truce is a tenuous one, but the jihadists watch and wait as a corrupt and inept government becomes ever more corrupt and inept.

This is not to suggest that accommodation is a flawed strategy but merely to note that it does have its risks. In particular, it requires that Islamic parties that gain power by peaceful means be allowed to rule. If the Algerian case is any example, efforts to deprive the moderate Islamic parties of their legitimate electoral victories will push the jihadists to the fore of the Islamic movement and result in an escalation of violence. On the plus side, the experience of Iran demonstrates that people soon tire of Islamic governments and their support wanes. It is far easier to criticize than it is to solve the mammoth economic and social problems of the Islamic world.

Ironically, the Egyptian government has used its truce with the jihadists to place greater pressure on the Muslim Brotherhood. While this may seem quixotic, the popularity of the Brotherhood probably poses a greater threat to the Mubarak regime than the jihadists.[86]

Why Jihadist Terrorism Has Decreased in the Islamic World

In contrast to the escalation of violence in Israel and the West, there has been a marked decrease of terrorist activities within the Islamic world. Egypt, long the focal point of the jihadist terror, returned to relative normality following a unilateral cease fire declared by the Islamic Group and its allies in 1997. Terrorist-related deaths dropped from 160 in 1997, the year of the truce, to fourteen the following year. They remain at minimal levels. On the other hand, casualties continue to mount in Algeria as the jihadist groups fight a rear-guard action, but the threat to secular rule has abated. Terrorist attacks against Christians and foreigners have increased in Saudi Arabia, the Gulf States, Indonesia, and Pakistan, but jihadist violence against Muslims continues to decline. Even the bloody attack on a tourist resort in Bali that killed 200 mostly Muslims civilians had been designed as an attack on foreign tourists. The war against terror in the Islamic world is far from over but, for the moment at least, it has eased.

Why has terror declined in the Islamic world? The answer may provide important guidelines to America's war on terror. One answer to this most intriguing of questions is the partial shift in jihadist strategy that occurred in the late 1990s. Rather than attacking other Muslims, the jihadists have increasingly shifted their focus to American, European, and Israeli targets. As a practical matter, the jihadists lack the resources to fight on all fronts at once. They also require a strong base of support for their operations, something that cannot be achieved if a hostile climate prevails in the Muslim world. Attacks on America and Israel have increased; attacks in the Islamic world have declined.

This, however, is only part of the picture. Self-evaluations by key groups within the Islamic movement also suggest that this shift in strategy was at least partially forced on the jihadist movement by the effectiveness of government anti-terrorist measures.[87] Terrorist organizations were suffering severe losses as defensive strategies improved and government forces, enhanced by Western training and technology, increased in effectiveness. Adding to their woes, as we have seen in earlier chapters, was their own ineptitude. The jihadists were terrorizing themselves out of business by killing innocent Muslims and causing severe economic hardship among Muslim populations who might otherwise have been sympathetic to their movement. One way or another, the jihadists were being forced to acknowledge that existing strategies were not working and had to adjust to new realities. Thus, truces were announced by the Islamic Group and its allies in 1997 and by Hamas and the Palestinian Islamic Jihad in 2003. It was time to regroup and reevaluate. A similar truce has been declared by the Philippines' Moro Islamic Liberation Front.

It would be a mistake to give too much credit to iron-fisted anti-terrorist measures as a cure for terror. A major reason terror is decreasing in the Islamic world is simply that the governments of the region have accepted the truce offered by the jihadists. No formal papers were signed, but both sides have increasingly withdrawn from the line of battle. In Pakistan, for example, major groups such as the HuM are closed down but allowed to resurface under a different name. The border provinces have also begun to institute Islamic laws that differ little in content from those of the Taliban.

There is, though, one interesting caveat to this scenario, that being al Qaeda. Top al Qaeda operatives are becoming too hot to handle for both the governments of the Islamic world and local jihadist groups. Local jihadist groups understand that it is dangerous for the governments of the region to shelter al Qaeda operatives or the groups that support them. The United States, after all, rules the world. Even Iran, the country mostly deeply involved in supporting jihadist terrorism, is delivering al Qaeda operatives to the West. There can be no truce between the two sides as long as al Qaeda is part of the picture. Local jihadists groups are also anxious to avoid American attack. They, too, have their own interests to protect.

This does not mean that al Qaeda is likely to disappear. It does suggest that al Qaeda is finding it more difficult to find shelter in "safe" countries and will be forced to place greater reliance on areas of turmoil where there is little centralized authority. It also suggests that the jihadist movement is moving toward decentralization and independent action. Groups that cooperate with al Qaeda now tend to be spin-offs that disappear once an attack has been carried out. Direct connections tend to be tangential. A different relationship also appears to be emerging between al Qaeda and its contractors. Earlier attacks appeared to have been planned by al Qaeda and contracted to local groups. More recent attacks appear to be the result of local groups coming to al Qaeda with projects. If approved, al Qaeda provides the funds and technology. In the meantime, bin Laden is using the core network of al Qaeda cells to plot against America and its allies.

With or without bin Laden, the pattern of mutual accommodation between the secular governments and the jihadists is probably a temporary expedient as both sides sort things out and lick their wounds. Israeli security agencies, for example, claim that Hamas is using the 2003 truce to build 1,000 kassam rockets.[88] Whether or not this is the case, it would be naive to expect the jihadists to sit idly by while governments plot their next moves.

Why, then, have the governments of the Islamic world found it necessary to accept truces with jihadists? The answer is simple. They haven't been able to stamp out the jihadists and their supporters. The terrorists are not winning, but neither are the secular governments of the Islamic world. Hence, the stalemate.

The problems are many. The brutality of anti-terrorist measures in the Islamic world was alienating their citizens and creating new generations of terrorists. Sweeps against suspected jihadists enclaves resulted in massive collateral damage, including "unintended" deaths and the wholesale incarceration of innocent civilians. The 2003 attacks on Jewish and Spanish sites in Morocco, for example, saw the Moroccan government arrest more than 700 suspects.[89] The Saudis, in turn, "questioned" some 12,000 suspects during 2003 in an effort to bring a recent spate of terrorist attacks under control.[90]

As a rule, most suspects arrested by security forces were released in a few weeks, but the interrogation process was not gentle and often involved beatings and "light torture." Anyone evenly remotely linked to the terrorists could expect to be interrogated by the police. The prisons themselves became breeding grounds for terrorism, building hatred toward the government and bringing despairing youth in contact with charismatic religious fanatics. Some jihadist leaders even managed terror campaigns from behind bars, issuing their orders via a network of Islamic lawyers. People of the Islamic world may have been wary of the jihadists, but they were not supporting the government. This was all the more so because governments in the Islamic world were using the war on terror as a pretext to crush all groups opposed to their rule, legitimate or otherwise. Rather than building bridges to the legitimate opposition, they were attempting to crush it.

Government efforts to crush jihadist groups have also been slowed by internal problems. Police and military units tend to be cautious and unwilling to take unnecessary risks. Many rank-and-file troops are either indifferent or sympathetic to the jihadist cause, leaving much of the battle to overtaxed special security units. Supporters of the jihadists also appear to enjoy at least covert support in high places, a problem pervasive in countries that maintain a high Islamic profile, such as Saudi Arabia. It is simply difficult to be the world's foremost sponsor of Islamic causes without inadvertently abetting local jihadist groups. Much the same is true of Pakistan, a country that attempts to suppress the domestic activities of the jihadists while simultaneously encouraging their external activities.

Egypt and other front-line countries in the war against terror also complain that the West has hampered their anti-terrorist efforts. When the heat on the jihadists becomes too strong within the Islamic world, their leaders find easy shelter in Europe and continue to direct their operations from abroad. London and Paris bristle under accusations that they have become the new center of the jihadist movement.

RELEVANCE OF THE EXPERIENCE OF ISRAEL AND THE ISLAMIC WORLD TO AMERICA'S WAR ON TERROR

Taken collectively, the experience of Israel and the Islamic world in fighting jihadist terror suggests certain patterns that are very relevant to America's war on terror:

1. Force alone cannot defeat jihadists who have strong allies and a broad base of mass support. As things currently stand, the jihadist groups fighting America enjoy both.
2. Excessive force tends to be counterproductive. Among other things, it intensifies mass hostility, pushes moderates into the hands of the extremists, generates new terrorists, and unleashes an outcry of international protest. Violence also begets violence, unleashing a cycle of terror and counterterror of ever-increasing intensity.
3. Closing down the operations of the jihadists and their allies requires a high level of international cooperation and coordination. Adequate levels of international cooperation and coordination do not currently exist. The jihads in the Occupied Territories, Kashmir, and Chechnya are all fueled by a high level of external support. This has become the case in Iraq as well.
4. Occupation is risky business. Occupying powers take heavy casualties and jihadists get easy victories. Evacuations become defeats and encourage greater violence. This was certainly the case of Israel's withdrawal from southern Lebanon. Occupation is also costly and places a tremendous strain on the defense budgets of the occupying country.
5. The most effective strategy for easing jihadist terror is a combination of force and accommodation. Force weakens the jihadists. Reasonable accommodation reduces their level of mass support. It will be recalled that Palestinian support for the second intifada reached the 80 percent level during the height of Israeli counterviolence in 2002. It dropped to almost half of that level during the truce that began during the summer of 2003.
6. Accommodation is a temporary solution as long as the underlying causes of jihadist terror remain. The causes of jihadist terror are diverse and include the desperation born of poverty, oppression, and lack of opportunity. They also include policies that deny the aspirations of large population groups, be they the desire for an independent state or a more Islamic country. Each seems to feed the other.

NOTES

1. Nathan Guttman, "U.S. Said Adopting Israeli Army Counter-Terror Tactics in Iraq," *Ha'aretz*, 9 Dec. 2003, at http://www.haaretz.com/hasen/spages/369772.html

(accessed 9 Dec. 2003); Arieh O'Sullivan, "IDF Training Software to Go to U.S. Forces in Iraq," *Jerusalem Post*, 17 Sept. 2003, at http://www.jpost.com/servlet/Satellite?pagename = JPost/A/JPArticle/ShowFull&cid = 406621551.html (accessed 17 Sept. 2003).

2. Martin Gilbert, *The Arab-Israeli Conflict: Its History in Maps,* 3rd ed. (London: Weidenfeld and Nicolson, 1979).

3. Maxime Rodinson, *Israel and the Arabs* (Middlesex, England: Penguin, 1969).

4. Theodor Herzl, *A Jewish State* (New York: American Zionist Emergency Council, 1896).

5. T. G. Fraser, *The Middle East 1914–1979* (London: Edward Arnold, 1980), 18.

6. William R. Polk, David M. Stamler, and Edmund Asfour, *Backdrop to Tragedy: The Struggle for Palestine* (Boston: Beacon Press, 1957).

7. Menachem Begin, *The Revolt: Story of the Irgun* (New York: Henry Schuman, 1951).

8. UN338 and the *Camp David Accords.* Both can be found in Fraser, *The Middle East 1914–1979.*

9. Frank J. Trapp, "Does a Repressive Counter-Terrorist Strategy Reduce Terrorism?: An Empirical Study of Israel's Iron Fist Policy for the Period 1968 to 1987 (unpublished Ph.D. dissertation, Tallahassee, Florida State University, 1994).

10. See: http://www.jpost.com.

11. See: http://www.haaretzdaily.com.

12. Amos Harel, "Easing Rules in Territories Will Focus on Creating Jobs," *Ha'aretz*, 2 Nov. 2003, at http://www.haaretz.com/hasen/spages/356061.html (accessed 2 Nov. 2003).

13. Caroline Glick, "Sharon: No Military Solution to the War with the Palestinians," *Jerusalem Post*, 26 Sept. 2002, at http://www.jpost.com/servlet/Satellite?pagename = JPost/A/JPArticle/ShowFull&cid = 200259421.html (accessed 26 Sept. 2002).

14. Jonathan Lis, "Not Much Success in Fighting Jewish Terror," *Ha'aretz,* 11 Apr. 2003, at http://www.haaretz.com/hasen/pages/ShArt.jhtml?itemNo = 282872.html (accessed 11 Apr. 2003).

15. "Labor Submits No-Confidence over Settlement Growth," *Jerusalem Post*, 30 Dec. 2003, at http://www.jpost.com/servlet/Satellite?pagename = JPost/A/JPArticle/ShowFull&cid = 51622761.html (accessed 30 Dec. 2003); Dan Izenberg, "Background: Illegal Outposts Gained Momentum under Sharon Government," *Jerusalem Post*, 20 Oct. 2002, at http://www.jpost.com/servlet/Satellite?pagename = JPost/A/JPArticle/Show Full&cid = 218581141.html (accessed 21 Oct. 2002).

16. Aluf Benn, Nadav Shragai, and Moshe Reinfeld, "Sharon, U.S. Reach Deal on Building in Territories," *Ha'aretz*, 11 June 2002, at http://www.haaretz.com/hasen/pages/ ShArt.jhtml?itemNo = 302189.html (accessed 11 June 2003).

17. James Bennet, "Israeli Official Labels Hamas Leader 'Marked for Death,'" *New York Times*, 16 Jan. 2004, at http://www.nytimes.com/ (accessed 16 Jan. 2004).

18. "Israel: Palestinian Population Statistics," *IPR Strategic Business Information Database*, 14 Jan. 2003, Infotrac A96419273 (accessed 24 Feb. 2004).

19. "Israel: Palestinian Population Statistics."

20. John Lancaster, "UN Envoy Calls Camp 'Horrifying,'" *Washington Post*, 19 Apr. 2001, at http://www.washingtonpost.com/wp-dyn/articles/A11963-2002Apr18.html (accessed 10 Apr. 2002).

21. Hassan Fattah, "Hamas Official: Islamic Group Is Ready to Take over from Arafat," *Washington Post*, 7 Feb. 2003, at http://www.washingtonpost.com/wp-dyn/articles/A39151-2003Feb7.html (accessed 7 Feb. 2003).

22. Aluf Benn, "The Plan Sharon Refuses to Consider," *Ha'aretz*, 29 Aug. 2002, at http://www.haaretzdaily.com/hasen/pages/ShArt.jhtml?itemNo = 202704.html (accessed 29 Aug. 2002).

23. Dore Gold, *Hatred's Kingdom: How Saudi Arabia Supports the New Global Terrorism* (Washington, D.C.: Regnery Publishing, 2003).

24. Corinne Heller, "Israeli Vice Premier Says Killing Arafat an Option," *Washington Post*, 14 Sept. 2003, at http://www.washingtonpost.com/wp-dyn/articles/A8813-2003 Sep14.html (accessed 14 Sept. 2003).

25. "Report: Elite Unit Has Been Ready to Snatch Arafat since April 2002," *Jerusalem Post*, 12 Sept. 2003, at http://www.jpost.com/ (accessed 12 Sept. 2003).

26. James Bennet, "Not Urging War, Sharon Says," *New York Times*, 11 Mar. 2003, at http://www.nytimes.com/2003/11/international/middleeast/11ISRA.html (accessed 11 Mar. 2003).

27. "Report: Mossad, IAF Have Plan for Iran Nuke Sites," *Jerusalem Post*, 11 Oct. 2003, at http://www.jpost.com/ (accessed 12 Oct. 2003).

28. Amos Harel, "Analysis: Questionable Censorship," *Ha'aretz*, 18 Nov. 2003, at http://www.haaretz.com/hasen/spages/362243.html (accessed 19 Nov. 2003); U.S. Department of State, "Israel and the Occupied Territories: Country Reports on Human Rights Practices," 4 Mar. 2002, at http://www.state.gov/g/drl/rls/hrrpt/soo1/nea/ 8222262pf .html (accessed 23 Jan. 2003).

29. Odai Sirri, "Peace Workers Shot by Israelis," Al-Jazeera, 26 Oct. 2003, at http:// english.aljazeera.net/NR/exeres/01AA7ECA-7018-447-A10D-9E4139D4.html (accessed 26 Oct. 2003).

30. Greer Fay Cashman, "FSU Jewish Immigration to Germany More than to Israel," *Jerusalem Post*, 17 July 2003, at http://www.jpost.com/servlet/Satellite?pagen ame = JPost/A/JPArticle/ShowFull&cid = 370360271.html (accessed 17 July 2003).

31. Nathan Guttman, "U.S. Campaign Challenges Jewish Consensus on Israel," *Ha'aretz*, 17 Nov. 2002, at http://www.haaretzdaily.com/hasen/pages/SHArt.jhtml?i-temNo = 231227.html (accessed 17 Nov. 2002).

32. Bob Deans, "Powell Warns Sharon against War," *Atlanta Journal-Constitution*, 7 Mar 2002, A3.

33. Janine Zacharia, "Bush: Security Wall 'A Problem,'" *Jerusalem Post*, 27 July 2003, at http://www.jpost.com/servlet/Satellite?pagename = JPost/A/JPArticle/ShowFull& cid = 376588991.html (accessed 27 July 2003).

34. Etgar Lefkovits, "Aharonishky: Terrorism Will Only Increase," *Jerusalem Post*, 11 Feb. 2002, at http://www.jpost.com/Editions/2002/02/11/News/News.43204.html (accessed 11 Feb. 2002).

35. Nina Gilbert, "1,000 Days of Conflict: 810 Dead in Palestinian Attacks," *Jerusalem Post*, 24 June 2003, at http://www.jpost.com/ (accessed 24 June 2003).

36. Amos Harel, "18% of 1,945 Palestinians Killed in Intifada Were Innocent Civilians, IDF Says; 130 Were Children," *Ha'aretz*, 13 Mar. 2003, at http://www.haaretz daily .com/hasen/pages/ShArt.jhtml?itemNo = 272310.html (accessed 13 Mar. 2003).

37. Joseph Algazy, "Red Cross: Stop Killing Civilians," *Ha'aretz*, 14 Mar. 2003, at http://www.haaretzdaily.com/hasen/pages/ShArt.jhtml?itemNo = 272855.html (accessed 14 Mar. 2003).

38. Danny Rubinstein, "Analysis: An Outdated Method," *Ha'aretz*, 27 Sept. 2002, at http://www.haaretzdaily.com/hasen/pages/ShArt.jhtml?itemNo = 213105.html (accessed 27 Sept. 2002).

39. Amos Harel, "Shin Bet: 50% Drop in the Number of Israelis Killed by Terror in 2003," *Ha'aretz*, 9 Jan. 2004, at http://www.haaretz.com/hasen/spages/381161.html

(accessed 9 Jan. 2004); Arieh O'Sullivan, "80% of Attacks Foiled," IDF Officer, *Jerusalem Post*, 20 Feb. 2002, at http://www.jpost.com/Editionsd/s002/022222/20/News/News .43733.html (accessed 20 Feb. 2002).

40. James Bennet, "Sharon Laments 'Occupation' and Israeli Settlers Shudder," *New York Times*, 1 June 2003, at http://www.nytimes.com/2003/06/01/international/middleeast/01MIDE.htm (accessed 1 June 2003).

41. Yossi Verter and Amos Harel, "PM Orders Release of 450 Palestinian Prisoners," *Ha'aretz*, 23 July 2003, at http://www.haaretz.com/hasen/pages/ShArt.jhtml?item No = 320959.html (accessed 23 July 2003).

42. Khaled Abu Toameh, "PA Condemns Knesset Resolution Saying Territories Aren't Occupied," *Jerusalem Post*, 17 July 2003, at http://www.jpost.com/servlet/Satellite?pagename = JPost/A/JPArticle/ShowFull&cid = 370359861.html (accessed 17 July 2003).

43. Herb Keinon, "U.S. Sees Palestinian State by 2005 If They 'Clamp Down on Terror,'" *Jerusalem Post*, 27 Jan. 2003, at http://www.jpost.com/serevlet/Satellite?page name = JPost/A/JPArticle/ShowFull&cid = 281405871.html (accessed 27 Jan. 2003).

44. "Ben-Eliezer Admits 'Despair' Motivates Suicide Bombers," *Daily Star-Lebanon*, 22 June 2002, at http://www.dailystar.com.lb/22_06_02/art20.asp (accessed 31 July 2003).

45. "West Bank Settlements: Swallowing All before Them," *Economist*, 2 Nov. 2002, 48.

46. "Almost as Many Settlers Are Leaving as Are Arriving," *Ha'aretz*, 30 Sept. 2002, at http://www.haaretzdaily.com/hasen/objects/pages/PrintArticleEn.jhtml?itemNo = 214141.html (accessed 30 Sept. 2002).

47. Amos Harel, "Ministries Defy AG to Go on Building at Illegal Outposts," *Ha'aretz*, 12 Nov. 2003, at http://www.haaretz.com/hasen/spages/359697.html (accessed 12 Nov. 2003).

48. "UN Expert: 'Without Malice,' Israel Nonetheless Creates 'Catastrophic Humanitarian Situation,'" *Jerusalem Post*, 18 July 2003, at www.jpost.com/ (accessed 18 July 2003).

49. Dispatches, "The Lost Children of Rafa," *The Observer-London*, 9 Feb. 2003, at http://www.observer.co.uk/worldview/story/0,1158,891849,00.html (accessed 9 Feb. 2003).

50. Amos Harel, "Focus: Regrouping Faster than They Can Be Stamped Out," *Ha'aretz*, 20 May 2003, at http://www.haaretz.com/hasen/pages/ShArt.jhtml?itemNo = 294819.html (accessed 7 Feb. 2002).

51. *Ha'aretz*, 27 Sept. 2002, at www.haaretz.com/ (accessed 27 Sept. 2002).

52. "Palestinian Kids Collect Terrorist Cards," *Jerusalem Post*, 25 Dec. 2003, at http://www.jpost.com/ (accessed 25 Dec. 2003).

53. Arieh O'Sullivan, "Analysis: Did Military Leaders Really Think No Innocent Civilians Would Be Hit?," *Jerusalem Post*, 24 July 2002, at www.//jpost.com/ (accessed 24 July 2002).

54. Lamia Lahoud, "80.6% of Palestinians Support Continuing Terror Campaign," *Jerusalem Post*, 28 Sept. 2002, at www.jpost.com/ (accessed 28 Sept. 2002).

55. Toameh Abu, "Most Palestinians Say They Want to Stop the Violence—Poll," *Jerusalem Post*, 28 Mar. 2003, at http://www.jpost.com/servlet/Satellite?pagename = J-Post/A/JPArticle/ShowFull&cid = 320123751.html (accessed 28 Mar. 2003).

56. *Ha'aretz*, 9 May 2000, at www.haaretz.com/ (accessed 9 May 2000).

57. Christopher Slaney, "Israeli Prisoner Swap Success," *Middle East Times*, 5, 31 Jan. 2004, at http://metimes.com/2K4/issue2004-5/reg/israeli_prisoner_swap.htm (accessed 31 Jan. 2004).

58. Amos Harel, "Dialogue Survey: Suicide Bombings Frighten Israelis More than Iraqi Scuds," *Ha'aretz*, 13 Feb.2003, at http://www.haaretzdaily.com/hasen/pages/ShArt.jhtml?itemNo026373.html (accessed 13 Feb. 2003).

59. Arieh O'Sullivan, "IDF Straitjacketed by Its Power," *Jerusalem Post*, 29 Oct. 2001, at http://www.jpost.com/Editions/2001/10/29/News/News.37106.html (accessed 29 Oct. 2001).

60. Gideon Alon, "Desertion from IDF Rises by 30% Last Year, Report Finds," *Ha'aretz*, 26 Feb. 2002, at http://www.haaretzdaily.com/hasen/pages/ShArt.jhtml?item No = 134638.html (accessed 26 Feb. 2002); "Checkpoints Don't Work, Says Internal IDF Report," *Ha'aretz*, 2 Nov. 2001, at http://www.haaretzdaily.com/hasen/pages/ShArt.jhtml ?itemNo = 89959.html (accessed 2 Nov. 2001).

61. Gideon Alon, "40 Percent of the Eligible Avoid IDF," *Ha'aretz*, 31 Jan. 2002, at http://www.haaretzdaily.com/hasen/pages/ShArt.jhtml?itemNo = 123974.html (accessed 31 Jan. 2002).

62. The line separating Israel and the Occupied Territories.

63. Tovah Lazaroff, "Reservists Refuse to Serve in 'War for Peace of Settlements,'" *Jerusalem Post*, 28 Jan.2002, at http://www.jpost.com/Editions/2002/01/28/News/News.42407.html (accessed 28 Jan. 2002).

64. Greg Myre, "27 Israeli Reserve Pilots Say They Refuse to Bomb Civilians," *New York Times*, at http://www.nytimes.com/2003/09/25/international/middleeast/25MIDE.html (accessed 25 Sept. 2003).

65. Lefkovits, "Aharonishky: Terrorism Will Only Increase."

66. Saud Abu Ramadan, "Document Includes Hamas in Government," UPI (12 Aug. 2002), 1008224w2461 (Infotrac article no. A90311463).

67. The poll had 7,500 respondents, 500 from each member state. See Peter Beaumont, "Israel Outraged as EU Poll Names It a Threat to Peace," *Guardian Unlimited*, 2 Nov. 2003, at http://www.guardian.co.uk/israel/Story/0,2763,1076084,00.html (accessed 2 Nov. 2003).

68. Amiram Barkat, "Most U.S. Jews Believe Arabs Want to Destroy Israel," *Ha'aretz*, 23 July 2003, at http://www.haaretz.com/ (accessed 23 July 2003).

69. Tovah Lazaroff, "Peres Urges Sharon to Pull Out of Territories," *Jerusalem Post*, 22 Sept. 2003, at http://www.jpost.com/servlet/Satellite?pagename = JPost/ A/JPArticle/ShowFull&cid = 410729771.html (accessed 23 Sept. 2003).

70. Suzanne Goldenberg, "Israelis Lose Faith in Military Solution," *Guardian Unlimited*, 18 Feb. 2002, at www.guardian.co.uk/Israel/Story/0,2763,652048,00.html (accessed 18 Feb. 2002).

71. Aluf Benn, "Analysis: No One Has a Solution," *Ha'aretz*, 12 Sept. 2003, at http:// www.haaretz.com/hasen/spages/339463.html (accessed 12 Sept. 2003).

72. Lily Galili, "Reserve Generals Back Unilateral Withdrawal," *Ha'aretz*, 18 Feb. 2002, at http://www.haaretzdaily.com/hasen/pages/ShArt.jhtml?itemNo = 131193.html (accessed 18 Feb. 2002).

73. "Supplement on Refugees, 2003," *Jerusalem Post*, 1 Feb. 2002, at www .jpost.com/ (accessed 1 Feb. 2002).

74. "Greed and Torture at the House of Saud," *Guardian Unlimited*, 24 Nov. 2002, at http://www.observer,co.uk/worldview/story/0,11581,846600,00.html (accessed 9 Aug. 2003).

75. Human Rights Watch, "Human Rights Watch World Report 2003: Middle East & Northern Africa Overview," Jan. 2003, at http://www.hrw.org/wr2k3/mideast .html (accessed 17 Jan. 2003).

76. Ahmed Ali, "Why Quiet Returns to Egypt," *Al-Wasat*, 18 Jan. 1999, 26–27, in Arabic.

77. Emily Wax, "Report Says Egypt Jails and Beats War Protestors," *Washington Post*, 25 Mar. 2003, at http://www.washingtonpost.com/wp-dyn/articles/A22135-2003 Mar25.html (accessed 25 Mar. 2003).

78. Hamdi D. Zaqzuq, "Interview with the Minister of Wafqs," *Al-Wasat* (4 Jan. 1999), 23–25, in Arabic.

79. Imams in Sunni Islam are the directors of mosques. Imams in Shi'a Islam are the leaders of the faith.

80. Diana Digges, "All Preachers Meek and Mild: The Government Schools the Next Generation of Imams in Apolitical Islam," *Cairo Times* 1 (18 Sept. 1997), 15.

81. Iqbal Ragataf, "Malaysian Government Takes over Mosques, Islamic Schools," *Islam Online*, 17 Feb. 2000, at www.islamonline.com/ (accessed 21 Dec. 2002).

82. "Over 100 Turkish Teachers Fired," *Tehran Times* in *Middle East News,* 14 Oct. 2001, at http://www.middleeastwire.com/turkey/stories/20011014_meno.shtml (accessed 19 Oct. 2001).

83. "Al Azhar Calls for Jihad in Case of an Attack on Iraq," Al-Jazeera, 10 Mar. 2003, at http://www.aljazeera.net/news/arabic/2003/655/eg7.htm (accessed 13 Sept. 2003).

84. Al-Auda, Sheik Suliman ben Fahd, "Saudi Religious Scholar Forbids Participation in U.S. Strike on Iraq," Al-Jazeera, 6 Mar. 6, 2003, in Arabic, at http://www.aljazeera.net/news/Arabic/2003/3/3-6-7.htm (accessed 6 Mar. 2003).

85. Jailan Halawi, "Releases and Arrests," *Al Ahram Weekly*, 655, 11–17 Sept. 2003, at http://www.weekly.ahram.org.eg/print/2003/655/eg7.htm (accessed 13 Sept. 2003).

86. Adel Hamouda, *Prayer of the Spies* (Cairo: Dar al-Farsan, 1995), in Arabic.

87. Mansour Al Zaiyat, "Sharia and Life Series: Islamic Groups and Violence," Al-Jazeera (11 Aug. 2002), in Arabic. Interviewed by Mahir Abdullah.

88. Matthew Gutman and Margot Dudkevitch, "Hamas Building 1,000 Kassam Rockets," *Jerusalem Post*, 21 July 2003, at www.jpost.com/ (accessed 21 July 2003).

89. Isambard Wilkinson, "700 to Be Tried for Casablanca Suicide Bombings," *Jerusalem Post*, 18 July 2003, at www.jpost.com/ (accessed 18 July 2003).

90. Brian Whitaker, "Saudi Arabia to Question '12,000 Citizens,'" *Guardian Unlimited*, 15 Aug. 2003, at http://www.guardian.co.uk/Saudi/story/0,11599,1019332,00.html (accessed 15 Aug. 2003).

9

THE FUTURE:
WINNING THE WAR ON TERROR

The war on terror is currently a stalemate. Americans have been stung by the jihadists, but neither their stability nor their ability to retaliate has been put at risk. By the same token, the jihadists remain undeterred in their determination to drive the United States from the Islamic world. The United States, in their view, is the major obstacle blocking the emergence of an Islamic state that spans the Middle East, if not the world at large. Stalemate, unfortunately, is not enough. America and its allies do not want to live under the constant threat of jihadist attack for decades to come.

The purpose of this final chapter is to examine the strengths and weaknesses of America's war on terror and to suggest modifications that will help the United States defeat the jihadists. We begin by examining America's strategy in the war on terror and then turn to an analysis of why U.S. strategy has not defeated the jihadists. This, in turn, is followed by an analysis of the influence of the war on Iraq on the war on terror. For better or for worse, Iraq has become a key test case in the struggle between the United States and the jihadists. We conclude by suggesting modifications in U.S. strategy that will enhance its ability to defeat the jihadists. Some of these modifications are based on the experience of the United States, Israel, and other countries in fighting jihadist terror. Others focus on exploiting the vulnerabilities of the jihadists, winning the hearts and minds of the moderate Muslims, and countering the allies of the jihadists.

U.S. ANTI-TERRORIST STRATEGY

The anti-terrorist strategy of the United States is guided by a long series of principles designed to defend America and defeat the jihadists.[1] Some are a reflection of U.S. experience in fighting communism and drugs, while others are dictated by the tactics of the jihadists. Most bear a marked resemblance to the Israeli anti-terrorist strategy.

The principles guiding America's struggle against jihadist terror are logical and for the most part, self-evident:

> Strengthen internal defenses.
> Attack the terrorists with maximum force.
> Close down the allies of the jihadists.
> Alleviate the root causes of jihadist terror.
> Build a world coalition to fight terror.
> Strengthen the capacity of friendly countries to combat terror.
> Persuade countries that support terror to alter their policies.
> Punish those countries that fail to heed American warnings.
> Sell America's cause to the world and especially the Islamic world.
> Let indigenous forces do the fighting whenever possible.

U.S. policy reflects an understanding that America's war on terror differs from earlier American wars. It can only be won by combining superior force with international cooperation and a concerted effort to alleviate the root causes of jihadist terror.

America's current anti-terrorist strategy also focuses on traps to be avoided in its struggle against the jihadists. They, too, are self-explanatory and bear a marked resemblance to Israeli anti-terrorist strategy.

1. Don't wait for the terrorists to act. If you see the smoking gun, it's too late. This policy came into full force with America's preemptive strike on Iraq and represents a major shift in American policy.
2. Don't allow the terrorists to hide behind civil-rights legislation. Civil rights are for the peaceful citizens of the world's democracies, not their enemies. Unfortunately, the peaceful citizens of the world, including those of the United States, have been forced to accept restrictions on their civil liberties.
3. Don't be deterred by fear of civilian casualties. Civilian casualties are an inevitable product of war, and America is at war. This is unfortunate, but the United States blames the terrorists who hide among civilian populations.
4. Don't allow international law and the resolutions of the United Nations to hamper anti-terrorist operations. America's war on ter-

ror has taken precedence over UN resolutions and has increased the disarray of the United Nations and the lack of resolve among its members.

5. Don't bend to external pressure. Well-intended allies object to U.S. policies, but their doubts have not been allowed to hamper America's war on terror. Much the same applies to mass demonstrations protesting U.S. policy. Demonstrations are a way of life in a democracy, but voters make policy, not mobs.

6. Don't be afraid to go it alone. U.S. anti-terrorist strategy has been marked by a pronounced lack of patience with potential allies.

America's efforts to avoid the traps inherent in fighting jihadist terror are controversial and have come to the fore in the aftermath of the September 11 attacks on the United States. By and large, they mark a major transformation in the pattern of U.S. policy that has prevailed since the end of World War II, but none more so than the Bush doctrine of preemptive strikes. The focus of U.S. policy represents frustration with the United Nations and the intricacies of international law. It also reflects the siege mentality that has gripped the United States in the aftermath of September 11 as well as the Bush administration's open admiration for Israel's no-nonsense approach to fighting terror.

ASSESSMENT: HOW WELL IS AMERICA DOING?

How well is America's strategy in its war against terror working? Making assessments in the heat of battle is risky, but necessary. Advantages have to be pressed and flaws rectified. Most assessments to date, including those of the U.S. government, give U.S. strategy a resounding so-so.[2] There have been many pluses, but for every plus there has been a grim downside. In a few instances, there have been no pluses at all.

Attacking the Jihadists

Heading the list of pluses is the fact that there have been no major terrorist attacks on the United States or Europe since September 11, 2001. Bin Laden and his al Qaeda network have been dislodged from their strongholds in Afghanistan, and the Taliban have been put to flight. U.S. pressure has resulted in the arrest of al Qaeda operatives in more than fifty countries spanning the globe from Europe and Asia to Latin America and Africa. The list of al Qaeda members arrested by the United States and its allies continues to grow and now includes some of bin Laden's senior lieutenants. The closing down of active terrorist cells has followed apace.

Despite clear signs of progress, all is not well. Failed attacks on the United States and Europe have given way to an unrelenting series of attacks on Western targets abroad. An impressive list of al Qaeda operatives has been arrested, but bin Laden and many of his senior lieutenants remain at large, despite a $25 million reward for their capture. This and the seemingly endless array of foiled plots, suggest that al Qaeda has survived the all-out attack on its operations. It may have fragmented, but that is not necessarily a good sign. Fragmentation reduces the coordination of the network, but it also diversifies the sources of attack and makes interdiction more difficult. FBI Director Robert Mueller has been particularly worried about the spread of al Qaeda to the countries of the Pacific Rim and candidly admitted that, "What we do not know is the extent of their support in South East Asia. . . . We don't know all we would like to know about their means of communications. We do not know all that we would like to know about the financial transfers, the money sources."[3]

The picture is much the same in Europe, as Germany, France, Belgium, Spain, Italy, Britain, and the Netherlands all continue to discover new and unknown cells. The arrests would be sources of comfort were it not for fears that the supply of potential terrorists appears to be unlimited. There is simply no evidence to suggest that U.S. anti-terrorist measures, for all their sophistication, are drying up the "swamp." In the meantime, the American government warns that some plots will eventually succeed.

Adding to the concern of American officials is the pattern of past jihadist attacks on the United States, each of which was followed by two or three year pauses as the jihadists ran for cover, regrouped, reassessed, and waited for the furor to die down. The furor following September 11 was far greater than that of earlier jihadist strikes, but the same principle could well apply.

Defense

Substantial progress has been made in strengthening U.S. defenses against terror. The Department of Homeland Security is now operational, albeit with serious glitches over funding, turf battles, disorganization, and questionable support from the White House.[4] Aircraft patrol sensitive areas, and air traffic routes are altered during periods of alert. U.S. intelligence and security agencies are now better coordinated than at any point in recent history. Stinging criticism that the September 11 attacks could have been prevented has also resulted in heightened sensitivity to terrorist operations at all levels of government, from the White House to local law enforcement agencies. The American public has also become involved, reporting suspicious activities and accepting new security restrictions without protest. Civil-rights activists suggest they may be too obliging. In any case, the United States is now a more difficult target for the jihadists than it was on the eve of the September 11 attacks.

Much, however, remains to be accomplished. The Department of Homeland Security incorporates twenty-two defense-related agencies, but excludes the CIA, FBI, and DEA. They are the lead units in the war on terror but must coordinate with Homeland Security via its secretary and other senior administrators. The same is true of state and local security agencies. As a result, the congressional report examining intelligence flaws in the lead up to the September 11 attacks concluded that "the U.S. Government does not presently bring together in one place all terrorism-related information from all sources."[5]

The problems, unfortunately, are far deeper than communication bottlenecks. In 2002, Coleen Rowley, a whistle blower within the ranks of the FBI hand delivered a thirteen-page memo to the Senate Intelligence Committee accusing the FBI, the lead agency in the war on terror, of having obstructed measures that might have stopped or lessened the impact of the September 11 attacks. The litany of charges was long and included accusations that senior FBI officials, including its director, ignored information from field agents and openly denied that they had any inkling of the impending attacks. Coleen Rowley's memo also included accusations that the behavior of FBI agents was shaped by careerism and a culture of fear. Most agents, it seems, were unwilling to rock the boat or take risks that might hurt their career. The FBI stamped the memo "secret," but its contents were incorporated in the congressional report examining intelligence flaws in the lead up to the September 11 attacks.[6]

Other senior FBI officials complain that agents in the field lack a focus on terror, with Bruce J. Gebhardt, the second-ranking official in the FBI, admonishing his leadership group "to instill a sense of urgency (in your agents). . . . They need to get out on the street and develop sources."[7] The director of the FBI has acknowledged that mistakes were made, as has the president. Both have pledged to do better in the future. The FBI director has launched a shake-up of the agency designed to fight the culture of careerism and has also promised to hire more analysts to follow up on reports from field agents. A "flying squad" of special agents is also being created to follow up on warning signals that were ignored in the past. Many of the problems outlined in the Rowley memo, however, are not subject to a quick fix. Careerism and fear are endemic problems that have survived past shake-ups. Senior officials also fault agents in the agency's fifty-six regional offices of finding it difficult to adjust to the new challenges posed by jihadist terrorism and clinging to their traditional concern of fighting drugs and bank robbers.[8]

Similar problems appear to be pervasive throughout the U.S. security establishment. Turf wars are legend; refusal to share information is endemic. The American Council on Education has branded the system installed by the Bureau of Immigration and Customs Enforcement to track foreign students as an "unmitigated disaster."[9] In 2003, the same agency began a frantic effort to register illegal migrants from a variety of Muslim countries, demanding that they register or face deportation. As a senior official in the Justice Department commented, "We need to have a better understanding of who exists and enters our country, and who these people are that have been identified as possible national security concerns for the United States."[10]

International Cooperation

Progress has been made on the international front, as most countries in the world have signed on to the war on terror and pledged their cooperation with the United States. On September 28, 2001, some two weeks after the September 11 attacks on America, the United Nations adopted UNSC Resolution 1373, calling on all member countries to fight terrorism with every means at their disposal. The Group of 20, a group of the world's major economic powers created in 1999 to deal with the crisis in the world's poorer countries, also pledged itself to attack the financial networks of the jihadists.[11] Less formal working groups have proliferated within the world's intelligence community. As a result of these agreements and extreme pressure from the United States, most countries of the world have now stepped up surveillance of suspected jihadists and their allies. Yemen, Pakistan, the Philippines, and several other countries have gone the extra mile and allowed the United States to "cooperate" with their police in the pursuit of terrorists.

Again, however, things are not as well as they might be. Agreements may have been signed, but tensions between the United States and its allies have hampered their effectiveness. Europeans are wary of America's cowboy tendencies and feel that they have not been adequately consulted in the formulation of global anti-terrorist strategy. Secretary of Defense Rumsfeld fueled animosities in Europe by referring to France and Germany as the "old Europe"[12] and reiterating the willingness of the United States to go it alone. Shouting matches have given way to European charges that the United States is not sharing data with its allies.[13]

The picture is much the same in the Islamic world. Governments in the Islamic world have been bribed and bullied, but cooperation with the United States has been slow and plodding. In many cases, overt support for terror has simply become covert support for terror. In the meantime, the corruption, ineptitude, and oppression of governments in the Islamic world continue to breed the mass frustration on which the jihadists feed. U.S. technical assistance designed to fight the jihadists is also being used to suppress legitimate voices of dissent. This aggravates an already severe problem and fuels the anti-Americanism endemic in the region.

Winning the Hearts and Minds of the Islamic World

Looking for bright spots in America's propaganda war is a dismal task. The reluctance of governments in the Islamic world to support America's war on terror is a reflection of the strident anti-Americanism in the region. The United States, by its actions and words, has convinced the Muslim world that it has declared war on Islam. It has also inflamed nationalistic sentiments by its occupation of Iraq, threatened attacks on Syria and Iran, unflinching support of Israel, and lengthy bombing of Iraq and Afghanistan. The United States believes that its policies are fully justified. Muslims do not. In their eyes, America is a neocolonial power intent on reshaping the map of the Middle East to its own strategic and economic advantage. Propaganda efforts to counter the ugly American image have been an unmitigated failure.[14]

Shutting Down the Allies of the Jihadists

The picture is much the same in regard to U.S. efforts to close down the allies of the jihadists. Progress has been made, but it has been sparing and has not eased the jihadist threat to America and its allies. Efforts to close down the money trail are a case in point. Islamic banks and charities in the United States and Europe have been brought under close scrutiny and a few closed down. Saudi Arabia and other Islamic countries have been pressured to follow suit. Agreements of cooperation have been signed, but compliance is difficult to monitor. In many cases, support for jihadist operations that was once overt has merely disappeared from view. A recent UN report called al Qaeda's financial network "fit and well" and said that efforts to close it down had reached a "dead end."[15] The White House disputed the UN findings, but U.S. officials admit that their task is a daunting one and that they don't know how much money al Qaeda needs to operate on an annual basis or how much money they can lay their hands on at any particular time. Officials estimate that the figure is close to $100 million per year, but acknowledge that they "don't really know."[16]

The difficulty in closing down the money trail is not hard to understand. Complexity, secrecy, the sensitivity of attacking religious institutions, the opaqueness of international financial dealings, loose border controls in Europe, international law, and the sovereign rights of nations all impede effective monitoring, as does confusion and competition within the U.S law enforcement community. With so many different agencies involved, information becomes "stove-piped," an in-house expression referring to information that doesn't get shared for one reason or another.[17] Not only are there are too many cracks for jihadist funds to fall through, but the jihadists have reduced their exposure to accounts that are easily traced and shifted to smaller sums and the use of gems. They have also become adept at informal transfers of money, including couriers and the hawala system.

Even less progress appears to have been made in U.S. efforts to alter the anti-U.S. content of Islamic education and sermons. Pledges have been made, supervision enhanced, and symbolic closures made, but the topic is simply too sensitive for either Islamic governments or the United States to pursue with vigor. Few governments in the Islamic world are capable of challenging the upsurge in Islamic emotions overwhelming their countries, and the United States is already fighting an uphill battle against charges that it has declared war on Islam. Civil-rights activists and religious leaders have found common ground in their fear that restrictions on Islam could result in restrictions of Christianity and Judaism as well. One way or another, the topic has dropped from view.

Alleviating the Root Causes of Jihadist Terror

All of the world's major anti-terrorist agencies admit that terror will exist as long as the causes of terror exist. Poverty and gross inequalities in wealth play their roles, as do the corrupt, oppressive, and incompetent leaders of the region. Some interpretations of Islam may flame anti-American terror, but so do hopelessness and frustration. The World Bank and International Monetary Fund statistics reluctantly indicate that the poor of the world are getting poorer. The United States gives less foreign aid per capita than most countries of the First World and 40 percent of that goes to Israel and Egypt. Afghanistan remains a disaster area two years after its infrastructure was pulverized by U.S. bombing, and the Taliban are reviving.[18]

WHY THE GLITCHES?

The glitches in America's war on terror reflect the urgency of the moment. America was attacked by the jihadists and had little choice but to respond with every weapon in its arsenal. Glitches and contradictions would be sorted out with time. The critical factor was repelling the jihadist threat. The glitches in the war on terror have also been the result of inexperience. Unlike earlier conflicts, the war on terror is not a war of massed tanks or clearly demarcated boundaries. The enemy is elusive, striking with stealth and fading into the broad mass of the world's more than one billion Muslims. The mobility and motivations of the terrorists also differ from those of earlier adversaries. Death is not a threat but a reward. The war on drugs is clearly relevant to the war on terror, but the drug lords are businessmen motivated by profit rather than salvation. It is not clear, moreover, that the United States is winning its war on drugs. The United States must win the war on terror.

It could also be argued that the jihadists had a head start. Their operations were promoted by the United States during Afghanistan's decade-long struggle against the Soviet Union. Part and parcel of this process was allowing the development of jihadist cells and financial networks in North America and Europe. The United States is now attempting to catch up.

America blames its so-so record in the war on terror on the lack of global cooperation. The global community responds in kind. The countries of the Islamic world complain that U.S. policy in the Middle East makes cooperation difficult, while the Europeans charge the United States with being impetuous, impatient, and power hungry.[19] They also say that America's war on terror lacks a clear strategy.

Perhaps they have a point. The rush to confront the jihadist enemy saw the United States develop the strategic guidelines outlined above.

America has yet to develop a coherent anti-terrorist strategy. Rather, it has responded by trying some of this and some of that in the hopes of finding something that works. This is in the best pragmatic tradition of American policy making, but the result has been inconsistencies and dramatic shifts in policies as the administration struggles to come to grips with contradictions within its guiding principles.

Going it alone with minimal regard for the United Nations has increased U.S. maneuverability, but it has also impaired its efforts to build an international coalition against terror. Preemptive strikes against jihadist targets lessen their ability to strike at the United States, but the strikes also undermine U.S. efforts to win the hearts and minds of the Islamic world. Clearly, America's anti-terror guidelines are not all on the same page.

U.S. policy has also displayed marked inconsistencies.[20] One day President Bush chastises Prime Minister Sharon for building settlements and using excessive force against innocent civilians. A few days later, the president calls Sharon a man of peace and suggests that settlement building may be allowed under certain circumstances. The eve of the joint U.S.-British invasion of Iraq would see President Bush promise to rebuild a democratic Iraq. A day later, the Department of State issued an internal memorandum saying there would be no democracy in Iraq. One day the administration takes a hard line against North Korea, the next it reverts to negotiations and bribes. The MKO, an anti-Iranian terrorist group, is placed on the U.S. list of terrorist organizations and then utilized to terrorize Iran. It now exists in limbo.

The War on Terror and the War on Iraq

Adding to the difficulty of forging a coherent anti-terrorism strategy have been the well-publicized conflicts within the Bush administration itself.[21] Secretary of State Powell, a man with broad international experience, stressed the need to focus on jihadist terror and emphasized coalition building. Other members of the president's team found Powell's view of the world unduly restrictive and see the war on terror as the opportunity to rid the world of rogue states that either possess weapons of mass destruction or are on their way to developing them.[22] Iraq, the most vulnerable of the rogue states was to be attacked first, followed, presumably, by other members of the "axis of evil."

As senior members of the Bush team who had long been pushing for preemptive strikes on rogue states openly admitted in the lead up to the Iraq

War, "Without Sept.11, we never would have been able to put Iraq at the top of our agenda. . . . It was only then that this president was willing to worry about the unthinkable—that the next attack could be with weapons of mass destruction supplied by Saddam Hussein."[23] Other goals for attacking Iraq seemed to include securing Middle Eastern oil supplies and reshaping the political map of the Middle East in a manner that would favor the United States and Israel. Military personnel also note that attacking Iraq was also the only way that the United States could extricate itself from a decade-long burden of patrolling the no-fly zones that it had established to protect Iraq's Kurds and Shi'a from the vengeance of Saddam Hussein.

President Bush's senior advisor on terrorism resigned in protest on the eve of the Iraq War, as did several members of Tony Blair's cabinet.[24] It has also become evident that the war in Iraq has undermined America's ability to pursue its war on terror. There are many reasons for this.

First, the war in Iraq has reinforced the image that the United States has declared war on Islam. In so doing, it has stoked anti-Americanism in the Islamic world to a feverish pitch and weakened the ability of friendly Islamic governments to cooperate with America's war on terror. Jihadist recruitment appears to have increased apace, but there are little hard data on this topic. Shi'a opposition surely has as U.S. forces in Iraq have found themselves facing an onslaught of terror perpetrated by Shi'a militias.

Second, the U.S. and British decision to go it alone in Iraq weakened the international coalition assembled to fight jihadist terror and challenged the effectiveness of the United Nations and NATO as effective agencies in the war on terror. In the process, the United States legitimized the right of other states to go it alone without the approval of the United Nations. This can only give solace to Iran and other states that support the jihadists.

Third, the occupation of Iraq has reinforced the lessons of Vietnam by demonstrating that the United States can be forced to take heavy casualties by small guerilla bands. By early 2004, more than 775 American personnel had died in Iraq. According to PBS, some 8,800 U.S. personnel had been evacuated from Iraq for medical treatment by the same date.[25] Few of these casualties appear to have been inflicted by the jihadists, but they are the ones who are claiming victory. Bin Laden has also joined the money game by reportedly promising 10,000 grams of gold for the murder of top U.S. and U.N. officials in Iraq.

Fourth, the United States appears to be confused, if not in retreat. Once excluding the United Nations and much of Europe from the administration of occupied Iraq, the United States has urged both to return. Efforts to privatize the Iraqi economy, including its oil, were scrapped, and the training of Iraqi police and military recruits was reduced to a minimum.[26] This proved to be a mistake. Many of the new recruits were unreliable while others refused to kill Iraqis. This, among other problems, led the U.S. to enlist a former Republican Guard general in its effort to quell the rebellion in the Iraqi city of Falluja. He showed up for duty in full Baathist regalia, suggesting that the U.S. had reached an accord with henchmen of Saddam Hussein. The Shi'a were not amused. He was demoted three days later. Diverse Iraqi militias, supposedly disarmed, have been invited to send troops to serve as the nucleus to a new Iraqi force. Among these are the militias of the pro-Iranian Supreme Council for the Islamic Revolution in Iraq (Hizbullah), the Dawa Party (Radical Shi'a), the Communist Party, and two Kurdish militias.[27] The loyalty of each is to its party rather than the country and seems to be a recipe for future chaos. Sensing the mood, the U.S.-appointed ruling council bucked the administration and demanded a U.S. evacuation. Little matter, the U.S. had agreed to the dissolution of its hand picked ruling council as part of a plan to reintroduce the U.N. to Iraq. It is now the U.N. that will guide Iraq to democracy, albeit with strong U.S. influence from behind the scenes. Far more embarrassing were the gruesome pictures of U.S. prison guards torturing Iraqi prisoners that flashed around the world's television screens in the spring of 2004. The President expressed his deep remorse, but the high moral ground had been lost. Rumors of a pending civil war abound. Should they prove true, yet another swamp for the breeding of terrorism will have been created.

The actual war against Iraq is reported to have cost just less than the $62.6 billion Congress approved, but the subsequent U.S. occupation of Iraq is costing some $4 billion a month, a far cry from earlier estimates of $390 million per month.[28] An additional $87.6 billion is now in the offing, all of which will have to be borrowed.[29] More funding requests are on the way.

The two major justifications for the war have proven to be erroneous. Iraq did not have credible WMD and a tangible link was not established between Saddam Hussein and the major jihadist groups. The cover of *Time* magazine on February 9, 2004, portrayed glum pictures of President Bush and his major advisors, while its headlines screamed "WE WERE ALL WRONG."[30] A very dour 2003 report by the Foreign Affairs Committee of the British House of Commons concluded, "We cannot conclude that these threats (terrorism and WMD) have diminished significantly, in spite of 'regime change' in Iraq and progress in capturing some of the leaders of al Qaeda."[31]

Ironically, the United States was within striking distance of Baghdad in the 1991 Gulf War and could have dispatched the Iraqi leader with ease. It chose not to, fearing Iraq would splinter and turn the region into chaos. The United States was also wary of occupying Iraq, a messy business that, as the Israelis can testify, leads to high casualties. The same concerns still apply today, with Washington seeming to admit that it lacked a clear end game for Iraq.[32] Things were to be sorted out once Saddam was gone.

Although the original justifications for the attack proved erroneous, the Bush administration can claim a number of pluses. The long-term threat of Iraqi aggression has been eliminated, the security of Israel has been strengthened, Iran and Syria have become markedly less belligerent, Saudi Arabia and other friendly countries have been bolstered in their struggle against the jihadists, and the forces of democracy in the region have been strengthened. Indeed, the war was supported by the grandson of the Ayatollah Khomeini as well as by Saad Ibrahim, Egypt's leading civil-rights activist.[33]

Whichever position one supports, there can be no question that the U.S./British occupation of Iraq has become a key test case in the war against jihadist terror. On one side stand the jihadists, the remnants of Saddam Hussein's forces, a growing body of Afghan Arabs, a variety of Shi'a groups anxious to seize control of Iraq, various Iraqi nationalists, and the rogue states presumably slated for attack by the United States. Of these, the most important is Iran, a country the United States accuses of both supporting terror and developing weapons of mass destruction. On the other side, stand the United States, Britain, and Israel. Watching intently from the sidelines are the Islamic countries, groups accused of abetting terrorism, and the broad range of more moderate Islamic groups that form the base of the Islamic movement. This category certainly includes Hizbullah, the Muslim Brotherhood, and the emerging Islamic parties of the Muslim world.

The stakes are high. Mounting U.S. casualties are victories for the jihadists and demoralize American morale. They also reduce the probability that the United States will rush into another lengthy invasion, be it Iran, Syria, or North Korea. If the United States runs, both the jihadists and the countries that support them will step up their activities, as will the Islamic movement as a whole. An American victory by contrast, will demoralize the jihadists and force them to further retrench. Islamic countries and groups will become infinitely more careful in their support of the jihadists and the way will have been paved for U.S. attacks on Iran and Syria.

Unfortunately, the picture does not look bright. As former general and member of a conservative think tank bluntly stated: "We have failed. The issue is how high a price we're going to pay. . . . Less, by getting out sooner, or more, by getting out later."[34] A number of unnamed U.S. officers in Iraq have similar views.[35] Spain apparently agreed, and withdrew its symbolic but psychologically important contingent (1,300 troops) from Iraq following bloody Jihadist attacks on Madrid in the spring of 2004. Honduras followed suit. Withdrawal, however, is risky business and in the spring of 2004 the Pentagon announced that it planned to keep 135,000 troops in Iraq through 2005.[36] Ironically, the problems faced by the U.S. occupation of Iraq are virtually identical to those faced by the Israeli occupation of the West Bank and Gaza Strip.

DEFEATING THE JIHADISTS

If America is to defeat the jihadists, it must improve its performance in each of the five key dimensions of the war on terror: defense, attacking the jihadists, closing down their allies, depriving them of their base of mass support, and alleviating the causes that give rise to jihadist terror. The United States fared better in some of these areas than others, but all, as we have seen, are seriously flawed.

The recommendations that follow are not a substitute for a coherent plan for fighting the jihadists, but they should result in marked improvements in all areas of the war on terror. They are based on earlier discussions of (1) the complexities within the Islamic religion; (2) variations in Muslim attitudes toward both the jihadists and the United States; (3) the patterns of evolution within the jihadist movement; (4) the vulnerabilities of the jihadists; (5) the nature of their allies; (6) the experience of Israel, the Islamic world, and the West in fighting jihadist terror; and (7) the U.S. experience in occupying Iraq.

Focus on the Jihadists

The United States was victorious in its struggles against Nazi Germany and the Soviet Union because its energies were focused on survival. If the United States is to win the war on terror, it must now focus its energies on the jihadists. This is not currently the case. The United States has declared war on jihadist terror, but it is simultaneously attempting to rid the world of pariah states intent on developing weapons of mass destruction, securing strategic oil resources, and reshaping the map of the Middle East in a manner compatible with the strategic interests of America and Israel. Although each of the four goals may be in the national interest of the United States, they require different strategies and pull in different directions.

Striking at Iran and other pariah states attempting to develop weapons of mass destruction requires a war plan similar to that used in the attack on Iraq, including saturation bombing, high collateral damage, and eventual occupation, to mention just the obvious. All fuel jihadist sentiments, alienate allies, divert much needed resources from the war on terror, and confuse the American public. Much the same is true of efforts to redraw the map of the Middle East in a manner compatible with the interests of the United States and Israel.

Not only must the United States give the war on terror its top priority, it must impose that priority on all key policy agencies. The public war between the State Department and the Defense Department causes confusion and delays and wastes resources. The same applies to widely publicized conflicts between America's various intelligence and defense agencies.

Rebuild the International Coalition against Terror

Jihadist terror is global in its reach, and the war on terror can only be won with the support of governments and security agencies throughout the world. This will require the United States to back away from its go–it–alone policy developed during the Iraq War and to be patient in working with its allies. The only other option is for the United States to patrol the world alone, hunting jihadists and their allies in seventy countries whose diverse cultures and political systems have little resemblance to its own. Not only is this a lonely and thankless task, but the United States lacks the knowledge, capacity, and resources to do so. If the United States finds it difficult to rule Iraq, how does it intend to rule the world? Even the national defense of the United States requires international cooperation. Unlike Israel, America cannot build a security wall around its borders, its dismal efforts to fence out illegal aliens from Latin America being a case in point. American defense against the jihadists requires the active support of Canada and Mexico, just as it depends on the ability of foreign countries to stem jihadist plots before they reach North America.

The same principle applies to the United Nations and international law. The United States is the major beneficiary of the United Nations and international law and is in an unparalleled position to shape the future direction of both. This requires accepting the constraints of international law until they can be modified. It also involves a greater willingness to listen to the suggestions of other countries and accommodating their interests.

Britain, America's staunch ally in the war against Iraq, also feels isolated from the world community. The Foreign Affairs Committee of the House of Commons minces no words on the topic, "In the wake of the Iraq war, we recommend that the Government make it a priority to work towards restoring the cohesion of the United Kingdom's international partnerships, better to face the daunting challenges of the continuing 'war against terrorism.'"[37]

Attack the Vulnerabilities of the Jihadists

The vulnerabilities of the jihadists have been discussed throughout this book and include heated debates over strategy, intense personalization of authority, distrust, turf wars, personality conflicts, excessive zeal, lapses of morale, questionable theological legitimacy, dependence on unreliable governments, overextended supply lines, secrecy, a narrow support base, and competition from more moderate Islamic groups. Some vulnerabilities are being exploited, but many are not.

1. Eliminate Jihadist Leaders. Eliminating jihadist leaders disrupts their chain of command and accentuates leadership struggles, turf wars, personality conflicts, and all other dimensions of the relationship between jihadist leaders and their followers. The organizational chart of jihadist organizations may resemble that of a modern army but, as noted in chapter 6, it can't act like one. Replacements are found, but it takes a long time to establish the patterns of trust and loyalty that make the jihadists effective. Splintering is also probable. In the meantime, their efficiency is reduced and jihadists have suffered a defeat. Morale declines accordingly. The same principle applies to midlevel leaders responsible for executing policy.

   However, the United States should avoid claiming responsibility for assassinations. Ambiguity plays on the intense distrust that permeates jihadist organizations and raises the possibility of betrayal or attack by a rival group. Denial of responsibility also avoids international crises and disputes with allies. In the language of international relations, it becomes a *fait accompli*. What is done is done and life goes on. Jihadist groups will vow revenge, but there is little they can do that they would not have done anyway. The United States can rest assured that the jihadists and their supporters will get the message. As we have seen in chapter 2, everything in the Middle East is blamed on the United States anyway.

Short of killing jihadist leaders, it is vital that the jihadists be kept on the run. This disrupts communications and logistics, spawns conflicts within and among jihadist groups, and has a debilitating impact on morale. Bin Laden may have become a folk hero by eluding American forces, but his al Qaeda network has been slowed down. The U.S. policy of putting a price on the heads of key jihadist leaders is an important step in this direction. Rewards may not have captured bin Laden and other jihadists leaders, but it has made them very nervous and accentuated distrust and suspicion within the jihadist community. The same suspicions and distrust disrupt ties between the jihadists and their allies.

2. Deny the Jihadists Publicity. The experience of Israel and the Islamic world suggests that arrests and imprisonment are less effective than the assassination of key jihadist leaders. Publicity is the core of the jihadists' psychological war plan, and lengthy trials are soon transformed into propaganda soap operas. Fair trials are interminable, while military trials set a bad precedent by violating U.S. provisions of due process. Arrest also transforms jihadist leaders into living martyrs who manage their affairs from prison. This is a harsh recommendation, but this is a harsh war. Maintaining large concentration camps such as Guantanamo Bay merely compounds the problem by creating an international human rights crisis. Of the 600 plus detainees at Guantanamo, only two had been formally charged by spring of 2004 and the United States was forced to find a new defense team as members of the original team resigned in protest over what they termed "unfair" trials.[38] The case has headed to the Supreme Court.

3. Deprive the Jihadists of Victories. Part and parcel of denying the jihadists publicity is depriving them of the victories on which they thrive. Victories against America send jihadist morale soaring, embolden supporters and allies, invite imitators, and sow doubts in the allies of the United States. Part of this equation is improving

U.S. defenses at home and abroad. Equally important is keeping Americans out of harm's way. The Israelis have demonstrated the effectiveness of assassinations. They have equally demonstrated the heavy price that one pays for occupation. The United States learned the lessons of occupation in Somalia and Beirut and is learning it again in Iraq.

4. Fragment the Jihadist Movement. The jihadists can be divided into three basic groups: those intent on attacking America and its allies, those who are tempted to renounce violence, and those who oppose attacks on the United States. Focusing on al Qaeda and other groups targeting America allows the United States to concentrate its resources on those groups that pose the greatest immediate threat to American security. Simultaneously, it drives a wedge between al Qaeda and other jihadist groups fearful of becoming the target of U.S. retribution. Less-threatening groups must be monitored to avoid the mistakes that led to September 11, but there is little need to take premature action that will embroil the United States in more crises than it can manage at one time. The same principle applies to the Muslim Brotherhood and other more moderate elements of the Islamic movement.

5. Undermine the Theological Legitimacy of the Jihadists. One of the weakest links in the jihadist armor is their questionable standing in Islamic jurisprudence. Most Muslims simply do not accept the jihadists' justification for killing Muslims and innocent civilians. The most effective way for the United States to exploit this vulnerability is for it to ease its criticism of the al-Jazeera network and the programming of Islamic tele-preachers. They are not pro-American, but neither are they kind to the jihadists. Tele-preachers, such as Sheikh Qaradawi, have led the charge against the jihadists by accusing them of perverting Islam and destroying the Islamic movement. Their voice is far more legitimate than that of the establishment clergy and cannot be matched by U.S. propaganda.

Avoid Public Intimidation of Governments in the Islamic World

The governments of the Islamic world are the front line in the battle against the jihadists. They must carry the battle to the jihadists and must bear primary responsibility for closing down the jihadists' allies. The United

States is placing intense pressure on the governments of the Islamic world to do both.

By and large, this pressure has taken the form of public threats and intimidation. Iran is part of the axis of evil, and Saudi Arabia is regularly chastised for its support of Islamic schools and Islamic charities. Press wars play well in the United States but they make it difficult for the leaders of Saudi Arabia, Iran, and other target countries to back down in the face of U.S. pressure. Saudi Arabia and Syria have made symbolic gestures but little more. In the meantime, anti-Americanism in the Islamic world continues unabated.

The United States might be better advised to adhere to the dictum of Theodore Roosevelt: "Walk softly and carry a big stick." Iraq and Afghanistan have already demonstrated that the United States has a big stick, and no one in the Islamic world doubts that it is willing to use it. Behind-the-scenes pressure will get the message across to the offending countries in a manner that allows them to take corrective measure without fear of losing face in front of their citizens. This strategy also provides the United States with maximum flexibility in dealing with noncompliance. It is dangerous for the United States to draw lines in the sand unless it is prepared to follow through. Given the present difficulties in Iraq, that may be difficult to do.

In the meantime, public pressure can be placed on target countries in a manner that does not offend Islamic and nationalistic sensibilities. For example, the United States can withdraw favor from Saudi Arabia on the grounds of the kingdom's lack of democracy and hideous record on human rights. The Saudis will get the message and the United States will have emerged as the champion of democracy.

Don't Create More Jihadists than You Are Eliminating

Attacking the jihadists loses much of its effectiveness if American policies are producing new generations of jihadists and strengthening their support within the Muslim community. That currently appears to be the case. The following suggestions will help.

1. Attack the Jihadists, Not Islam. The United States has not declared war on Islam, but the Muslim world believes that it has. As a result, the emotions of moderate Muslims are inflamed, the Islamic movement is solidified, the jihadists gain recruits and supporters, cooperation between Shi'a and Sunni is strengthened, and the

governments of the Islamic world shy away from cooperating with America in its war on terror.

An important step in countering the impression that the United States has declared war on Islam is for the United States to stop its press war against Islam, Islamic charities, Islamic education, and Islamic countries. As suggested above, the United States does have a big stick and doesn't need screaming headlines to achieve its objectives. The same message can be delivered behind the scenes with greater effectiveness. Criticizing governments for their lack of democracy and human rights, by contrast, would help the United States build a broad base of support in the region.

Greater efforts should also be made to separate bin Laden and al Qaeda from the broader Islamic movement. As a rule, Muslims believe that America is more than justified in going after the perpetrators of September 11. Revenge is part of the culture. They have no difficulty with that. Indeed, the United States would be perceived as a paper tiger if it did not destroy bin Laden and al Qaeda. What the Islamic world does not understand is the excessive bombing of Islamic countries and the occupation of Islamic lands.

2. Decouple Islam from anti-Americanism. Much of the animosity toward the United States in the Islamic world is based on nationalistic emotions rather than threats to Islam, although the two are sometimes difficult to disentangle in the Middle East. Not only do Muslims believe that the United States is anti-Islamic, they also believe that it is a neo-imperialist power intent on seizing control of the region. The occupation of Iraq has furthered this view, as have continuing verbal threats against Syria and Iran. Again, press wars are counterproductive and merely exacerbate behind-the-scenes negotiations.

Particularly upsetting to Muslim emotions is the Arab-Israeli conflict, an unrelenting source of anti-Americanism that has endured for more than fifty years. Even Paul Wolfowitz, the Pentagon's number-two official and one of the authors of the war on Iraq, has called the Arab-Israeli conflict the huge obstacle to U.S. goals.[39] It would be ludicrous to suggest that there is an easy solution to the problem, but the Oslo Accords initiated by Israeli Prime Minister Yitzhak Rabin came closer to success than any proposal before or after his unfortunate assassination. The Oslo Accords enjoyed broad support among both Israelis and Palestinians and offer the best opportunity for America to eliminate a major obstacle to its war on terror. Implementation of the Oslo Accords would also ease Syrian support for the jihadists and isolate Hizbullah and its Iranian sponsors. This, as we have seen, was part of Rabin's logic.

3. Avoid Excessive Violence. Attacks against jihadist positions that result in high collateral damage (civilian casualties and material damage) bring an international uproar, fuel anti-Americanism, and create new generations of jihadists. Mass arrests also tend be counterproductive, netting few hard-core jihadists, inflaming public opinion, and putting children in detention camps that serve as schools for terror. Covert and low-intensity operations carried out in cooperation with local governments inflict losses on the jihadists, while simultaneously minimizing hostility toward the United States.

4. Empower the Natural Enemies of the Jihadists. The vast majority of the world's Muslims don't want to live in a jihadist state. Even the large voter turnout for Islamic political parties in the flawed elections of the Islamic world has more to do with protest than a desire for the tyranny of extremist clerics. Unfortunately, most moderate groups in the Islamic world have little impact on the governance of their countries. By supporting nondemocratic regimes, such as those ruling Egypt, Saudi Arabia, Jordan, and Pakistan the United States is marginalizing moderate groups and preventing them from fighting the jihadists and their allies.

The United States can remedy this situation by using its persuasive power to force the empowerment of moderate groups in the Muslim world, a category that includes moderate Islamic parties. Empowerment means more than phony elections to parliaments that do not legislate. It means the power to shape policy and try new experiments. It also means the power to throw out corrupt bureaucrats and generals. This, of itself, will go a long way toward generating a sense of hope in the Islamic world.

Does this entail an element of risk? To be sure, but propping up decaying dictatorships only fuels support for the jihadists and makes their defeat that much more difficult in the long run. Empowering moderate groups inspires the natural enemies of the jihadists to get involved in the war on terror and makes the United States their friend rather than their foe.

The dangers of empowering the moderates can also be alleviated by a staged push for democracy. Democracy is not going to happen overnight, but genuine progress toward democracy is exhilarating and provides a tremendous stimulus for getting the enemies of the jihadists involved in the political process. Rather than chastising the governments of the Islamic world for supporting the jihadists, the United States should issue highly publicized demands for ever-greater democracy. Lapses should be punished by a withdrawal of U.S. aid and behind the scenes arm-twisting. This probably would not be so difficult. Friendly dictators are eager to please the United States. It is their best hope for sticking around.

Establishing democracy involves a degree of accommodation. If Islamic parties do well, so be it. Moderate Islam is tremendously popular in the Muslim world and attempting to crush popular views merely fuels extremism. It is also the nature of democracy. Even the Israelis are reluctantly moving in the direction of accommodation by acknowledging that there will be an independent Palestinian state of some form or another. Better the moderates than the jihadists.

Build Hope for a Better Future

Democracy is only part of the problem. The long-term struggle against the jihadists also requires a marked improvement of the quality of life in the poorer countries of the Islamic world. It might be recalled that the jihadists have flourished in areas of poverty and social turmoil, a list that includes the Sudan, Somalia, Egypt, Pakistan, Indonesia, Afghanistan, and Iran.

Improving the quality of life in the poorer countries of the Islamic world and elsewhere requires that the United States provide more foreign aid, give it to the countries that need it the most, administer it with far greater effectiveness, and coordinate it with other aid-granting countries and agencies. America's program of foreign assistance presently fails on all counts. U.S. foreign assistance is minimal, goes to a few close allies, is poorly administered, and often benefits American contractors more than the populations affected. Much the same applies to America's global aid effort. Coordination, while much discussed, gives way to jealousy, competition, duplication, and waste.

We close by noting that America's war on terror is both military and political. The military war is being won. The political war—dealing with the people and governments of the world—is being lost. Force alone cannot win the war on terror.

NOTES

1. United States Government, *National Strategy for Combating Terrorism* (Feb. 2003).

2. "Joint Inquiry into Intelligence Community Activities before and after the Terrorist Attacks of September 11, 2001," *Report to Congressional Committees*, The United States General Accounting Office, S. Rept. No. 107–351, 107th Congress, 2nd Session, H. Rept. No. 107–792, December 2002.

3. "Agents Uncover Islamic Terrorist Network Stretching across Pacific," *Guardian Unlimited*, 17 Mar. 2002, at http://www.observer.co.uk/international/story/0,6903 ,668836,00.html (accessed 17 Mar. 2002).

4. John Mintz, "Government's Hobbled Giant: Homeland Security Is Struggling," *Washington Post*, 7 Sept. 2003, at http://www.washingtonpost.com/wp-dyn/articles/ A36519-2003Sep6.html (accessed 7 Sept. 2003).

5. "Joint Inquiry into Intelligence Community," xvii.

6. Romesh Ratnesar and Michael Weisskopf, "How the FBI Blew the Case," *Time*, 3 June 2002, at http://www.time.com/time/covers/1101020603/story.html (accessed 3 June 2002).

7. Eric Lichtblau, "FBI Officials Say Some Agents Lack a Focus on Terror," *New York Times*, 21 Nov. 2002, at http://www.nytimes.com/2002/11/21/politics/ 21INQU.html (accessed 21 Nov. 2002).

8. Lichtblau, "FBI Officials Say Some Agents Lack a Focus on Terror."

9. Diana Jean Schemo, "Problems Slow Tracking of Students from Abroad," *New York Times*, 23 Mar. 2003, at http://www.nytimes.com/2003/03/23/international/ wordspecial/23STUD.html (accessed 23 Mar. 2003).

10. Dan Eggen and Karlyn Barker, "Registration Stirs Panic, Worry," *Washington Post*, 10 Jan. 2003, 10(A).

11. "G-20 Nations Agree to Fight Terrorist Funding," *Washington Post*, 23 Nov. 2002, at http://www.washingtonpost.com/wp-dyn/articles/A29772-2002Nov23.html (accessed 23 Nov. 2002).

12. John Hooper and Ian Black, "Anger at Rumsfeld Attack on 'Old Europe,'" *Guardian Unlimited*, 24 Jan. 2003, at http://www.guardian.co.uk/france/story/0,11882 ,881375,00.html (accessed 21 Jan. 2003).

13. Desmond Butler, "U.S. Is Slow to Share Leads on Qaeda Cells, Germans Say," *New York Times*, 4 Nov. 2002, at http://www.nytimes.com/2002/11/04/international/ europe/04GERM.html (accessed 4 Nov. 2002).

14. David Hoffman, "Beyond Public Diplomacy: U.S. Propaganda in Muslim Countries," *Foreign Affairs* 81, no. 2 (Mar.–Apr. 2002):83 (Infotrac A82782323, 14 Feb. 2004).

15. Edmund L. Andrews, "Traces of Terror: The Money Trail, White House Denies Report al Qaeda Funds Are Flowing," *New York Times*, 30 Aug. 2002, at www .nytimes.com/ (accessed 30 Aug. 2002).

16. Karen De Young and Douglas Farah, "Infighting Slows Hunt for Hidden Al Qaeda Assets," *Washington Post*, 18 June 2002, at http://www.washingtonpost.com/ wp-dyn/articles/A1813-2002Jun17.html (accessed 18 June 2002).

17. Jeremy Scott-Joynt, "U.S. Terror Fund Drive Stalls," *BBC News*, 3 Sept. 2002, at http://www.news.bbc.co.uk/1/hi/business/2225967.stm (accessed 11 Dec. 2002).

18. Steven R. Weisman, "Resurgent Taliban Threatens Afghan Stability, U.S. Says," *New York Times*, 19 Nov. 2002, at www.nytimes.com/ (accessed 19 Nov. 2002).

19. Mark Steyn, "Europeans Are Worse than Cockroaches: There Is a Cold War between the U.S. and the EU Says Mark Steyn, and It Will End with the Collapse of

Old Europe," *Spectator* 293, no. 9144 (20 Mar. 2003):12(A) (Infotrac A111203887, 14 Feb. 2004).

20. Bob Woodward, *Bush at War* (New York: Simon and Schuster, 2002).

21. Glann Kessler, "State-Defense Policy Rivalry Intensifying," *Washington Post*, 22 Apr. 2003, at http://www.washingtonpost.com/wp-dyn/articles/A7581-2003Apr21 .html (accessed 22 Apr. 2003).

22. David Frum and Richard Perle, *An End to Evil: How to Win the War on Terror* (New York: Random House, 2003).

23. Steven R. Weisman, "Pre-emption: Idea with a Lineage Whose Time Has Come," *New York Times*, 23 March 2003, at http://www.nytimes.com/2003/03/23/ international/worldsecial/ 23PREE.html (accessed 23 Mar. 2003).

24. Karen DeYoung and Peter Slevin, "Counterterror Team's Turnover Continues," *Washington Post* (18 Mar. 2003):A12 (Gulf/2000); Glenn Frankel, "Three Britons Quit Cabinet in Protest," *Washington Post*, 18 Mar. 18, 2003, at http://www.washingtonpost .com/wp-dyn/articles/A44706-2003Mar18.html (accessed 21 Mar. 2003).

25. Michele Norris (host) and Daniel Zwerdling (reporting), "Analysis: Elusive Numbers of U.S. Troops Evacuated from Iraq Due to Serious Injury or Illness," NPR, *All Things Considered*, no. 200401072002 (7 Jan. 2004).

26. Rajiv Chandrasekaran, "Attacks Force Retreat from Wide Ranging Plans for Iraq," *Washington Post*, 28 Dec. 2003, at http://www.washingtonpost.com/wp-dyn/ articles/A3505-2003Dec28.html (accessed 28 Dec 2003); David Sanger and Eric Schmitt, "Bush in a Hurry to Train Iraqis in Security Duty," *New York Times*, 30 Oct. 2003, at http://www.nytimes.com/2003/10/30/politics/30PREX.html?hp (accessed 30 Oct. 2003).

27. Edward Wong, "Iraqi Political Parties Will Form Militia to Work with American Forces," *New York Times*, 4 Dec. 2003, at www.nytimes.com/ (accessed 4 Dec. 2003).

28. Thom Shanker, "Rumsfeld Doubles Estimate for Cost of Troops in Iraq," *New York Times*, 10 July 2003, at http://www.nytimes.com/2003/07/10/international/ worldspecial/10MILI.html (accessed 10 July 2003).

29. David Firestone, "Dizzying Dive to Red Ink Poses Stark Choices for Washington," *New York Times*, 14 Sept. 2003, at http://www.nytimes.com/2003/09/14/ politics/14DEFI.html?hp (accessed 14 Sept. 2003).

30. The headlines were a quote from David Kay, former head of the U.S. Arms Inspection Team in Iraq in 2004, *Newsweek*, 9 Feb. 2004.

31. Report by the Foreign Affairs Committee of the British House of Commons (2003), 8.

32. Mona Ziade, "U.S. Admits It Lacks Post-Saddam Plan," *Daily Star-Lebanon*, 11 Sept. 2002, at http://www.dailystar.com.lb/11_9_02/art18.asp (accessed 11 Sept. 2002).

33. Neil MacFarquhar, "A Khomeini Breaks with His Lineage to Back U.S.," *New York Times*, 6 Aug. 2003, at http://www.nytimes.com/2003/08/06/international/ middleeast/06KHOM.html (accessed 6 Aug. 2003); Paul Simao, "Brahim Sees Positive Side to U.S. Action in Iraq," *Middle East Times*, 23 Aug. 2003, at http://www.metimes- .com/2K3/issue2003-34/eg/Ibrahim_applauds_us.htm (accessed 23 Aug. 2003).

34. Retired General William E. Odom, cited in John Harwood, "Capital Journal," *The Wall Street Journal*, 28 April 2004: A4.

35. Thomas Ricks, "Dissension Grows in Senior Ranks on War Strategy," *Washington Post*, 9 May 2004 at http://www.washingtonpost.com/ac2/wp-dyn/A11227-2 (accessed 9 May 2004).

36. Thom Shanker, "U.S. Commander to Keep 135,000 Troops in Iraq through 2005," *New York Times*, 5 May 2004 at http://www.nytimes.com/2004/05/05/ international.middleeast.htm (accessed 5 May 2004).

37. The Foreign Affairs Committee of the House of Commons (2003), 8.

38. James Meek, "U.S. Fires Guantanamo Defence Team," *Guardian Unlimited*, 3 Dec. 2003, at http://www.guardian.co.uk/international/story/0,3604,1098523,00.html (accessed 3 Dec. 2003).

39. Paul Wolfowitz, "Mideast Conflict Huge Obstacle to U.S. Goals," *Jerusalem Post*, 31 Oct. 2003, at www.jpost.com/ (accessed 31 Oct. 2003).

SELECTED BIBLIOGRAPHY

Abdul-Jabar, Faleh, ed. *Ayatollahs, Sufis, and Ideologies: State, Religion, and Social Movement in Iraq.* London: Al Saqi Books, 2002.

Abdullah, Mahar. "Will the Islamic Street Explode after the Strike on Afghanistan?" Interview with Abdullah Al Hamid II Sheikh Mubarak, Royal School of Islamic Jurisprudence. *Al Jazeera.* October 30, 2001, at http://www.aljazeera.net/programs/shareea/articles/2001.10/10-30-1.htm (accessed November 5, 2001). In Arabic.

Ajami, Fouad. *The Arab Predicament.* 2nd ed. Cambridge: Cambridge University Press, 1992.

Al-Auda, Sheik Suliman ben Fahd. "Saudi Religious Scholar Forbids Participation in US Strike on Iraq." *Al-Jazeera* (March 6, 2003), at http://www.aljazeera.net/news/Arabic/2003/3/3-6-7.htm (accessed March 6, 2003). In Arabic.

Al-Azm, Sadiz Jallal. *Self-Criticism after the Defeat.* Beirut: Dar Al Taliah, 1969. In Arabic.

Al-Baiya'nooni, Ali Sadr Eddin. "The Political Future of the Muslim Brotherhood in Syria." *Al Jazeerah* (July 7, 1998). In Arabic. Transcripts of interview with Ahmed Mansour, at http://www.aljazeera.net/programs/no_limits/articles/2001/11/11-29-2.htm (accessed November 29, 2001).

Al-Hadidi, Salah Addin. *Witness to the Yemen War.* Cairo: Madbouli, 1984. In Arabic.

Al-Hamid, Berlinti Abdul. *The Marshall and I.* Cairo: Madbouli, 1992. In Arabic.

Ali, Tariq. *The Clash of Fundamentalism: Crusades, Jihad, and Modernity.* London: Verso, 2002.

Al-Katib, Ahmed. "The Events in Najaf: Will They Ignite Riots or an Intifada?" *Al-Wasat* (March 1–7, 1999): 14–15. In Arabic.

Allievi, Stegano. "Converts and the Making of European Islam." *The Netherlands ISIM Newsletter,* no. 11 (December 2002): 25–26.

Al-Qassem, Fysal. Moderator. "The Arab Street: Panel Discussion." *Al Jazeera* (April 16, 2002), at www.aljazeera.net/programs/op_direction/articles/2002/3/4-25-1.htm (accessed May 6, 2002). In Arabic.

Al-Shaibi, Kamil. *Sufism and Shi'ism.* England: LAAM, Ltd., 1991.

Al-Tamimi, Azaam. "Failures of the Islamic Movement." *Al Jazeera* (November 11, 2001). Interviewed by Mahir Abdullah, at http://www.aljazeera.net/programs/shareea/articles/2001/11/11-11-2.htm (accessed August 24, 2002). In Arabic.

Al-Turabi, Hassan. "Islamic Fundamentalism in the Sunna and Shi'a Worlds." *Sudan Foundation Religious File Number 6.* London, 1997.

Al-Zaiyat, Mansour. "Sharia and Life Series: Islamic Groups and Violence." *Al Jazeera* (August 11, 2002). Interviewed by Mahir Abdullah, at http://www.aljazeera.net/programs/shareea/articles/2002/8/8-11-1.htm (accessed August 11, 2002). In Arabic.

Aoude, Ibrahim G. "From National Bourgeois Development to Infitah: Cairo 1952–1992." *Arab Studies Quarterly* 16, no. 1 (1994): 1–23.

Anderson, James. "International Terrorism and Crime: Trends and Linkages." Washington, D.C.: William R. Nelson Institute for Public Affairs, James Madison University, n.d.

Anonymous. *Through Our Enemies' Eyes: Osama Bin Laden, Radical Islam, and the Future of America.* Washington, D.C.: Brassey's, 2002.

Arian, Asher. *Politics in the Israeli Second Republic.* London: Chatham House, 1997.

Arjomand, Said Amir. *The Shadow of God and the Hidden Imam.* Chicago: University of Chicago Press, 1984.

Armajani, Yahya. *Middle East: Past and Present.* Englewood Cliffs, N.J.: Prentice-Hall, 1970.

Armanios, Febe. "Islamic Religious Schools, Madrasas: Background." Congressional Research Service, Library of Congress, October 29, 2003.

Aronoff, Myron J. *Israeli Visions and Divisions: Cultural Change and Political Conflict.* New Brunswick, N.H.: Transaction Publishers, 1989.

Ayrout, Henry Habib. *The Egyptian Peasant.* Translated by John Williams. Boston: Beacon Press, 1962.

Ayubi, Nazih. "The Political Revival of Islam: The Case of Egypt." *International Journal of Middle East Studies* 12 (1980): 481–99.

Awad, Hassan. "Jihad Names for Armed Groups." *Al-Wasat*, no. 622 (December 29, 2003), 10–11. In Arabic.

Banuazizi, Ali, and Myron Weiner, eds. *The State, Religion and Ethnic Politics.* New York: Syracuse University Press, 1986.

Barber, Benjamin R. *Jihad vs. McWorld: Terrorism's Challenge to Democracy.* New York: Ballantine Books, 2001.

Baram, Amatzia, and Barry M. Rubin. *Iraq's Road to War.* New York: St. Martin's Press, 1993.

Batatu, Hanna. *The Old Social Classes and the Revolutionary Movements of Iraq.* Princeton, N.J.: Princeton University Press, 1978.

———. "Iraqi Underground Shi'a Movements: Characteristics, Causes and Prospects." *Middle East Journal* 35, no. 4 (1981): 578–94.

Beeley, Brian, ed. *Turkish Transformation: New Century: New Challenges.* London: Eothen Press, n.d.

Begag, Azouz. "Les relations France-Algerie vues de la diaspora algerienne." *Modern and Contemporary France* 10(4) (November 2002): 475–82.

Benjamin, Daniel, and Steven Simon. *The Age of Sacred Terror: Radical Islam's War Against America*. New York: Random House, 2003.

Begin, Menachem. *The Revolt: Story of the Irgun*. New York: Henry Schuman, 1951.

Bergen, Peter L. *Holy War, Inc.: Inside the Secret World of Osama bin Laden*. New York: The Free Press, 2001.

Bill, James A. *The Eagle and the Lion: The Tragedy of American-Iranian Relations*. New Haven, Conn.: Yale University Press, 1988.

———. "Resurgent Islam in the Persian Gulf." *Foreign Affairs* 63, (Fall 1984): 108–27.

Bill, James A., and Robert Springborg. *Politics in the Middle East*. New York: HarperCollins, 1997.

Bill, James A., and John Alden Williams. *Roman Catholics and Shi'i Muslims: Prayer, Passion, and Politics*. Chapel Hill: University of North Carolina Press, 2002.

Bodansky, Yossef. *Bin Laden: The Man Who Declared War on America*. Roseville, Calif.: Prima Publishing, 2001.

Boukra, Liess. *Algérie la terreur sacrée*. SA Lausanne: FAVRE, 2002.

Brockelmann, Carl. *History of the Islamic People*. New York: Capricorn Books. 1960.

Burgat, Francois. *Face to Face with Political Islam*. London: IB Tauris, 2002.

Burke, Jason. *Al Qaeda: Casting a Shadow of Terror*. London: IB Tauris, 2003.

Busse, Herbert. *Islam, Judaism and Christianity: Theological and Historical Affiliations*. Princeton, N.J.: Markus Wiener Publishers, 1997.

Butler, Richard. *Saddam Defiant: The Threat of Weapons of Mass Destruction and the Crisis of Global Security*. London: Weidenfeld & Nicolson, 2000.

Campagna, Joel. "From Accommodation to Confrontation: The Muslim Brotherhood in the Mubarak Years." *Journal of International Affairs* 50, no. 1 (Summer 1996): 278–304.

Carapico, Sheila. "Yemen and the Aden-Abyan Islamic Army." *Middle East Report Online*. October 18, 2000, at http://www.merip.org/mero/mero101800.html (accessed July 19, 2003).

Carmi, Shulamit, and Henry Rosenfeld. "The Time when the Majority in the Israeli Cabinet Decided 'Not to Block the Possibility of the Return of the Arab Refugees' and How this Policy was Defeated." *State and Society* 2, no. 3 (December 2002): 371–400.

Cavender, Gay, Nancy C. Jurik, and Albert K. Cohen. "The Baffling Case of the Smoking Gun: The Social Ecology of the Political Accounts in the Iran-Contra Affair." *Social Problems* 40, no. 2 (1993): 152–65.

Clarke, Richard A. *Against All Enemies: Inside America's War on Terror*. New York: Free Press, 2004.

Cole, Juan Ricardo. *Colonialism and Revolution in the Middle East*. Princeton, N.J.: Princeton University Press, 1993.

Combs, Cindy. *Terrorism in the 21st Century*. 2nd ed. Englewood Cliffs, N.J.: Prentice Hall, 2000.

Cordesman, Anthony H. *Terrorism, Asymmetric Warfare, and Weapons of Mass Destruction.* Westport, Conn.: Praeger, 2001.

Cronin, Stephanie. *The Army and the Creation of the Pahlavi State in Iran, 1910–1926.* London: IB Tauris, 1997.

Daragahi, Borzou. "Financing Terror," *Money* 30, Issue 12 (Nov. 1, 2001): 120 (Infotrac A79304052, accessed Sept. 2001).

Davis, Eric. "The Concept of Revival and the Study of Islam and Politics." In *The Islamic Impulse,* edited by Barbara F. Stowasser. London: Croom Helm, 1987.

Dawish, Adeed. "Requiem for Arab Nationalism." *The Middle East Quarterly* 10 (Winter 2003), at http://www.meforum.org/article/518 (accessed November 3, 2003).

De Corancez, Louis A.O. *The History of the Wahabis: From Their Origin until the End of 1809.* Translated by Eric Tabet. Reading, UK: Garnet Publishing, 1995.

Dekmejian, R. Hrair. *Fundamentalism in the Arab World.* Syracuse, N.Y.: Syracuse University Press, 1985.

———. *Islam in Revolution.* Syracuse, N.Y.: Syracuse University Press, 1995.

Del Carmen, Alejandro, ed. *Terrorism: An Interdisciplinary Perspective.* 2nd ed. Toronto, Ontario: Wadsworth Publishing, 2003.

Doran, Michael Scott. "The Saudi Paradox." *Foreign Affairs* Jan/Feb. 2004, at http://www.foreignaffairs.org (accessed January 1, 2004).

Dorraj, Manocheht. "Symbolic and Utilitarian Political Value of a Tradition: Martyrdom in the Iranian Political Culture." *The Review of Politics* 59, no. 3 (1997): 489–521.

El Halim, Tarig. "Views on the Transformation of the Islamic Movement in Egypt: The Muslim Brotherhood in Half a Century." *Al Manar al Jadeed,* no. 15 (December 2001). In Arabic.

El Khazen, Farid. *The Breakdown of the State of Lebanon, 1967–1976.* London: IB Tauris, 2000.

Elliot, Matthew. *Independent Iraq: The Monarchy and British Influence, 1941–58.* London: IB Tauris, 1996.

El-Nawawy, Mohammed, and Adel Iskander. *Al Jazeera: How the Free Arab News Network Scooped the World and Changed the Middle East.* Boulder, Colo.: Westview Press, 2002.

Ernst, Carl W. *The Shambhala Guide to Sufism: An Essential Introduction to the Philosophy and Practice of the Mystical Tradition of Islam.* Boston: Shambhala, 1997.

Esposito, John. *Unholy War: Terror in the Name of Islam.* New York: Oxford University Press, 2002.

Esposito, John L., ed. *The Iranian Revolution: Its Global Impact.* Miami, Fla.: Florida International University Press, 1990.

Ezrahi, Yaron. *Rubber Bullets: Power and Conscience in Modern Israel.* Berkeley, Calif.: University of California Press, 1998.

El Safty, Madiha, Monte Palmer, and Mark Kennedy. *An Analytical Index of Survey Research in Egypt.* Cairo: Cairo Papers in Social Science, 1985.

Fahmy, Ninette. *The Politics of Egypt: State-Society Relationship.* Richmond, Surrey, UK: Curson Press, 2002.

Fairbanks, Steve, and Bill Samii. "Iran: Weak Economy and High Unemployment Worry Tehran." *IPR Strategic Business Information Database*. 30 April 2003. Info-Prod, Middle East Ltd. at http://infotrac-college.thomsonlearning.com/itw/ (accessed February 6, 2004).

Farid, Abdel Majid. *Nasser: The Final Years*. Reading, UK: Ithaca Press, 1994.

Fathaly, Omar, and Monte Palmer. "Change Resistance Among Rural Libyan Elites." *International Journal of Middle East Studies* (1980): 247–61.

Fisher, Sydney N. *The Middle East: A History*. New York: Alfred A. Knopf, 1964.

Fraser, T.G. *The Middle East 1914–1979*. London: Edward Arnold, 1980.

Frum, David, and Richard Perle. *An End to Evil: How to Win the War on Terror*. New York: Random House, 2003.

Fuller, Graham F. *The Future of Political Islam*. New York: Palgrave Macmillan, 2003.

———. *The Arab Shi'a*. New York: Palgrave, 2001.

Gause, F. Gregory. "Getting It Backward on Iraq." *Foreign Affairs* 78, no. 3 (May 1999): 54.

———. *Oil Monarchies: Domestic and Security Challenges in the Arab Gulf States*. New York: Council on Foreign Relations Press, 1994.

Gieling, Saskia. "The Marja'iya in Iran and the Nomination of Khamanei in December 1994.' *Middle Eastern Studies* 44, no. 4 (Dec. 1997): 777–87.

Gilbert, Martin. *The Arab-Israeli Conflict: Its History in Maps*. 3rd ed. London: Weidenfeld and Nicolson, 1979.

Graham-Brown, Sarah. *Sanctioning Saddam*. London: IB Tauris, 1999.

Gold, Dore. *Hatred's Kingdom: How Saudi Arabia Supports the New Global Terrorism*. Washington, D.C.: Regnery Publishing, 2003.

Goldberg, Jeffrey. "In the Party of God: The Meeting." *The New Yorker* (October 14, 2002): 21.

Goodson, Larry P. *Afghanistan's Endless War: State Failure, Regional Politics, and the Rise of the Taliban*. Seattle: University of Washington Press, 2001.

Gunaratna, Rohan. *Inside Al-Qaeda: Global Network of Terror*. New York: Columbia, 2002.

Habib, Kemal As-Said. "The Experience of the Islamic Movement in Egypt." *Al Manar*, no. 21 (2001), at http://www.almanar.net/ussues/12/121.htm (accessed December 13, 2001). In Arabic.

Hadar, Leon T. "Israel in the Post-Zionist Age: Being Normal and Loving It." *World Policy Journal* 16, no. 1 (1999).

Haddad, Sami. Moderator. "Panel Discussion: The Future of the Afghan Arabs After the Defeat of the Taliban." *Al Jazeera*. 23 November 2001, at http://www.aljazeera.net/programs/opinions/articles/2001/11/11-25-1.htm (accessed December 1, 2001).

Halliday, Fred. *Two Hours That Shook the World*. London: Saqi Books, 2002.

Halm, Heinz. *Shi'a Islam: From Religion to Revolution*. Translated from German by Allison Brown. Princeton: Markus Wiener Pub., 1997.

Hamzeh, Nizar, and Harir Dekmejian. "A Sufi Response to Political Islamism: Al-Ahbash of Lebanon." *International Journal of Middle East Studies* 28 (1996): 217–99.

Hamouda, Adel. *Prayer of the Spies*. Cairo: Dar al-Farsan, 1995. In Arabic.

Hatina, Meir. *Islam and Salvation in Palestine: The Islamic Jihad Movement*. New York: Syracuse University Press, 2001.

Heikal, Mohammed H. *Autumn of Fury: The Assassination of Sadat*. London: Andre Deutsch, 1983.

Herzl, Theodor. *A Jewish State*. New York: American Zionist Emergency Council, 1896.

Hertz, Todd. "Riots, Condemnation, Fatwa, and Apology Follow Falwell's CBS Comments," *Christianity Today Magazine* (October 14, 2002), at http://www.christianity today.com/ct/2002/140/41.0.html (accessed December 7, 2003).

Hidar, Asaad. "As Sadr in the Week Before." *Al-Wasat* (March 1–7, 1999): 13–14. In Arabic.

Hitti, Philip K. *History of the Arabs from the Earliest Times to the Present*. 6th ed. London: Macmillan, 1956.

Hoffman, Bruce. "The Leadership Secrets of Osama bin Laden." *The Atlantic* (April 2003): 291–93.

———. "Beyond Public Diplomacy: US Propaganda in Muslim Countries." *Foreign Affairs* 81, no. 2 (March–April 2002): 83 (Infotrac A82782323, 14 Feb. 2004).

House of Commons Foreign Affairs Committee. *Foreign Policy Aspects of the War against Terrorism: Tenth Report of Session 2002–03*. Report, together with formal minutes, oral and written evidence. HC 405. London: The Stationery Office, Ltd., 15 July 2003.

Hudson, Rex A. *Who Becomes a Terrorist and Why: The 1999 Government Report on Profiling Terrorists*. Guildord, Conn.: The Lyons Press, n.d.

Human Rights Watch. *Human Rights Watch World Report 2002: Middle East and North Africa*. New York: Human Rights Watch, 2001.

Huntington, Samuel P. *The Clash of Civilizations and the Remaking of World Order*. New York: Simon and Schuster, 1996.

Ibrahim, Farhad. *Confessionalism and Politics in the Arab World: The Shi'a Program in Iraq*. Translated from German into Arabic by the Center for Cultural Studies and Translations. Cairo: Library Madbouli, 1996.

Ibrahim, Saad Eddin. *Egypt, Islam, and Democracy*. Cairo: American University of Cairo Press, 1996. In Arabic.

———. "Anatomy of Egypt's Militant Islamic Groups: Methodological Note and Preliminary Findings." *International Journal of Middle East Studies* 12, no. 4 (1980): 423–53.

Jerichow, Anders. *Saudi Arabia: Outside Global Law and Order*. Richmond, Surrey, UK: Curzon Press, 1997.

———. *The Saudi File: People, Power, and Politics*. NY: Palgrave Macmillan, 1998.

Johnson, Haynes. *The Best of Times: The Boom and Bust Years of America Before and After Everything Changed*. New York: Harcourt, Inc., 2002.

Jones, Owen Bennett. *Pakistan: Eye of the Storm*. New Haven: Yale University Press, 2002.

Joseph, Nevo. "Religion and National Identity in Saudi Arabia." *Middle Eastern Studies* (July 1998): 34.

Juergensmeyer, Mark. *Terror in the Mind of God: The Global Rise of Religious Violence*. Los Angeles: University of California Press, 2000.

Kaplan, Robert D. *The Arabists: The Romance of an American Elite*. New York: The Free Press, 1995.

Karsh, Efraim. *Israel in the International Arena*. London: Frank Cass, 2002.

Keilani, Musa. *The Islamic Movement in Jordan*. Amman, Jordan: Dar Al Bashir, 1990. In Arabic.

Kelidar, Abbas. "The Shi'I Imami Community and Politics in the Arab East." *Middle Eastern Studies* 19, no. 1 (1983): 3–16.

Kelly, Laurence. *Diplomacy and Murder in Tehran*. New York: IB Tauris, 2002.

Kepel, Gilles. *Jihad: The Trail of Political Islam*. Cambridge, Mass.: Belnap Press of Harvard University Press, 2002.

Khadduri, Majid. *War and Peace in the Law of Islam*. Baltimore: Johns Hopkins Press, 1955.

———. *Independent Iraq, 1932–1958*. London: Oxford University Press, 1960.

Khalid, Kemal. *They Killed Sadat: Secrets of the Legal Proceedings in the Case of the Jihad Organization*. Cairo: Preservation House, Dar I'tisam, 1988. In Arabic.

Khan, Amil. "Brotherhood Faces Crisis." *Middle East Times*, no. 45 (November 2002), at http://www.metimes.com/2K2/issue2002-45/eg/brotherhood_faces_crisis.htm (accessed November 9, 2002).

Kharishan, Mohammed. Moderator. "First War of the Century: Organization of Al Qaeda and its Relation with the Taliban." *Al-Jazeera* (October 29, 2001), at http://www.aljazeera.net/programs/first_Cent_wars/articles/2001/11/11-1-1.html (accessed November 5, 2001). In Arabic.

Kharishan, Mohammed. Moderator. "Changing the Arab Educational Program at the Request of the United States." Panel Discussion *Al-Jazeera* (December 22, 2001), at http://www.aljazeera.net/programs/first_Cent_wars/articles/2001/12/22/1.html (accessed December 29, 2001). In Arabic.

Khashan, Hilal. *Arabs at the Crossroads: Political Identity and Nationalism*. Gainesville, Fla.: University Press of Florida, 2000.

———. *Inside the Lebanese Confessional Mind*. Lanham, Md.: University Press of America, 1992.

Khashan, Hilal, and Monte Palmer. "The Social and Economic Correlates of Islamic Religiosity." Paper presented at the annual meeting of the Middle East Studies Association for North America, Chicago, December 1998.

Kimmerling, Baruch. *The Invention and Decline of Israeliness: State, Society, and the Military*. S. Mark Taper Foundation Book in Jewish Studies, December 2001.

Kinzer, Stephen. *All the Shah's Men: An American Coup and the Roots of Middle East Terror*. Hoboken, N.J.: John Wiley and Sons, 2003.

Klardman, Daniel, Ichael Isikoff, and Mark Hosenball. "Investigators Link Last Week's Attacks, Embassy bombings in Africa and USS Cole." *Newsweek Web Exclusive*, Sept. 20, 2001, at http://www.msnbc.msn.com/id/3066931 (accessed February 24, 2004).

The Koran: Interpreted. Translation by A.J. Arberry. New York: Touchstone: Simon & Schuster, 1955.

Lacy, Robert. *The Kingdom: Arabia and the House of Sa'ud.* New York: Harcourt, Brace and Jovonovich, 1981.

Levitt, Matthew. *Targeting Terror: US Policy Toward Middle East State Sponsors and Terrorist Organizations, Post Sept. 11.* Washington, D.C.: The Washington Institute for Near East Policy, 2002.

Lewis, Bernard. "The Roots of Muslim Rage." *The Atlantic Monthly* 266, no. 3 (Sept. 1990): 47–60.

———. *What went Wrong? The Clash between Islam and Modernity in the Middle East.* New York: Oxford University Press, 2002.

———. *The Crisis of Islam: Holy War and Unholy Terror.* New York: The Modern Library, 2003.

Lintner, Bertil. "Religious Extremism and Nationalism in Bangladesh." Paper presented at the international workshop on Religion and Security in South Asia at the Asia Pacific Center for Security Studies in Honolulu, Hawaii, August 2002.

Lippman, Thomas W. *Inside the Mirage: America's Fragile Partnership with Saudi Arabia.* Boulder, Colo.: Westview Press, 2004.

Looney, Robert. "Hawala: The Terrorists' Informal Financial Mechanism." *Middle East Policy* 10, no. 1 (Spring 2003): 164–67.

Lynch, Marc. "Beyond the Arab Street: Iraq and the Arab Public Sphere." *Politics and Society* 31, no. 1(2003): 55–92.

Mackey, Sandra. *The Iranians: Persia, Islam and the Soul of a Nation.* New York: Dutton, 1996.

Mango, Andrew. *Ataturk: The Biography of the Founder of Modern Turkey.* New York: The Overlook Press, 2002.

Mehta, Mandavi, and Ambassador Teresita C. Schaffer. "Islam in Pakistan: Unity and Contradictions." Report from the CSIS Project Pakistan's Future and US Policy Options. October 7, 2002.

Miller, John, and Michael Stone, with Chris Mitchell. *The Cell: Inside the 9/11 Plot and Why the FBI and CIA failed to Stop It.* New York: Hyperion, 2003.

Miller, Judith. "Faces of Fundamentalism: Hassan al-Turabi and Muhammed Fadlallah (Sudanese and Lebanese Islamic Fundamentalist Leaders)." *Foreign Affairs* 73, no. 6 (Nov.–Dec.): 123–43.

Milton-Edwards, Beverly. *Islamic Politics in Palestine.* London: IB Tauris Academic Studies, 1999.

Mitchell, Richard. *The Society of Muslim Brothers.* London: Oxford University Press, 1969.

Mordechai, Gazit. *Israeli Diplomacy and the Middle East Peace Process.* London: Frank Cass, 2002.

Moussalli, Ahmad. *Moderate and Radical Islamic Fundamentalism: The Quest for Modernity, Legitimacy, and the Islamic State.* Gainesville, Fla.: University Press of Florida, 1999.

Mozaffari, Mehdi. "Changes in the Iranian Political System after Khomeini's Death." *Political Studies* XLI, no. 4 (1993): 611–17.

Mullaney, Francis Cabrini. *The Role of Islam in the Hegemonic Strategy of Egypt's Military Rulers (1952–1990)*. Ann Arbor, Mich.: UMI Dissertation Information Service, 1995.

Munson, Henry Jr. *Islam and Revolution in the Middle East*. New Haven, Conn.: Yale University Press, 1988.

Muslih, Muhammed. *The Foreign Policy of Hamas*. New York: Council on Foreign Relations, 1999.

Mustafa, Hala. *The Political System and the Islamic Opposition in Egypt*. Cairo: Markaz Al-Mahrusa, 1995. In Arabic.

———. "Les Forces Islamiques et l'Experience Democratique en Egypte." In *Democratie et Demoncratizations dans le Monde Arabe*. Le Caire: Dossiers de CEDEJ, 1992, 379–97.

Nada, Joseph, "Dimensions of the American Attack of Islamic Financing," *Al Jazeera*. 19 Nov. 2001. Interviewed by Ahmed Mansour, at http://www.aljazeera.net/programs/no_limits/articles/2001/11/11-19-1.htm (accessed November 23, 2001). In Arabic.

———. "Interview with Joseph Nada, Commissioner of International Political Affairs for the Muslim Brotherhood." Part 1 of six interviews by Ahmed Mansour. *Al Jazeera*. (August 4, 2002) at http://www.aljazeera.net/programs/century_witness/articles/2002/8/8-4-1.htm (accessed September 9, 2002). In Arabic.

———. "Interview with Joseph Nada, Commissioner of International Political Affairs for the Muslim Brotherhood." Part 2 of six interviews by Ahmed Mansour. *Al Jazeera*. (August 13, 2002), at http://www.aljazeera.net/programs/century_witness/articles/2002/8/8/13-1.htm (accessed September 9, 2002). In Arabic.

———. "Interview with Joseph Nada, Commissioner of International Political Affairs for the Muslim Brotherhood." Part 3 of six interviews by Ahmed Mansour. *Al Jazeera* (August 18, 2002), at http://www.aljazeera.net/programs/century_witness/articles/2002/8/8/18-1.htm (accessed September 9, 2002). In Arabic.

———. "Interview with Joseph Nada, Commissioner of International Political Affairs for the Muslim Brotherhood." Part 4 of six interviews by Ahmed Mansour. *Al Jazeera* (August 28, 2002), at http://www.aljazeera.net/programs/century_witness/articles/2002/8/8-28-1.htm (accessed September 9, 2002). In Arabic.

———. "Interview with Joseph Nada, Commissioner of International Political Affairs for the Muslim Brotherhood." Part 5 of six interviews by Ahmed Mansour. *Al Jazeera* (September 9, 2002), at http://www.aljazeera.net.programs/century_witness/articles/2002/9/9-5-1.htm (accessed September 9, 2002). In Arabic.

———. "Responses to Testimony of Youssef Nada." Part 6 of six interviews by Ahmed Mansour. *Al Jazeera*. (October 5, 2002), at http://www.aljazeera.net/programs/no_limites/articles/2002/10/10_5_1.htm (accessed October 13, 2002). In Arabic.

Naipaul, V.S. *A Million Mutinies Now*. New York: Viking, 1990.

Nakash, Yitzhak. *The Shi'is of Iraq*. Princeton, N.J.: Princeton University Press, 1994.

National Commission on Terrorism. *Countering the Changing Threat of International Terrorism*. Pursuant to Public Law 277, 105th Congress, n.d.

Nehme, Michel. *Fear and Anxiety in the Arab World*. Gainesville, Fla.: The University Press of Florida, 2003.

No Name. "Turkish Republic at Seventy Years: The Progress—Development—Change." Papers presented at the 75th Anniversary of the Founding of the Turkish Republic. London: Eothen Press, n.d.

————. "Unfulfilled Promises: Pakistan's Failure to Tackle Extremism," *International Crisis Group Asia Report*, no. 73 (January 16, 2004).

————. "US Officials Poised to use the Internet as a Lethal Weapon," *Al Wasat*, Issue 618 (December 1, 2003): 1–2. In Arabic.

Nonneman, Gerd. *Iraq, the Gulf States, and the War*. London: Ithaca Press, 1986

Norton, Augustus R. *Amal and the Shi'a: Struggle for the Soul of Lebanon*. Austin, Tex.: University of Texas Press, 1987.

Norris, Michele (host) and Daniel Zwerdling (reporting). "Analysis: Elusive numbers of US Troops Evacuated from Iraq due to Serious Injury or Illness." National Public Radio, All Things Considered, no. 200401072002, (January 7, 2004).

Oleson, Asta. *Islam and Politics in Afghanistan*. Richmond, Surrey, UK: Curzon Press, 1995. Nordic Institute of Asian Studies monograph series no. 67.

Oliver, Haneef James. *The 'Wahhabi' Myth: Dispelling Prevalent Fallacies and the Fictitious Link with Bin Laden*. Online Publishing: Trafford, 2002.

Orlinsky, Harry M. *Ancient Israel*, 2nd ed. Ithaca, New York: Cornell University Press, 1960.

Palmer, Monte. *Politics of the Middle East*. Itasca, IL: F.E. Peacock Pub., Inc./Wadsworth, 2002.

————. *Political Development: Dilemmas and Challenges*. 5th ed. Itasca: F.E. Peacock Pub., Inc./Wadsworth, 1997.

Palmer, Monte, Madiha El Safty, and Earl Sullivan. "The Relationship between Economic and Religious Attitudes in Egypt." Paper presented at the annual Meeting of the Middle East Studies Association of North America, Providence, R.I., 1996.

Palmer, Monte, Ali Leila, and El Sayed Yassin. *The Egyptian Bureaucracy*. Syracuse, New York: Syracuse University Press, 1988.

Palmer, Monte, Mima Nedelcovych, Hilal Khashan, and Debra Munro. *Survey Research in the Arab World: An Analytical Index*. London: Menas Press Ltd., 1982.

Pike, John, Interviewee, *ABC News*, Dec. 20, 2002, at http://www.abcnews.go.com/sectons/world/Daily_News/binladenterror_000918.html (accessed December 20, 2002).

Pillar, Paul. R. *Terrorism and US Foreign Policy*. Washington, DC: Brookings Institution Press, 2001.

Polk, William R., David M. Stamler, and Edmund Asfour. *Backdrop to Tragedy: The Struggle for Palestine*. Boston: Beacon Press, 1957.

Pollack, Kenneth. *The Threatening Storm: The Case for Invading Iraq*. New York: Random House, 2002.

Prokop, Michael A. "Saudia Arabia: The Politics of Education." *International Affairs* 79, no. 1 (2003): 78–79.

Qaradawi, Yousef. "Violence and the Islamic Groups, Part 1." *Al Jazeera* (July 7, 2001). Interviewed by Hamid Al Ansari, at http:www.aljazeera.net/programs/shareea/articles/2001/7/7-7-1.htm (accessed August 24, 2002). In Arabic.

———. "Violence and the Islamic Groups, Part 2." *Al Jazeera* (7 July 2001). Interviewed by Hamid Al Ansari, at http:www.aljazeera.net/ programs/shareea/articles/2001/7/7-7-1.htm (accessed August 24, 2002).In Arabic.

Qauwisi, Ahmed. "The Islamic Movement on the Doorstep of the 21st Century." *Al Manar al Jadeed*, no. 15 (December 2001). In Arabic.

Radwan, Zeinab. *Appearance of the Hijab among University Students*. Cairo: National Center for Social and Criminal Research, 1982.

Rahman, Anisur. "Tabligh Jamaat Host Biggest Congregation of Muslims after Hajj." *Islam Online* (January 30, 2000), at http://www.islamonline.net/completesearch/English/mDetails.asp (accessed October 21, 2002).

Rahman, B. "Harkat-ul-Mujahideen: An Update," at www.ict.org.il (accessed March 20, 1999).

———. "Islamic Jihad and the United States," SAPRA, 2000, at http://www.subcontinent .com/sapra/terrorism/terrorism20001029a.html (accessed June 5, 2002).

Ramadan, Abdel Azim. "Fundamentalist Influence in Egypt: The Strategies of the Muslim Brotherhood and the Takfir Groups." In *Fundamentalisms and the State: Remaking Polities, Economies, and Militance: The Fundamentalism Project,* vol. 3. Edited by Martin E. Marty, and Scott Appleby. Chicago: University of Chicago Press, 1993.

Ramazani, R.K. "The Shifting Premise of Iran's Foreign Policy: Towards a Democratic Peace?" *The Middle East Journal* 52, no. 2 (1998): 177–87.

Rashid, Ahmed. *Taliban: Militant Islam, Oil and Fundamentalism in Central Asia*. New Haven, Conn.: Yale University Press, 2001.

———. *Jihad: The Rise of Militant Islam in Central Asia*. New York: Penguin Books, 2002.

Reesa, Maria A. *Seeds of Terror: An Eyewitness Account of Al-Qaeda's Newest Center of Operation in Southeast Asia*. New York: The Free Press, 2003.

Rizk, Hamdi. "Egyptian Muslim Brotherhood." *Al-Wasat*, 31 (October 30, 1999). In Arabic.

Roberson, B.A., ed. *Shaping the Current Islamic Reformation*. London: Frank Cass, 2003.

Rodinson, Maxime. *Israel and the Arabs*. Middlesex, England: Penguin, 1969.

Roth, Cecil. *History of the Jews*. New York: Schocken Books, 1963.

Rubin, Barry, ed. *Revolutionaries and Reformers: Contemporary Islamic Movements in the Middle East*. Albany, New York: State University of NY Press, 2003.

Rubin, Barry, and Metin Heper, eds. *Political Parties in Turkey*. London: Frank Cass, 2002.

Rubin, Elizabeth. "The Cult of Rajavi." *New York Times Magazine* (13 July 2003): 5.

Rugh, Andrea B. *Reveal and Conceal*. Cairo: American University of Cairo Press, 1987.

Saadeq, Mahmoud. "For the First Time: Thoughts of a Social Islamic Party in Egypt." *Al-Waton Al-Arabi* (2 April 1999): 4–8. In Arabic.

———. "Wanted Dead or Alive." *Al-Waton Al-Arabi* (28 May 1999): 4–7. In Arabic.

Sachedina, Abdulaziz. *The Islamic Roots of Democratic Pluralism.* Oxford: Oxford University Press, 2001

Saeed, Abdul Karim Qassem. *The Muslim Brotherhood and the Fundamentalist Movement in Yemen.* Cairo: Madbouli, 1995.

Sahliyeh, Emile. *In Search of Leadership: West Bank Politics Since 1967.* Washington, D.C.: The Brookings Institution, 1988.

Saleh, Heba. "Undercover: Why are More Egyptian Women Wearing Veils? Social Scientists Suggest a Variety of Reasons." *Cairo Today* (February 1990): 67–69.

Salem, Jihad. "Important Emergency Meeting in the Majlis As Shoura (Hezbullah Lebanon) to Discuss the Disaster of the Decrease in Iranian Support." *Al-Waton Al-Arabi* (9 April 1999): 32–33. In Arabic.

Samii, William. "The Nation and Its Minorities: Ethnicity, Unity, and State Policy." *Comparative Studies of South Asia, Africa, and the Middle East* 20, nos. 1–2 (2000): 128–37.

Sarour, Mustafa. "Assassination of As-Sadr Preceded by a Deadly Telephone Debate: Preemptive Strike or Provocation to Civil Strife." *Al-Wasat* (March 1–7, 1999): 10–12. In Arabic.

Satloff, Robert B., ed. *War on Terror: The Middle East Dimension.* Washington, D.C.: The Washington Institution for Near East Policy, 2002.

Saud, Al-Rais. "Saudi Arabia: Lifting the Veil on Implicit Sympathy with the Extremists." *Al-Wasat* (22 Dec. 2003): 11.

Saurash, Sami. "Muktadar As-Sadr Shuffles the Cards: Shi'a War against America or Shi'a War Against Shi'a." *Al-Wasat* (20 Oct. 2003): 4–6. In Arabic.

Schwartz, Stephen. *The Two Faces of Islam: The House of Saud from Tradition to Terror.* New York: Doubleday, 2003.

Schwedler, Jillian. "The 'Street' and the Politics of Dissent in the Arab World." *MERIP* 226, no. 3 (Spring 2003): 10–17.

Sellers, Jef M. "Religious Cleansing." *Christianity Today.* 15 April 2003, at http://www.christianitytoday.com/ct/2003/004/27.98.html (accessed July 18, 2003).

Senate Testimony. Rand Beers, Assistant Secretary for International Narcotics and Law Enforcement Affairs; Francis X. Taylor, Ambassador-at-Large for Counter-Terrorism. March 13, 2002.

Sharabi, Hisham. *Neopatriarchy: A Theory of Distorted Change in Arab Society.* New York: Oxford University Press, 1988.

Sharett, Moshe. *Yoman Ishi (Personal Diary).* Tel Aviv: Maariv 1024–1025, 1978. Reprinted as "Israel's Foreign and Middle Eastern Policy." In *Israel in the Middle East: Documents and Readings on Society, Politics and Foreign Relations, 1948–Present.* Edited by Itamar Rabinovich and Jehuda Reinharz. Oxford: Oxford University Press, 1978.

Sharkansky, Ira. "Religion and Politics in Israel and Utah." *Journal of Church and State* 38, (1997): 523–41.

Shemesh, Haim. *Soviet-Iraqi Relations, 1968–1988.* Boulder, Colo.: Lynne Rienner Publishers, 1992.

Shepard, William. "Islam and Ideology: Towards a Typology." *International Journal of Middle East Studies* 19 (1987): 307–36.

Shihab, Zaki. "Iraq." *Al-Wasat*, (March 21, 1999): 18–19. In Arabic.

Shipler, David. *Arab and Jew: Wounded Spirits in a Promised Land.* New York: Penguin Books, 2003.

Shlaim, Avi. *The Iron Wall: Israel and the Arab World.* New York: WW Norton and Co., 2001.

Shlaim, Avi, and Avner Yaniv. "Domestic Politics and Foreign Policy in Israel." *International Affairs* 56 (1980): 242–62.

Snowden, L.L. "How Likely are Terrorists to Use a Nuclear Strategy?" *American Behavioral Scientist* 46, no. 6 (Feb. 2003): 699–713.

Stern, Jessica. *The Ultimate Terrorists.* Cambridge: Harvard University Press, 1999.

———. *Terror in the Name of God: Why Religious Militants Kill.* New York: Harper Collins, 2003.

Tessler, Mark. *A History of the Israeli-Palestinian Conflict.* Bloomington, Ind.: Indiana University Press, 1994.

Thomas, Gordon. *Gideon's Spies: The Secret History of the Mossad.* New York: Thomas Dunne Books/St. Martin's Press, 1999.

Tibi, Bassam. *The Challenge of Fundamentalism: Political Islam and the New World Disorder.* Berkeley, CA: University of California Press, 1997.

Tierno, Philip M., Jr. *Protect Yourself Against Bioterrorism.* New York: Pocket Books, 2002.

Trapp, Frank J. *Does a Repressive Counter-Terrorist Strategy Reduce Terrorism?: An Empirical Study of Israel's Iron Fist Policy for the Period 1968 to 1987.* Unpublished Ph.D. dissertation: Florida State University, 1994.

The United States Commission on National Security/21st Century. *New World Coming: American Security in the 21st Century: Supporting Research and Analysis.* The Phase I Report on the Emerging Global Security Environment for the First Quarter of the 21st Century. September 15, 1999.

The United States General Accounting Office: Report to Congressional Committees. *Combating Terrorism: Selected Challenges and Related Recommendations.* GAO-01-822, September 2001.

The United States General Accounting Office. *Joint Inquiry into Intelligence Community Activities Before and After the Terrorist Attacks of September 11, 2001.* Report to Congressional Committees, S. Rept. no. 107-351, 107th Congress, 2nd Session, H. Rept. no. 107-792, December 2002.

The United States General Accounting Office: Report to Congressional Requesters. *Combating Terrorism: Issues to be Resolved to Improve Counterterrorism Operations.* GAO/NSIAD-99-135, May 1999.

United States Department of Justice. "Press Release: Khobar Towers." June 21, 2001, at http://www.fbi.gov/pressrel/pressre101/Khobar.htm (accessed July 19, 2003).

United States Department of State. *Patterns of Global Terrorism, 1999.*

United States Government. *National Strategy for Combating Terrorism.* February 2003.

U.S. Senate Select Committee on Intelligence and US House Permanent Select Committee on Intelligence. "Joint Inquiry into Intelligence Community Activities Before and After the Terrorist Attacks of September 11, 2001." Congressional Report, 107th Congress, 2D Session, S. Rept. no. 107-351, H. Rept. no. 107-792, Dec. 2002.

Vakili-Zad, Cyrus. "Conflict among the Ruling Revolutionary Elite in Iran." *Middle Eastern Studies* 30, no. 3 (1994): 618–31.

Weaver, Mary Ann. *A Portrait of Egypt: A Journey through the World of Militant Islam.* New York: Farrar, Straus and Giroux, 1999.

White, Jonathan. *Terrorism: An Introduction, 4th Edition.* Belmont, Calif.: Wadsworth Publishing, 2003.

Wiley, Joyce N. *The Islamic Movement of Iraqi Shi'as.* Boulder, Colo.: Lynne Rienner Publishers, 1992.

Winrow, Gareth. *Turkey in Post-Soviet Central Asia.* Washington, D.C.: Brookings Institution, 1995.

Woodward, Bob. *Bush at War.* New York: Simon and Schuster, 2002.

Wright, Larence. "The Man Behind Bin Laden." *The New Yorker* 78, no. 27 (16 Sept. 2002): 1–46. Infotrac, February 7, 2004.

Yamani, Hani A.Z. *To be a Saudi.* London: Janus Publishing Co., 1998.

Yazdi, Majid. "Patterns of Clerical Political Behavior in Post-War Iran, 1941–1953." *Middle Eastern Studies* 26, no. 3 (1990): 281–308.

Young, Michael. "Hizballah Outside and In." *MERIP* (26 Oct. 2002), at http://www.merip.org/pins/pin37.html (accessed May 9, 2002).

Zakaria, Rafiq. *The Struggle within Islam: The Conflict between Religion and Politics.* London: Penguin Books, 1988.

Zaqzuq, Hamdi D. "Interview with the Minister of Wafqs." *Al-Wasat* (4 Jan. 1999): 23–25. In Arabic.

Zisser, Eyal. "Hizballah in Lebanon: At the Crossroads," *MERIA* 1, no. 3 Sept. 1997, at http://www.biu.ac.il/SOC/besa/meria/journal/1997/issue3/jv1n3a1.html (accessed May 9, 2002).

Zonis, Marvin. *Majestic Failure: The Fall of the Shah.* Chicago: University of Chicago Press, 1991.

Zonis, Marvin, and Cyrus Amir Mokri. "The Islamic Republic of Iran." In *Politics and Government in the Middle East and North Africa.* Edited by Tareq Y. Ismael and Jacqueline S. Ismael. Miami, Fla.: Florida International University Press, 1991.

INDEX

Abdullah II, King, 48

Abdul-Rahman, Sheikh Omar, 89, 90, 116, 158

Abu Sayyaf, 157

Afghan Arabs: and al Qaeda, 104, 151; Bosnian Civil War, role in, 117; defined, 99; Iraq, activities in, 138, 259; jihadists, support of, 166, 170; origin of term, 98; Taliban, relations with, 119; Turabi's PIO, relations with, 105

Afghanistan, 96–100; bin Laden as hero of, 160; chaos in, 138; cultural terror in, 137; jihadists in, 138; opium trade, 187; Taliban rule in, 14, 138; U.S. support of, 192–96

Ahli Hadith, 93, 94, 95

Akef, Mohammed Mahdi, 51

al-Abash of Lebanon, 28

al-Aqsa Martyr Brigade, 114, 222, 225

al-Asad, Hafez, 134

al-Bana, Hasan, founder of the Muslim Brotherhood, 17

al-Bashir, Omar, 102, 118

Al-Gama'a al-Islamiyya. *See* Islamic Group

Algeria, 106–10

Ali, (ibn-abi-Talib) 14, 70

al-Khoei, Sheikh, 75

al-Misri, Abu Hamza, 180

al'Owhali, Muhammed, 170

al Qaeda: Al-Zawahiri's role in, 162; and American Embassy, Nairobi, 170; arrests of members of, 249–50; influence of on Assam, 120; biological warfare and, 140; businesses and, 187; compared to Turabi's network, 121; and threat of cyber-warfare, 137; decentralization of, 239; discipline of soldiers in, 171; drug business and, 189; Egyptian Islamic Jihad and, 88; financial contributions to, 185; financial network of, 254; and gems network, 190; interaction with other Jihadist organizations, 124; as an international terrorist network, 121; relations with Iran, 194; leadership of, 160; militia of, 151; myth building of, 162; method of operations, 85–86; organizational structure of, 152–56; origin of term, 98; Pacific Rim operations of, 250; physical plant of, 172–73;

strength of, 29; vulnerabilities of, 164; and weapons of mass destruction, 139
al-Zawahiri, Ayman Mohammad, 88–89, 120, 153, 162
Amal, 58–59, 61, 67
Amer, Field Marshall Abdel Hakim, 87
anti-Americanism, 31, 40; and Muslim countries, 9; Muslim perceptions of, 32; opinion polls about, 26; religion and, 10–12; in Saudi Arabia, feelings of, 200
Arab–Israeli War, 1967, 18
Arafat, Yasir, 112, 211, 218, 225
as-Sadr, Mohammed Sadiq, 74–75
as-Sadr, Muqtada, 73–74
Assirat al Moustaquim (The Religious Path), 154
Ataturk, 16
axis of evil, 256
Azzam, Abdullah, 98, 120

Badr Corps, 68, 69
Balfour Declaration, 208
Barelvi, 93
Begin, Menachem, 209
bin Laden: Afghanistan, activities in, 97–100; Al Zawahiri, influence of, 89; business network of, 187; dirty bombs, access to, 139; drug business of, 189; and fatwas condemning 9/11 attack, 141; and fatwas supporting terrorism, 159; and jihadist movement in Bangledesh, 96; leadership style of, 161; leaving Saudi Arabia of, 100; militia of, 151; obsessions of, 145; relations with HuM and LT, 95; religious leader credentials of, 159; return to Saudi Arabia of, 99; Saudi Arabia, support of, 26; and September 11 attacks, 134, 179; Somalia, activities in, 117; Sudan, activities in, 103–4; Taliban, relations with, 119–24; and terrorist attacks, in

Saudi Arabia, 118; and Turabi's network, 118; U.S. support of, 192–93; vulnerabilities of leadership of, 164; war plan of, 146
Blair, Tony, criticizes Bush, 34
Bush, George W.: administration of, conflicts among, 256; condemnation of Israeli security fences, 214; crusade against terrorists and, 5; democratic Iraq and, 256; drugs and terrorism and, 190; Iran, attack of, 201; Israel, support of, 33–34, 221, 249, 256; and preemptive strike, 249; resignation of senior terrorism advisor and, 257; influence of Sharon on, 218; Syria and Golan Heights and, 199; weapons of mass destruction and, 258

Carter, Jimmy, 210
charisma, defined, 156–57
Christianity, defined, 10–12
Christian missionaries in Iraq, 76
Colombia drug gangs, 3
Copts, in Egypt, 90
crusade against Muslims, 5

Dawa Party, 68, 69, 73
Deobandi, 93–96

economic globalization, 21
El-Hodeibi, 51
European Union, 64
Fadlallah, Ayatollah Sayyed Mohammed Hussein, 58, 63, 65, 66, 73, 179
FARC. *See* Revolutionary Armed Forces of Colombia
FIS. *See* Islamic Salvation Front
FLN. *See* National Liberation Front

GIA. *See* le Groupe islamique arme

Hakim, Ayatollah Mohammed Baqer, 69, 73

Hama, 232

Hamas, 49, 68, 110–13, 145

Harakat ul-Mujahedeen (HuM), 95, 154

hawala (or hundi), defined, 188

Herzl, Theodore, 208

Hidden Imam, 56, 158

Hizbullah, 39, 173; commercial activities of, 63; Iran and, 55, 56–58; Iraq and, 68–71; Lebanon and, 55, 58–63; and martyrs, 65, 67; and obstacles and expansion in Iraq, 71–74; organization of, 63–66; strengths and vulnerabilities of, 66–68; U.S. strategy against, 74–76

Holy Jihad, 110, 114

HuM. *See* Harakat ul-Mujahedeen

Hussein, (Ali's martyred son), 70

Hussein, King, 111

Hussein, Saddam: as-Sadr, support of, 74–76; bin Laden, relations with, 100; Iran, invasion of, 57, 164; Kurds, torture of, 232; MKO, relations with, 193; SCIRI, relations with, 68–71; Shi'a, torture of, 232; Turabi, support of, 103; U.S. relations with, 68; weapons of mass destruction and, 257, 258

Ibn Taymiyyah, 14–15

idealists, 78

IMF. *See* International Monetary Fund

India, 92, 96

International Monetary Fund, 21

Iran–Iraq War, 68

Iraq, occupation of, 253

Iraq War: cost of, 258; goals of, U.S., 257; House of Commons views on, 262; inconsistent U.S. policies and, 256; Israeli support of, 218; jihadist terror in, 259; Muslim discontent and, 23–26; no fly zones and, 257; as preemptive strike, 248; Shi'a militias in, 257; U.K. cabinet members resign due

to, 257; U.N. role in democracy during, 258; U.S. senior terrorism advisor resigns due to, 257; U.S. go-it-alone policy and, 261; war on terror, effect on, 256–57; Iraqi Liberation Act, 69

ISI. *See* Pakistani Intelligence

Islam: Ahli Hadith and, 93, 94, 95; Ali and, 13, 14; Ayatollahs and, 13; Christians and Jews, relations with, 10–12; declaring war on, 26, 30, 34–35, 40; Deobandi and, 93–96; evolution of, 12; extremism and, 14; fundamentalism of, 17; hidden Imam and, 13; institutions of, 10; Koran and, 11; Mohammed and, 11; Muawiyah and, 13; religiosity, measuring of, 25; religious intensity, levels of, 27–31; Shi'ism and, 13; Sunnism and, 13

The Islamic Army for the Liberation of Holy Places, 154

Islamic Army of Mohammed, 153

Islamic Association, 112–13

Islamic Deterrence Forces, 153

Islamic education, 180–83

Islamic Group, 19, 87–91, 116, 130, 145

Islamic Jihad, 19, 88–89, 167

Islamic Movement, Algeria and, 106–109; axis of evil according to, 144; bin Laden views of, 121; conferences about, 104–105; control of, 77; as counterweight to the Jihadist, 76; defined, 30; government support of, 236; jihadist view of, 55; jihadist violence, effects of, 48, 264; mobilization of, 101; moderate Islamic groups and, 259; Muslim Brotherhood, relations with, 48, 53, 144; opposition to politics of Muslim world, 21; PLO and, 105; religiosity and politics of, 30; suggestions to strengthen, 265–266; supporters of, 195; Turabi as leader of, 102; Unity of, 77; U.S. support of, 264

Islamic Revolution, Iran, 31, 56–57, 91–92
Islamic Salvation Front (FIS),107
Israel: American Jewish support of, 229–230; anti-terrorist strategy of, 212–220; Arafat, planned removal of, 218; collective punishment and, 215–16; declining morale and, 227–28; European relations with, 229; history of, 207–212; Iraq War, support of, 218; settlers in, 214; maximum force attacks and, 214–15; occupation of Beirut, 58; options to stop violence in, 231; Palestinian Authority, relations with, 218; strategic traps of, 219–220; terrorist attacks and, 221
Izz al-Din al-Qassam, 113

Jemaah Islamiya, 154
jihad, 35n4; defined, 1, 7n1, 11; and Muslim Brotherhood, 42
Jihadist Movement, 85–87
jihadists: allies of, governmental, 192–202; allies of, holy 178–89; allies of, unholy, 189–92; authority patterns of, 160–63; decision making procedures of, 163–64; effective leaders of, 160–63; Hizbullah's role in, 63, 92; leadership of, 156–60; money trail of, 183–89; Muslim Brotherhood, view of, 54–55; organization of, 149–52; physical plant of, 172–73; psychology of terror and, 129; religious authority and, 159–60; soldiers of, 165–72; Shi'a and, 91; Sunni and, 57–93; support of, 30; U.S. support of, 58; violence and, 130; war plan, 127–29
Judaism, 10–12

Karbala, 70
Kemal. *See* Ataturk
Khamenei, Imam, 64, 73–74, 158, 202

Khomeini, Ayatollah: anti-Americanism and, 200; charisma of, 158; communist support of, 31; hidden Imam and, 56, 158; Hizbullah, support of, 218; Islamic Revolution and, 56, 91–92; jihadist movement, influence on, 113; jihadists, support of, 218; MKO and, 193; Pakistan, relations with, 97; Saudi Arabia, relations with, 99; Turabi, influence on, 102
Khoui, Grand Ayatollah, 74
Koran, 11

Lakshkar-e-Toiba (LT), 162, 164
Le Groupe islamique arme (GIA), 109, 150, 152

Machivellian view, 77
Middle East, defined, 7
Mohammed, Prophet, 85, 130, 132, 143, 160, 198
Mubarak, Hosni, 25, 48, 51, 53, 134, 235
Mujahedeen Kalq (MKO), 193
Musharaf, General, 196, 197
Muslim. *See* Islam
Muslim Brotherhood: and democracy, 46; charity and welfareof , 44–45; comparison to jihadists, 42–43; elections and, 25; goals of, 18, 41; indoctrination and, 44; membership of, 41; on violence, 48; on Israel, 48–50; organization of, 50–53; political activism and, 45–47; strengths and vulnerabilities of, 53–55; Syrian slaughter of, 49; teaching and preaching of, 43–44; testament of, 42
Muslim Extremists: defined, 23; measuring religiosity of, 24; religious dress of, 24
Muslim World: anti-Americanism and, 235; anti-terrorist strategies and, 231–33; anti-terrorist treaties and, 233;

decrease in Jihadist terror in, 237; effect of Israel on, 23
governments becoming more Islamic in, 234–35; psychological warfare in, 235–36; support for moderates of, 236; use of maximum force in, 232

Nada, Joseph, 41, 50–53, 187–88
Najaf, 70, 72, 74–75
Nasrallah, Sheik Hassan, 59, 64, 66, 74
Nasser, President Abdul, 18, 51, 86–87, 112, 134, 217
National Liberation Front (FLN), 106

Occupied Territories settlements in, 223–234; support for intifada in, 226
oil as a weapon, 135
Omar, Mullah, 119, 160
Oslo Accords, 210–12, 224–25, 230, 266–67

Pakistan, 92–96
Pakistani Intelligence (ISI), 97, 196
Palestine, history of, 208
Palestinian Authority, 114–15, 211–12, 215, 225, 228
Palestinian desperation, cause of: land as, 223–234; water as, 224; economy as, 224
Palestinian Intifada, 48, 61, 115, 210–12, 221
Palestinian Islamic Jihad, 113–14
Palestinian Jihadists, 64, 110–11, 115–16
Palestinian Liberation Organization (PLO), 112, 114–15, 225
Palestinian Refugees, 62
PLO. *See* Palestinian Liberation Organization
PIO. See Popular International Organization
Popular Liberation Organization: purpose

of, 105; members of, 105; Muslim world, impact on, 105
Powell, Colin, 221, 256,

Qadaffi, Muammar, 103, 134
Qaradawi, Sheikh, 179, 182, 184, 198, 264
Qum, 70, 75
Qutb, Sayyed, 19, 86–87

Reagan, Ronald, 58
radical moderates, 77–78
Rabin, Yitzak, 211–12, 266–67
Rahman, Fazul, 153
Revolutionary Armed Forces of Colombia (FARC), 3
Russian mafia, 191

Sadat, Anwar: assassination of, 24, 57, 88, 113, 116; The Islamic Group, relations with, 89; Muslim Brotherhood, relations with, 87; Nobel Peace Prize and, 210; Peace Accords and, 210
Salafia Jihadia, 154
Salafiya, 14–15, 36n11
SCIRI. *See* Supreme Council for the Islamic Revolution in Iraq
September 11 attacks: al Qaeda and, 122, 190–91; al-Zawahiri and, 89; bin Laden and, 1; future attacks and, 264; jihadist message and, 2; Muslim world reaction to, 179, 185, 195, 266; opinion polls about, 25–26; origin of, 9; perpetrators of, 30; post–September 11 era, 221, 223, 249; reorganization of intelligence after, 251; security measures after, 31; siege mentality as a result of, 249
Sestani, Ayatollah, 75
Shah of Iran, 31, 56, 91, 158
Sharon, Ariel, 60, 212, 214, 230
Sheba Farms, 60

Shehata, Tharwat Salah (Abu Sama), 89
Shi'a. *See* Islam
Shi'a prisoners, 70
Sudan, 100–105
Sunni. *See* Islam
Supreme Council for the Islamic Revolution in Iraq, 68–69, 71–73, 201

Tabligi Jamaat, 93
Taliban, 14, 119
terror, components of: catastrophic terror as, 138; cultural terror as, 137–38; economic terror as, 135–37; political terror as, 132–35; random terror as, 131–32; revolutionary terror as, 138
terrorism: defined, 7; patterns in fighting in, 241
Turabi, Hassan Abdullah: Algeria, influence on, 106–109; America, views of, 101; America, and terrorism in, 117; Ayatollah Khomeini, influence of, 102; background of, 101; bin Laden, work with, 103–104; Bosnia, terrorism in, 117; goals of, 101; Iran and, 103, 104; Jihadist movement, influence on, 102–103; network of destroyed, 118; Palestinian Jihadists, support of, 110; Popular International Organization (PIO) and, 104–105; Somalia, terrorism in, 117; World Trade Center attack and, 116
Turkomans, 72

ul-Haq, General Zia, 94
UN Security Council Resolution, 238, 229
UN Security Council Resolution, 242, 209, 229
UN Security Council Resolution 1373, 252
USS *Cole*, 89, 136, 154–55
US War on Terror: anti-Americanism and Islam and, 266; anti-terrorist principles and, 248; attacking the Jihadists and, 249, 262–63, 265; defense against, 259; excessive violence, 267; glitches, 255; improve quality of life, 268; international coalition, 261; international cooperation, 252–53; intimidation of govt. in Islamic World, 264–65; jihadist allies, 253; recommendations for victory, 260–68; root causes for terror, 254; traps to avoid, 248–49; using democracy, 267–68; war on Iraq, 256–57. *See also* Iraq War.

Wahhabi, 93; Abdal–Wahhab, 15; doctrine, 15; schools, 182
World Bank, 21
World Trade Organization, 21

Yemeni Society for Reform, 49

Zionism, 208

ABOUT THE AUTHORS

Monte Palmer has had more than 30 years of experience working in the Middle East including his recent tenure as the Director for the Center for Arab and Middle Eastern Studies at the American University of Beirut. His earlier associations include the Al-Ahram Center for Strategic and Political Studies in Cairo, as well as associations with the bir-Zeit Univeristy in the West Bank and Libya's Arab Development Institute. He is currently Professor Emeritus at Florida State University. His recent publications include *Politics of the Middle East* (Peacock/Wadsworth, 2002); *Political Development: Dilemmas and Challenges*, 5th ed. (Peacock/Wadsworth, 2001); and *The Egyptian Bureaucracy*, with Ali Leila and El Sayed Yassin (Syracuse University Press, 1988).

Princess Palmer has traveled extensively in the Middle East and has taught at numerous schools in the area including Cairo American College, the American Community School at Beirut, and the Lebanese American University. She has also served as a consultant for The World Bank and as Director of the Florida State University Reading Clinic. Her specialty is reading and education in the Arab World.